AREA HANDBOOK

for the

FEDERAL REPUBLIC OF GERMANY

Coauthors

Eugene K. Keefe

William Giloane
Anne K. Long
James M. Moore, Jr.
Jean E. Shema
Neda A. Walpole
Howard C. Weizmann

Research completed August 1974

First Edition

Published 1975

ʊ 9 3 ᦲ 9

DA Pam 550-173

Library of Congress Cataloging in Publication Data

Keefe, Eugene K
Area handbook for the Federal Republic of Germany.

"DA Pam 550-173."
"One of a series of handbooks prepared by Foreign Area Studies (FAS) of the American University."
Bibliography: p. 355–372.
Includes index.
1. Germany (Federal Republic, 1949-   ) I. American University, Washington, D.C. Foreign Area Studies. II. Title.

    DD259.K38   943.087   75-22146

For sale by the Superintendent of Documents, U.S. Government Printing Office
Washington, D.C. 20402

Stock Number 008-020-00578-9 / Catalog Number D 101.22:550-173

FOREWORD

This volume is one of a series of handbooks prepared by Foreign Area Studies (FAS) of the American University, designed to be useful to military and other personnel who need a convenient compilation of basic facts about the social, economic, political, and military institutions and practices of various countries. The emphasis is on objective description of the nation's present society and the kinds of possible or probable changes that might be expected in the future. The handbook seeks to present as full and as balanced an integrated exposition as limitations on space and research time permit. It was compiled from information available in openly published material. An extensive bibliography is provided to permit recourse to other published sources for more detailed information. There has been no attempt to express any specific point of view or to make policy recommendations. The contents of the handbook represent the work of the authors and FAS and do not represent the official view of the United States government.

An effort has been made to make the handbook as comprehensive as possible. It can be expected, however, that the material, interpretations, and conclusions are subject to modification in the light of new information and developments. Such corrections, additions, and suggestions for factual, interpretive, or other change as readers may have will be welcomed for use in future revisions. Comments may be addressed to:

The Director
Foreign Area Studies
The American University
5010 Wisconsin Avenue, N.W.
Washington, D.C. 20016

iii

PREFACE

More than fourteen years have passed since publication in 1960 of the *Area Handbook for Germany*, which treated both Germanys in a single volume. The continued separation of the two parts of the German nation plus the remarkable changes in their economic, political, and social structures warranted preparation of separate updated studies. A volume dealing with the German Democratic Republic was published in 1972 as the *Area Handbook for East Germany*. Since publication of that volume, the two Germanys have recognized each other as separate states, and both have been admitted to membership in the United Nations; hence the decision was made to use the formal title Federal Republic of Germany rather than the vernacular West Germany. Future editions of the East Germany handbook will also use the title German Democratic Republic.

In the spring of 1974 Willy Brandt, the popular and respected chancellor of the Federal Republic, resigned after a spy scandal touched his chancellery. But the transition to the administration of his successor, Helmut Schmidt, was smooth, and the stability of the government was unshaken. The Federal Republic continued to be a dynamic partner in West European economic communities and an important ally in the North Atlantic Treaty Organization. In late 1974 the economy and the currency remained strong despite worldwide inflation and fears of recession. The country's rates of inflation and unemployment were lower, and its foreign exchange reserves higher, than those of any other important industrial nation in the world.

The present study attempts to provide an objective analysis and a concise exposition of the evolution of dominant political, social, and economic aspects of society in that part of the former German Reich that has been the Federal Republic since 1949. This handbook is designed to give the reader an understanding of the forces that operate in the society and an insight into the goals and values of the people.

In Chapter 15, Agriculture, area measurements have been given in hectares rather than acres, and all tons are metric; United States equivalents are provided in the text and in the Glossary. The spelling of place names conforms to the rulings of the United States Board on Geographic Names except for the use of widely accepted English terms, such as Bavaria for Bayern, Munich for München, and Cologne for Köln.

In Chapter 9, Artistic and Intellectual Expression, titles of various artistic works have been cited in German unless the works have become well known to American and English readers under translated titles, as for example, *All Quiet on the Western Front* and *The Three Penny Opera*.

Grateful acknowledgment is made to John E. Dockham, who wrote Chapter 10, Mass Communications, and to Chester F. Low, who wrote Chapter 13, Foreign Relations.

COUNTRY SUMMARY

1. COUNTRY: Federal Republic of Germany (Bundesrepublik Deutschland—BRD), founded in 1949. Basic Law (Grundgesetz), ratified in 1949, serves as a constitution.

2. SIZE AND LOCATION: Area 95,975 square miles, including West Berlin. Located in north-central Europe; bounded by the North Sea, Denmark, Baltic Sea, German Democratic Republic, Czechoslovakia, Austria, Switzerland, France, Luxembourg, Belgium, and the Netherlands.

3. TOPOGRAPHY: Terrain rises from lowlands in the north to a belt of central uplands, descends slightly in the Danube River basin, and rises sharply in the Alpine region of the extreme south. Northward flowing Rhine River is the most prominent physical feature.

4. CLIMATE: Westerly winds and maritime climate predominate, but continental conditions, with greater temperature extremes, prevail to a degree that increases with the distance inland and to the south.

5. POPULATION: About 61.5 million in early 1973. Density 641 people per square mile. Rapid growth after World War II resulted mainly from resettlement of European German population, inflow of industrial labor. Natural growth was negative in early 1970s.

6. ETHNIC GROUPS AND LANGUAGES: Over 99 percent of the indigenous population shares the German language and cultural traditions. Apart from the large foreign worker population (over 2 million), there are no significant ethnic populations. Of those remaining after World War II, the largest are the Danes of Schleswig-Holstein and the Jews, who live in sixty-nine communities scattered throughout the country.

7. RELIGION: Almost 95 percent of the population claims affiliation with Protestant (overwhelmingly Lutheran) or Roman Catholic churches. Lutherans make up about 49 percent of the population; Roman Catholics, just under 45 percent. Jews constitute only about 0.1 percent of the population; Protestants other than Lutherans and non-Christian religious communities account for almost 2.5 percent. The remainder of the population—almost 4 percent—claim no religious affiliation.

8. GOVERNMENT: Democratic parliamentary republic. President serves as chief-of-state; executive power vested in chancellor as head-of-government. Chancellor assisted by cabinet of ministers. Legislative branch composed of Bundestag (Federal Diet) and Bundesrat (Federal Council).

9. POLITICAL SUBDIVISIONS: Federal system includes ten *Länder*

(states), two of which—Bremen and Hamburg—are city-states. Certain administrative and legislative powers accorded to the *Länder* were intended to deemphasize extreme centralization of the Nazi government. *Länder* are subdivided into thirty districts, 540 counties, and 21,900 communities. West Berlin is administered separately.

10. JUSTICE: Federal Constitutional Court (Bundesverfassungsgericht) is highest court. Four-level civil and criminal court system consists of local, *Land*, higher *Land*, and federal courts. Special courts handle administrative, labor, social security, and financial affairs.

11. INTERNATIONAL ORGANIZATIONS: Member of United Nations (UN) and its specialized agencies, Western European Union (WEU), North Atlantic Treaty Organization (NATO), and Organization for Economic Cooperation and Development (OECD). Member of European Community, which includes European Coal and Steel Community (ECSC), European Economic Community (EEC, known as the Common Market), and European Atomic Energy Community (EURATOM).

12. COMMUNICATIONS: Press is privately owned. Radio and television are controlled by *Länder* based public corporations. The film industry is privately owned but governmentally subsidized. Aside from restraints against libel, pornography, and subversion, government interference is forbidden by the Basic Law. Public libraries are supported by universities and municipal and *Länder* governments.

13. EDUCATION: Full-time education compulsory for nine years. Three additional years also compulsory but may be full-time or part-time. Operation of the system is a function of the *Länder*. Secondary schools are divided into vocational and academic. Higher education is professional or technical.

14. ECONOMY: Among world's strongest, maintaining sizable balance-of-payments surpluses despite increasing value of Deutsche Mark. Long-term effects of anti-inflation measures, energy shortages, and world economic situation not known in 1974.

15. LABOR: Over 65 percent of the 39.1 million working-age population are employed, about 13.1 million of them in industry. High percentage of indigenous labor is skilled; about 15 percent of industrial labor force, much of it unskilled, consisted of foreign workers.

16. AGRICULTURE: Crop yields are high, 54 percent of the country's area is agricultural land; 56 percent of total agricultural land is arable; and farm output provides about 75 percent of domestic food requirements. Agriculture, however, employs only about 7 percent of the economically active population and contributes less than 3 percent of the gross domestic product (GDP).

17. INDUSTRY: Dominant sector of the economy, accounts for more than one-half of the GDP. Dependent upon exports, is vulnerable to domestic increases in production costs, tight credit, international monetary instability, and worldwide changes in economic conditions.

18. FINANCE: Strong Deutsche Mark (DM) valued at DM2.66 per

US$1 on August 31, 1974, having changed, during successive devaluations of the dollar, from the rate of DM4.00 per US$1 that prevailed until October 1969.

19. FOREIGN TRADE: Major industries are export oriented; value of exports was the equivalent of nearly 20 percent of GNP in 1973. About 80 percent of foreign trade is with other Western industrial nations; politically important trade with the German Democratic Republic is only 2 percent of the total.

20. RAILROADS: About 18,300 miles of rail line, 42,000 miles of track; 5,000 miles are electrified. Main line German Federal Railways system is state owned and operated.

21. ROADS: Network consists of about 2,550 miles of limited access autobahn, 20,000 federal, 40,000 state, and 38,000 miles of county roads. Highway traffic is most dense in Europe.

22. INLAND WATERWAYS: About 2,700 navigable miles. Rhine River system carries larger volume of traffic than any other European waterway.

23. CIVIL AVIATION: About sixty of world's airlines carry 30 million passengers into or out of seven international airports annually. Federally controlled Lufthansa airline carries about one-fourth of the total.

24. PORTS: Hamburg handles approximately one-half of merchant shipping, the Bremen and Bremerhaven complex about one-fourth, Emden and Lübeck the remainder. Merchant marine consists of about 2,500 ships totaling 8.4 million tons.

25. ARMED FORCES: Bundeswehr (Federal Armed Forces) numbered about 475,000 in 1974, 70 percent in army, 20 percent in air force, 10 percent in navy. All major units—twelve army divisions, twenty-six air force squadrons, and combat naval vessels—committed to NATO.

26. SECURITY: Local, local criminal, and emergency police units organized under *Länder* governments. Federal Border Police and small special forces are under federal control.

THE FEDERAL REPUBLIC OF GERMANY

TABLE OF CONTENTS

LIST OF ILLUSTRATIONS

LIST OF TABLES

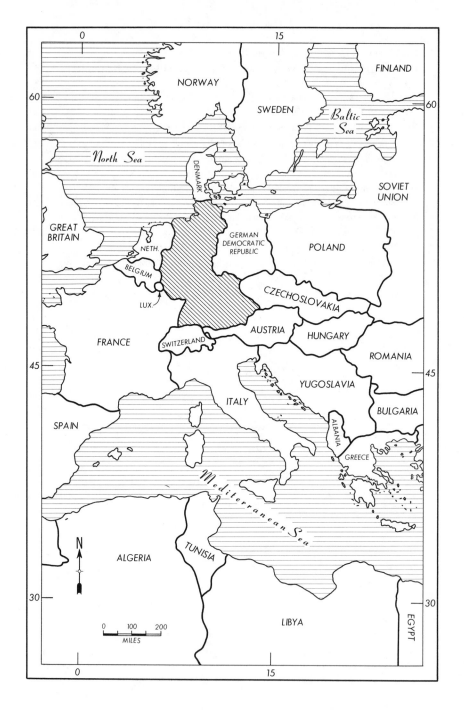

Figure 1. The Federal Republic of Germany: Its Geographical Setting

SECTION I. SOCIAL

CHAPTER 1

GENERAL CHARACTER OF THE SOCIETY

Adolf Hitler boasted in 1934 that his Third Reich would last for a thousand years, but in its thirteenth year, having been led by Hitler into a disastrous war, the Third Reich collapsed in utter defeat. Germany was left devastated and destitute and occupied by foreign armies. By May of 1945 Hitler was dead by his own hand and his successors had capitulated unconditionally as demanded by the victorious World War II Allies. Germany was divided into four zones of occupation—American, British, French, and Soviet—and Berlin, its capital, was placed under four-power control. In 1949 the zones of the three Western Allies were constituted as the Federal Republic of Germany (Bundesrepublik Deutschland—BRD) and the Soviet Zone became the German Democratic Republic (Deutsche Demokratische Republik—DDR). Berlin remained under four-power control, each sector being administered in practice under the authority of the respective occupying power.

The part of the former Third Reich that became the Federal Republic extends southward from the North and Baltic seas to the Austrian and Swiss Alps, and shares borders with Denmark, the Democratic Republic, Czechoslovakia, Austria, Switzerland, France, Luxembourg, Belgium, and the Netherlands (see fig. 1). The western sector of Berlin, which lies 100 miles inside the borders of the Democratic Republic, is constitutionally a part of the Federal Republic but has not been granted the full status of a *Land*. The country encompasses 95,790 square miles plus 185 square miles in West Berlin. The population was estimated in mid-1974 to be approximately 62 million, including more than 2 million in West Berlin.

The native-born population is over 99 percent ethnic German and shares the same language and cultural traditions. The native-born population that is not ethnic German consists principally of Danes and Jews. Most of the Danes, who live in Schleswig-Holstein just south of Denmark, are being gradually assimilated into the German society, using the German language in daily communication and often intermarrying with Germans in the area. The Jews, who had been the most important ethnic minority in pre-World War II Germany, were practically eliminated by the Nazis under Hitler's racial policies.

Much larger ethnic minorities live in the country but are not citizens.

1

These are foreign workers who have been recruited by labor-short German industries, usually for semiskilled and unskilled jobs, in what has been a booming West German economy since World War II. The *Gastarbeiter* (guest workers), as they are called, began migrating to the Federal Republic at the end of the 1950s, but they were usually recruited for a specified term of employment after which they would return to their countries of origin. Many of the *Gastarbeiter*, however, brought their families and settled in the country on a semipermanent basis. Official estimates in 1974 placed the number of *Gastarbeiter* at well over 2 million, unofficial estimates range considerably higher. In 1974 the largest single group was the Turks who numbered over 500,000. In descending numerical order the Turks were followed by Yugoslavs, Italians, Greeks, and Spaniards. Smaller numbers of Portuguese, Moroccan, and Tunisian workers had also been recruited, plus a sprinkling of French, Dutch, Belgian, and English. In November 1973, because of a downturn in the economy, the federal government halted the recruitment of foreign workers.

The ethnic Germans of the Federal Republic are descended from Teutonic tribes that inhabited the region between the Rhine and Oder rivers many centuries before the Christian Era. The Bavarians, Franks, Frisians, Saxons, Swabians, and Thuringians assimilated lesser tribes and, although differing greatly in racial characteristics, these tribal peoples shared a common language that made them the nucleus of a German nation. Many of the regional characteristics and the differences in dialects in modern Germany resulted from the differences that existed among the ancient Germanic tribes. The most important unifying factor since the Middle Ages was the common language despite the existence of distinctive dialects. The use of a standard written language first became widespread after the publication of Martin Luther's voluminous works in the sixteenth century. A standardized spoken language was much slower in developing because of the tenacity of the people in holding to their dialects. In modern times the influence of radio, television, the cinema, and the theater has spread the use of standard or High German, and young people in the post-World War II period have been less interested in retaining distinctive dialects.

Almost 95 percent of the population claims affiliation with Roman Catholic or Protestant churches in the country. The ratio of church members slightly favors Protestants over Catholics with Protestants generally predominating in the north and Catholics in the west and south. Most Protestant churches are Lutheran and are associated with the Evangelical Church in Germany. There are also congregations of Methodists, Baptists, Mennonites, and Quakers. Since World War II, denominational differences among the Christian churches have been less important than ever before, particularly in political affairs.

The Jewish community, which numbered about 530,000 in all of Germany at the beginning of the Hitler period, had about 26,000 adherents in the Federal Republic in 1974. There were sixty-nine congregations scattered throughout the country with many established in traditional centers of Jewish settlement, such as Frankfurt, Munich, Stuttgart, West Berlin, and Wiesbaden. The largest Jewish community, numbering about 6,000, is in West Berlin.

The people of the Federal Republic, the Democratic Republic, Austria, and German-speaking areas of Switzerland constitute a cultural community that is bound together not only by a common language but also by a common cultural legacy, which the members of the community prize very highly. German achievements in every field of artistic expression have contributed significantly to the mainstream of Western civilization. German philosophers and scientists rank among the world's foremost. To list only a few German artists and thinkers who have made an impact on world history necessarily omits the names of many others whose contributions were also of great importance; but the names of a few serve to highlight past contributions, which the modern German-speaking community remembers with fervent pride. Martin Luther, Immanuel Kant, Ludwig van Beethoven, Johann Wolfgang von Goethe, and Albert Einstein are five whose works may be expected to last as long as civilization. Generations to come will no doubt ponder how the land that produced such giants of artistic, philosophic, and scientific expression could also produce a Hitler, whose monstrous policies and activities threatened for a time to eclipse the glories of the past.

The Federal Republic and the Democratic Republic came into being because the World War II Allies could not see eye to eye on reconstituting a government for all of Germany. The assembly that met in 1948 to formulate plans for a federal government in the American, British, and French zones of occupation called itself the Parliamentary Council rather than a constitutional convention, and the document produced is still known as the Basic Law (Grundgesetz) rather than a constitution. These semantic maneuvers were designed to emphasize that the Basic Law was only temporary, and a true constitution would be forthcoming only after reunification of the country. The Parliamentary Council, with Konrad Adenauer as chairman, labored through the winter of 1948 and 1949 and finally agreed on the document in late spring. The occupation authorities quickly approved the Basic Law, and it was promulgated on May 23, 1949.

By means of the Occupation Statute of May 12, 1949, France, Great Britain, and the United States reserved to themselves rights in the fields of disarmament, displaced persons, foreign affairs, and reparations. In all other respects the new Federal Republic was to exercise all executive, legislative, and judicial powers. Elections to the Bundestag (Federal Diet) and appointments to the Bundesrat (Federal Council) took place in August 1949, and in September civil government was restored with Theodor Heuss as the first president and Konrad Adenauer as the first chancellor. Bonn was chosen as the capital of the new republic.

The Federal Republic, as it has evolved in the first twenty-five years of its history, is made up of ten *Länder* (states, sing. *Land*) plus West Berlin, which is administered separately. The federal executive branch consists of the president as head of state, the chancellor as head of government, and several ministries or executive departments, the ministers of which form the chancellor's cabinet. The legislature is bicameral and consists of the Bundestag and the Bundesrat. The judiciary is a separate branch consisting of a Federal Constitutional Court (Bundesverfassungsgericht) and local, regional, and appeals courts. *Länder* governments were assigned specific powers and functions by the Basic Law in order to avoid the extreme centralization of the Hitler era.

The president is elected by the Federal Assembly (Bundesversammlung), which consists of all members of the Bundestag plus an equal number of members chosen by the *Land* legislatures. The Federal Assembly meets once every five years for the sole purpose of electing the president. The office of president as constituted by the Basic Law has more prestige than power; real political power is in the hands of the chancellor.

The chancellor is nominated by the president and must be confirmed by an absolute majority of the Bundestag. Customarily, the chancellor is the leader of the party holding the majority of seats in the Bundestag or the leader of a coalition of parties holding such a majority.

Adenauer, as leader of the strongest political party—the Christian Democratic Union (Christlich-Demokratische Union—CDU)—ruled the Federal Republic with a strong hand for the first fourteen years of its existence. Reconstruction and economic recovery were the major problems facing the new chancellor, and the rebuilding of the entire country presented a truly monumental task to the new government. A combination of currency reform, Marshall Plan aid, and German determination brought about the spectacular recovery that the Germans labeled *Wirtschaftswunder* (economic miracle). Aside from his interest in the recovery of the domestic economy, Adenauer's special forte was in foreign affairs. Under the auspices of the American, British, and French high commissioners, who retained actual control of foreign policy until 1955, Adenauer pursued his drive to make the Federal Republic a secure member of the Western economic and military alliances.

During the entire tenure of Chancellor Adenauer, close association with the West was the key to West German policy. Adenauer favored the economic integration of Western Europe and the rearmament of the Federal Republic. Under the Hallstein Doctrine, named for one of Adenauer's chief foreign policy advisors, the Federal Republic refused to deal with any government that recognized the Democratic Republic. An exception was made in 1955 when Adenauer went to Moscow to establish formal diplomatic ties with the Soviet Union. In the same year,

Adenauer's government was granted full sovereignty by the Western Allies and became a member of the North Atlantic Treaty Organization (NATO).

Under Adenauer's successors, Ludwig Erhard (1963–66), Kurt Georg Kiesinger (1966–69), Willy Brandt (1966–74), and Helmut Schmidt (1974–), the strong orientation toward the West continued, but overtures toward Eastern Europe were gradually increased until, during Brandt's term as chancellor, *Ostpolitik* (Eastern Policy) had also become a major thrust of West German foreign policy. Under Brandt, treaties were concluded with the Soviet Union, Poland, and the Democratic Republic that recognized the de facto boundaries of the post-World War II era. Brandt's government also acknowledged that the Democratic Republic was a sovereign state, and in 1973 both Germanys gained admission to the United Nations.

The most outstanding political feature of the Federal Republic during its first quarter century has been the stability of its government. From its founding in the fall of 1949 to the fall of 1974, the Federal Republic has been ruled by only five chancellors. Although Willy Brandt resigned in 1974 under a cloud of scandal, as one of his closest aides was exposed as an East German spy, the stability of the government was not threatened. The transfer of power to the new chancellor, Helmut Schmidt, was orderly and peaceful. This remarkable stability of the Federal Republic, which had only one chancellor during its first fourteen years, is in great contrast to the Weimar Republic, which during its entire history—also fourteen years—had twenty-one governments.

One of the chief reasons for the stability of the government has been the dominance of only two major political parties and one minor party, as opposed to the six major parties and the myriad of minor parties that existed during the Weimar era. The two major parties are the CDU, which held power alone or in coalition for twenty years, and the Social Democratic Party (Sozialdemokratische Partei Deutschlands—SPD), which came to power in coalition in 1969 and continued to hold the chancellery in late 1974. The only minor party continually represented in the Bundestag has been the Free Democratic Party (Freie Demokratische Partei—FDP), which through the years has formed coalitions with both major parties and since 1969 has been part of the government in coalition with the SPD. A Bavarian party, the Christian Social Union (Christlich-Soziale Union—CSU), maintains a separate organization and elects its own leadership but votes in the Bundestag with the CDU and is referred to as the "sister party" or the "Bavarian wing" of the CDU.

The social structure of the Federal Republic has undergone drastic changes from the traditional German system that was characterized by rigid class divisions based on family and property. The post-World War II social system, which is still developing, is based on achievement, income, and education. Social stratification is multidimensional, and it is no longer possible to divide the society into neatly labeled categories of upper, middle, and lower classes. Classes exist but there is much greater social mobility than ever before in German history.

Sociologists make various categorizations of the society. Some see a vast leveling process, which will result in a broad middle class with only minor differentiations at the extremes. Others contend that a more or less rigid structure still exists in which traditional attitudes concerning social distinctions are prevalent. No matter what categorization is made, however, in the postwar era West German society has been extremely mobile because of the economic boom and the increased opportunities for education. The greatest upward mobility has been effected by unskilled workers from factory and farm, who have been trained or educated for better positions.

Over a long period of time education has been highly prized by Germans but, for various reasons, the number of university graduates has always been small, often resulting in an elitist attitude and outlook. In the Federal Republic of the 1970s, education is the most important determinant of a person's social status, but the number of students aspiring to higher education far exceeds the number that can be accommodated. Wealth and family background are still indicators of social position to some extent despite the partial breakdown of class barriers since World War II, but education is of primary importance. The comparatively small number of students who graduate from academic secondary schools, as opposed to the vast majority who receive vocational or technical schooling, are already marked, at an early age, as belonging to a small, prestigious class of citizens. The much smaller number who acquire university degrees gain entrée into the highest paying professions and occupations, and their prestige in the society—but not necessarily their wealth and power—is ensured.

The economy of the Federal Republic resembles those of most other Western European countries although, for various reasons, it has outdistanced all others in the post-World War II era. It is most often described by the West Germans themselves as a social market economy, that is, one of free initiative in competitive industry combined with the principles of social progress. Free enterprise operates within a framework of government regulation designed to protect workers against insecurity, to protect entrepreneurs against unfair competition, and to protect consumers against fraudulent practices. Except in the fields of transportation, communications, and utilities, the government is not an important entrepreneur, but its regulatory activities are of great importance to the operation of the economy.

The economy is predominantly industrial, and West German industry is highly advanced in technique and provides the great bulk of exports that pays for the large quantities of food and raw materials that must be imported. In contrast to industry, agriculture provides only a small portion of the gross national product (GNP) and must be subsidized.

In the fall of 1974, only a few months after the demise of the Brandt government and the succession of Helmut Schmidt as chancellor, the West Germans, along with most other people of the West, were concerned about the world economic situation and the possibility of recession. Government controls had kept inflation at a much lower rate than in other industrialized, noncommunist countries during 1973, but climbing unemployment rates have brought demands for a loosening of controls. High interest rates have hurt the building industries, and automobile sales in 1974 were running much behind those of the previous year. Since taking over the government, however, Schmidt has concentrated almost entirely on economic affairs, which raised his stock in public opinion polls but which led some foreign observers to wonder about the future of *Ostpolitik*.

Militarily, the Federal Republic is committed to NATO, and official spokesmen continually stress that the mission of the Bundeswehr (Federal Armed Forces) is completely defensive. Maintaining somewhat fewer than 500,000 men in uniform, the Bundeswehr is roughly made up of 70 percent army, 20 percent air force, and 10 percent navy. Civilian control of the forces is rigidly adhered to, and the basic rights of individuals conscripted to serve are guaranteed by the Basic Law. In the postwar era the West German citizenry has been less than enthusiastic about maintaining a large military establishment, and this attitude has affected young men of draft age, many of whom enter the Bundeswehr reluctantly and some of whom declare themselves to be conscientious objectors. The latter are assigned to alternative service in various social agencies.

The antimilitary attitude has placed additional burdens on military professionals who have only a short time to train recruits (conscripts serve only fifteen months); nevertheless, the Bundeswehr is considered to be an efficient defense force and its personnel are considered to be well trained, loyal, and reliable. In 1974 elements of six foreign armies were still maintained in the Federal Republic. American, Belgian, British, Canadian, and Dutch troops stationed in the country were committed to NATO, but French forces numbering almost 60,000 men were not under NATO command.

CHAPTER 2

HISTORICAL SETTING

German unity was long in coming, owing to a variety of factors that inhibited the evolution of a nation-state. The German lands lay in the paths of early invaders from the east and came to occupy a mediating position between classical western civilization and semibarbarous cultures of the east and north. After a period during the Middle Ages when German kings were the most powerful monarchs in Europe, political fragmentation weakened Germany, leaving it vulnerable to papal intervention and French incursions.

Religious struggles affected several centuries of German life. In the eleventh and twelfth centuries the controversy over state versus church authority brought more chaos and further weakened secular authority. The issue was partially settled in 1122 by a compromise that granted the church the right to bestow spiritual authority on the clergy and permitted nobles to invest political authority on clerics.

Martin Luther rekindled the religious debate in the early 1500s by criticizing church conditions and practices and papal authority. Dissension followed for more than 100 years and left Germany not only divided into a predominantly Protestant north and Roman Catholic south but weakened politically and economically.

As Prussian influence grew in the seventeenth century under Hohenzollern rule, its absolutist regime spread throughout Germany. By the time of Friedrich the Great, in the mid-eighteenth century, Prussia was strong enough to challenge Austria for hegemony among the more than 200 German sovereignties, but it was still unable to develop a unified nation-state. Only in the second half of the nineteenth century, under Otto von Bismarck's vigorous leadership, was the country united in the North German Confederation and was able to match its western neighbors politically and economically through national unification and industrial development. Modernization under the autocratic Prussian crown took its toll. Despite the crown's avowal of individual rights and a political role for the people, authority remained in the hands of a governing clique unfettered by popular mandates.

The outbreak of World War I resulted in a superficial coalescence of conflicting interests in support of the state. The deep cleavage however, between the rationale of state power and the demand for a free and possibly socialistic society survived to plague Germany's first experiment in republican government.

After World War I the unstable Weimar Republic patched governments together until the attempt at democratic government was finally ripped apart by the economic crash of 1929. Both political extremes—the Communist Party and the National Socialist German Workers' Party (Nazi Party)—gained followings. In desperation President Paul von Hindenburg turned to the demagogic solutions offered by Adolf Hitler and his reactionary supporters.

The rise of the Nazis to power ended the remnants of German freedom and marked the beginning of rampant expansionism in foreign relations. As Hitler embarked on the road to total war, Germans were lulled into false security by the economic recovery that followed war preparations dating from 1936. After the ultimate defeat of Germany—the devastation of war was aggravated by Hitler's apparent determination to carry the country with him into oblivion—the Germans were once again controlled by outside forces.

The Allies could not agree on the restructuring of Germany. Four occupation zones soon developed into two major divisions—the United States, Great Britain, and France uniting their zones into the Federal Republic of Germany, and the Soviet Union controlling what would become the German Democratic Republic.

The Federal Republic has been described as an "economic giant but a political pygmy." Although an economic upsurge, which began in the late 1940s, has placed the state among the major economic powers, its leaders have, for the most part, refrained from using financial aid as a lever to implement the country's political aims in other nations. This restraint is motivated by the country's dependence on the West for defense, its geographic vulnerability, and the volatility of Berlin. Moreover, as Willy Brandt has noted, Germany continues to be burdened by distrust and doubt among foreigners who question the country's determination to maintain peace and a democratic process.

THE ANCIENT PERIOD TO A.D. 800

During the second century B.C., as Roman authority was extended throughout the Mediterranean area and into Western Europe, Germanic tribes began to move westward and southward from central Europe and collided with Roman forces, inaugurating several centuries of hostilities between the so-called barbarians and the Romans. Eventually, the Rhine and Danube rivers constituted the frontier beyond which Roman power did not extend. Rome fortified the frontier and, after a severe defeat of three Roman legions east of the Rhine in A.D. 9, was content to defend the frontier rather than try to extend it into German territory. Until the final collapse of the Western Roman Empire in the latter part of the fifth century A.D., Roman forces generally fought off the incessant incursions of Germanic raiders. At the same time, however, many thousands of German settlers crossed the frontier and lived peacefully under Roman rule. During the fifth century, Roman power was so weakened that

German marauders and other invaders crossed the frontiers at will, and before the end of the century the Roman Empire in the west had disintegrated.

Gradually, as the power of the Romans declined, a group of closely related Germanic tribes known as Franks became the dominant power in the Rhine River area and, under King Clovis I, expanded their territory through military conquests and became the successor to the Roman Empire in much of western Europe. Under Clovis, who converted to Christianity in 496, the expansion of Frankish temporal power was accompanied by the spread of the Roman religion and the establishment of new monasteries and churches. At the time of his death in 511, Clovis' Merovingian dynasty was firmly entrenched in the former Roman province of Gaul, but he had little success in subjugating the Germanic peoples east of the Rhine.

After Clovis a series of weak Merovingian kings dissipated Frankish power, but the dynasty survived for two centuries until Charles Martel, a councillor to the king, led a Frankish army to an important victory by halting invading Muslims at Poitiers in 732. Martel subsequently became the most powerful leader in the kingdom, although he did not take the throne. His son, Pepin the Short, finally deposed the last Merovingian king and became the first ruler in the new Carolingian dynasty. Once again the Franks were united under a powerful ruler and began to expand when Pepin's son Karl (Charlemagne) succeeded to the throne in 768.

THE HOLY ROMAN EMPIRE

Charlemagne succeeded through relentless military and missionary campaigns in bringing the areas of present-day Germany, France, Switzerland, Austria, northern Italy, and the Low Countries within a precariously unified administration. His coronation as emperor by Pope Leo III in Rome on Christmas day, A.D. 800, marked the emergence of a successor in western and central Europe to the defunct western Roman Empire, which could protect the papacy and assume equality with the Byzantine successor of the empire in the east. Charlemagne's empire remained, however, essentially a Frankish kingdom having its center in Aachen. The centrifugal forces of such Germanic tribes as the Saxons and Bavarians were too strong to permit more than a tenuous and uneasy unity. The death of Charlemagne in 814 was followed by the rapid dissolution of the empire. One or two generations of Frankish administration had been insufficient to fashion a cohesive political tradition centering on royal authority in the comparatively newly conquered regions of Germany as it had in France. The lack of a clear rule of succession led to the division of the empire among rival heirs of Charlemagne's son, Louis the Pious. In 843 the three chief claimants signed the Treaty of Verdun, which divided the empire into three strips running north to south: the westernmost constituting roughly medieval France, the easternmost roughly the German lands east of the Rhine, and a central strip of territory stretching from the North Sea to the city of Rome.

In 855 the ruler of the Middle Kingdom died, and within a few years that territory had been divided between the remaining two, making boundaries similar to those of modern France and modern Germany. The two regions quickly developed different solutions to the problem of rule. In the German area, where both rulership and individual free status had retained greater vitality, feudalism came later than it did in France. Power devolved upon those Carolingian administrators who stood out as effective military leaders. Five great German duchies—Franconia, Bavaria, Swabia, Saxony, and Thuringia—evolved and gradually assumed the trappings of petty kingdoms. The ties of legitimacy were broken when the Carolingian line died out, and the imperial crown faced the continuing problem of asserting its power successfully against the territorial dukes.

Two great dynasties, the Saxon and the Salian, which dominated during the tenth and eleventh centuries reversed the particularist trend. The Saxon homeland was the Schleswig-Holstein area of present-day Germany, and the Salian center was the Rhineland. The territorial dukes were circumvented by a monarchy that succeeded, during the tenth century, in governing with major assistance from a German church subservient not to the dukes but to the crown and during the eleventh century through a developing Salian imperial administration. Strong central authority went far toward eliminating regional peculiarities and loyalties, and rising trade and cultural advances introduced a new sense of kinship among the German provinces. At the same time, however, absorption in the conflict with the dukes caused the monarchy to ignore the classes of freemen and aristocracy—neither of them bound as yet by feudal hierarchical ties—which were developing a political consciousness that would later cause trouble for the empire.

The Saxon kings, who ruled from 919 to 1024, revived the idea of an "empire." Inheriting a tradition of kingship and monarchical rights from the Carolingians, the Saxon empire was, nevertheless, far different from the Frankish kingdom. Lacking the ecumenical motive of Charlemagne and superseding old tribal loyalties, it became under the forceful leadership of the Saxon kings a truly German empire. The Saxon kings established the hereditary principle of succession, increased the crown lands, important as a basis of power, and extended their influence in several directions.

One great enterprise during this period was the conquest of eastern territories, accompanied by limited settlement. The church moved along in the wake of conquest, ostensibly to convert the pagans, but it was motivated at least as much by a chance to increase holdings and gain an economic advantage. The severe treatment accorded the conquered Slavs aroused their hostility and stimulated the political cohesion of Poles and Bohemians. As they gained strength they successfully prevented further German expansion at the end of the tenth century.

The formal revival of the Holy Roman Empire dates from 962, when Otto I (the Great) received the title "Imperator et Augustus" in Rome. The Saxon kings turned their attention southward toward Burgundy and, even more, toward Italy, which was a wealthy but weak neighbor. Their aims in Italy were limited, whereas the legacy of the imperial tradition greatly strengthened the crown in its northern home. The German hold on Italy waned in the eleventh century.

The Salian rulers, inheriting the accomplishments of the Saxon dynasty, were the most powerful kings in Europe during the eleventh century. At this time Germany was well ahead of both France and England in the modernity of its political and governmental conceptions. Under Conrad II, Heinrich III, and Heinrich IV, from 1024 to 1106, the constructive features of monarchy reached fruition.

The most obvious of the Salian accomplishments was the development of a permanent administrative system based not on personal or dynastic relations but on a class of "ministeriales," officials of the crown. The Salian administrative machinery proved effective, though not as directly influential on the people as in feudal France. The monarchy was challenged unsuccessfully in 1075 by an uprising of the peasantry, which sided with the nobility in opposing the administrative burdens imposed by the monarchy.

A more compelling challenge, the Investiture Contest, which endangered the throne itself, came to a climax in 1077. The controversy was a clash between church and state, between Pope Gregory VII and Heinrich IV, that pitched Germany into disorder for a generation. Essentially it was a struggle for the German church, which recognized the emperor as its head and was, hence, largely outside papal authority. Gregory insisted that Heinrich IV give up his rights over the church, eventually extending his argument to an outright attack on divine right of kings and hereditary monarchy. The pope was joined by large elements of the German aristocracy whose motives were not reform of the church but release from imperial control. Heinrich IV was eventually forced to submit to the personal humiliation of his famous journey to Canossa to conciliate the pope and outwit the German opposition. But he did not renounce his imperial role as head of the German church, and the struggle was prolonged beyond the deaths of both opponents.

The contest was accompanied by rampant civil war, devastation of religious establishments, and general loss of central control. The disorder lasted, to some degree at least, until the middle of the twelfth century and the rise of the Hohenstaufen dynasty. The crown had become dependent upon the aristocratic factions. Its control over Italy was lost; its control over Germany was so impaired that the governing edifice built up over two centuries by Saxon and Salian kings was scarcely viable when

Friedrich I, also known as Friedrich Barbarossa, began to restore the empire in 1152.

Exploiting their opportunity fully, the aristocracy took over administration and organized it around increasing numbers of castles, which came to form the visible expression of territorial fragmentation and a particularism that was to influence eight centuries of German history. Feudalism advanced rapidly, making vast inroads on the class of freemen. A full-fledged German feudal order eventuated, lacking only the capstone of the hierarchy; the monarchy had lost, at least for the time being, its preeminence in the German lands.

During the century of Hohenstaufen rule over the empire, the reigns of Friedrich I (1152–90) and Heinrich VI (1190–97) constituted a period of brilliance and were followed by a period of decline.

Friedrich I's accession in 1152 was welcomed as a remedy for the disorder that had characterized the empire for more than a generation. The loyalty that he engendered, even among dukes and clergy, was proof against further interference by the papacy in imperial affairs. By combining favorable conditions and a firm but circumspect policy he was able to refurbish and extend the empire. Through his efforts the crown was restored to its position of preeminence in the feudal organization; concessions to the feudal aristocrats as well as gains to the crown were implied in the policy.

His son, Heinrich VI, continued the vigorous Hohenstaufen policies, though more recklessly than Friedrich. His addition of Sicily to the empire as a result of marriage, although constituting a further check on anti-imperial papal ambitions, was to prove fateful for Germany, for later Hohenstaufens would ignore Germany in favor of Italy where they felt more at home.

What the first two Hohenstaufen emperors gained, however, their successors either lost or neglected. The decay of the empire as a genuine political force—it remained a compelling idea for centuries—left Germany thoroughly disunited and subject to the desires of territorial interests. The decline, however, coincided with a period of cultural enlightenment; the towns gained in economic strength; German literature was introduced; architecture developed rapidly; and German influence moved steadily eastward with the colonizers. For most of the thirteenth century, as a contrast, Germany was relatively powerless in European politics, while both France and England had developed viable central monarchies and political institutions.

The early thirteenth century was a transitional period in German history. The empire, neglected in favor of Italy, was allowed by the Hohenstaufens to decay at the center. With the passing of the Hohenstaufens the empire entered a period of decline. The houses of Luxembourg, Wittelsbach, and Habsburg succeeded each other, and the Habsburgs retained the imperial throne from the mid-fifteenth century until the end of the empire at the hands of Napoleon Bonaparte in 1806.

Beginning in the fourteenth century, the ruling houses based their strength upon dynastic holdings rather than upon imperial claims or prerogatives; consequently, their policies were dynastic rather than imperialistic in character, and specifically German interests were usually ignored by the crown. The Luxembourgs had established Bohemia as their dynastic center, and it was under their tutelage that Prague became a cultural and educational center. Charles IV founded the first German university in Prague in 1348 on the pattern of Oxford, Paris, and Bologna, setting in motion an educational movement of profound importance for the future of Germany. The universities of Vienna, Heidelberg, Cologne, and Erfurt were founded within the century. In 1356 Charles promulgated the Golden Bull, which accepted the reduction of imperial power by establishing the elective principle of monarchy, granting the territorial princes virtually regal powers in such matters as coinage and foreign policy and setting up the seven electors as the keys to imperial stability. The Golden Bull, by tacit exclusion of the papacy from any role in the election, also brought to an end the extended and, for Germany, destructive history of papal intervention in imperial affairs. This compromise in favor of the status quo left effective power securely in the hands of the princes, and German political history developed, henceforth, in the principalities.

The territorial state, which thus succeeded the personal bonds of the feudal order as the chief agency of government in the territories, became the carrier of political developments leading to the emergence of the nation-state. But that process, which was proceeding so vigorously in France and England during the fourteenth and fifteenth centuries, was late in developing in Germany for several reasons. All but the most vigorous territorial sovereignties in Germany were limited by their fragmentary nature and their lack of land, wealth, and military power; they were also challenged by the counterclaims of cities and emerging commercial classes for political power. The result, in the west at least, was that the German states became pawns in great power rivalries, suffering particularly from French incursions along the western frontier, which were a constant feature of French policy from the time of Philip the Bold at the end of the thirteenth century through Cardinal Richelieu and Louis XIV to Napoleon. In the long run, however, the course of events in the east was to be more decisive.

Colonization had been moving eastward ever since the organization of marches for defensive purposes by Charlemagne. It had been especially intense in the region later comprising Austria, but by the Hohenstaufen period the emphasis was in the northeast. As the German center of power shifted to the east, the princes were increasingly freed from imperial control by basing their power on holdings beyond the imperial frontiers. In general, colonization was carried out with little bloodshed or racial animosity. The Slavs often welcomed and profited from the methods introduced by German settlers and worked with them in developing the areas east of the Elbe River.

Not only did this movement lay the foundations for later development of Prussian and Austrian domains; it also provided impetus for the spreading of German influence along the Baltic area. An example was the colonization of East Prussia and Livonia by the Teutonic Knights in the thirteenth and fourteenth centuries. The Teutonic Order's rule—despite its demise after its defeat at Tannenberg in 1410 by the rising Polish state—resulted in the effective germanization of East Prussia and the establishment of German cities along the Baltic, such as Danzig, Riga, Dorpat, and Reval.

For most of the individual German colonizer's the eastward move meant an opportunity to obtain their own land and to enjoy comparative freedom. Many of the later Prussian landowners, the Junkers, were descended from the colonizers who had amassed large holdings. Another major element in the extension of German influence eastward was the commercial league known as the Hanse, a group of cities generally dominated by Lübeck, of paramount importance to Baltic trade from about 1350 to 1500. Like the colonization of the east, the Hanse developed on private initiative without reference to, or significant assistance from, the empire. Comprising at its peak some seventy north German cities, plus Novgorod and other non-German trade centers, the Hanse not only carried on its lucrative trade operations, it even maintained its own foreign policy and fought a war with Denmark over trade privileges. Only toward the end of the fifteenth century did Hanse dominance over northern trade decline because of national competition from Holland and England. The fall of the Teutonic Order contributed to the loss of Hanse power, as did the lack of agreement among the cities, the closing of Novgorod by the Russians in 1494, and the absorption of many of the cities in the expanding territorial German states.

The German cities, although not as advanced as those of northern Italy or Flanders, had long been in the center of a developing commercial bourgeois culture. With the protection granted by the crown and despite opposition from territorial princes and clerical authorities, the cities flourished as commercial centers and developed a distinctive order characterized by the commercial law that was to form the basis for city law, by guilds of artisans, and by bourgeois freedom contrasting markedly to the dependent condition of the peasantry. In the thirteenth and fourteenth centuries some of the trading cities formed leagues for the protection of their special privileges against the territorial princes. But these centers fell prey to the rising power of the princes at a time when the empire was powerless to protect them. By the mid-seventeenth century, however, only Lübeck, Bremen, and Hamburg remained as members of the Hanse diet.

At the end of the medieval period no single political force represented anything that could be called a German interest. The Habsburg dynasty, which kept the empire alive, was concerned with its Austrian base and with its status in Spain; Germany figured in dynastic policy only as a possible tool in its rivalry with France. The princes pursued particularist interests without reference to the whole of Germany, and the middle class, having risen during the commercial revolution, had no channel through which to become a unified or unifying force.

THE REFORMATION

The Reformation was an attempt at readjustment between religious and secular forces. It also involved a reconciliation between the hierarchical social organization of feudalism and a new emphasis upon the individual arising out of Renaissance humanistic thought.

Martin Luther (1483–1546), an Augustinian monk and professor of theology at the University of Wittenberg, was one of the purifiers who tried from within church polity and discipline to reform ecclesiastical practices. In objecting to such abuses as the sale of indulgences, Luther was a loyal cleric striving for reform. From the outset Luther's ideas contained a fundamental challenge to the Roman Catholic hierarchy—the belief in justification by faith that lay at the center of his teaching. In this respect, Luther was a heretic.

The ground had been prepared for Luther's deviation by the influence of the Renaissance; by the teachings of humanists such as Erasmus; by a popular, mystical religious revivalism growing out of frustration with the religious examples offered the people by the church; and by social and economic grievances. Not least among the factors accounting for the success of the Reformation was the spread of printing, which enabled the reformer's message to reach the masses.

Luther's strong personality and leadership catalyzed conditions that were ripe for revolution. His famous ninety-five theses, nailed to a church door in Wittenberg in 1517, included criticism of conditions within the church, several teachings that contradicted official dogma, and an attack on the assumption of papal authority to grant indulgences. Within a short time the theses were known throughout Germany, and Luther was called before the papal legate where he refused to renounce his position. In 1520 Luther published his three great reformist pamphlets. They called for the destruction of papal power by the German princes and the rejection of the orthodox system of the seven sacraments and stated the conviction that every man is his own priest, requiring gospel and faith but not priestly intercession.

In 1521 Luther again refused to recant before the Emperor Charles V at the Diet of Worms. The emperor was opposed to Luther's teachings, but Luther had the support of most of the princes and the people. Charles outlawed Luther and his teachings, but the reformer was given sanctuary by one of the imperial electors, Friedrich the Wise of Saxony.

Despite Luther's strong language in condemning princely misrule, he stated that a Christian must obey the ruler even if his commands are unjust. The peasants, however, had read into his religious teachings a message of social reform and were stimulated to revolt. The Peasant War of 1524–25 testified to their depressed condition but was crushed by the princes and nobility, with the support of Luther, who relied essentially on upper class support to effectuate his religious revolution.

Nevertheless, the Reformation was important for Germany because it involved all elements of the population. Princely support was based on resistance to papal authority over churches in their domains; popular support, on grievances against clerical abuses of power in both temporal and spiritual realms; and intellectual support, on the congruence of Lutheran teaching along with the contemporary trend toward individualistic emphasis in science and thought.

The political working out of the implications of the Reformation occupied the remainder of the sixteenth century and culminated early in the next century in the Thirty Years' War (1618–48). External pressure from the Turks, defeated near Vienna in 1529, and the repeated wars of Charles V against France preoccupied the emperor and permitted the ideas of the Reformation to spread without arousing overt violence. A legal solution to the growing religious disunity was the Augsburg Religious Peace in 1555, which enunciated the doctrine *cuius regio, eius religio*, meaning that the religion of subjects was determined by that of the prince.

But this formula did not quiet religious dissension, which was further stimulated by the Counter-Reformation under Jesuit leadership and by disagreement among Protestants of Lutheran, Calvinist, and sectarian persuasion. The Counter-Reformation had great success in the south and west of Germany, as well as in Poland and France, and by the early 1600s Germany was sharply divided, the Catholic League led by Bavaria in opposition to the Protestant Union led by the Palatinate. The Protestant churches had by this time become territorial institutions and served ultimately to reinforce the princely regimes. But the religious passions engendered by the Reformation remained much in evidence as contributing factors to the devastating series of battles and depredations known as the Thirty Years' War.

The several sets of opposing forces active during the years from 1618 to 1648 included Roman Catholic imperial Austria-Spain under the Habsburgs against the Protestant countries; the empire against the estates (classes) represented in the Reichstag; and the Habsburgs against France. Furthermore, Sweden found itself having an opportunity to extend its power in the German areas of northern Europe in the absence of a unified national power that could prevent its incursions on the continent.

Most of the wars that resulted were fought on German soil. The devastation was enormous; thousands of towns, villages, and castles were destroyed. The economy received a setback that was not reversed until the nineteenth century. The population was reduced by perhaps one-third, and the general level of culture fell markedly as life became a simple struggle for survival. Except for Johann Sebastian Bach and Gottfried Wilhelm von Leibniz, the renewal of a flourishing German culture had to wait for the age of Johann Wolfgang von Goethe and Johann Christoph Friedrich von Schiller.

Despite the brilliant exploits of the emperor's military leaders, Albrecht von Wallenstein and Johann Tserclaes Tilly, the Counter-Reformation as embodied in the Habsburg forces registered no gains in the series of wars. The mixture of religious discord and national rivalry dictated the outcome as incorporated in the Peace of Westphalia ending the war in 1648. It did not end religious strife, but it established a workable formula for the German territories, essentially a reaffirmation of the Augsburg principle of *cuius regio, eius religio* and, therefore, a confirmation of German fragmentation.

Political atomization was also enhanced by assuring the sovereign status of each principality. This meant the final nullification of the empire as a political force and the establishment of numerous incipient German nation-states too weak to compete with the modern European powers. France and Sweden were left in a position to interfere at will in German affairs. Among the German states only Brandenburg emerged from the wars with a foundation for growth. But in European perspective it, too, remained a second-rate power for another century. More than ever, Germany was a mere geographical expression. The consciousness of national purpose and identity, awakened at times in the past by external threats to the empire, was stultified in the atmosphere of petty absolutism that followed the Thirty Years' War. The German people, except for the few bureaucrats and professional men employed by the system, ceased to count as a political factor, becoming merely an object of exploitation. Popular endorsement was neither granted to nor sought by the princes.

ABSOLUTISM AND THE RISE OF PRUSSIA

After papal interference had been largely eliminated, the urban middle class ruined, and imperial power shunted to the sidelines, the principal force the princes had to appease after 1648 was that of the aristocratic landowners. This they did by extensive grants of privilege and authority.

Modeling their courts and conduct of state affairs on the resplendent example of Versailles, the principalities required efficient bureaucracies and some semblance of military strength, but most of all they needed abundant financial resources to support what was more often extravagant display than constructive state activity. To secure the resources, the courts imposed crushing taxation upon the peasantry.

Owing to the decay of the commercial bourgeoisie and the deterioration of the status of the peasantry, the older commercial centers declined; new cities grew around local courts, and in the rural areas landholdings were markedly consolidated in the hands of wealthy landowners. It was the period when the Junkers, the landed aristocracy, developed as an independent, conservative political power in the east, while the middle class was being increasingly subordinated to the state. Large-scale appeasement of the Junkers in the form of privileges of rule over their domains often secured their acquiescence in the destruction of the remaining organs of parliamentary expression. Moreover, the ruling class had such a monopoly of power that it could, in its petty concern for self-protection, bring about a rigidity of social stratification hitherto unknown. The era of absolutism was, for the most part, only a system of preserving privilege, unrelieved by major cultural advance or renewal.

In the late seventeenth century Prussia appeared as a new political power, although it was not until a century after the Peace of Westphalia that it emerged as a great European power under the strong rule of the Hohenzollerns. The erection of a powerful Prussian state did not alter the repressive, socially and politically rigid pattern of absolutism; on the contrary, the reactionary order was strengthened by the expansion of Prussian influence throughout Germany. And the very success of Prussia as a European power made its illiberal social organization seem justified as a prop of effective state policy.

In 1618 the Hohenzollern rulers of Brandenburg inherited the Polish fief of Prussia, as they had, in equally passive fashion, acquired possessions on the Rhine a decade earlier. But Friedrich Wilhelm, who became elector in 1640, began to pursue a more active policy of expansion. Known as the Great Elector because of his vigorous fostering of Brandenburg's interests, he pressed the Hohenzollern claim to Pomerania during the settlement after the Thirty Years' War and acquired the eastern portion of it despite Sweden's conflicting claims. The victory over Sweden at Fehrbellin in 1675 confirmed the state as a power in the Baltic area. In 1701 Friedrich Wilhelm's successor took the title of king of Prussia and was crowned at Königsberg. The new title indicated clearly the eastern outlook of the leading German Protestant state.

The Hohenzollerns were distinguished from other German ruling houses by their concept of duty to the state. The regime of austerity established in Brandenburg by Friedrich Wilhelm was designed to stabilize the finances of the state while permitting it to undertake mainly military projects that would make it a power to be reckoned with. And because the ruling house followed the same spartan regimen, it was able to awaken a sense of loyalty among its subjects that had no particular relation to their economic well-being. The Hohenzollern rulers, sparing neither themselves nor their subjects in a century of building were able to establish Prussia's power and its tacit claims to German leadership.

The extent of Brandenburg-Prussian territory, coupled with its lack of internal cohesion and shared tradition, required an efficient administrative apparatus for its management. Its internal problems had to be solved before it could presume to genuine great power status. Along with centralizing the administration, Friedrich Wilhelm had to impose his terms on the still viable estates, especially the landholders and their parochial and selfish interests. Although conceding to the Junkers their right to keep the peasants in virtual serfdom, Friedrich Wilhelm succeeded in forcing the Junkers to accept the burden of maintaining a standing army, which he had concluded was required to meet the political needs of the state. The well-trained permanent professional Prussian army may be dated from 1655.

Friedrich Wilhelm I (who bore the same name as the Great Elector of Brandenburg) ruled Prussia from 1713 to 1740 and devoted himself largely to the army and to inculcating the population with the idea of unconditional obedience. At the end of his reign he had an army of 80,000, half recruited at home from a population of roughly 2 million. His financial austerity enabled him to leave a surplus in the treasury, which was increased by his successor, while maintaining the army out of Prussian resources without the foreign subsidies that rendered many other German states so vulnerable. The army, like the administration, was rigidly hierarchical; the officers stemmed exclusively from the nobility and enjoyed enormous social prestige. The army was probably the best drilled army in Europe, but it constituted an enormous burden on the taxpayers because it consumed two-thirds of the state budget. As the landholders were largely tax exempt, the peasants and the middle class assumed most of the tax burden.

Under the stern rule of Friedrich the Great (1740–86), Prussia emerged clearly as a European power and as the counterweight to Austria among the more than 200 parochial sovereignties that had formed the crazy-quilt German map since the Peace of Westphalia. Internally, Friedrich continued to build on the foundation of the earlier Hohenzollerns. Keeping administrative authority completely in his own hands, he devoted himself wholly to efficiency, frugality, and absolutism. He was not despotic toward his subjects in the sense of needless repression, but the peasants were kept above the threshhold of starvation mainly so that the Prussian state might continue to enjoy tax revenues and the supply of soldiers.

Friedrich's devotion to the Enlightenment, symbolized by his friendship with Voltaire, was a matter of private indulgence more than a policy of state, for nothing mitigated the stern Prussian doctrine of service to the state. Friedrich called himself the first servant of the state.

Externally, during Friedrich's reign Prussia acquired territory that made it an extended but continuous area spreading across northeastern Europe from the original Brandenburg province to East Prussia; Silesia stretched southeastward along the Oder River; and there were scattered possessions in the western areas. Friedrich's major acquisitions were Silesia, separated from Austria in 1742 in a major test of strength, and West Prussia, Prussia's portion resulting from the first partition of Poland in 1772.

The growth of Prussian territory was of secondary importance compared to the profound implications of Friedrich's reign in terms of power. Prussia became a power to be reckoned with in European perspectives, and before the end of Friedrich's reign it had become the leading German power, supplanting a weakened Austria, which was increasingly absorbed in its multinational empire in Italy and the Balkans. Foreign influence was not diminished; on the contrary, the inability of either Prussia or Austria to gain clear hegemony enabled other powers—chiefly France and the Russia of Catherine the Great—to assume the function of arbiter in Germany. But Prussian power ended Germany's role as a mere pawn in great power manipulations.

After twenty years of pursuing an aggressive foreign policy, which kept Prussia almost constantly at war, Friedrich spent the last half of his reign maintaining a balance of power in Europe. Prussia needed time to recover from the devastating effects of the Seven Years' War (1756–63) and time to solidify its economic base. To this end Friedrich was instrumental in founding the League of German Princes, including the rulers of Prussia, Saxony, Hannover, and other smaller states, to oppose Austrian attempts to upset the power balance. Because neither side expressed a genuinely German policy, the league cannot be regarded as foreshadowing a unified German state. It was not until Napoleon and the ideas of the French Revolution were introduced that the pioneers of German nationalism and patriotism were awakened.

Within Prussia the most significant developments were the stricter differentiation of the estates—nobility, middle class, and peasantry. The landed aristocracy was increasingly dependent upon either military or administrative service to the state as a source of privilege. Constructive economic measures were made, including the attraction of new settlers in the sparsely settled areas; improvement of the peasants' lot without eliminating serfdom; and mercantilistic furtherance of Prussian industries, such as weaving and silk manufacture. The preparation of a common Prussian law that spread throughout the land after 1794 replaced the diverse and often outmoded systems of custom and law.

Under strong leadership the Prussian system had proved itself a capable defender of its own interests within the absolutist state pattern of the eighteenth century. Friedrich's successors, however, were not strong leaders. And, more important, at the turn of the century Prussia and all of Germany were confronted with a new set of ideas introduced in the wake of Napoleon's national army. Prussia withdrew from the Rhine as early as 1793 to avoid a conflict with the volunteer army of the French Revolution and devoted itself exclusively to interests in the east. When Austria also, after resisting somewhat more resolutely, gave way before the French, Napoleon had a free hand to reconstitute the entire pattern of German politics in the west.

THE DEVELOPMENT OF NATIONAL SENTIMENT

In the absence of any spirit of nationalism in Germany until the early nineteenth century, the country's cultural and intellectual life was dominated by a cosmopolitan spirit that rose above the petty concerns of the principalities. This spirit set an example for all of Europe in its breadth of vision and universal appeal.

The spirit of the Enlightenment, the first great intellectual movement to sweep across modern Europe, reached a pinnacle in the Germany of Immanuel Kant, Goethe, and Schiller. Germany's backwardness in terms of economic development and political consolidation probably made it easier for its great minds to remain free from patriotic passion. Goethe disdained national sentiment, refused to compose hortatory, patriotic poetry, and regarded the appearance of German nationalism as the enemy of the cultural growth that in his view was paramount in Germany's future. But these geniuses of the free and universal human spirit remained loyal to the absolutist political forms of the past and failed to show the way in which humanist, liberal ideals might be applied to the achievement of concrete political objectives. German thought never again took the lead in European intellectual life; on the contrary, in the nineteenth century German philosophy and literature drifted even further from the mainstream of Western thought. This breakdown in communication between Germany and the West encouraged German thinkers in arrogant, self-pitying, and self-deceiving notions that their power-oriented ideas were deliberately misconstrued or rejected by a hypocritical Western idealism.

The romantic movement, which had its inception in Germany at the close of the eighteenth century, stressed the importance of the German past and German uniqueness. This predilection passed into glorification of the nation and deliberate rejection of both German Enlightenment and Western liberalism.

Another stimulus was added to the formulation of characteristically German political thought of the nineteenth century by the philosophers Johann Fichte and Georg Hegel. Fichte subordinated both individual and state to the integral notion of a "higher freedom" for the nation. Hegel built his philosophical position on the state as the primary feature of historical development. For him freedom could be achieved only in the nation, the effective organizational agency of which was the state. This conception also left little room for the free play of private interest or individual self-assertion except as it accorded with the interest of the state.

The intellectual ferment of the early nineteenth century was confined to a small segment of the population. But as these ideas filtered into popular thought throughout the century, the cosmopolitanism and humanism of the Enlightenment were buried under the statist and nationalistic attitudes stimulated, at least in part, by the imposition of Napoleonic rule over large areas of Germany. The War of Liberation that followed represented a genuine awakening of national consciousness within the limited sphere of effective public opinion. At the same time, there is little evidence that the reaction against foreign domination reached very far down into the masses of the people. Particularly in the western portions of Germany, French examples proved highly durable; even the educated statesmen and intellectual leaders often preferred French to Prussian models. Throughout Germany the peasantry remained essentially indifferent to the struggle against Napoleon.

Napoleon dominated the early nineteenth century in Germany. The welcome accorded him displayed a lack of national feeling. The French Revolution had aroused intellectual enthusiasm in Germany, and Napoleon was described by Goethe as the "expression of all that was reasonable, legitimate, and European in the revolutionary movement." Beethoven originally dedicated his *Eroica* Symphony to him, although growing evidence of despotism caused the composer to withdraw that homage. More important than the intellectuals, however, were the German princes who flocked to Napoleon's camp in preference to Prussian or Austrian hegemony.

Napoleon's policy in Germany was to isolate the two principal powers, Prussia and Austria, and to erect a third force, the Confederation of the Rhine, which would be dependent on him. Prussia's failure to act against this move meant the technical end of the Holy Roman Empire. Prussian neutrality after 1795 gave Napoleon a free hand to defeat Austria in the field and strengthen his alliance on the Rhine by rewarding the princes of Bavaria, Baden, Württemberg, and Hesse-Darmstadt generously for their support. With Prussia's influence sharply delimited within its own borders, Friedrich Wilhelm III roused himself and his armies to fight the French less than a year after Napoleon's victory over the Austro-Russian forces at Austerlitz (1805). The Prussian army was routed at Jena in October 1806, and presently the French troops were "sharpening their swords on the statue of Frederick the Great" in Berlin. Prussian humiliation was emphasized by the maintenance of French garrisons in Prussia until 1813.

The Holy Roman Empire was formally dissolved in 1806. The Confederation of the Rhine, including all German states but Austria and Prussia, took its place under French protection. Napoleon's principal allies gained lands, and the electors of Bavaria, Saxony, and Württemberg were elevated to kingly status. The number of sovereign entities was reduced from about 1,800 to fewer than forty.

Some of the direct reforms that Napoleon brought to Germany, as to his other domains, survived the restoration that followed the Congress of Vienna. He abolished the lingering feudalism that had prevented the growth of a class of peasant proprietors, as well as the anachronistic ecclesiastical states. The Napoleonic Code was introduced in western Germany and, thereafter, remained the basis of law in that area. Napoleon removed the legal disabilities affecting the Jews and inaugurated freedom of worship. His influence was also visible in the spread of a decimal system of coinage and the adoption of the metric system of weights and measures.

Although Napoleon desired a unified Europe contiguous with the area of his conquests, his measures elicited national responses making him at least the godfather of the discrete nation-state pattern of Europe. He also released forces of secularism, middle-class political awareness, and commercial striving. The first evidence of a German counteraction to Napoleon's system was the reform movement in Prussia. Reform of the military system was undertaken by Friedrich Wilhelm III's military leaders Gerhard von Scharnhorst, Karl von Clausewitz, and August von Gneisenau. Their program was to build an army of patriots on the French model, eliminating the earlier dependence of mercenaries and the exclusion of all but nobles from the officer ranks.

Like the military regeneration, administrative reforms were stimulated by French example and carried through by men, such as Heinrich vom und zum Stein and Prince Karl von Hardenberg, who had entered Prussian service from other states. The French stimulus consisted mainly in the recognition by the reformers, many of whom detested the French Revolution, of what energies the Revolution had loosed in France. These men were not democrats, although Stein owed much to English constitutional precedents, and they worked to devise an efficient system that would prolong the authoritarian rule so characteristic of Prussia. Accordingly they abolished the rigid caste system that had kept nobles out of the bourgeois professions and the lower classes out of vocations and property holding reserved for their superiors.

The remnants of feudal obligation were eliminated and the status of serfdom abolished, although the landowners were generally confirmed in their manorial privileges, local manorial police power surviving until 1872. Municipal reform set up a system of municipal self-government and opened up an avenue of civic training and political experience, although a limited one as Prussia was still predominantly a rural country. The civil service was modernized and set in the pattern that was to be a model of efficiency throughout the century. The reforming impulse also extended to the educational system; Wilhelm von Humboldt attempted to found a system that would serve his ideals of the freely developing individual while permitting state initiative and aid. He was responsible for the plans to organize the University of Berlin as a center of scholarship serving the cause of liberation.

In 1812 Napoleon's forces were in retreat from Moscow. Napoleon's Confederation of the Rhine dissolved as he fled westward, and the states joined a resurgent Prussia in the alliance with England and Russia against their former patron in return for the preservation of their territory and sovereignty. The Congress of Vienna had begun its deliberations when Napoleon returned in 1815, calling forth another coalition against him. His second defeat at the hands of the English and Prussian forces resulted in the second Paris peace treaty, which gave Prussia additional territories along the Rhine but left France in the position of a great power.

The Congress of Vienna, designed to reestablish the shattered European order, awarded Prussia, as one of the victors, the remainder of Pomerania, the northern half of Saxony, part of Westphalia, and the Rhenish province. Prussia thus became a westward-looking country and, at England's behest, a bulwark against French ambition along the Rhine. Conservatism predominated at Vienna and was further mirrored in the Holy Alliance advocated by the Russian tsar; Russia, Austria, and Prussia were the exponents of a return to the prerevolutionary order and combined their forces in protection of absolute monarchy. This backward-looking policy was initiated by the representative of Habsburg Austria, Clemens von Metternich, whose leadership Prussia accepted. It also characterized the constitutional arrangement devised for Germany.

Metternich's creation, the German Confederation, consisted of thirty-nine states and, in spite of the rule of unanimity, only Austria and Prussia had de facto power to guide policy. The confederation was largely powerless except to support restoration of the old order, but it carried the seed of conflict for hegemony between the two dominant members in Germany.

Reform agitation grew for a constitutional order and German unification. A desire for German nationalism was growing but lacked large-scale support. It was a time of frustration for liberals and reformers. By 1820 five states had constitutions that granted the people representation in parliamentary government, but sovereign authority remained in the hands of the monarch.

Unification, along with trade and transportation, was hindered by numerous customs barriers among the German sovereign states. Prussia took the initiative in forming a German customs union (*Zollverein*), which eventually encompassed all German states except Austria. This union provided the impetus for industrialization, which became widespread in the 1850s, and it also served as the economic basis for eventual unification.

In 1848 discontent was stimulated by revolutionary events in France. The ideas and social forces contributing to the unrest were mixed. In the southwest of Germany the uprising was particularly influenced by liberal ideals and republican goals of opening politics to popular participation. In the Rhineland Karl Marx and Friedrich Engels were involved. Proletarian agitation occurred in Berlin and Leipzig. Extensive pamphleteering among the workers injected social and economic demands into the struggle for political change. The unrest included strains that were primarily nationalistic rather than liberal and even some peasant discontent that was essentially reactionary and often anti-Semitic. The central issues of the movement consisted of middle-class demands for a political role.

Uprisings in Vienna and Berlin in 1848 elicited from the Prussian monarch a promise of aid in achieving German unification. On the basis of general elections a German national assembly convened in May 1848 in Frankfurt, although the assembly was powerless against state authorities. It substituted a central authority for the Confederation diet and adopted the Declaration of Fundamental Rights, modeled on the French Declaration of Rights of Man and the United States Declaration of Independence. The Revolution of 1848 failed, but the document on fundamental rights assumed importance as an indigenous liberal tradition after both world wars when new political forms were being sought.

The constitutional problem revealed division within the assembly over the question of including Austria in a unified Germany. Opponents of inclusion, who also wished to enthrone the Prussian monarch, won. Effectuation of the constitution, however, depended on the willingness of the Prussian king to accept the proffered crown, but Friedrich Wilhelm IV refused the crown unless offered by his peers, the sovereign princes of the states, thus reasserting monarchical authority.

The actual failure of the Revolution of 1848 often obscures its importance in German history. The partial realization and partial frustration of the ideas and aims expressed by the Frankfurt assembly form the substance of German history up to World War I. That liberalism largely gave way before nationalism is only partly attributable to the failure of the revolution, although the subsequent repression drove some of liberalism's best spokesmen into exile.

BISMARCK AND UNIFICATION

The prerevolutionary lack of a broad middle-class economic base and parliamentary governments was resolved in the 1850s. Not only was there a burst of economic energy, but commercial interests were encouraged by the state. Although parliaments were restricted, they existed in Germany before unification. Another significant change before unification was the transformation of political thought; much of the liberal tradition in Germany had been diluted.

In this setting Otto von Bismarck was named chief minister of Prussia. He was a conservative Prussian Junker who believed that Germany would profit from anything that was good for Prussia. His objective on assuming office was to strengthen the power of the crown over military matters and to defeat the attempts of the Prussian diet to infringe upon the authoritarian nature of the Prussian state. Public opposition to him mounted as he ignored the diet in some matters, restricted the press, and limited the actions of some local governments that criticized his policies.

Bismarck resorted to war, and this action silenced some liberal opposition. The wars of 1864 to 1866 proved decisive not only for Bismarck's policy but also for Prussia's position within Germany. Bismarck collaborated with Austria, the enemy of German unity, to wrest Schleswig from the Danes and to resolve the question of the rule of

Schleswig-Holstein. The German campaign was successful, and the two powers agreed that Austria would manage Holstein and that Prussia would administer Schleswig.

Difficulties over the joint governance of the northern provinces gave Bismarck a pretext to initiate war with Austria in 1866. The Prussian forces defeated Austria in less than one month, and the Treaty of Prague confirmed the end of the German Confederation and Austria's role in German affairs.

The North German Confederation was established in 1867 under the presidency of the Prussian king, and Bismarck served as chancellor and the only responsible minister (see fig. 2). Bismarck supplied a constitution that stipulated equal, direct, and secret elections to the Reichstag (Lower House), which was empowered to participate in legislation and budget approval.

Bismarck remained occupied primarily with foreign affairs. He was convinced that war with France was inevitable, and the question of possible Hohenzollern succession to the Spanish throne served as provocation. The outbreak of war in 1870 received popular approval in both Germany and France, but by January 1871 the German victory had stemmed French enthusiasm.

The Germans immediately proclaimed the new German Empire—the Second Reich—and Wilhelm I was crowned emperor. Bismarck had united Germany and had obtained the nearly unanimous support of the people while maintaining the predominance of the Prussian state. Elections took place for a Reichstag genuinely representative of all Germany. The Reichstag adopted the Constitution of 1867.

Bismarck found it difficult to preserve the balance he desired, and beginning in 1871 he had to shuffle alliances to stave off war. Conflict over political strategy developed between Bismarck and the last German emperor, Wilhelm II. Bismarck's forced resignation in 1890 left European nations with no one to restrain the power that had developed during the previous twenty years. The degeneration of Bismarck's system eventually led Europe, which was in an age of national self-assertion, into World War I, which nobody wanted but nobody knew how to avoid.

Bismarck was equally skilled in the maneuvers of domestic politics, the consequences of which were as far reaching for Germany as World War I and directly attributable to Bismarckian fallacies. He was bent on preserving the authority of the crown and thwarting the people from actively participating in the governing processes. This was at a time when the people were strong enough to contribute to national solidarity and to modify the narrow official orientation to consideration of state power alone, which prevented Germany from undergoing a further stage of modernization in responsible political operation. Bismarck's frustration of republican and democratic tendencies was probably the most damaging part of his legacy to Germany.

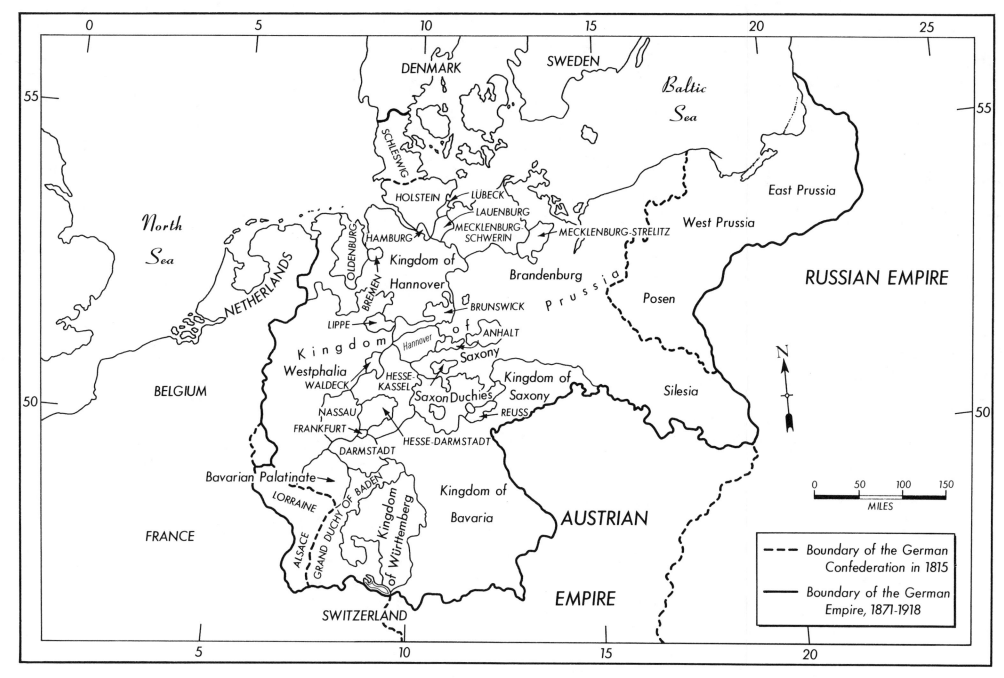

Source: Adapted from *Rand McNally Historical Atlas of the World*, Chicago, 1965, p. 26

Figure 2. Germany in the Nineteenth Century

Nevertheless, he made concessions to calm the demands of domestic forces. He acceded to the expansionists and inaugurated a colonial program, although he limited the program and the colonies were not a source of economic strength. He provided social legislation to aid the sick and aged in response to radical agitators. These measures failed to come to grips with the socialist movement, but they increased the paternalistic role of the state in the people's welfare. In the final analysis Bismarck's internal policies failed because they were anachronistic; they constituted a holding operation against new forms and new accommodations required by the rising German industrial society.

Bismarck was faced with a basic division in German society and economy. Western Germany was modern and industrialized, and eastern Germany was agrarian, semifeudal, and autocratic. Makeshift measures and superficial constitutionalism could not abolish this split. In fact, the reactionary policy of Prussia intensified the splintering of Germany into incompatible segments by treating all opposition as a force hostile to the state. Political parties thus came to represent not competing interests or programs but incompatible ideologies, each of which wished to eliminate the others. Parliament, without effective power either to direct or restrain the government, became a debating society in which the opposed ideologies were aired to no particular purpose. Bismarck used it largely as a tribunal for berating and bullying the members and for conveying his messages to the public.

The principal political parties in the Second Reich were: the Conservative Party, anticapitalist, devoted to inequality and military virtues, and becoming increasingly anti-Semitic as it allied itself with the Christian Social Movement, which was avowedly anti-Jewish; the Free Conservative Party, which split off from the Conservative Party and represented large capitalists and non-Prussian landholders; the National Liberal Party, a strong middle-of-the-road party composed largely of liberals whose devotion to the nation exceeded their espousal of individual rights, although they never abandoned their liberal trademark; the Progressive Party, subject to frequent splits but loyal to liberal principles and free trade and opposed to militarism and statism; the Catholic Center Party, victim of legal restrictions; and the Social Democratic Party, which was declared illegal. Opposition to Bismarck was futile, as the emperor remained the actual power in Germany having a veto over all legislation through his power to appoint or dismiss the chancellor. The parties and the parliament had to wait until the Weimar Republic to obtain real authority.

The conflict with the Roman Catholic Church, the so-called *Kulturkampf* of 1872 to 1878, originated in Bismarck's belief that the Roman Catholic Church and the Center Party were potential threats to German unity under the crown. The Center Party was antagonistic toward a secular Prussian monarchy, protective of its own religious schools, and it advocated federalism and social harmony. In order to restrain the party, laws were passed to reduce the authority of the bishops, ease apostasy, and interfere with the educational prerogatives of the church. Yet the Center Party continued to increase its parliamentary strength in each election, and the church adopted an effective passive resistance to restrictive measures. Conservative Lutherans, who feared Bismarck might include them in his anticlerical moves, supported the Center Party. By 1878 Bismarck wanted to seek a way out of the impasse, and some of the anticlerical measures were repealed. Bismarck's defeat on the religious issues made a popular party of the Center Party.

Germany became economically prominent among the industrial nations of Europe under the Second Reich. By 1870 its iron, steel, and textile industries were highly developed; rail and canal transportation facilities were being expanded rapidly; and banks and joint-stock companies were flourishing in support of the capitalist boom. After unification the government gradually became responsive to the needs of the national economy, and by 1879 agricultural opposition to high tariffs diminished enough to allow tariff protection for new industries. By World War I Germany had become Europe's foremost iron and steel producer. Governmental policy was closely related to economic interest by this time, and the state was deeply involved in the economy through ownership of many public utilities and transportation facilities.

One consequence of the economic changes was the increased importance of economic issues in politics. The rise of a commercial middle class injected a new element of conscious self-interest into the political process and heralded a broadening of issues. The government still considered the labor movement to be of questionable loyalty. Organized labor became closely identified with socialism and was repressed as a threat to state security and stability.

Among the socialist intellectuals whose doctrines were propagated in the second half of the nineteenth century in Germany was a middle-class Jewish lawyer, Ferdinand Lassalle, who supplied the stimulus for formation of a socialist party. His personal concern was to create a mass party to take over the power of the state. He was called on to organize a new workers' party in 1863, but his death in a duel the following year left the organizational task to another state-oriented Socialist, Johann von Schweitzer.

The General Workingmen's Association organized by Lassalle and Schweitzer in north Germany was soon joined by a Marxist counterpart in the south, organized and led by August Bebel and Wilhelm Liebknecht. Bebel arrived at Marxism through Lassalle's teachings and, like Liebnecht, he was hostile toward Bismarck and the Prussian state tradition. The Social Democratic Labor Party, founded in 1869, provided the channel through which Marxist thought penetrated German socialism. The party's early growth, early in terms of the growth of an industrial proletariat, helped it to forge and maintain bonds of solidarity with the labor movement as it developed out of artisans' associations and guilds. The program emphasized not revolution but the emancipation of labor and the attainment of a democratic political order. Marxism was evident mainly in the stressing of international working class ties and in the party's affiliation with the Socialist International.

In 1875, spurred on by growing official repression of socialism, the two parties combined in the Socialist Labor Party of Germany. The common program, though criticized by Marx and Engels for its concessions to Lassale, represented the initial acceptance of Marxism as German socialist doctrine.

The socialist parties had been gaining votes rapidly since 1870, and by 1877 the Socialist Labor Party received almost 500,000 votes and elected twelve deputies to the Reichstag. Bismarck began to look for means of suppressing socialism. By exploiting an attempt on the emperor's life as a socialist plot, Bismarck secured passage of the Socialist Law, giving the government power to suppress labor organizations and publications. The party was forced underground and became more radical. It continued to register electoral gains until Bismarck's dismissal and its reconstitution as a legal party in 1890. The more radical party program of 1890 bore the imprint of the new leader Karl Kautsky and followed the main tenets of Marxist ideology.

The Social Democrats under Bebel's leadership enjoyed such notable growth and discipline that it became the model socialist party within the Socialist International until the outbreak of war in 1914. It also became the largest single party in the Reichstag in 1912. Beginning in 1890, however, there was growing evidence of disunity within the party. A revisionist, Eduard Bernstein, believed that as the status of workers generally improved economically and politically, the revolutionary motive should be dropped in favor of democratic and parliamentary methods of coming to power. This theory corresponded to the conservative views of the trade unions, which had perceived their stake in the existing economic order, and to the experience of southern German Social Democrats. The result was to preserve the slogans of a revolutionary Marxist party while pursuing a democratic and legal course. By 1914 there were several poorly concealed cleavages within the party. A group in Bremen joined the future Spartacists, Karl Lieb-knecht and Rosa Luxemburg, part of the left-wing; Kautsky and Bebel maintained a precarious middle position; and the trade unionists and revisionists advocated a conservative course. By the end of the war the divisions had crystallized, and the prized unity of the Social Democrats was a thing of the past.

In one major respect the reign of Wilhelm II (1888–1918) departed from the Germany of Bismarck. The emperor cloaked his uncertainty in brash and intemperate displays of power. The resulting tendency toward national assertiveness and imperialism supported a new trend in foreign policy. The desire for a commanding role in world affairs was rooted in the conviction held by many German leaders at the time that Germany had been denied its place in history because of the predominance of France and England. The historian Ludwig Dehio observed that Germany entered upon an imperial course having no motive other than national self-assertion, a mission that could not secure allies in its undertaking. Germany, striving for colonies and for a commanding naval position, brought its policy into conflict with every major power except Austria.

With the possible exception of England, all of the powers were intoxicated with national power during the late 1800s and early 1900s and were determined to advance their national goals at all costs. Rivalries were exacerbated by the rising nationalism of eastern Europe. The diplomatic record shows an even distribution of responsibility for the outbreak of war in 1914. Germany's responsibility, however, is determined by the reckless spirit of its policy and its determination to overthrow rules of diplomacy, if necessary, to achieve its objectives. Because these objectives were conditioned by an exaggerated estimate of German military strength, the country was led into war against superior powers.

Germany entered the war in a jubilant mood. Its generals were confident of the superiority of the German military forces, and its people were convinced of the rightness of their cause. The nation closed ranks and refrained from pressing partisan interests. A group of ninety-three prominent writers, scholars, and scientists issued a manifesto in support of the war. Pacifist voices were few and despised.

The army failed in the opening phase of the war to achieve the lightning victory in the west that German strategists intended. The war soon settled into a slogging campaign in the trenches, and only the news of brilliant victories in the east under the leadership of Paul von Hindenburg and Erich Ludendorff compensated the civil population for its patriotic sacrifices. By 1916 this team of generals had taken over the civil government as well as the conduct of the war. Ludendorff, the more dynamic individual, became, in effect, a military dictator. The High Command was completely lacking in political insight and failed to perceive the breaking of civilian morale. The war economy was held together by the skillful management of Walther Rathenau, but the growing desire for a negotiated peace was dividing the political front.

The High Command refused to tolerate any break in its total aims and pressed for the unrestricted submarine warfare that resulted in arousing the United States against the Central Powers. In Germany more and more people, not only radical socialists, were disillusioned about war aims, military leadership, and prospects for victory. Among other evidences of disillusionment was the growing demand for political reform based on the realization that modern warfare requires the unflinching support of all elements of the population and that they must, therefore, be permitted to have a voice in policy determination.

The breakdown of the final German offensive in March 1918 and the defection of Germany's allies persuaded Ludendorff that the military cause was hopeless. With unrest at home bordering on revolution and with mutiny in the navy, Ludendorff decided to turn command over to a broadly constituted government under the chancellorship of the liberal Prince Max of Baden. This government presided during October and November 1918 over the liquidation of the empire, the abdication of the emperor, and the initiation of peace negotiations.

THE WEIMAR REPUBLIC

A variety of irreconcilable forces contended for postwar leadership. The German Revolution of November 1918, which was fomented by some of these incompatible groups, culminated in Prince Max relinquishing the chancellorship to the Social Democrat Friedrich Ebert, a nonrevolutionary interested in restoring a democratic order through the National Assembly.

Ebert's provisional government stood on precarious ground. Several areas of Germany were presided over by soldiers' and workers' councils, patterned after the soviets of the Russian Revolution. Rootless soldiers, who were unprepared to admit defeat and return to their homes, were already forming into contingents that would fight private wars and support reactionary interests throughout the duration of the republic.

Many Socialists wanted to push the revolution further. In December, 1918 the Spartacists formed the Communist Party of Germany (Kommunistische Partei Deutschlands—KPD). They were led by the Polish-born revolutionary Rosa Luxemburg, long active in the German socialist movement, and Karl Liebknecht, the son of a cofounder of German socialism.

Fighting and disorder increased. In January 1919 the KPD attempted another revolution, but the government quelled the uprising during which Luxemburg and Liebknecht were arrested and murdered. Order was restored in March but at the cost of permanently alienating left-wing Socialists.

Ebert's hope for convening a national assembly was finally realized in Weimar on February 6, 1919. This marked the reestablishment of comparative order and the extension of central control over the entire country. Although the new order and control represented victory for the conservative wing of the revolution, many features illustrated the sharp departure from the recent German past and foreshadowed the future. The parties of the Right and Center had been reorganized into four main groups: Democrats, Nationalists, People's Party members, and Centrists.

The Social Democrats, who favored a parliamentary government, formed the largest single group in the assembly. By closing ranks with the Democrats and Centrists, the Socialist Democrats formed a coalition, although a short-lived one.

The National Assembly had three main tasks: to establish a legal government, to conclude peace with the victors, and to draft a constitution. The first act was to elect Friedrich Ebert to the Reich presidency. Phillipp Scheidemann then formed a coalition cabinet composed of Social Democrats, Centrists, and Democrats, whose forces were dedicated to a democratic Germany.

The second task of concluding a peace agreement was more difficult. The peace terms imposed on Germany seemed unacceptable to Germans of all political persuasions. Acceptance of the terms was accompanied by complaints among responsible elements of the population and by vows of vengeance among the pan-Germanists. The question then arose whether to fulfill the treaty terms, a problem that would plague the republic until the depression of 1929.

The constitution that the assembly adopted embodied democratic and parliamentary principles and a unitary state pattern. The document paid less attention to the fundamental rights of individuals and more to a just social and economic order. On the whole, it was as democratic a constitution as could have been desired, but the transition from an emperor's state to a people's state was not sufficiently grounded in civic responsibility and general agreement on democratic principles.

Within a year of the German Revolution of 1918 dissension was evident, none of it caused by the terms of Versailles, but all of it intensified by a treaty that Germans could only regard as unjust. The bureaucracy had been reinstated, along with the judiciary, in positions where it could attenuate if not defeat the democratic process. The army, limited in size and armaments by the treaty, was devising means of training large numbers of reservists, and General Hans von Seeckt was spreading the doctrine that Germany should seek its destiny in the East, chiefly at Poland's expense. The Communists were continuing their efforts to mobilize revolutionary forces.

Meanwhile, new ideological currents were forming. Oswald Spengler, Moeller van den Bruck, and others were supplying ideological ammunition for antidemocratic and anti-Western positions. The appearance of General Ludendorff in support of Hitler's infant National Socialist German Workers' Party (Nazi Party) in Munich when the party staged its Putsch of 1923 endorsed these currents. As early as 1920 right-wing elements had attempted to overthrow the government. Some organizations were primarily militaristic in orientation, attempting to stimulate the resurgence of German military strength. Anti-Semitism was a prominent feature of the propaganda circulating at the time, appearing frequently in conjunction with the *Dolchstosslegende* (literally, the stab in the back myth), which assigned Jews a prominent place in the "plot" that betrayed the German military forces in World War I.

The period from 1921 through 1923 was one of hardship and disorder in Germany. Growing inflation was a constant burden for most of the people; only a few wealthy industrialists reaped gains from the increasing poverty of the rest of the population. French demands for reparations exceeded the possibilities of the moment, and parts of the Rhineland were occupied by French forces in retaliation. Germany had already lost major portions of its arable land and mineral resources through the provisions of the Versailles Treaty, and the government was powerless either to meet French demands or to halt the inflationary spiral that was making it less and less possible to restore the economy. Additional French sanctions in the Ruhr led to passive resistance and then to outbreaks of violence that provided martyrs for exploitation by rightist elements in Germany.

In August 1923 Gustav Stresemann was chancellor. A National Liberal, he was the outstanding political figure to emerge from Weimar Germany, and his brief tenure coincided with the ending of resistance in the Ruhr and the stabilization of German currency. The end of 1923 was a period of transition to a time of economic improvement and political stabilization. After 1924, although there were frequent changes of government in the confused and fragmented political party configuration, domestic politics settled into familiar conservative channels. By 1929 the economic revival had restored Germany's prewar position, especially regarding industrial production, which was increasingly concentrated in such powerful combinations as I. G. Farben, Siemens electrical manufacturing, and United Steel Works (Vereinigte Stahlwerke). The market crash of that year was to introduce a new and fateful period.

The five years of relative stability were made possible in part by the easing of relations with the West. The United States provided extensive assistance to help Germany regain a firm economic footing. The Dawes Plan, signed by Germany in 1924, fixed annual reparations payments, and the Young Plan of 1929 set the final terms of settlement. By this time Germany's economic well-being had made it possible to meet the payments agreed upon and had helped to restore German respectability in the West. Because the country was excessively dependent on United States loans, the economic boom that preceded the 1929 crash was deceptive.

Political accommodation between Germany and the West had been expressed in the Locarno Treaty of 1925 whereby the western frontier was guaranteed, and Germany gave up any claim to Alsace-Lorraine and renewed the Versailles obligation of Rhineland demilitarization. This was followed the next year by Germany's entry into the League of Nations. Although nationalists still protested the indignity of supervision under the Dawes Plan and the losses of territory, Germany had resumed its place as a leading European nation.

The counterpart of the Locarno policy toward the West was the Rapallo policy toward the East. Germany and the Soviet Union were thrown together initially by their common status as pariahs in Europe. Each needed help the other could offer, and the policy of accommodation had many advocates on both sides. The informal side of Soviet-German collaboration is still veiled in mystery as to detail, but in general it entailed mutually profitable arrangements as to training of military leadership, production of arms, and exchange of military missions. The political side of the rapprochement was developed during 1921 and 1922. When it seemed that the West would do nothing to relieve the situation in Germany, Foreign Minister Walther Rathenau and his Soviet counterpart, Georgi Chicherin, signed the treaty at Rapallo. The provisions of the pact were simple and inoffensive. The two countries renounced all claims against each other, established full diplomatic relations, and laid the basis for the development of trade. The treaty was renewed in 1926 but, except for continuing trade relations, had served its main purpose from the German point of view when an alarmed West realized that Germany would not remain an outcast forever.

Although the West and East had contributed to the revival of Germany's economy, military capacity, and self-respect, little had been done to repair the political structure. Proportional representation in the Reichstag accentuated political instability; Prussia retained its predominant role over Germany, and authority was exercised by the same class that had held office under the emperor. Industry, the army, and the Junkers were subject to little restraint because of the weakness or indolence of the ever-changing governments, and the judiciary had not been reformed. Paul von Hindenburg was elected Reich president in 1925. Tied emotionally to the old order, von Hindenburg was unable or unwilling to act resolutely in defense of the republic. Consequently, there was no widespread sense of patriotism, and the series of nineteen administrations that governed during the Weimar years failed to muster public support.

By 1930 three professedly antirepublican and antiparliamentary parties—Nationalist, Nazi, and Communist—were enjoying unusual support as a result of popular despair and together held nearly half the seats in the Reichstag, which they transformed into a mere caricature of a democratic legislature. The government was forced to rely increasingly upon decrees as a means of effectuating any policy and had unwittingly discredited democratic procedures before its members were forced out of office by the intrigues of men close to the president. The aged von Hindenburg installed Franz von Papen as chancellor and granted him the aid of presidential decree to govern without Reichstag endorsement or consent.

In the 1932 election the Nazis won 230 seats in the Reichstag, making it the largest single party. Von Hindenburg rejected Hitler's claim to the right to form the next government in the mistaken belief that the Nazis, who were engaged in daily exercises of violence against Communists and Social Democrats, could be tamed before being taken into the government. The Nazis went into opposition and lost the generous financial support of heavy industry and also lost thirty-four seats in the second election of 1932. This party crisis was possibly the last time the Nazis could have been crushed. Instead, von Papen proposed making

Hitler chancellor in a cabinet composed of Nazis and friends of the president. A slightly chastened Hitler accepted the offer and formed a cabinet containing only two other Nazis—Wilhelm Frick as minister of the interior and Hermann Göring as minister without portfolio and Prussian minister of the interior. Once the police were under control, the Nazis unleashed a reign of terror, which enabled them to complete the revolution and assume unlimited authority.

NAZI GERMANY

A wide range of factors aided Hitler in coming to power. The rise of the Nazi Party reflected the continued crisis within Germany as well as the interwar crisis of the West in general. But its appeal was carefully tailored to German conditions and weaknesses. The party evolved from a Munich radical fringe to a commanding position within the Reich and a threat to all its neighbors. As the political bankruptcy of the country grew more pronounced and viable republican government was no longer possible, the German people turned in either despair or hope to the solutions promised by the Nazis.

Hitler was imprisoned at Landsberg fortress after his unsuccessful uprising in 1923 and spent his time there dictating *Mein Kampf* (My Struggle) to his lieutenant, Rudolf Hess. This rambling treatise became the cornerstone of Nazi ideology. It made irrationality an ideological base and the manipulation of power, unrestrained by any moral consideration, the basis of strategy. The Nazi movement was essentially anti-intellectual, and it made no great effort to elaborate its theory in detail. It took over whatever writings could be used to good effect, drawing upon the ideas of Spengler, Ernst Jünger, Friedrich Nietzsche, Richard Wagner, Houston Stewart Chamberlain, Alfred Rosenberg, and Joseph Arthur de Gobineau, among others. Nietzsche was grossly misrepresented, and Spengler and Jünger were not pleased about their popularity with the Nazis.

The variety in sources of Nazi ideology has led some observers to conclude that it was a smokescreen used purely for propaganda purposes. Ideology proved a pliant instrument in the face of power requirements, as demonstrated by the Axis pact with Japan that seemed to contradict the Nazi emphasis on racial purity, but Nazi doctrines had certain fixed points that were not subject to maneuvering. The racial doctrines formed one such point as far as internal matters were concerned. Anti-Semitism was both a set belief of the movement and a calculated appeal to popular acclaim on the basis of a scapegoat approach to all German misfortunes. In attitudes toward the outside world the Nazis seldom strayed far from deliberate rejection of Western humanistic values in favor of irrational appeals to racial and folk solidarity. The tactical nonaggression treaty with the Soviet Union did not really distract them from a basic hostility toward Bolshevism, though this suggests strategic more than ideological reasons. Most probably, the basis of anti-Soviet sentiment was embodied in the notion of folk superiority over all Slavs. Hitler played a large part in determining what was fixed dogma and what tenets could be manipulated. Ideology and propaganda were both utilized to form a united Germany unquestionably obedient to their one indispensable leader *(Führer)*.

This fairly simple ideological base was buttressed by an eclectic body of propaganda, the apostle of which was Josef Goebbels, designed to attract the sympathetic attention of all Germans. The best illustration may be the name of the party itself which, though it may have been national and German, was neither a socialist nor a workers' party. Hitler's usual tactic was to promise all things to all people, provided only that they give him their obedience and faith. The promises were spiced with emotional attacks against Versailles, Jews, Bolsheviks, and anyone else who could serve as scapegoats. It is impossible to isolate definite economic principles except the need for a strong Germany; the Nazis used already existing state control measures to construct a national economy geared to war. The party made some use of pagan religious appeals to counteract the Christian churches, but few of the leaders took this mock theology seriously.

Historians admit the difficulty of determining what degree of popular support the Nazi Party enjoyed. Strict hierarchical control was exercised from within the Nazi Party. The party received substantial electoral support in the last free elections before the end of the republic. Thereafter, coercion was liberally employed to elicit the appearance of unanimous endorsement required by the dictator. The success of the ruling powers in overcoming the depression by sponsoring public works and finally by preparing for war was a potent factor in securing mass support for what seemed a truly national regime. Moreover, the Nazis revealed just enough of their atrocities in concentration camps to serve as a threat without disclosing enough to arouse a conscientious reaction on the part of a largely docile population. At least until the enormity of Hitler's crimes became clear during the latter stages of the war, it is probable that he had the backing of most Germans.

It took the Nazis about two years to consolidate their system politically. The combined terrorism of the party's Storm Troops (Sturmabteilung—SA) and the police forces at their command took care of potential opposition. Concentration camps were gradually filled with Jews, Communists, the more recalcitrant Social Democrats, and church leaders. By 1935 the whole mechanism of government had been coordinated. Nazi-controlled organizations moved into all cultural, professional, and economic areas to assure totalitarian rule in strict accordance with Hitler's wishes. Göring added to the terror apparatus by forming the Secret State Police (Geheime Staatspolizei—Gestapo) in 1933 to give special attention to political crimes.

The more sinister aspects of the anti-Jewish campaign began in 1935 when the Nürnberg laws were passed depriving Jews of German citizenship and forbidding marriage between Jews and so-called Aryans. These were followed by more severe measures, such as confiscating property, requiring the wearing of the Star of David as identification, and eventually full-scale deportation to the concentration camps and extermination centers.

Economic success was achieved more slowly. Unemployment was substantially reduced by 1935, and by 1936 production reached 1929 levels. The introduction of concentrated war production enabled Germany to rise rapidly to first place in industrial output among European countries. Germany was no longer primarily an agricultural country, and it proved impossible for the Nazi government to achieve self-sufficiency in agricultural production.

The effectiveness of Hitler's domestic measures was gradually improved by the extension of Goebbels' propaganda machine to control all sources of information, by the gathering of all police power in the hands of Heinrich Himmler with the Elite Guard (Schutzstaffel–SS) as the nucleus of terroristic control, and by the assertion of unlimited political control over the Wehrmacht (Armed Forces). Whereas the majority of Germans suffered no immediate ill effects and therefore felt pride in the accomplishments of the new and efficient regime, others—victims and potential victims—were forced to flee or retire into the relative safety of private life. Resistance was present but limited because of the effectiveness of police control. Many Germans chose the alternative of emigration, that is, so-called inner emigration, or withdrawal.

The dictator's audacity aided by the unwillingness of the Western Powers to risk a decisive move against him permitted successes in foreign affairs that strengthened his prestige within Germany, especially in the Wehrmacht. Hitler's first important foreign policy move was withdrawal from the League of Nations and the World Disarmament Council in 1933. Two years later the Saar voted to rejoin the Reich and, soon after, Hitler renounced the Locarno Treaty and unilaterally ended the demilitarized status of the Rhineland. Finding no opposition, Hitler formed the Axis partnership with Italy and signed the Anti-Comintern Pact with Japan. In 1936 Hitler was also testing his armed forces in the Spanish Civil War. In 1938 German troops moved into Austria, and German-Austrian unification (*Anschluss*) was proclaimed.

Western powers acceded to Hitler's expansion, and he continued his policy in Czechoslovakia. About 3 million to 4 million ethnic Germans lived in Czechoslovakia along the western border, an area known as the Sudetenland, where Nazi agitators had maintained a state of unrest against the Czech government in preparation for Hitler's move. Four European heads of state, Neville Chamberlain of Great Britain, Edouard Daladier of France, Benito Mussolini of Italy, and Hitler, met in Munich to resolve the Czech crisis. It was agreed that the Sudetenland would become German territory. This foothold in the Sudetenland was quickly expanded in early 1939 when Hitler recognized the independence of Slovakia and established a protectorate over the Czech provinces of Bohemia and Moravia. This last move lacked even an ostensible justification of the right of self-determination and shattered the last remnant of Western trust in Hitler's word.

In August 1939, when both the Western powers and Germany sought to ensure Soviet benevolence in the event of war, Josef Stalin decided that his interests would be better protected by an understanding with Hitler. Vyacheslav Molotov and Joachim von Ribbentrop signed the German-Soviet Non-Aggression Pact containing secret agreements as to respective spheres of interest. The pact was also the basis for the division of Poland. Hitler had already issued his orders to the Wehrmacht on the invasion of Poland, an action that he alone wanted—even his own generals opposed the move—and for which he was willing to risk not only general war but the presence of Soviet forces in direct proximity to his own area of control.

At this point it became clear that Hitler's aggressive intentions were without visible limits. His expansionist activities had been accompanied by constant efforts to unite all ethnic Germans and citizens of other nations having German backgrounds in support of Nazi aims. Wholesale emigration had publicized the extent of German war preparation and internal repression; the anti-Jewish measure had been pushed to new extremes at the end of 1938. When German troops invaded Poland in September 1939 without a declaration of war, Great Britain and France responded by declaring war on Germany. Hitler's power drive had unleashed a second world war.

The period from 1939 to 1942 was one of impressive lightning victories for the well-prepared, -trained, and -equipped German forces (see fig. 3). Hitler directed his war using intuitive cleverness that bore no relationship to the traditional military thinking of many of his generals. The superiority of the force at his command contrasted sharply to his unprepared opponents. His strategy was to conquer France and the Low Countries quickly, thus neutralizing Great Britain and the West, and then proceed in the East to erect the "Greater Germany" of his dreams. The basic ideas for these plans had been described in *Mein Kampf*.

By June 1941, when the Wehrmacht had initially penetrated the Soviet Union, Hitler was in effective command of the continent, but the Soviet undertaking imposed a strain on German armed might and industrial reserves that exceeded its capabilities. The turning point was the defeat at Stalingrad in late 1942, which coincided roughly with the Anglo-American landing in North Africa. Thereafter it was mainly a question of how long the German homeland could support its drastically extended military positions. By mid-1944 the pressure was increasing; the Red Army was advancing along the eastern European front, the Western Allies were moving in from Italy and France, and German industries were undergoing constant aerial bombardment.

42

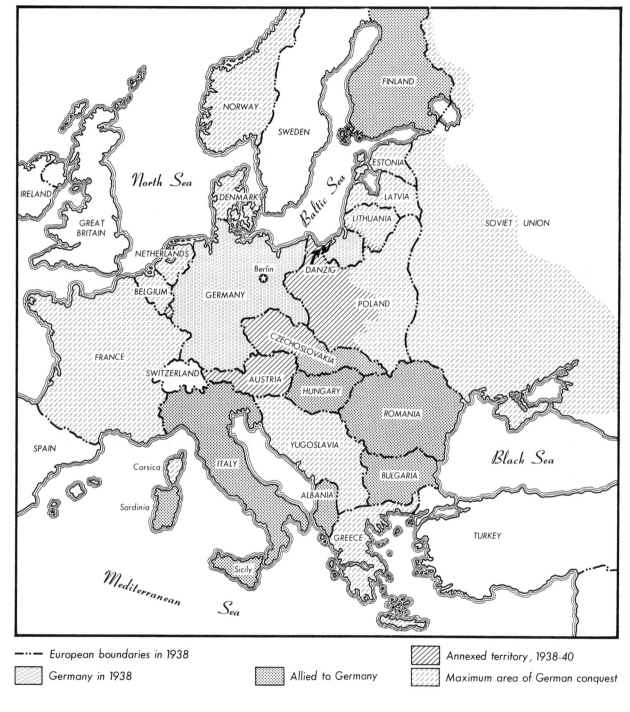

North Sea

Baltic Sea

Black Sea

Mediterranean Sea

IRELAND
GREAT BRITAIN
NORWAY
SWEDEN
FINLAND
DENMARK
ESTONIA
LATVIA
LITHUANIA
SOVIET UNION
NETHERLANDS
BELGIUM
Berlin
GERMANY
DANZIG
POLAND
FRANCE
CZECHOSLOVAKIA
SWITZERLAND
AUSTRIA
HUNGARY
ROMANIA
SPAIN
YUGOSLAVIA
Corsica
ITALY
BULGARIA
Sardinia
ALBANIA
GREECE
TURKEY
Sicily

–··– European boundaries in 1938

Germany in 1938

Allied to Germany

Annexed territory, 1938-40

Maximum area of German conquest

Figure 3. Extent of Nazi Germany Expansion in 1942

OCCUPATION PERIOD

The chaos that Germans faced was evidence enough of their total defeat and unconditional surrender. During the war the Allies had met to evolve common policies and postwar aims. The Yalta Conference laid down five guiding principles: total disarmament, destruction of Nazism and militarism, punishment of war criminals, removal or control of industrial potential for war, and compensation for damages caused by German aggression. The development of the cold war and disagreements among the Allied commanders later revealed a lack of genuine agreement even on these principles.

Several wartime conferences were devoted to the issue of dividing Germany into occupation zones. Leaders of Great Britain, the United States, and the Soviet Union had intended to control the zones, but before the war ended they granted a zone to France. The governing authority was the Allied Control Council, which was composed of the Allied military commanders of each zone. Berlin was also divided into four occupation sectors under inter-Allied control.

Reparations and supply provisions were to be coordinated among the occupying powers on the basis of unanimous agreement, but disagreement between the Western Allies and the Soviet Union erupted. At issue were the forms that postwar German political, economic, and social systems should assume. The Soviets favored a strong central government, whereas the United States intended to establish a democratic federal state, and the British, a unitary state. The French, who wanted to keep Germany as weak as possible, opposed attempts to develop a central administration. Continued disagreements caused the demise of the Allied Control Council in 1948, which served as a factor in the East-West division of Germany.

Each zone established a government. Local government was revived first. The *Land* (state; pl., *Länder*) was reconstituted as the largest governmental division within each zone. Although it was more difficult to revive the administration at higher levels, in the American zone the Council of States (*Länderrat*) was functioning by the end of 1945 to cope with matters beyond the power of the local organs. Similar progress was made in the British and, more slowly, in the French zones.

One point on which all Western Allies agreed was the necessity of screening public officials to prevent former Nazis from holding important administrative positions, but the denazification program was only partially successful because the method of judging a person's degree of Nazism by his length of service and membership or by his rank failed to reveal the degree of responsibility an individual held for specific actions. Denazification was intended to exclude formerly active Nazis from industry, commerce, agriculture, finance, education, journalism, and government. Consequently, there was a lack of qualified personnel to fill vacancies. There were also instances of discriminating in favor of some Nazis who were willing to cooperate with the Allies.

The attendant confusion damaged the prestige of the Allied occupation forces in the eyes of the Germans and made many of them reluctant to participate in restoring political life. Gradually, however, German personnel came forward to fill in the administrative framework of the occupation, and some continuity was achieved by appointing officials whose political training and convictions dated to the Weimar years.

Political parties were permitted in the occupation zones, and by 1949 there were fourteen parties. Two parties dominated: the Christian Democratic Union (CDU—see Glossary), which replaced the Center Party; and the Social Democratic Party (SPD—see Glossary), which had its roots in the Socialist party of the same name of the Weimar Republic (see ch. 12). The vague program of the CDU and its ties to Christian principles gave it broad appeal. At first the SPD put forward a platform favoring nationalization of industry, but as the economy improved the party's emphasis shifted. In general, the parties were notable for their lack of extremism and their adherence to middle-of-the-road policies and to democratic practices.

The immediate postwar years were a time of extreme hardship. In addition to wartime destruction the people suffered from a lack of basic goods and services. The currency reform of 1948, the most popular of the occupation measures, brought immediate results. Stores filled with goods, shortages disappeared, food rationing ended, and the cigarette was no longer a substitute for currency. Small businessmen, shopkeepers, and entrepeneurs were able to expand their businesses. Coincident with the renewed concentration on economic recovery was the erection of new political forms, a return of self-respect and confidence, and a revival of scholarship and cultural activities.

EARLY YEARS OF THE FEDERAL REPUBLIC OF GERMANY

Gradual steps were taken toward unifying the three Western zones. In mid-1946 the American occupation authorities proposed to unite the Western zones for economic reasons. The following year the British and American zones were united both economically and politically. As economic cooperation began to quicken the pace of Germany's recovery, France was persuaded to join in the establishment of a west German state, and the French zone merged with the two others in 1948.

Village elections had been held as early as January 1946, and three *Länder* had established parliamentary governments and were operating under popularly approved constitutions by 1947. After the three Western occupation authorities agreed to combine zones, they instructed the German administrators of the *Länder* in the Western zones to call a constituent assembly to draft a democratic constitution for a federal government. The ministers-president of the *Länder* wanted to avoid being held responsible for perpetuating the division of Germany and, therefore, requested that the constituent assembly be named instead the Parliamentary Council and that the resultant document be called the

Basic Law (Grundgesetz) rather than a constitution. These changes were intended to emphasize the temporary nature of the document and to allow for the eventual reunification of Germany. The Parliamentary Council met in Bonn, September 1, 1948, and chose Konrad Adenauer, chairman of the conservative CDU in North Rhine-Westphalia, to serve as chairman. The Basic Law was ratified by all the *Land* diets except Bavaria's, although Bavarians accepted the jurisdiction of the document. The law was promulgated May 22, 1949, and within a few months the organs of the federal Republic of Germany were in operation (see fig. 4).

According to the Basic Law sovereignty rests with the people, and maintaining the individual's freedom and dignity is the highest goal of the

Figure 4. States of the Federal Republic of Germany

state (see ch. 11). The Federal Republic has a cabinet form of government and a bicameral legislature. The president serves as chief of state, and the chancellor exercises executive authority. Theodor Heuss and Konrad Adenauer were the first president and chancellor, respectively.

Such matters as disarmament, reparations, denazification, and foreign policy remained under Allied control by the Occupation Statute, but when the republic was founded the high commissioners agreed that the statute could be phased out gradually. Full sovereignty was granted to the republic by the Western occupying powers in 1955. The Western Allies retained only the right to maintain troops in the country. Sovereignty, however, strengthened the East-West division of Germany because it was accompanied by political, economic, and military links to Western Europe and the United States.

Economic survival was of prime concern in postwar Germany. Western influence was important in reintegrating the Federal Republic into Western economic and military alliances as an equal. The country was welcomed into international organizations and became an important member of European communities. Among the first cooperative actions was the placing of German and French steel under joint control in 1950. This cooperation expanded and led to the founding of what was originally known as the European Economic Community (EEC, also known as the Common Market), which was gradually to abolish internal tariffs. Further roles were undertaken by joining some of the economic and social agencies of the United Nations (UN), despite the fact that the state was not as yet a member of the UN. The Federal Republic participated in agencies, such as the Food and Agriculture Organization, the World Health Organization, the International Bank for Reconstruction and Development (IBRD, commonly known as the World Bank), the International Labor Office, and the United Nations Educational, Scientific and Cultural Organization (UNESCO).

The Federal Republic's gradual integration into the Western community culminated in its entry into the North Atlantic Treaty Organization (NATO) upon acquiring its sovereignty in 1955. It has since become one of the leading members of the alliance, serving as host for most of NATO's combat-ready forces, including those of the United States.

The economic upsurge in the 1950s reflected the country's success in utilizing foreign aid, particularly the Marshall Plan, and the skills and determination of its citizens. Also, the dismantling of factories that was undertaken by the occupying powers had the unforeseen effect of aiding the economy. Industries that might otherwise have continued on a low production level were rebuilt using modern, efficient equipment. Increased production set off beneficial waves throughout the state. The Federal Republic became an international conference center, universities became multilingual educational centers, tourism boomed, and southern Europeans migrated to the state in search of employment.

48

THE ADENAUER ERA

Konrad Adenauer's life spanned nearly a century of political and social upheavals. He was born in 1876, was raised in a middle-class family of civil servants, and served as mayor of Cologne during and after World War I. The Nazis terminated his mayoralty, and he was later imprisoned. Adenauer's career fluctuated immediately after the war. He was reappointed mayor of Cologne by the American occupation authorities only to be dismissed by the British.

Adenauer's paternal and authoritarian airs fit the father-figure the Germans welcomed after World War II. His self-confidence was reflected at the first meeting of the CDU in the British zone in 1946 when he strode to the vacant chairman's seat and announced that as he was the oldest member present, he would preside over the meeting. He was subsequently elected chairmen of the CDU in the British zone.

Adenauer realized that disputes among Western European countries would have to be relegated to the past if order were to be restored to the postwar world. Once he was elected chancellor, Adenauer played an important role in advising British, French, and American occupation actions to alleviate tensions with the Soviet Union in Germany. Concessions were made by the Western zones at Adenauer's suggestion.

Adenauer led a Christian Democratic Union-Free Democratic Party (FDP—see Glossary) coalition, but his administration was often described as being "chancellor democracy," or governing through the chancery rather than through the Bundestag (Federal Diet) or the cabinet. One writer defined chancellor democracy as "the complex system of relationships which Adenauer established and sought to exploit for the purpose of consolidating the weak and unstable body politic." Others saw it only as reflecting the chancellor's authoritarian tendencies. Unquestionably, strong leadership was needed. Even stronger charges, those of dictator of demagogue, were made against him. The chancellor, however, viewed his role differently. It was not that he disregarded public opinion but rather that he was responsible for making decisions. Then he chose methods to make his actions palatable to the people.

The chancellor guided his country through economic recovery and the revival of an international role. A stable government was established, and in 1955 full sovereignty was attained. Adenauer's primary interest was foreign affairs. European unity and close ties to the United States received priority. Difficulties with the Soviet Union and the German Democratic Republic (DDR—see Glossary) plagued the Federal Republic throughout the 1950s and culminated in the Soviets' constructing the Berlin Wall in August 1961.

A more successful relationship was established between France and the Federal Republic. France had claimed the Saar after World War II, but in 1957 the area was officially reintegrated into Germany. Six years later another important step toward reconciliation with France was taken. The two countries signed a treaty of friendship, which covered such items as joint consultations on some foreign policy issues and cooperation in economic and educational affairs.

During his final years in office, Adenauer's popularity and prestige dwindled. One cause of this decline was his turnabout in the 1961 election. At first Adenauer sought the candidacy for the presidency, but he later revoked his decision in order to block Ludwig Erhard from becoming chancellor.

Another blow to Adenauer was an article in the popular magazine, *Der Spiegel*, that questioned the military readiness of the country. The government accused the magazine editors of treason but failed to support these charges, thereby weakening its case. Because of Adenauer's acquiescence in the case, the FDP ministers forced him to promise to resign by the end of 1963.

Adenauer's resignation brought Erhard to the chancellorship. Although the new chancellor improved relations with his coalition partners and with the opposition and granted more authority to the Bundestag, he lacked the political acumen necessary to carry out a successful program. On the plus side he began trade programs with five communist countries, but on the minus side relations with France worsened and efforts toward reunification were at a standstill. When he lost a majority of CDU support, Erhard resigned.

THE GRAND COALITION, 1966–69

The summer of 1966 brought increasing unemployment and, as production fell, so did confidence in business. Chancellor Erhard's resignation brought new elections in which the prime minister of Baden-Württemberg, Kurt Georg Kiesinger, became chancellor; and the mayor of West Berlin, Willy Brandt, was named vice chancellor and foreign minister. Their government, called the Grand Coalition, was so named because it was composed of the two major parties, the CDU and the SPD.

The program of the Grand Coalition outlined new diplomatic initiatives in taking positive steps to improve relations with Eastern European countries to the extent of opening diplomatic relations. Economic expansion and international détente were other facets of the plan. Steps were taken to ease tensions over the division of Germany, but Willi Stoph, premier of the DDR, and Kiesinger failed to reach agreement on common grounds. In particular, Stoph required acceptance of the Oder-Neisse line as the eastern border of the DDR. Diplomatic relations were resumed with Yugoslavia and were established with Romania. An economic upswing in 1968 and 1969 enhanced the coalition's popularity, but unity was fleeting. The 1969 election terminated the Grand Coalition and welcomed a Socialist-Liberal coalition. Willy Brandt, the newly elected chancellor, promised to continue the Grand Coalition's policy of détente with the Eastern European countries.

STATUS OF BERLIN

Berlin was the capital of the German Empire in 1871. After the post-World War II division of Germany and Berlin into four occupation zones, the Soviet Union regarded Berlin as the capital of its zone and intended to establish a communist government. Tensions increased when the Soviets blocked or slowed transportation into the city. The supposed issue that stimulated Soviet harassment was the kind of currency that should be circulated in Berlin. The Soviets wanted the same currency for the city and for the Democratic Republic. The Western Allies were willing to acquiesce but stipulated that the West also have the authority to issue the currency. Later it was clear that Soviet intransigence was primarily to force the Allies to withdraw from Berlin or to prevent them from setting up a government in the Western zones.

Berlin became a symbol of freedom and a showplace of Western rights. In response to the Soviet blockade of Berlin in 1948 American and British planes flew supplies to the besieged area, defeating Soviet maneuvers and renewing the Berliners' feelings of solidarity with the Western Allies. The blockade cemented the split in the city's government. The Soviets walked out of the Four Power Control Body for Berlin (Kommandantura) and forced the city government to move to headquarters in the American sector. East Berlin was then led by a communist mayor and West Berlin, by an SPD mayor.

When the East Germans, with Soviet support, erected a wall dividing East and West Berlin in 1961, reunification of Germany became less likely. The focus of Western Allies for the next several years shifted to concern with access to Berlin.

Responding to United States calls for new efforts to resolve the Berlin-access problem and reduce tensions in the area, representatives of France, the Soviet Union, the United Kingdom, and the United States began negotiations in 1970 that eventually resulted in the Berlin Quadripartite Agreement, the final protocol of which was signed in June 1972. The agreement did not in any way change the legal status of Berlin or the rights and responsibilities of the four powers in the city. West Berlin is not a constituent part of the Federal Republic and is not governed by it; but there are very close ties between the city and the Federal Republic in political, economic, and cultural areas, and the agreement provides that these may be strengthened. The agreement also provides that transit traffic of civilians and freight from the Federal Republic to Berlin will be unimpeded.

Berliners have a voice in electing the president of the Bundestag, but their vote in electing a federal chancellor is merely symbolic. Berliners have representatives in the Bundestag who participate in debates but do not vote.

POPULAR ATTITUDES TOWARD THE COUNTRY'S HISTORY

Since World War II German historians have taken sharp turns in revising historical analyses. Motives for the shifts vary. Some wrote to counteract what they believed was the biased condemnation of German wartime leaders by the Western Allies. Others viewed the 1937–47 period "as a chain of evil actions and reactions." Strong moralizing was present in the writings of the immediate postwar years and during the 1950s. Freedom for individuals was emphasized, and writers shied away from accounts of concentration camps and mass murders. By passing off the actions of the Third Reich as fulfillments of *Mein Kampf* proposals, historians avoided the awkward situation of explaining the concurrence of conservatives, members of the middle class, and industry. Rationales for participation or acceptance of the regime were ignored.

A reversal came in the 1960s when historians began questioning established ideas. They conducted research in such fields as economic, domestic, and diplomatic interrelationships to examine their effects on events. A more realistic and balanced view of the past was advanced. For example, some writers conceded that certain weaknesses of the Weimar Republic permitted a man such as Hitler to attain power.

Until the 1960s it was feared that studies of the 1930s and wartime would revive nazism but, after suppressing memories of life under Hitler for over thirty years, people in their fifties were coping with a reexamination of his role, and some were viewing him as a man rather than a monster. Feelings were mixed. Some were ashamed of the past; condemnation of Hitler often focused on what he perpetrated on fellow citizens rather than on his crimes toward other nations. Others believed his only error was to be defeated.

Evidence of increased interest in the Nazi period appeared in the fourteen major books about Hitler and his era that were published in the Federal Republic in 1973. Interest in the revival of Hitler studies was widespread but did not lack voluble opposition and reluctance on the part of some to openly admit their interest. Booksellers revealed that clients would telephone to order a Hitler book rather than appear in person to make the purchase.

Among young people there is little interest in the Hitler revival. A twenty-eight-year-old university student summarized his peers' attitude: "As Germans, we all have responsibility for what happened, of course, but I feel no special guilt on my shoulders. The older generation does because they feel their own conduct during that time was wrong." Many youths cannot comprehend why their parents were mesmerized by Hitler.

CHAPTER 3

PHYSICAL ENVIRONMENT AND TRANSPORTATION

The Federal Republic is a post-World War II German state that evolved from the occupation zones of France, the United Kingdom, and the United States. The zone occupied by the Soviet Union became the German Democratic Republic. The 95,975 square miles within the borders of the Federal Republic and West Berlin include a wide variety of terrain, from coastal lowlands and plains in the north through uplands and low mountains in the center and the south to the high Alps along the extreme southern rim of the country. The country is bounded on the north by the North Sea, Denmark, and the Baltic Sea; on the east by the Democratic Republic and Czechoslovakia; on the south by Austria and Switzerland; and on the west by France, Luxembourg, Belgium, and the Netherlands. The longest single frontier of the Federal Republic is the one that divides it from the Democratic Republic. The western two-thirds of the city of Berlin—West Berlin—is a part of the Federal Republic, but it is isolated from the remainder of the country by nearly 100 miles.

The Federal Republic's geography is almost devoid of distinctive dividing lines. Few of its political boundaries are natural, and the physical regions within the country tend to fuse gradually into one another. The flat lowlands of the northwest become rolling green hills to the northeast and inland to the south, where they blend into the uplands of the central part of the country. The low mountains and great forests of the central regions give way to more gentle terrain in the Danube River basin and once again become hilly at the approaches to the Alps. The Bavarian Alps and the Rhine Valley are impressive features of the Federal Republic's landscape—the mountains for their beauty and ruggedness and the Rhine valley for its importance as a commercial artery and its physical beauty.

Land (state; pl., *Länder*) borders conform roughly to regions that date back to the Holy Roman Empire. Eight of the ten *Länder* divide most of the country's territory. Two of them—Hamburg and Bremen—are large urban complexes requiring so many administrative functions differing from the largely rural areas adjacent to them that they have been made into separate *Länder*. West Berlin and its 2.1 million population are administered separately.

GENERAL SETTING

The location of the Federal Republic in north-central Europe places it at the center of nearly all aspects of that region's physical environment.

The country shares its coastal lowlands with all of the lands that border on the North and Baltic seas; its central range of low mountains and their band of rich mineral resources, with France, Belgium, the Democratic Republic, Czechoslovakia, and Poland; and its high mountains, with Austria, Switzerland, France, and Italy.

The climate of the Federal Republic is influenced largely by the maritime systems that originate to the west, but it is also affected by polar and continental air masses that reach it from eastern Europe and the Soviet Union. The boundaries of the Federal Republic have no greatly isolating physical barriers, and major transportation arteries extend beyond the borders into the larger industrial community of which it is a part.

Although soils are not the best, precipitation and climate are favorable enough so that crop yields are good, and natural vegetation is luxuriant. Where the terrain is too rugged for cultivation, most of it can be made into pasture or productive forests. Mineral resources are not overabundant but are adequate to stimulate and to support one of the world's greatest industrial economies.

NATURAL FEATURES

Topography

For the purpose of topographic discussion, the country is divided into five major physical regions: the northern lowlands, central uplands, Alpine foothills, Bavarian Alps, and the Rhine Valley and western highlands (see fig. 5). The northern lowlands encompass the territory of three *Länder*—Schleswig-Holstein, Hamburg, and Bremen—and most of a fourth, Lower Saxony. The lowlands are part of a great plain that extends across north-central Europe, broadening from northern Belgium and the Netherlands until, by the time it reaches the Ural Mountains, it has encompassed a large part of Poland and the European portion of the Soviet Union.

South of the northern lowlands, the terrain rises to a hilly region commonly known as the central uplands. The central uplands incorporate the remainder of Lower Saxony, adjacent hills in the *Land* of North Rhine-Westphalia, and most of the *Land* of Hesse. This is a part of the Hercynian massif, a range of eroded low mountains extending from northern France, through southern Belgium, the Federal Republic, the Democratic Republic, and into southern Poland.

The greatest part of the *Land* of Bavaria and the eastern two-thirds of the *Land* of Baden-Württemberg are hilly or have low, forested mountains that are foothills of the Alps. This Alpine foothill region contains the upper Danube River basin and the country's most beautiful lake area. Where the foothills give way to an abrupt rise in terrain, the Bavarian Alps region begins. This area is part of the Alps proper.

The remainder of the Federal Republic, the western and southwestern

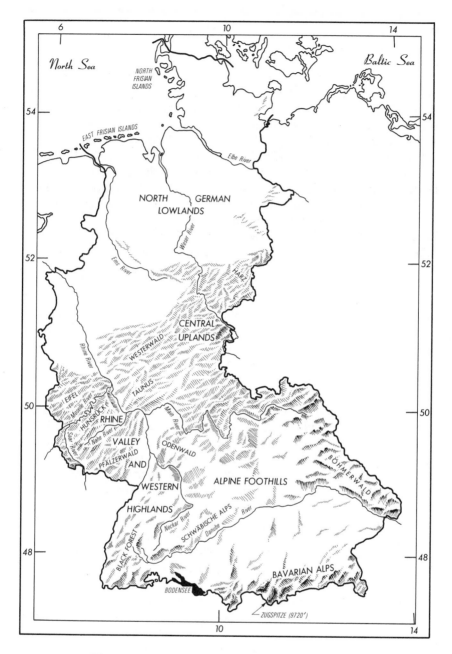

Figure 5. Topography of the Federal Republic of Germany

section, is largely hilly country and is dominated by the Rhine River, which drains almost all of the area. This section contains the Rhine Valley and most of the terrain beside it from the Swiss border to the Ruhr River. It is a varied region that includes the wide and terraced valley of the upper Rhine, the narrow gorges of the river between Bingen and Bonn, the Saar, the Black Forest (Schwarzwald), and the low mountains on both sides of the river north of the Black Forest.

Northern Lowlands

Hills in eastern Schleswig-Holstein rarely exceed 500 feet in elevation, and those in the central and western parts seldom reach 300 feet. Particularly in the northeast and all along the southern side of the region—wherever there is a little elevation or where the terrain is rolling and drainage is satisfactory—the land is highly productive.

Commerce and industry that thrive around the great port of Hamburg and the combined ports of Bremen and Bremerhaven have brought a large number of people to the region. In the lower, flatter areas, the land itself, however, is ill suited to support a substantial population. Before extraordinary reclamation measures were taken, the dry areas were heath, a wasteland characterized by peat or scrubby plant life on acid, infertile soil. Wet areas were equally infertile moor, characterized by peat bogs and coarse grasses.

The lowlands slope almost imperceptibly toward the sea. The North Sea portion of the coastline is devoid of cliffs and has wide expanses of sand, marsh, and mud flats. The mud flats (*Watten*) between the Elbe estuary and the Netherlands borders are believed to have been above sea level during Roman history and to have been inundated when the shoreline sank during the thirteenth century A.D. In the western area, the former line of inshore sand dunes then became the East Frisian Islands. The mud flats between the islands and the shore are exposed at very low tides and are crossed by innumerable channels varying in size from those cut by small creeks to those that are the estuaries of the Elbe and Weser rivers. The mud and sand are constantly shifting, and all harbor and shipping channels require continuing maintenance. Harbors are better regulated in the present day than in the past, when the shoals and sand dunes caused many shipwrecks and accounted for much loss of life. Ship access to small fishing villages and even to the major ports remains treacherous, and only pilots familiar on a day-to-day basis with the latest shifting of sands can safely navigate the estuaries.

The offshore islands have maximum elevations of less than 100 feet and have been subject to eroding forces that have washed away whole sections during severe storms. In 1854, for example, the only village on Wangerooge, the easternmost of the main East Frisian group, was washed away. Shorelines most subject to eroding tides were stabilized during the late nineteenth and early twentieth centuries.

Although the East Frisian Islands are strung along the coast in a nearly straight line, having long axes roughly parallel to the coast, those in the North Frisian group are irregularly shaped and are haphazardly positioned. They were also a part of the mainland, and much of the mud flat between the islands and the coast is exposed during low tides. In slight contrast to the East Frisian Islands, their basic rock structure is exposed in some places. The island of Sylt has red sandstone cliffs on its outer exposure to the sea.

Mud flats do not altogether dominate the scenery of the islands, and several of them have sandy beaches that are popular with summer vacationers. Vegetation is dense, flowering plant life is beautiful, and the settlements tend to be picturesque.

Helgoland, in the North Sea between the two Frisian island groups about thirty miles from the coast, is unique among the islands and has one of the more unusual histories. It was probably not a part of the mainland, as were the Frisian Islands. Records from about A.D. 800 show that Helgoland and Düne—now a separate sandy islet to the east—were a single island with a periphery of about 120 miles. Subsidence of the area in the thirteenth century reduced this periphery to about forty-five miles; and erosion occurring between the thirteenth and seventeenth centuries further reduced the periphery to about eight miles. The separation into two islands occurred still more recently, and the major part of Helgoland is now less than a mile long and only about one-third as wide.

The Schleswig-Holstein coast on the Baltic Sea exposure differs markedly from that on the North Sea side. It is indented by a number of small fjords, which have steep banks, rising abruptly to wooded slopes. Rivers emptying through the fjords are small, but they are usually quite deep because of conditions that existed when they were formed. At that time the land was covered with glacial ice, and the streams, which were held within relatively narrow confines, tunneled beneath the ice. This usually resulted in quite straight courses having fairly constant widths and depths. The deep water and shelter of the fjords provide safer sailing conditions, and there are several more fishing villages on the Baltic coast than on the North Sea.

Central Uplands

Hundreds of picturesque villages nestle in the hills of Hesse. This region has inspired the legends, children's stories, and folklore of the Grimms' fairy tales and other literature. The lower hills north of Hesse in Lower Saxony and North Rhine-Westphalia contain a large portion of arable land. The forests thin out, and much of the rich land is sown to wheat and root plants—sugar beets and potatoes—supporting a considerably greater population than either the lowlands to the north or the forests to the south.

Alpine Foothills

All of Bavaria and the eastern portion of Baden-Württemberg, except the Black Forest and the Odenwald, constitute the country's Alpine foothills. Relatively little of this area is forest, and a high proportion is extremely productive crop and pasture land.

Except for small areas in Baden-Württemberg and the part of Bavaria to the north of Nürnberg, most of the region is in the upper Danube River basin. The Danube is not as important a river in the Federal Republic as it is in the countries along its lower courses.

Lakes that range in size from less than an acre to a little more than thirty square miles were created throughout the region when glacial moraine blocked the valleys. Typical lakes have clear, clean water, are deep, and have steep, heavily wooded banks. Swimming in them is usually enjoyed only by the most hardy of vacationers, as the waters are usually very cold, but the lakes are favorite holiday resorts.

Bavaria, which makes up the major part of the Alpine region, has for most of its history been separate from the rest of the country. It has been a part of Germany continuously only since the Bismarck era in the nineteenth century. Bavarians have a temperament, life-style, and set of values that are different from those found in other sections of the country. Bavarians constitute most of the population that is native to their *Land*, but the people of Franconia in the northern section of the foothills, for example, have an altogether different, Frankish ancestry (see ch. 6).

Because industry developed later in the region than in the areas of the country near transportation arteries and coalfields, the Bavarians have been used to making their living from the land. To do so they have used every square inch of productive soil, and the careful attention given to the hilly pastures and forest floors results in a pastoral beauty seldom equaled.

Bavarian Alps

The Bavarian Alps are the small fringe of high mountains that extend in a narrow strip along the southern boundary of the Federal Republic. They range eastward from the Bodensee, a lake on the border shared with Switzerland, to the Austrian border just west of Salzburg. The Bavarian Alps have the same origin, structure, and features as the main Alpine ranges of Switzerland, Austria, Italy, and France, but the western part of the Bavarian portion is separated from the rest of the range by the Inn River valley. The range rises very steeply from the foothills.

Valleys are dotted with small cultivated fields, and slopes are usually forested with coniferous trees or are pastureland. The area supports less local population than is average for the country, but it is extremely popular as a holiday resort at all seasons of the year. The highest peak, the Zugspitze (9,720 feet), is near the Austrian border south-southwest of Munich. There is year-round skiing on the Zugspitze and a few other of the higher slopes.

On typical mountainsides, above the meadows and pasturelands, the coniferous forests yield again to Alpine meadows above the tree line. Base rock predominates where ascents are more precipitous and where the peaks are sharp. Meadows, however, may occur at nearly the highest of elevations if the slopes are not too steep and if the summits are rounded.

The Rhine Valley and the Western Highlands

To many who study Germany and begin to appreciate the many ways the river contributes to the country, the Federal Republic is in essence the Rhine River basin. The Rhine is the most important waterway in

Europe, overshadowing the Danube and the great rivers of the Soviet Union, and its valley is perhaps the greatest single commercial artery in the world. Although the Rhine rises in Switzerland and, for the final 130 miles of its lower course to the sea flows through the Netherlands, the river is nevertheless the single great unifying feature of the Federal Republic.

The upper Rhine region consists of a valley plain some twenty to thirty miles wide, flanked on both sides by heavily forested mountainous areas. This 190-mile portion of the valley is often called the Rhine rift valley, because it originated as a result of a sharp fracture of the region's terrain at the same time the Alps were formed. Until then the region had consisted of a single mountain massif that had included the Black Forest and the Vosges range in France.

This upper valley is also referred to as the terraced country. The name derives from the fact that the rift valley is about twenty to thirty miles wide and has an upper level that is fairly uniform in elevation until it rises to the hilly regions on both sides. This terrace level was formed during glacial periods when ice blocked the river from the lower courses and sediment was deposited in the valley. As the river established these courses, it cut into the softer sediment, leaving the upper level as a distinctive flat-topped terrace region. The channel and floodplain at the lower level are only from 1½ to three miles wide in most places.

The Rhine has been artificially regulated since the late nineteenth century, and its length in the rift valley cut by more than one-half, isolating many of the terraces. The steep slopes from the floodplain to the terraces are usually wooded. Where the area has been extensively fragmented, these terraces may appear as a number of little hills; in other places they amount to small plateaus.

The Black Forest in the extreme southwestern corner of the country is so named both because the fir trees that predominate in its natural forest present a deep green color and because their thick canopies form a cover that shield much of the light from the forest floor, giving an aura of semidarkness. Elevations in the Black Forest approach 5,000 feet, making it the highest of the areas bordering the Rhine.

Between the Black Forest and the Rhine River, just northwest of Freiburg and contrasting markedly with the neighboring terrain, is the Kaiserstuhl (the Kaiser's Chair). It is, as its appearance suggests, an extinct volcano, one side of which has been eroded by the Rhine River. The old volcanic form has withstood this weathering not because it has escaped erosion but because, where its softer rocks have been eroded, they have been replaced by loess deposits. As a result the Kaiserstuhl has become one of the richest agricultural spots in the country. Its terraced slopes are rich with orchards, vineyards, and a variety of other gardens, and wine cellars have been dug back under many of the soft slopes.

The Rhine's upper valley ends abruptly in the vicinity of Frankfurt, Wiesbaden, and Mainz, where the river turns sharply to the west. Below

Mainz, past Bingen—where it turns northward again—and nearly to Bonn, it flows through narrow gorges. This is the region of steeply wooded slopes and of vineyards on carefully terraced banks where dozens of the rocky hilltops are crowned with medieval castles.

To the east of the river north of Mainz are the Taunus Mountains and the Westerwald, which blend into the lower hills northeast of Bonn that continue to the Ruhr. Although some of the world's busiest commerce passes nearby and there are some of the world's greatest industrial concentrations at either end of the middle river's course, much of this region remains wooded or in pastureland and is unspoiled.

West of the Rhine River, immediately northeast of Karlsruhe, is another largely forested, hilly region called the Pfalzerwald. Its shorter streams in the east flow in torrents to the Rhine. The land slopes more gently to the west, and the streams that flow in that direction and eventually join the Moselle River are less violent. Because it is between the heavily industrialized Saar region and the Rhine valley, the population of the Pfalzerwald is relatively dense.

The Saar region, now one of the Federal Republic's *Länder*, is notable primarily for its rich coalfield and the industry that has developed around it. Located on the French border southeast of Luxembourg, the Saar area has changed hands between France and Germany on several occasions (see ch. 2). The coalfield that has made it the source of contention is about twenty-five miles long and about eight miles wide. This field extends from the southwest to the northeast, north of the cities of Saarbrücken and Neunkirchen. To the east and north of the coalfield the terrain increases in elevation, and in the north it blends into the Hunsrück mountain range. The Nahe and Saar river valleys, which enclose the Hunsrück range on the south and west, have cut deep valleys with steep banks, but the Saar hills and the Hunsrück are geologically old, and long erosion as well as the forests have softened their outline.

Across the Moselle River, which is a winding stream flowing between steep banks whose course has only been regulated since World War II, is the considerably steeper, more rugged Eifel region. This area extends from the western border of the country and blends into the lowland region north of Bonn and Aachen. Because of its central location the high Eifel—known as such only in relation to the surrounding terrain, because its elevations at no point reach 3,000 feet—drains into the Moselle, Rhine, and Meuse rivers. The eastern portion of the range west of Andernach reveals its volcanic origin—remnants of volcanic cones, crater lakes, and larger lakes formed in the valleys, while lava flows formed dams across mountain streams.

The Taunus Mountains are low, and their highest point is only 2,887 feet above sea level. They occupy the area north of the Rhine and Main rivers as those rivers flow westward past Frankfurt and Wiesbaden, and they extend to the Lahn River valley, about twenty-five miles to the north. Southern slopes of the Taunus are frequently steep but, where they can be terraced, the climate and their exposure to the southern sun encourage vineyards. Wine from this part of the Rhine valley, the other Rhine terraces, the Moselle valley, and the Franconian area north of Nürnberg constitute a large share of export wines. The terrain of the northern Taunus slopes more gradually toward the Lahn River valley.

The Westerwald, to the north and northwest of the Taunus, more nearly resembles the Eifel area across the Rhine than it does the uplands adjacent to it on the eastern side of the river. The terrain in the region is lower, as it blends into the northern lowlands, and rarely reaches 2,000 feet. The most prominent peak, the Drachenfels, is isolated in an area of lower elevation that makes it stand out, even though it reaches a height of only 1,066 feet. The Westerwald has much forest, steep gorges, and few people; therefore, small pastures and cultivated areas are restricted to land that is reasonably level.

Drainage

The greater part of the country drains to the North Sea via the Rhine, Ems, Weser, and Elbe rivers, and by lesser local streams in the northwest. A small area north and northeast of Hamburg drains to the Baltic Sea, and a considerable area in the southeast lies in the Danube River basin. The Danube flows eastward across south-central Europe into the Black Sea.

The divide separating the watersheds of the Danube and Rhine basins winds around Baden-Württemberg and Bavaria in a line that is difficult to define in some places. The Danube basin includes the greater portion of Bavaria and southeastern Baden-Württemberg. Water that it collects from the Federal Republic comes from the Bavarian Alps, the Black Forest, and the Alpine foothills. A small area north of the Bodensee, however, drains to the Rhine River. There are short streams flowing to the lakes, and the area along the Swiss border west of the lake drains directly to the Rhine.

The Danube rises in the Black Forest just east of Freiburg. Here again the Rhine basin intrudes upon what would appear to be a part of the Danube's drainage area. The Neckar River, the tributary of the Rhine that joins it just below Heidelberg, also rises in the Black Forest, only about five miles from the headstream of the Danube. In some of the upper course, while it remains a smaller stream, the Danube crosses porous limestone terrain in the Schwäbische Alps. During some seasons the river loses more water underground than it picks up from inflowing streams. The stratification of the subsurface rock is such that much of the Danube's lost water flows westward underground, eventually making its way to the Rhine.

Starting from the Bodensee, where the divide between the Rhine and Danube basins can be determined, the divide follows the high ridge of the Black Forest to a point a few miles northeast of Freiburg and then dips to the Southeast. After passing between the headwater points of the

Neckar and Danube rivers it turns again to the northeast, following the high ridge of the Schwäbische Alps, and continues in that general direction to the Böhmerwald and the Czechoslovak border.

The Danube's seasonal flow varies greatly because the tributaries from the Bavarian Alps are torrents during the spring and early summer thaws, but they contribute very little water during the autumn and winter. Streams that flow to the Danube from the north are minor. Summer precipitation throughout the area is also much greater than during the winter.

The Rhine River drains an area of the Federal Republic that is small in relation to the importance of the river to the country. Unlike the Danube, however, the water it collects from outside the country—in particular from Switzerland and France—contributes greatly to the river's importance to the Federal Republic. Tributaries of the upper river contribute much to its volume, and the seasonal flow of the upstream water complements that of the lower tributaries and in large degree accounts for the river's highly regular annual flow. Rivers in Switzerland flow at maximum in the early summer and join the Rhine at a time when there is relatively little water being contributed by its downstream tributaries. The lower streams are much more responsive to seasonal variations in precipitation and tend, as a result, to maintain the river's commercial channels at near equal water levels throughout the remainder of the year.

The western tributaries, the most important of which are the Nahe and the Moselle, drain that portion of the western highland country that does not drain to the west into France and through France to the English Channel. The more numerous and more important eastern tributaries —including the Neckar, Main, Lahn, Sieg, and Lippe—drain a larger area.

A large portion of the northern country is drained by the Ems, the Weser, and other northward-flowing streams. The Ems flows almost directly northward only a few miles inside the Federal Republic, paralleling the Netherlands border. The Weser, which flows into the North Sea at Bremerhaven, about fifty miles east of the mouth of the Ems, is a longer river and drains a much larger part of the central uplands. It is also joined by more and larger sized tributaries. The Elbe is a far greater river than the Weser, but the most important parts of its basin are in the Democratic Republic. It does collect some water from the small streams in the vicinity of Hamburg. The northern section of Schleswig-Holstein is drained by other lesser rivers and streams, some of which flow to the North Sea and some to the Baltic.

The lowland rivers are fed by spring thaws and heavy summer precipitation, but their winter flow is much greater than the summer. This apparent contradiction is accounted for by the fact that evaporation from the terrain in the winter is only a fraction of what it is in the summer months.

Climate

The entire country falls into a climatic zone where westerly winds and a maritime climate prevail for a substantial majority of the year. Maritime influences are effective a greater percentage of the time in the northwest, especially along the coast. Continental conditions and greater temperature extremes between day and night and between summer and winter are experienced increasingly inland, to the south, and to the southeast. The change to an increasing influence from continental weather systems over Europe as a whole is experienced more noticeably from west to east but, because the Federal Republic is narrow in this direction and its north-south axis is more than three times as long, continental climate is more apparent at increasing distances from the sea and in the higher elevations of the south.

In addition to the maritime and continental climates that predominate over most of the country, the Alpine regions in the extreme south and, to a lesser degree, a few of the upland sections of central and western areas, have a so-called mountain climate. This climate is different because temperatures decrease with higher elevations, and because precipitation increases when moisture-laden air is forced to lift over higher terrain. Variable local winds develop as high and irregular terrain deflects prevailing winds. Such terrain also creates local areas of differing shelter and exposure, in relation both to the winds and to the sunshine.

The major air masses contributing to the maritime weather are the Icelandic low-pressure and the Azores high-pressure systems. The Icelandic lows originate in the North Atlantic Ocean, rotate in a counterclockwise direction, and tend to move to the east and southeast as they approach Europe. The Azores highs form in the vicinity of the Azores Islands or in their 30° to 40° latitude band. They move eastward and rotate in a clockwise direction. Both of these air masses furnish western Europe with moisture-laden clouds propelled by westerly winds.

The northern lowlands frequently experience a situation (more often during the winter months) when they are between these air masses and are simultaneously influenced by both. At such times winds are westerly and usually strong. When only one of the systems is dominant, it is more often the Icelandic low. In spite of their nearly polar origin, the Icelandic lows are warmed by the Gulf Stream, and areas on the Federal Republic's North Sea coast have midwinter temperatures averaging more than 35°F. This is more than fifteen degrees above the average for that latitude, which is shared by central Labrador, the lower part of Hudson Bay, the Aleutian Islands, and some bitterly cold regions in Siberia.

When continental weather systems originating to the east are responsible for the weather in the Federal Republic, conditions are markedly different. In the winter months these systems have high-pressure air masses that bring bright, clear, cold weather. The local people describe these air masses as Siberian highs and usually expect them to prevail for about two weeks. They may dominate for only a week or less, and there are seasons when longer lasting ones will succeed each other. This occurred during the 1945–46 winter season and added acutely to the misery of the population in the first post-World War II months.

An occasional condition arises when the center of a low-pressure system deviates to the south of its usual path and crosses the central part of the country. This causes what is called föhn, or warm wind. Warm tropical air is drawn across the Alps and loses its moisture on the southern slopes of the mountains. The air warms significantly as it compresses during its descent from the northern slopes. In the springtime these winds dissipate the cloud cover and melt the snows. The föhn of Bavaria and Baden-Württemberg rarely are comparable in velocity or in desiccating effect to those that occur in Switzerland or to the mistral winds, which are of the same origin and type, that roar up the Rhone River valley in France.

The yearly mean temperature for the country is about 48°F. It varies with shelter and elevation, but otherwise the annual mean is almost constant throught the country. Temperature extremes between night and day and summer and winter are considerably less in the north.

During January, the coldest month, the approximately 35°F average temperature in the north decreases to less than 27°F in the south. In the higher mountains, where elevation is the dominant factor, the average may be as low as 20°F. In July, the warmest month, the situation reverses, and it is cooler in the north than in the south. The northern coastal region has July temperatures averaging between 61°F and 66°F, at some locations in the south the average is 68°F or slightly higher.

Annual precipitation varies between about twenty inches and more than eighty inches, and over most of the country it averages between twenty-five inches and thirty inches. The lowest totals are experienced in the extreme northeast and smaller isolated spots in the central uplands. The highest totals occur in the Bavarian Alps in small local areas on the higher Alpine slopes. Most of the moderately elevated upland areas receive annual averages of thirty inches or more.

Soil

Almost all of the land in the country that is not built upon or that does not have nearly vertical bare rock slopes is put to some economic use by the people. If soils are good, the land is cultivated, if marginal, the land is put into pasture, if poor, the area is retained as timber-producing forest.

The finest soils occur in scattered places of varying size. The best and largest of these are in the area where the central uplands blend into the lowlands to the north and in central Bavaria. Small areas of excellent soils are found in the river valleys and in the region of low hills between Hamburg and Kiel Bay.

The northern portion of the central uplands has a wide variety of soils, and many of them are rated good to excellent. Soils vary according to the kinds of rock from which they have formed, the steepness of the slopes, the elevation, and the amount of shelter from streams and prevailing winds. Brown earths are most prevalent, having been formed beneath earlier stands of deciduous forest. The humus and mineral content have mixed with loess deposits to form rich soil that crumbles easily and drains well. Some darker soils occur that are even richer in humus and lime, but these are usually found in thinner layers than are the black earths of similar composition in the Democratic Republic and Poland. Even where soil bases are clay or shale, the topsoil of the region is usually good and can be used for the production of good crops when the land is artificially drained.

The largest expanses having generally poor soils are on the flatter terrain of the northern lowlands. Poor drainage, either too fast or too slow, has usually been the main reason for the inferior quality of the soil. In generial, soils have derived from glacial deposits and river alluvium, the basic sedimentary rock having been buried beneath the surface far enough so that its main effect is to determine the amount or rapidity of drainage from upper soil layers. Alluvial deposits predominate in and near the river valleys. Elsewhere glacial moraine and older alluvium have been undisturbed and have decayed in place, over the millennia, forming geest, a soil that is clayish, impermeable, infertile, and difficult to improve. When these upper soils are waterlogged and boggy, they are usually highly acid. Sphagnum moss flourishes in such an environment, however, and centuries of its growth are responsible for the many peat bogs that are a prominent characteristic of the region.

Where the soil is overly coarse alluvium, drainage is so rapid that plant life has been unable to take hold. In other places, typically those where alluvium is fine or clayish, soils tend to be badly leached podzols. Humus and minerals have washed from the surface layer, usually being deposited a foot or more down in the base hardpan, a granular but closely compacted layer that is extremely difficult to work.

In the areas where spaghum moss and the other humus-producing plant life have been able to survive on the moister lowlands, the density of their decayed matter has further inhibited natural drainage. Reclamation and development of good soils in some places have, nonetheless, been successful. Until the requirement for more land becomes critical, it has been more economical to improve drainage of larger areas to a limited degree, converting them first to forest or pasture.

The larger river valleys, particularly those of the Weser and Elbe, have alluvial soils that have been more recently deposited. In these instances the less mature soils are superior to those that are older but that suffer from drainage problems.

Throughout the country, uplands that are subject to more rapid erosion and upon which loess has not collected have, as is always the case, thinner layers of surface soil. Podzol soils in hilly regions have a thin layer of partially matured humus at the surface but, as fast as they become water soluble, soil nutrients leach through the layers of clayish earth below if they are not washed off by rainwater. This type of podzol soil prevails over much of the land that is retained as permanent forest.

Agricultural and forestry practices tend to improve the fertility of marginal land and to reclaim wasteland when feasible. The quality of land under cultivation is seldom allowed to deteriorate. As the population has increased and the need has grown, the tendency has been to improve and to recover additional acreages of poorer land.

Vegetation

The country divides into vegetation zones that relate closely to the topographic regions but, because of soil and climatic factors, they are not identical (see fig. 6). Also, the Rhine River, which dominates a sizable portion of the country's topography, has only local effects upon vegetation. Maritime vegetation occurs over all of the areas of low elevation in the north where weather is predominantly maritime. This region extends farther to the south in the extreme west, not only to the Ruhr district but into the Rhine Valley as far south as Bonn. Natural vegetation in the central parts of the country consists largely of beech and some other mixed deciduous forests. The southwest and a large part of southern Bavaria have substantial stands of fir and spruce forest. The highest places in the country—parts of the Harz Mountains, a strip along the Czechoslovak border, the Black Forest, and the Bavarian Alps —retain their natural Alpine vegetation including sub-Alpine stands of spruce, pine, and fir forests. Other natural Alpine vegetation consists of coniferous forest to the tree line, above which are scrub and native grassland, giving way to bare rock.

The country has a great variety of plant-life species and conditions that encourage a large number of plants to grow profusely. For example, the Federal Republic has nearly three times as many flowering plants as do the British Isles and many times more than those countries having less precipitation or where there are more barriers to plant migration than is the case on the middle European continent.

Coastal vegetation, which is less significant than the other kinds because it is native to less of the country and is less adaptable to modification, occurs along the northern coast. Saltwater marshes penetrate several miles inland in many places because of low terrain, high tides, and frequent storms producing high tides. Most such vegetation consists of plants having succulent leaves and, if leaves are not large, succulent stems. Only varieties that tolerate high salinity survive in this environment.

On poorer parts of the lowlands in from the coast, the natural plant life consists mostly of scrub growth that could survive on heath land and grasses and tufted sedge plants that are common to the moors. Where drainage is better, there are stands of native coniferous trees, usually pine. As the population increased, the better lands became pastures and, beginning intensively in the nineteenth century, efforts were directed at

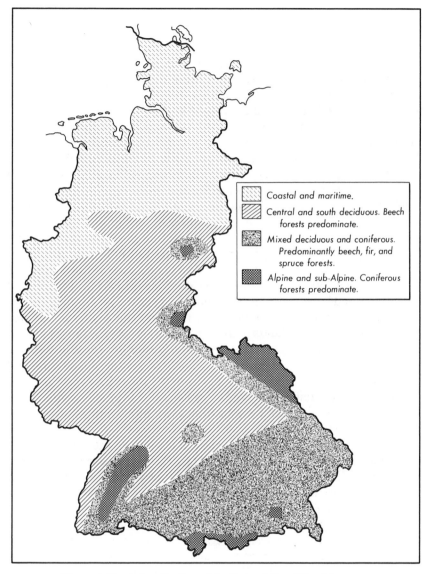

Figure 6. Vegetation Regions of the Federal Republic of Germany

reclaiming land. Much draining and soil conditioning have been accomplished. Land that responded best has been brought under cultivation. Marginal areas have been afforested. Conifers are almost invariably planted in these areas, not only because they produce quicker yields but also because they do better on poorer soils. Regions near the sea have been protected by dikes to prevent periodic inundation by salt water. Polders have been created on drained land that is not too saline. Since they are expensive to reclaim and require constant maintenance to drain and to control salinity, polders are made from only the most promising lands. They are used as improved pastureland or are cultivated.

Scrub, sometimes similar to the varieties that occur on the northern lowlands, is also found in the extreme south where trees cannot get a footing on steep mountainsides or above the tree line. Heather and dwarf trees cling to infertile places that are not too moist. Mosses, reedy growth, and the like do well in damper areas.

The only truly natural grasslands are found above the tree line in Alpine regions. On many hillsides and valley floors pasture grasses have become dominant after trees have been cut and grazing animals have been introduced in fairly large numbers. As long as animal life remains on the hillsides, the grasses will probably remain.

Most of the central and southern country is ideal forestland and, unusual in a land with so dense a population, nearly 30 percent of the entire country is still forest. This fraction will probably remain unchanged to any significant degree. Six varieties of large conifers and practically all of the temperate zone deciduous trees are native to the region. The conifers include three species of pine, silver fir, spruce, and larch. Pine and larch occur most frequently in natural stands in the north where the soil is mediocre. Pine is now the dominant conifer in the vast majority of reforested stands in the north. Natural spruce predominates in large areas at higher elevations along the border between the Federal Republic and the Democratic Republic, in southern Bavaria and Baden-Württemberg, and in some places in the Bavarian Alps. Spruce is important for its lumber and is often replanted. Fir predominates in the natural forests of the Black Forest and shares high elevations with spruce and pine in Bavaria.

Beech thrives from sea level to about 2,000 feet in the central region and up to 4,500 feet in the Bavarian Alps. It does not survive repeated severe frosts late in the spring and needs a fairly long growing season. Where beech predominates it makes beautiful forests, having little but mosses, grass, and early flowering spring flowers on the forest floors. Beech tree canopies are full and blend together and, after their leaves come out, discourage growth of plants that need more than a little sunlight. Much of the beech root system stays close to the surface of the ground, and shrubs find it difficult to compete with them for soil.

In spite of the predominance of beech, deciduous trees are frequently found in mixed forests, made up of oak, ash, elm, hornbeam, and other varieties in addition to beech. This is usually the case in the areas where conditions are not altogether favorable to beech.

Reforestation has also changed the character of some of the forests. Conifers grow faster and produce lumber more quickly and are often planted in place of the slower maturing deciduous varieties. Also, trees whose lumber is more valuable are frequently preferred over native types of conifers. Spruce, however, is an economically desirable tree, and new plantings are adding to its native stands. Scotch pine is replacing many other trees, including the native dark-canopied fir of the Black Forest. What this may do to the character of that forest is not yet known, but the canopies of the Scotch pine are a lighter green and are less dense than the native fir. The pine will give sections of the forest a lighter appearance and will allow more sunlight to reach the forest floor beneath it, which may cause a change in the vegetation on the forest floor.

Wildlife

The country's location makes its wildlife similar to that of central Europe. The absence of natural physical barriers allows it to be invaded from all directions by bird and animal life.

Nearly all bird species from the British Isles and Scandinavia find conditions suitable in some part of the country. Other species that are native to milder regions in southern, western, and southeastern Europe are found in lesser numbers. Larger bird species include the great bustard, which is found in the northeast, and the capercaillie, which inhabits the coniferous forests of the south. Fowl take to the wetter parts of the northern lowlands in great numbers. The cuckoo abounds in forests and wooded places in the Black Forest and throughout Bavaria. The great stork often makes its home close to the populated areas, where it builds nests of large sticks on the chimney tops of village houses.

Small mammals—mice, hamsters, and other rodents—thrive in all regions, as do several varieties of bats. The muskrat, which is not native to the country, and beaver live along the many rivers and small streams. Deer, including a number of small species, live in the deciduous woodlands but are numerous enough so that, when their natural foods are scarce, they invade village gardens. Wildcats, pine martens, and wolves live in the pine or spruce forests; these animals avoid contact with humans as much as possible. Wild boars are plentiful in the deciduous forestlands at lower elevations in the central regions.

Species of birds and animals that are feared to be nearing extinction are protected. Lynx and cranes are protected wherever they are found, and in a few areas the cranes' natural habitat is preserved.

Natural Resources

The country shares the variety of mineral resources that occurs in a band across north-central Europe on the northern slopes of the central uplands. Although there are many local deviations from the generalized pattern, the higher southern side of the band contains most of the metallic ores and, where the highlands blend with the flatter terrain to the north, the richer coalfields are found. On the lowlands there are occasional oil and natural gas deposits.

The most prevalent metallic ores are iron, lead, and zinc. Iron reserves are adequate for long-term production, but the ores are of relatively low grade and, as a result, more than one-half of the country's iron has been imported for some years. The largest iron deposits are southeast of

Hannover, northwest of Frankfurt, and northeast of Nürnberg. When better grades become scarcer elsewhere in the world, these local ores can again be exploited to a greater extent. Lead and zinc are found in more isolated areas near Bonn and in the central uplands.

Potash, an important ingredient in fertilizer, is mined and processed in large quantities. Before World War II, Germany contributed more than 95 percent of the world's total potash and, although the greater portion of it is in areas to the east of the country, it is also taken from a number of places in Lower Saxony and Baden-Württemburg. Salt is extracted in large amounts from mines in southeastern Bavaria. Oil fields on the northern lowlands provide less than 10 percent of the petroleum that the country consumes.

Water power is available and is dependable in much of the upland region, especially in the south, and is extensively exploited. It accounts, however, for only about 1 percent of the country's total power production.

Coal is the mineral and fuel resource of greatest value and importance to the economy. It is available in quantity in all of its natural forms; it can be easily mined; and its measured reserves will last for centuries. Lignite (brown coal) is found in the Cologne area, in Hesse, and in Bavaria. Large fields of harder coals are responsible for the great industrial complexes in the Ruhr and Saar regions.

BOUNDARIES AND POLITICAL SUBDIVISIONS

Boundaries

The country shares boundaries with nine neighboring states: Czechslovakia (221 miles), Austria (498 miles), Switzerland (208 miles), France (280 miles), Luxembourg (80 miles), Belgium (94 miles), the Netherlands (357 miles), Denmark (42 miles), and the Democratic Republic (856 miles). The number of neighbors is considerably larger than is the case for any other country having as small an area and as short a periphery—95,975 square miles and 2,636 miles, respectively. None of the nine borders was officially disputed in 1974. The last boundary in serious contention was settled when the Federal Republic and the Democratic Republic established formal relations, but not full diplomatic relations, in 1972.

For the most part, the borders reflect political decisions rather than adherence to features of the natural terrain, although the difference is not as great as might at first be expected. The North and Baltic sea coasts are wholly natural. The boundary with Czechoslovakia follows ridges in the Böhmerwald, and the southern boundary has some natural justification for its entire length. It adheres to the first high ridge in the Bavarian Alps on the Austrian border and runs through the Bodensee and continues along the Rhine River, sharing both of them with Switzerland. The Rhine also becomes the French border to the place where the border turns westward near Karlsruhe.

The Saar, a part of Lorraine, and a German-speaking region southeast of Liège in Belgium have changed hands politically on various occasions. The border with the Democratic Republic was formed by political accident, as the line separating the Soviet Union's post-World War II occupation zone from those of the Western Allies. No party to the drawing of that line admitted that it might become the border between two separate sovereign states.

In spite of the conditions under which much of the border has been drawn and the fact that the Germans have had little to say during the two more recent postwar settlements, only the border with the Democratic Republic separates great numbers of people who may consider themselves to be part of the larger German nation. This is also true, to a relatively insignificant extent, in the case of the German-speaking enclave in Belgium.

Political Subdivisions

The Federal Republic is divided into ten *Länder* (states) plus West Berlin, which is administered separately but at the same level (see ch. 2; ch. 11). Eight of the *Länder* are sizable territorial units; two are city-states (see fig. 4).

Schleswig-Holstein and Lower Saxony occupy roughly the northern one-third of the country, and Baden-Württemberg and Bavaria occupy the southernmost one-third. In the central area between them are North Rhine-Westphalia, Hesse, the Rhineland-Palatinate, and the Saar.

The two city-states are Hamburg and Bremen. Hamburg is an enclave between Schleswig-Holstein and Lower Saxony encompassing the city and little, if any, more than its immediate suburban area. The *Land* of Bremen, except where it borders the Weser River estuary, is altogether within Lower Saxony. It consists, however, of two physically separate enclaves. The larger encompasses the city of Bremen, and the smaller is the port city of Bremerhaven. Like Hamburg, the area includes little, if anything, that is not within the cities.

Within the *Länder* there are *Regierungsbezirke* (districts), *Kreise* (counties), and *Gemeinden* (communities). The smaller administrative subdivisions are potentially subject to further subdividing, combining, or redistricting and, hence, to changes in their numbers. During the early 1970s, however, there were thirty *Regierungsbezirke*, about 540 *Kreise*, and about 21,900 *Gemeinden*. The *Gemeinden* are the smallest governmental units. They are the municipalities, urban districts, parishes, and boroughs of the cities and the countryside.

TRANSPORTATION

The highly developed industrial economy of the country has owed as much to its efficient transportation system as it has to its natural resources. The major carriers, in the order in which they have become important to the region's economy, have been the waterways, railroads, highways, airways, and pipelines (see fig. 7). Although the waterways have been superseded in importance by the railroads and highways, until the middle 1800s heavy cargo could be moved only by water. Most of the railroad network was developed between about 1850 and the end of that century. Not only could the railroads move large amounts of cargo, but they moved it faster and were able to surmount terrain over which natural waterways did not exist and on which canals could not readily be built. Roads could be built almost anywhere, but extensive use of them was impossible before lightweight and fully mobile vehicles became reliable and cheap. As a result, they became of major importance for transport of cargo and passengers after World War II.

During the early 1970s railroads carried nearly 45 percent of the approximately 900 million tons of medium- and long-haul cargo traffic. Inland waterways carried between 25 and 30 percent, and highway transport about 20 percent. Pipelines accounted for most of the remainder. The airlines' share, although important to the national economy, was statistically very small.

As of 1970 the government estimated that the country's investment in its various transportation systems amounted to more than DM300 billion (for value of the Deutsche Mark—see Glossary). The investment is necessarily a continuing one, and in the two decades after 1950 it amounted to considerably more than DM175 billion. Of this, more than DM80 billion was invested in roads and another DM26 billion in commercial and passenger highway vehicles and facilities. The already well-developed railroads and waterways had received first priority to repair World Was II damages, and during the succeeding period —between 1950 and 1970—they received about DM37 and DM5 billion, respectively. Ocean transport, benefiting from subsidies and an effort to acquire a larger share of the world's seagoing shipping trade, received about DM22 billion. About DM6 billion was invested in air transport.

Railroads

The first railroad in the country, a five-mile line between Nürnberg and Fürth, was built in 1835. Germany had by then become important industrially, but it was still politically fragmented. Major lines were built during the mid-1800s and particularly after 1870.

As of the middle 1970s the network consisted of about 18,300 miles of rail line; there were nearly 42,000 miles of track, over 5,000 miles of which were electrified. In addition to over 375 million tons of freight, its trains carried about 1.5 billion passengers per year. Although lines constructed after 1870 were designed to serve the larger German nation between then and 1918 and continued to do so within its 1918 to 1945 boundaries, some lines were made less effective by the division of the country after 1945.

Most of the system is owned and operated by German Federal Railways (Deutsche Bundesbahn), but there are about 2,550 miles that

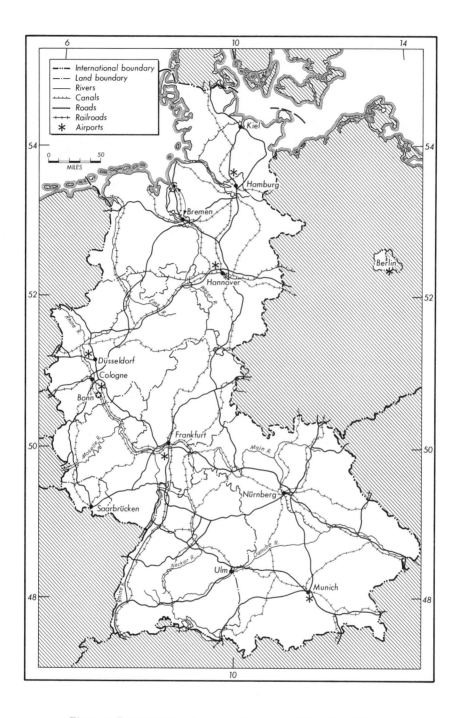

Figure 7. Transportation Systems of the Federal Republic of Germany

are not part of the federal railroad system; they carry about 70 million tons of cargo and about 70 million passengers annually.

Steam locomotives accounted for less than 10 percent of train miles in 1970. Diesel-powered trains accounted for 35 to 40 percent, and trains with electric traction for about 55 percent.

The railroads lost both passenger and freight traffic to the highways and their trucks, buses, and private motorcars after about 1950. Partly as a result of lost traffic and also to streamline operations, the railroads scaled down their routes and the number of their employees. Employees were cut by about 60,000 after 1964, to a total of about 410,000 in 1970. By 1970 it appeared that the trend to change from train to bus and passenger cars had been arrested, and both systems appeared to be carrying increasing amounts of traffic.

Local and urban rail service was receiving increased attention during the early 1970s. Underground and city railway systems were operating in fifteen cities or metropolitan areas in 1970 and were under construction or planned for eight more.

Special high-speed trains, trans-European expresses, that are easily identified by a large insignia (TEE) on the front of their streamlined locomotives, operate between major cities in the country and make connections with trains to principal cities in neighboring countries. The Germans have nicknamed these trains *Bonzenschleuder*, which translates loosely as VIP catapults, alluding to their extensive use by hurrying business executives and government officials. These high-speed trains are capable of attaining speeds of nearly 125 miles per hour. The train between Munich and Hamburg makes the 522-mile trip in seven hours, averaging about seventy-five miles per hour.

Upgrading plans for the railroad system call for increases in the capacities of main line track that will enable it to accept train speeds of 125 miles per hour with safety and comfort. Some routes are to get a speed rating of 185 miles per hour. About 6,800 miles of line are to be electric by 1976. Freight trains are providing a rapidly increasing amount of container service. Over 28,750 miles of continuously welded rail were in service in 1970.

Roads

The road and highway network is over 100,000 miles in length. Roads are classified as limited access expressways, or autobahns, and—in descending order of their importance and, generally, of their quality and maintenance—as federal, state, and county roads. There were 2,550 miles of autobahns, and 20,000, 40,000, and 38,000 miles, respectively, of the federal, state, and county routes in 1970.

The number of road vehicles is the highest in Europe, both in actual numbers and in relation to the highway mileage, and road traffic is dense. Of approximately 18 million registered vehicles in late 1971, 14 million were privately owned automobiles.

The development of motor transport came about early and is more mature in the Federal Republic than elsewhere on the European continent. This maturity shows in the relatively small annual increases in the use of highway vehicles since the early 1960s. In the eight-year period between 1962 and 1970, for example, bus passenger traffic remained nearly constant, and passenger and cargo traffic in other vehicles increased by only about 25 percent each.

The autobahns, the first of which were constructed by Hitler in the 1930s—to enhance the development of motor transportation, as status symbols, and as military roads—were the first limited-access expressways and were by far the most advanced highways of their time. Division of the country after World War II rendered those in existence of less service to the Federal Republic because of the closed border between it and the Democratic Republic. Construction of new routes since about 1950 has been aimed at, and has succeeded in, making the roads more useful, and they now carry heavy traffic. In the ten years after 1974, plans call for expanding the autobahn system to nearly 3,000 miles and for adding nearly 1,900 miles of other expressways.

Speed limits have been vehemently resisted by German motorists, and accident rates and death tolls have been high. This has been particularly true because vehicles with very high and low performance capabilities travel together on excellent highways having few, if any, restrictions upon their operation. After the Arab-Israeli conflict of late 1973 and the subsequent interruption in shipments of Middle East oil, speed limits were imposed on autobahn traffic in order to save motor fuels. A mandatory sixty-two mile-per-hour speed limit was imposed briefly. It was replaced within six months by a voluntary limit of seventy-eight miles per hour. Efforts at that time to impose a mandatory seventy-two mile-per-hour limit, to be effective for three years, were defeated in parliament.

Inland Waterways

The Rhine River system, including its major tributaries, the Moselle, Main, and Neckar rivers, carries a larger volume of traffic than any other waterway in Europe and tends to draw attention from the fact that the Rhine and the other rivers and canals in the country form an integrated system that serves a considerably larger area. The Rhine and the Ems rivers are connected by canalization of the Weser and the upper Ems rivers that in turn are connected by a canal. From the Ems, the Mittelland Canal proceeds eastward, connecting with the Weser River and joining the Elbe River system, most of which is in the Democratic Republic.

The Rhine itself accounts for only about one-sixth of the total navigable system. It is considered navigable from Rheinfelden, a few miles east of Basel, Switzerland, to the sea, a distance of 437 miles within the Federal Republic.

Terrain in central and southern parts of the country is less suitable to canalization, but the Rhine-Main to Danube Canal will, by 1981, connect the Rhine and Danube basins. The section of that route between the Main River and the city of Erlangen was open to shipping in 1970. When the remainder of the link is completed, shipping will be able to ply between the North and Black seas.

The Moselle was the last of the major rivers to be regulated. Only a short portion of it—about seventy miles—is in the Federal Republic, and it winds and loops through hilly, sparsely settled land. In 1956, when a joint program was agreed upon with France, it became feasible to proceed with the necessary work.

About 2,700 miles of the Federal Republic's inland waterways are considered navigable. The Rhine River can be used by 4,000-ton barges from the sea to Duisburg, and by barges of 2,000 tons from Duisburg to Basel, Switzerland. The Neckar River can accommodate 1,200-ton barges from the Rhine River to Stuttgart. The Mittelland Canal's capacity is 1,000 tons. The Weser River can take large barges downstream, but only 600-ton barges can reach Kassel.

The waterways have increased their relative importance among the major cargo carriers since the 1930s, when they carried approximately one-fifth of the cargo for Germany, and the navigable river and canal system included the frequently more extensive routes in areas to the east. The regions of the Democratic Republic and Poland that were included in that system were generally less hilly, and waterways in them were well developed. War damage to canal locks and inland port facilities and the loss of ships and barges were more difficult to repair and replace than the damage to railroads and highways, but by 1970 one-fourth of the Federal Republic's cargo was carried by inland waterway.

Passenger traffic on interior water routes is negligible. Principle cargo shipments consist of those that are heavy or that can be carried in bulk and those for which speedy delivery is not required. Such cargo includes ore, grain, oil, timber, coal, and heavy iron and steel products.

Airways

Lufthansa, the country's federally controlled airline, is one of the world's major air carriers. By 1970 it had routes calling at nearly 100 cities in sixty countries. It was then transporting 7 million passengers and about 150,000 tons of freight and mail annually. Lufthansa has had a good record for dependability and for freedom from serious incidents.

Most of the other major airlines in the world also have routes into the Federal Republic. About sixty of the airlines fly into Frankfurt, making the airport at Rhine-Main the country's, as well as one of the world's, busiest airports. Of the nearly 30 million passengers who arrived at or departed from the seven major international airports in 1970, more than 9 million were recorded at Rhine-Main; 5 million, at Berlin; and in descending order lesser numbers, at Düsseldorf, Munich, Hamburg, Hannover, and Cologne-Bonn.

Merchant Marine

Much of the country's oceangoing shipbuilding facilities and port installations was damaged or destroyed during World War II, and ship tonnage that was not sunk was lost as war reparations. For a few years after the war severe restrictions were placed on the shipbuilding industry for security reasons.

As port and shipbuilding facilities were rebuilt and restrictions against shipbuilding were removed, the all-new ships placed the Federal Republic's merchant marine in a highly competitive position in international ocean commerce. In addition, the country's rapidly expanding economy provided a local impetus to foreign trade. The combined result was that the country's ports soon came to be among the world's busiest, and a substantial amount of the tonnage was carried on its ships.

By the early 1960s tonnage of new merchant vessels had already exceeded that possessed by the German nation of 1939. In 1973 the Federal Republic had more than 2,500 ships totaling 8.4 million tons. Hamburg was the country's busiest port, handling approximately one-half of the shipping. Bremen and Bremerhaven handled about one-fourth, and Emden and Lübeck accounted for most of the remainder.

CHAPTER 4

POPULATION

The population of the country at the time of the May 1970 census was 60,650,599, including about 2.1 million in West Berlin. Estimates for mid-1973 placed the population at approximately 62 million. The increase of a little more than 425,000 per year was attributable to an excess of immigration over emigration, inasmuch as birthrates and death rates alone would have resulted in a negative growth rate after about 1970. Deaths have exceeded births by nearly 30,000 per year during the early 1970s, and the infant mortality rate has been relatively high for a northwestern European state.

German officials believe that the country's population has probably reached its highest point for the foreseeable future. They do not think it probable that there will be a reversal of trends in births and deaths, and they consider that continuing growth from immigration is unlikely.

The structure of the population by age and sex has been heavily affected by casualties and low birthrates caused by two great wars, by an influx of millions of people involved in the resettlement of most of Europe's ethnically German population after World War II, and by social factors causing a rapid decline in the birthrate since the mid-1960s. Females outnumber males considerably more than is usual in most countries; some age-groups include much smaller percentages of the total population than is usual; and there is an unusual deficiency of population in the preschool age-group.

Nearly seven-eights of the population is considered urban. Excellent transportation and industrial enterprises that are widely distributed throughout the country permit urban occupations for residents of small communities. As a consequence, the urban population is defined arbitrarily as that which resides in towns having populations of 2,000 or more.

Barely 8 percent of the working force is employed in agriculture, although much of the land is arable, the climate is favorable, and all of the productive land is intensively farmed. Industry uses about 50 percent of the working force, and about 42 percent is employed in service occupations. Most indigenous workers are considered skilled. The scarcity of native unskilled labor has accounted for the relatively heavy immigration that has been the most important contributor to the increase in population since about 1959.

STRUCTURE

Age and Sex

The composition of the population by age and sex in early 1972 shows a number of departures from the norm that are attributable to the national calamities and fundamental social changes that have occurred in the Federal Republic during the lifespan of its population (see fig. 8). The top of the population pyramid shows many more females than males, although males are in the majority in the young population and through age forty-four (see table 1). Below age forty-five there are only ninety-four females for each 100 males. The excess of females occurs abruptly at about age forty-five largely because of the loss of males in World War II.

The forty-five-year to forty-nine-year age-group shows 127 females for each 100 males, and the ratio is greater in the older age-groups, although it does not increase at a regular rate. In the eighty to eighty-four age bracket, for example, females outnumber males by more than two to one. Above age eighty-five the excess of females is slightly less extreme. The change in the trend at that age means only that, for the very old, extra

Table 1. *Population Statistics of the Federal Republic of Germany, 1971*
(in thousands)

Age	Male	Female	Total[1]	Females per 100 Males
Under 5	2,240	2,132	4,372	95
5–9	2,614	2,486	5,100	95
10–14	2,376	2,255	4,631	95
15–19	2,111	2,007	4,118	95
20–24	2,112	2,005	4,117	95
25–29	2,012	1,848	3,861	92
30–34	2,697	2,443	5,139	91
35–39	2,210	2,011	4,221	91
40–44	2,025	1,924	3,949	95
45–49	1,645	2,101	3,746	128
50–54	1,260	1,762	3,021	140
55–59	1,354	1,906	3,260	141
60–64	1,521	2,136	3,657	140
65–69	1,363	1,869	3,232	137
70–74	928	1,468	2,396	158
75–79	505	996	1,501	197
80–84	264	531	794	201
85–89	103	201	303	195
90 and over..................	29	56	85	193
TOTAL[1]	29,367	32,135	61,503	109[2]

[1] Columns do not add to totals because of rounding.
[2] Ratio for entire population

Source: Adapted from *Statistisches Jahrbuch für die Bundesrepublik Deutschland, 1973,* Wiesbaden, 1973, p. 45.

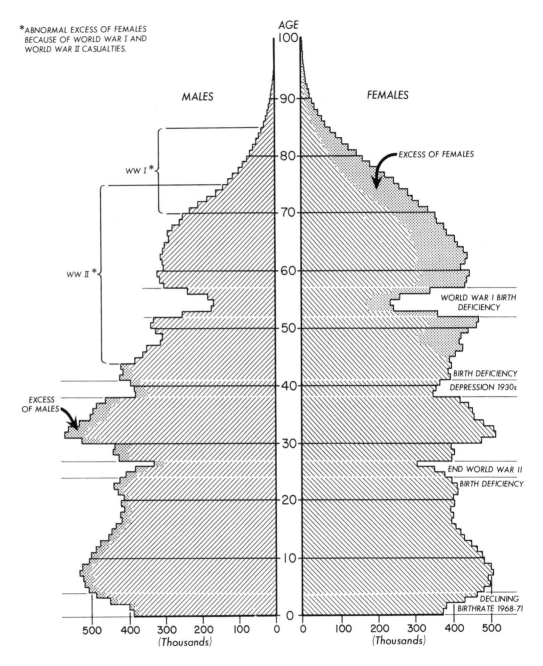

Source: Adapted from *Statistisches Jahr buch für die Bundesrepublik Deutschland, 1973,* Wiesbaden, 1973, p. 47.

Figure 8. Population Pyramid by Age and Sex, the Federal Republic of Germany, 1971

81

years result less from factors that create general statistical data than from such things as unusual health or family tendencies to longevity.

The pyramid also appears to rest on a narrow base. This reflects a decreasing birthrate since approximately 1964, which also contributes to an unusually high median age—between thirty-four and thirty-five years. Irregularities in the middle sections of the pyramid reflect the lower than usual birthrates that occurred during World War I, the depression years of the early 1930s, and the difficult years at the end of World War II. It is interesting to note that, whereas the birthrate was affected during World War I because large numbers of young men were away at war, there was little or no effect on the birthrate during the early and middle years of World War II because of the greater mobility of fighting men; the impact of the war became noticeable only near its end and in the early postwar years.

The various factors contributing to the phenomenal drop in the birthrate after 1968 had been widely discussed but not completely analyzed by the early 1970s. It seems apparent, however, that the factors are general throughout the country and that they are economic and sociological. Religion does not appear to be a factor. Although the birthrate in predominantly Roman Catholic Bavaria is slightly higher than the country average, the Saar, which is also predominantly Roman Catholic, has the lowest birthrate in the country.

Urban-Rural

Urbanization of the population is not a recent phenomenon. About 50 percent of the German population was classified as urban in 1860, over 70 percent in 1939, and by the early 1970s the figure in the Federal Republic had reached about 86 percent. There was an interruption in the movement to the cities at the end of World War II that was caused by wartime destruction within the cities and by the influx of immigrants. The tendency on the part of the early postwar immigrants was to settle initially as close as possible to the source of food. Movement in the direction of the towns began again with postwar recovery but, because so much of the population was already urban, it has continued at a slow rate.

Although the percentages of urban and rural population are based arbitrarily upon the percentages of people who live in towns having more than or less than 2,000 inhabitants, the percentage of persons dependent on agriculture has remained reasonably close to the percentage of the rural population while those dependent on industry have become a much smaller segment of the urban population. In 1860, for example, when about 50 percent of the people were rural, about the same percentage was dependent on agriculture. In 1972 about 14 percent of the population was rural, and about 8.2 percent was dependent on agriculture.

While the percentage of urban population was increasing from about 50 percent to 86 percent between 1860 and 1972, however, those dependent on industry increased by less than 10 percent—from a little more than 40 percent in 1860 to a little less than 50 percent in 1972. A third category—the number of people dependent on service occupations that were usually but not necessarily urban in character—has increased greatly, from about 6 percent of the population in 1860 to about 40 percent in 1972.

In 1972 there were 4,095 towns having populations of 2,000 or more; their total population of 52.9 million contributed the 86 percent of the country's population that is defined as urban. Of this urban group, about 30 million lived in the 4,035 towns of between 2,000 and 100,000 people; nearly 23 million lived in the sixty larger cities. The fact that only West Berlin, Hamburg, and Munich have populations of over 1 million is indicative of the decentralization of the urban population.

The dispersion of the urban population into a large number of towns reflects both the nature of the country's political history and the character of its industrial development. Until 1870 the area consisted of a number of independent or partially independent regions that had a corresponding number of regional capitals or administrative centers. Munich, for example, is in the center of a largely rural area having few mineral resources, and it is on no major waterway. Roads and railroads have come to Munich, rather than the city having developed along them. It has, however, been a provincial center since the thirteenth century, the capital of Bavaria before Bavaria's incorporation with the other German states in 1870, and a regional and *Land* (state; pl., *Länder)* capital since that date.

Density

Bavaria and Lower Saxony, with nearly identical densities, have the fewest people per square mile, followed by Schleswig-Holstein and the Rhineland-Palatinate (see table 2). These four *Länder* have a lower density than the country average, which was 641 people per square mile in 1971.

North Rhine-Westphalia, which includes the huge Ruhr industrial complex, the busiest section of the Rhine River valley's commerce, and nearly one-half of the better soils on the northern portion of the central uplands, has the greatest population of the *Länder*. It is also the most densely populated of the large *Länder* and has the highest percentage of urban population. The Saar, Hesse, and Baden-Württemberg have, in declining order after North Rhine-Westphalia, densities of population that are above the country's average.

The city-state *Länder* of Bremen and Hamburg and the city of West Berlin are considered separately in statistical analyses. Their populations are classified as altogether urban and, having essentially no rural areas, their densities are extremely high. In each of them and in the Saar the ratio of females to males is also high. The preponderance of females is

Table 2. Regional Distribution of the Population of the Federal Republic of
Germany, 1971

Land	Area (in square miles)	Population (in thousands)	Density (per square mile)	Percentage of Total Population	Urban Percentage of Population
Schleswig-Holstein.......	6,054	2,543	420	4.1	76
Hamburg	290	1,782	6,145	2.9	100
Lower Saxony...........	18,303	7,181	392	11.7	71
Bremen................	156	739	4,737	1.2	100
North Rhine-Westphalia..	13,148	17,138	1,303	27.9	95
Hesse	8,152	5,490	673	8.9	74
Rhineland-Palatinate	7,660	3,679	480	6.0	67
Baden-Württemberg	13,803	9,055	656	14.7	78
Bavaria................	27,238	10,690	392	17.4	66
Saar...................	991	1,122	1,132	1.8	83
West Berlin	185	2,084	11,265	3.4	100
TOTAL...........	95,980	61,503	641*	100.0	86*

*Average for entire country, not of column.

Source: Adapted from *Statistisches Jahrbuch für die Bundesrepublik Deutschland, 1973,*
Wiesbaden, 1973, pp. 36-40, 44.

below the country's average in Hesse and in Baden-Württemberg; in all
other *Länder* it is within 1 percent of the average.

Ethnic Composition

About 1 percent of the native population is not ethnically German, and
the largest element in this group is the Danish population living just south
of the Danish-Federal Republic border. There are a few French, who
have lived on the German side of the border with France for many years,
but most of the non-German people permanently in the country are there
for professional or other purely individual reasons.

There is a large group of migrant workers, most of whom entered the
country to do temporary or seasonal work, and the number that will take
up permanent residence cannot be determined. Such workers have been
encouraged to accept work in the Federal Republic in varying numbers
each year since about 1959, when the burgeoning economy began to
experience an acute need for unskilled labor. In 1973 about 2 million were
residents in the country. ·

Most of the migrant workers have come from southern Europe and
Asia Minor. In 1973 about 25 percent were Turks; 23.5 percent were
Yugoslavs; 21 percent were Italians; 13.5 percent were Greeks; 9 percent
were Spaniards; and a few were French, Dutch, or English (see ch. 6).
Because of rising unemployment during the early 1970s, the government
took steps in 1973 to discourage the immigration of industrial labor from
countries outside the European Community, and it can be presumed that

85

the number of migrant workers entering the country will decrease, at least temporarily.

DYNAMICS

Although the area that is now the Federal Republic has existed as that particular entity only since World War II, regional statistics have been maintained in sufficient detail so that the population of the area since early in the nineteenth century can be arrived at with reasonable accuracy (see table 3). Since 1819 the population of 14.2 million has more than quadrupled, growing to 62 million in 1973. The periods of most rapid growth occurred between about 1880 and 1910 and between 1939 and 1970. The population increased from about 22.8 million in 1880 to about 35.6 million in 1910, an increase of over 55 percent. In 1939 the population of the area was about 43 million; the increase between that date and 1970 amounted to about 40 percent. The largest factor in that increase was, however, the resettlement in the Federal Republic of great numbers of ethnic Germans from areas to the east.

Natural Growth Rates

Vital statistics for 1972 showed 11.4 births and 11.8 deaths per 1,000 of the population. Equivalent figures for the ten *Länder* were 11.5 and 11.7, and for West Berlin they were 9.1 and 19. Life expectancy for males in the ten *Länder* is sixty-eight years, and for females it is seventy-four years; in West Berlin it is sixty-six and seventy-two, respectively. Infant mortality in West Berlin is twenty-eight deaths in the first year for each 1,000 live births; for the remainder of the country it is 23.2.

Birthrates during the early 1970s were the lowest since such statistics have been recorded. A rapidly increasing population accompanied the industrial development of the country, the greater part of which occurred during the late nineteenth and early twentieth centuries. Birthrates averaged about thirty-five per 1,000 during the latter half of the nineteenth century; they began a slight decline during the years before World War I and plummeted sharply during the war years but recovered quickly after the war, although they have never again equaled the prewar rates. A slowly decreasing trend set in during the later 1920s, and another low point occurred during the depression years of the early 1930s. The Nazi government attempted to encourage population growth during the 1930s but had limited success. The birthrate in 1930, for example, was 17.6 per 1,000, and in 1939 it was 20.4.

World War II had less immediate impact on the birthrate than World War I, but the destruction that was visited upon the country in the war's last days and the chaos that followed the war caused the rate to fall again. Accurate statistics cannot be ascertained for the years 1944 and 1945, but by 1946 there were 16.1 births per 1,000 of the population. Except for a period in the early 1950s, the rate then tended to increase, reaching 18.3

86

*Table 3. Growth and Density of the Population of the Federal Republic of Germany,
Selected Years, 1819–1973*

Year	Population (in thousands)[1]	Density (per square mile)
1819	14,150	148
1831	15,860	166
1840	17,010	177
1849	17,970	187
1861	19,050	200
1871	20,410	213
1880	22,820	239
1890	25,433	265
1900	29,838	312
1910	35,590	372
1925	39,017	408
1930	40,334	421
1939	43,008	450
1946	46,190	483
1950	50,173	523
1960	55,433	579
1970	60,651	633
1973[2]	61,967	645

[1] Area is that of the Federal Republic of Germany in 1974.
[2] Estimated population, June 30, 1973.

Source: Adapted from *Statistisches Jahrbuch für die Bundesrepublik Deutschland, 1973,*
Wiesbaden, 1973.

in 1963. Since the mid-1960s, especially after 1968, the birthrate has taken an unprecedented drop, reaching 11.4 in 1972.

During most of the period of the declining birthrate after 1900, natural growth was maintained because a decline in the death rate counteracted the lower numbers of births. Improved sanitary conditions and advancements in medical science also lowered the incidence of infant mortality and added to the years of life expectancy. Losses during the great wars, however, reduced the number of productive males during the several years after those wars and also caused the higher than usual excess of females in the population.

Increased life expectancy, however, contributed to the creation of an older population and, since about 1950, the death rate has been gradually increasing. It was relatively high, at thirteen per 1,000 of the population, in 1946 but dipped to 10.4 in 1949 as postwar living conditions improved. The general trend has been upward since that time; in 1972 it was 11.7 per 1,000.

The overall rate of natural growth resulting from a combination of birth and death statistics remained high from the early 1800s until World War I. It slowed slightly during the 1920s and rose somewhat again during the decade before World War II. Natural growth has declined since World War II, and by 1972 the rate was negative.

Migration

Most of the 14 million people added to the population of the country between 1946 and 1970 came from outside its borders (see table 4). Other than migrant workers, most consisted of two groups of Germans, which official sources continued to list in separate categories.

The larger group of these ethnically German immigrants are called expellees *(Heimatvertriebene*—those who were expelled from their homelands). A majority of this group came from former German territories east of the Oder and Neisse rivers that now separate the German Democratic Republic from Poland. Representatives of the four major Allied powers who met at Potsdam, a western suburb of Berlin, in 1945 agreed in principle to cede a part of those territories to the Soviet Union but placed most of the area under Polish administration.

Table 4. Refugee and Expellee Population, Federal Republic of Germany, 1965

Land	Population (in thousands)	Refugees and Expellees (in thousands)	Percent of Population of Länder
Schleswig-Holstein	2,423	744	30
Hamburg........................	1,857	336	18
Lower Saxony	6,892	1,967	29
Bremen	738	146	20
North Rhine-Westphalia	16,661	3,207	19
Hesse..........................	5,137	1,120	22
Rhineland-Palatinate	3,567	404	11
Baden-Württemberg	8,360	1,620	19
Bavaria	10,053	1,940	19
Saar	1,123	41	4
West Berlin	2,201	532	24
TOTAL	59,012	12,057	20*

*Percentage for the country as a whole, including West Berlin.

Source: Adapted from T. H. Elkins, *Germany: An Introductory Geography*, New York, 1968, p. 115; and *Statistisches Jahrbuch für die Bundesrepublik Deutschland, 1973*, Wiesbaden, 1973.

The Allied Control Council, set up later, authorized the transfer of people from these territories and also from Czechoslovakia, Hungary, and Austria. They anticipated that the transfers would involve about 6.65 million people. The actual number of Germans who were forced to move, however, was about double that figure, and by far the greater number of them were sent, or eventually found their way, to the Western-occupied zones that became the Federal Republic.

More than 6 million Germans reached the Federal Republic between the end of the war and the autumn of 1946. Lesser numbers continued to arrive after 1946, and by 1950 the expellee group numbered nearly 8 million. Because a few more continued to arrive and because the group's offspring were counted with them, at maximum in about 1960 there were nearly 10 million expellees settling or still to be settled in the Federal Republic.

The Germans in the Federal Republic understandably remain bitter about the expulsion of millions of their people during the cruel days at the end of the war. With the passage of time, however, they have accepted the fact that a return to the prewar status would cause dislocations and hardships nearly as great as those experienced at the end of World War II.

Immigrants from the Democratic Republic—which was the Soviet Union's occupation zone in Germany until 1949—are classed as refugees. Totaling approximately 3 million, including the children that came with them or that were born before they were assimilated into the population, they arrived in a less torrential stream than did the expellees and over a longer period of time. They were also easier to assimilate into the population. All had come into the country willingly if not eagerly, and a far greater percentage of them were ready and able to enter the country's labor force. About 50 percent of them were under twenty-five years of age, and more than 20 percent were between twenty-five and forty-five. The stream of immigrating refugees was almost totally cut off by the erection of the Berlin Wall in 1961.

Later immigration was encouraged after the expellees had become settled and the inflow of refugees was insufficient to satisfy the demands for labor generated during the period of unusual economic expansion and prosperity that accompanied the country's recovery from World War II. Few of those arriving after 1961 were ethnically German. The need for increased numbers of laborers had diminished by late 1973, and in the future the government is expected to encourage immigration only of those who can be assimilated into the labor force.

As late as 1969 more than 1 million people came into the country. About 90 percent of them came from Europe, and most of the remainder from Asia Minor and the Middle East. Migration between the Democratic Republic and the Federal Republic and the movement of Germans from the other eastern territories that had been a part of pre-World War II Germany consisted mostly of older people and spouses or children of Federal Republic residents, whose government permitted them to migrate. Few economically active persons were permitted to make the move unless they had reasons more compelling than a desire to share in the reputed affluence of the Federal Republic.

Emigration from the Federal Republic has been on a smaller scale, and in every year since World War II except 1967 it has been exceeded by immigration. The overall population increase remained a substantial one until the early 1970s, even after the flow of expellees and refugees was terminated.

Of those who have emigrated from the country, a large majority have settled elsewhere in Europe. Many of them had been immigrants who had failed to become assimilated into the local population or, for some other reason, decided to return from whence they had come. Of the approximately 1.5 million who left the country for overseas destinations between 1946 and 1961, about one-half settled in the United States and almost one-third in Canada. Lesser numbers went to Australia, Brazil, and South Africa.

Population Projections

Population projections based on natural factors, that is, vital statistics only, and excluding migration, indicate that the population will start a decline that will be noticeable by the mid-1970s. Official German sources publish a double projection, part of which is based on the rate of growth (or decline) for the latest year for which all appropriate statistics have been tabulated. A second projection is based on a trend that is established by comparing the vital statistics for the preceding few years. The projection based on 1972 information indicates that between 1972 and 1990 the population will decrease by some 400,000. The projection based on the trends for several years preceding 1972, however, indicates that the 1990 population will be lower than that of 1972 by approximately 1.5 million.

The projections indicate that the working-age population between the ages of fifteen and sixty-four will increase. This is the case not only when 1972 vital statistics are projected but also when the lower growth rate is projected. In both estimates the working-age population increases from 39.1 million to 41.1 million. The greater share of the loss of population occurs in both cases in the youthful age-group, this loss being much more pronounced in the second projection, which calls for lower birthrates.

Both projections also predict a lessening of the 1972 imbalance between the male and female populations. This imbalance is the result of war casualties, mostly from World War II. World War I casualties are still a factor in the statistics, although to an increasingly smaller degree each year. In 1950 there were 114 females to each 100 males; in 1961 there were 113; and the 1970 census showed 110. The 1972 population was about 52 percent female—109 females to each 100 males. By 1990, barring major catastrophes, a more standard balance between the sexes will have developed. By either projection there will be about 106 females to each 100 males. This is near the norm when the difference in life expectancy is on the order of that in the Federal Republic.

Neither projection attempts to estimate the effect of external migration. This is largely because immigration will be encouraged or discouraged and emigration undertaken in relation to the country's economic conditions. Whether those conditions will be such that a larger labor force will be needed or, on the contrary, that a portion of the local population may seek better conditions elsewhere cannot be estimated with any confidence.

WORKING FORCE

The working force comprises people between the ages of fifteen and sixty-four who are physically capable of working and available for employment. In 1972 the working-age group consisted of 39.1 million people, including 19 million males and 20.1 million females (see table 5).

Because the Federal Republic occupies an area that had one of the earliest developed of the modern industrial economies, a large portion of the indigenous working population is considered skilled. Therefore, in the expanding economy between about 1959 and 1970, enough of the force could find employment in skilled positions so that there was a chronic shortage of unskilled domestic labor.

By 1974 there was little apparent need for serious concern over the availability of labor for the near or foreseeable future. The declining birthrate was not expected to affect the size of the indigenous working force appreciably for fifteen years or more, and the percentage of males within it would increase. No shortage of skilled labor was anticipated and, if demands for unskilled labor were to exceed the number available locally, migrant workers could be attracted. A leveling-off of the economy could be dealt with without too great an impact on the domestic population by discouraging migrant labor from entering the country.

Until about 1955 it was difficult to persuade expellee and refugee populations to settle in areas where they could best be absorbed into the labor force. This difficulty having been largely resolved, it is anticipated that changing regional demands for labor will be on a scale so small that they will be dealt with without undue stress.

The government creates as little publicity as possible about its attitude concerning the growth of the population. There are few publicly stated official policies on the subjects of birth control, family planning, and natural population growth. Governmental family allowances have been an effort to spread the social burden of raising a family, rather than to encourage parents to have more children.

SETTLEMENT PATTERNS

The first peoples who have been identified as German—whose continuity can be traced and whose identity with the modern German people is generally undisputed—were settled on the Baltic Sea coast and in the British Isles. In about 500 B.C. they began to encroach upon the lands to the south. Even during the days when the Roman Empire was most powerful, the land in the upper Danube and Rhine river basins that is now the southern part of the Federal Republic was in dispute between Rome and the Germanic people.

Such a dispute occasionally involved warfare between organized forces but, in Rome's view, most often consisted of raids by barbarians against

Table 5. *Working Force of the Federal Republic of Germany, 1971*
(by age, sex, and nonworking segments)*

Land	Nonworking Age		Working Age		Total Population
	Under Fifteen	Over Sixty-four	Male	Female	
Schleswig-Holstein............	601	375	759	808	2,543
Hamburg....................	325	309	543	605	1,782
Lower Saxony................	1,738	1,004	2,152	2,287	7,181
Bremen.....................	157	109	227	246	739
North Rhine-Westphalia.......	3,938	2,177	5,352	5,671	17,138
Hesse	1,197	751	1,744	1,798	5,490
Rhineland-Palatinate	888	492	1,110	1,189	3,679
Baden-Württemberg	2,179	1,089	2,829	2,958	9,055
Bavaria.....................	2,485	1,417	3,285	3,503	10,690
Saar........................	270	136	343	373	1,122
West Berlin.................	324	452	604	704	2,084
TOTAL..............	14,102	8,311	18,948	20,142	61,503

*In thousands.

92

the territory and forces of the empire. The Germans remained a confused pattern of tribes and tribal confederations throughout the Middle Ages, although about six larger groupings of ethnically Germanic people were emerging. Much of the country is still named for these groups, although their distinctive characteristics have become much less apparent over the centuries.

The Frisians were a fierce tribe of fishing, trading, and seafaring people who settled and tended to remain along the North Sea coast. Most of the land now referred to as Frisian is in the Netherlands, but some is within adjacent lowlands of the Federal Republic. Two of the Frisian island groups belong to the Federal Republic and include nearly all of the country's islands in the North Sea west of the Danish peninsula.

The Saxons settled the northern lowlands west of the Elbe River, and their early holdings included rich loess lands that constitute roughly the region now known as Lower Saxony. The influence of the Saxon tribes varied through the centuries and sometimes encompassed a much larger area. As a consequence, a separate area to the southeast that is now within the Democratic Republic is still referred to as Upper Saxony.

The Thuringians settled to the southeast of the early Saxons, occupying the basin that bears their name. Only a small portion of their region, north of the headstream of the Werra River and extending to the foothills of the Harz Mountains, is in the Federal Republic; most of Thuringia is to the east in the Democratic Republic.

The Franks were among the more powerful of the Germanic tribes and occupied much territory in addition to what is present-day Franconia. They also figured prominently in history. Charles the Great (Charlemagne) was "King of the Franks," and his empire was considered Frankish—neither German nor French. The region considered Franconia is at the confluence of the Rhine and Main rivers. It includes a part of Hesse and some of the Main River basin to the east.

The Bavarians also had times of greatness and times when their power was in total eclipse. The modern *Land* of Bavaria encompasses the territory of the Alpine foreland and the Danube River basin in the southeastern part of the country. The *Land* is somewhat larger than the area that is considered Bavarian, but the *Land* includes all of Bavaria.

The Alemanni, or Swabians, occupy the region to the west of Bavaria in the southern Rhine and Neckar river basins. The area includes the Black Forest and the Alpine forelands in Baden-Württemberg.

During the early industrial period the expanding population was first attracted to the commercial arteries and to the sites of the best mineral and soil resources. Hamburg and Bremen developed as seaports. Hannover is located near the greatest concentration of the country's mineral resources and in one of the better agricultural regions. The rich coalfields and the Rhine River generated the agglomeration of large towns in the Ruhr area of North Rhine-Westphalia. Other densely settled areas have formed in the middle Rhine Valley and along its Main and

Neckar tributaries. The Saar's coalfields and an industrial complex in the Nürnberg area of northern Bavaria have also attracted dense populations. The best commercial and agricultural locations have been densely settled for many years, however, and both industry and agriculture have spread to more marginally suitable places until every part of the country has a population density greater than that in all but a few countries of the world.

Some change in the trend to ever-larger cities has been observed by population analysts since the middle 1960s. The populations of towns of between 10,000 and 50,000 have increased more rapidly than, and occasionally at the expense of, those of larger towns. This has been the greatest contributing factor in the evolution of the larger population centers into urban agglomerations. Suburban or satellite communities around the large cities have grown more rapidly than any other kind of settlement. Officials have expressed concern over the "flight from the cities" as a few of the older city centers have tended to lose population and to decay.

Of the nine areas qualifying as agglomerations *(Ballungsgebiete* or *Verdichtungsgebiete)*, the largest by far is that of the Rhine-Ruhr, which has nearly 10.5 million people. Those of more moderate size are Hamburg, Rhine-Main, Stuttgart, Rhine-Neckar, Munich, Hannover, and Nürnberg. Their populations range in descending order from 2.3 million to 1 million. Bremen is the smallest, having only about 800,000.

Even between 1870 and 1945 Berlin was not the center of the German nation to the degree that Paris, London, and many other European capitals are the centers of their countries. In the absence of an overshadowing capital center the Federal Republic has a greater number of large towns and cities than is found in any other area of equivalent size in the world. In 1972, for example, it had sixty cities with populations greater than 100,000. Of these, twenty-eight had populations greater than 200,000, and eleven, greater than 500,000. There were another 820 towns or cities having between 10,000 and 100,000 people. Although a greater number of the large cities were in or near the Rhine River valley, no one in the country had to travel more than a short distance to a city.

Approximately 32 percent of the people lived in the sixty largest cities, but about 40 percent lived in the ten population agglomerations. This is because the agglomerations encompassed a good share of the larger individual cities as well as a great many of the smaller and medium-sized towns.

Housing in the country was critically short from the end of World War II until the mid-1950s. About one-fifth of the people in the country occupy housing that is 100 or more years old. About one-fourth was built between 1870 and 1918, and approximately the same amount was built between the two great wars. Nearly one-third has been built since 1948, the greater part in the larger cities. The post-World War II construction has been needed not only to cope with the larger population but also to replace housing destroyed during the war.

CHAPTER 5

LIVING CONDITIONS

In the fall of 1974, as the Federal Republic celebrated its twenty-fifth anniversary, the country bore no resemblance to the war-ravaged land of the 1940s. When the republic was founded in 1949, millions of its citizens were jobless, homeless, and undernourished, and a steady stream of refugees from the East served to exacerbate an already desperate situation. Twenty-five years later the refugees had been absorbed, and most people enjoyed a high standard of living although there were nagging worries about unemployment and inflation.

The people of the Federal Republic are among the world's healthiest and are proud of the low incidence of disease and the extended life expectancy. By 1960 all signs of the desperately poor health and sanitation levels of the immediate postwar era had disappeared and, in the ensuing years, the people pursued affluence and material well-being. Good medical care has been readily available and accessible to all through health insurance plans. The quality of medical service in the mid-1970s compared favorably with that of any country in the world.

A long tradition of state-sponsored welfare programs, dating from the late nineteenth century, has made Germans regard security against want and sickness as their inalienable right. Systematic planners and savers, they consider it essential to provide for a rainy day and do not mind paying taxes for social benefits. Private welfare organizations are also active in supplementing the government programs and are supported by the population. Almost all citizens of the Federal Republic are covered by social insurance on either a voluntary or a compulsory basis. Benefits cover pensions, accident and health insurance, unemployment insurance, maternity care, and special subsidies for children.

The people lived better in the mid-1970s than ever before in their history despite such temporary setbacks as the recessions of 1966 and 1967 and the energy crisis that followed the Arab-Israeli War of October 1973. Employment remained high and steady although 1974 witnessed disturbing signs of economic slowdown and increased unemployment. Consumer goods and services of high quality were readily available and, although prices have risen steadily, wages have increased at an even greater rate, thereby increasing the purchasing power of the average consumer. The diet during the postwar years has undergone a steady shift from bread and potatoes to such foods as meat, milk, and green vegetables; starches, however, continue to be a staple, and the people continue to indulge themselves in rich desserts and great quantities of beer.

HEALTH AND SANITATION

The crude birthrate in the Federal Republic in 1971, based on 778,526 live births, was 12.7 per 1,000 population, and the infant mortality rate was 23.3 per 1,000 live births. Life expectancy at birth was between sixty-nine and seventy for men and between seventy-four and seventy-five for women. In provisional figures for 1972, live births had dropped to about 701,000, and the crude live birthrate to 11.4 per 1,000 live births.

There has been a marked reduction in the incidence of serious disease during the post-World War II era (see table 6). As the country recuperated from the devastation caused by the war, health and sanitation authorities stressed preventive measures, and during the 1950s the drop in the incidence of serious disease was remarkable. Since about 1960 the health picture has remained fairly stable. Tuberculosis is by far the most common serious disease, followed by scarlet fever, the incidence of which has remained nearly constant since the mid-1950s. The death rate from tuberculosis has declined steadily during the postwar period, but the disease continues to be a major health problem. Hepatitis, for which there are no early figures available, and enteritis, the incidence of which has risen steadily, are also continuing problems for health authorities.

A slight increase in the overall death rate from year to year resulted from an increasing number of heart attacks and traffic accidents, both characteristic of many modern societies (see table 7). The number of deaths from cancer has also climbed steadily in the postwar period, but

Table 6. Prevalent Diseases in the Federal Republic of Germany, Selected Years, 1951–72

Disease	Number of Cases			
	1951	1958	1967	1972
Tuberculosis	117,546	80,128[1]	54,671	45,325[2]
Scarlet fever	65,123	30,354	38,767	36,058
Infectious hepatitis	n.a.	n.a.	21,328	23,321
Infectious enteritis	2,393	2,213	8,749	14,458
Contagious meningitis	n.a.	n.a.	9,190	6,517
Dysentery	1,025	2,245	1,070	593
Typhus	4,806	1,648	753	419
Paratyphoid	5,114	1,902	938	394
Diphtheria	27,156	5,091	117	34
Poliomyelitis...................	1,269	1,508	54	15

n.a.—not available.
[1] 1957 figure.
[2] 1971 figure.

Table 7. *Most Common Causes of Death in the Federal Republic of Germany, 1951, 1958, and 1971*
(per 100,000 of population)

Cause of Death	1951	1958	1971
Heart disease............................	178.7	228.1	307.5
Cancer....................................	175.7	192.6	236.7
Cerebrovascular	131.2	155.1	176.8
Accidents	49.2	57.9	62.7
Bronchitis, emphysema, and asthma	n.a.	n.a.	37.5
Pneumonia	49.2	43.1	26.1
Cirrhosis of the liver	n.a.	n.a.	24.8
Suicide...................................	18.4	18.4	20.9

n.a.—not available.

Source: Adapted from *Statistisches Jahrbuch für die Bundesrepublik Deutschland, 1973*, Wiesbaden, 1973.

deaths from pneumonia and children's diseases have declined. The most common causes of death in the early 1970s were heart disease, cancer, and circulatory disorders, often characteristic of an aging population, all of which contributed heavily to the overall death rate of 11.9, or slightly below 1,200 deaths per 100,000 population in 1971. Infant mortality has dropped sharply from the prewar and early postwar levels. In 1938 over 6 percent of all infants born alive died before their first birthday. In 1951 the rate was still high—5.5 percent—but by 1957 it had dropped to 3.6 percent; and in 1971 it was down to 2.3 percent.

In 1971 there were 3,545 hospitals and clinics: 1,340 of these were public facilities maintained by federal, state, and municipal authorities; 1,248 were operated for public benefit by various charitable organizations; and the remaining 957 were private institutions. The total number of beds was 690,236, or almost 11.1 beds for each 1,000 inhabitants. Of these, 377,477 were in public hospitals, 251,780 were in institutions maintained by religious and welfare organizations, and 60,979 were in private facilities.

In addition to regular hospitals and clinics, in 1972 there were over 900 sanatoriums and asylums managed by public authorities, charitable organizations, trade unions, industrial enterprises, and private individuals. A large number were devoted to caring for tubercular patients. Because Germans have traditionally placed high value on the curative powers of mineral waters and fresh mountain or sea air, there were also a great many health resorts and spas. The hotels, inns, and baths at such resorts are usually privately owned and operated.

At the end of 1971 there were 103,910 doctors practicing medicine in the Federal Republic, or one doctor for every 581 inhabitants. Of the total number of doctors, 51,159 were in private practice, 42,245 constituted the country's hospital staffs, and 10,506 were in some kind of official government service. There were also 31,405 dentists, 22,551 pharmacists, and 212,396 nursing personnel in 1971. In the winter semester of the 1972 school year there were 34,684 students in general medical studies (about 25 percent women) and 6,320 in dental studies (about 17 percent women). The vast system of vocational schools in the Federal Republic annually turned out great numbers of medical technicians, dietitians, and physiotherapists.

CONSUMPTION PATTERNS

In the early 1970s workers were enjoying the fruits of the oft-heralded economic miracle that had raised the country's gross national product (GNP) tenfold since the founding of the Federal Republic in 1949. The country's workers earned higher salaries for shorter workweeks than did the workers of any other country in the European Community.

In 1970 the so-called statistical four-person worker household had at its disposal DM1,089 (for value of the Deutsche Mark—see Glossary) to spend every month. The largest percentage of this amount—35.3 percent—was expended on food and *Genussmittel* (luxury items), which included such items as coffee, chocolate, wine, and cigarettes. The next largest expenditure of the average worker's available money was for rent, which took 15.5 percent of his funds. Clothing and footwear required 10.8 percent, as did transportation and communications. General household goods accounted for 9 percent of the worker's funds; education and entertainment, 7.3 percent; utilities, 4.7 percent; hygienic and cosmetic articles, 3.6 percent; and miscellaneous purchases, 3 percent.

HOUSING

In the area of Germany that became the Federal Republic, about one-fourth of the housing was destroyed during World War II. This great loss plus the influx of almost 10 million refugees during the pre-1961 era created a housing shortage of critical proportions. A housing census in 1950 revealed that 2 million people were living in hovels and makeshift shelters. Of a total of about 15.5 million families, only two-fifths had use of a dwelling unit for themselves; the remaining three-fifths were crowded into single units that sometimes accommodated two or three families. The immediate need was estimated at 5 million housing units.

With the founding of the republic in 1949, the federal Ministry of Housing was established, and its first task was the preparation of legislation that could serve as a basis for a very ambitious housing program. The first Housing Act, approved by the legislature in 1950, provided for the construction of 1.8 million housing units during the years 1951 to 1956. This act was amended in 1953 to provide for an additional 200,000 units. Other legislation followed, and during the 1950s a total of 4 million housing units were constructed. As the country's economic boom accelerated during the early 1960s, so did the housing construction and, even during the recession of the 1966–67 period, building went on apace; by 1970, with 11.6 million units completed, the Federal Republic claimed world leadership in the rate of housing construction over the previous twenty-year period.

At the beginning of the 1970s there were still over 2 million housing units considered substandard by housing authorities. The ambitious building program of some 500,000 units annually during the early years of the decade, however, resulted in a considerable reduction of the number of substandard units even as more units fell into that category each year. The housing picture, of course, was not all bright; some families on the lower end of the income scale still endured crowded or inadequate facilities, and in many cities the foreign *Gastarbeiter* (guest workers), who number more than 2.5 million, have crowded into ghettos that place a great strain on all facilities including housing.

WELFARE ACTIVITIES

With the passage of the Law on Health Insurance of Workers in 1883, Germany became the first country to introduce a national social insurance system. Health insurance was followed by accident insurance in 1884 and old-age and disability pensions in 1889. Through these and other welfare programs, Chancellor Otto von Bismarck sought to counteract the growing influence of socialism among German workers.

The Federal Republic has a comprehensive social security system inherited almost completely from the Bismarck era. It encompasses health insurance, accident insurance, old-age and disability pensions, unemployment insurance, family assistance, and a number of special schemes to assist war victims and refugees. Most of the social insurance schemes are obligatory for wage earners and salaried employees; however, since each scheme is an autonomous entity, there are differences in coverage. All schemes are self-administered through elected representatives of the employees. Claims and disputes are adjusted by independent courts on local, district, and federal levels.

In 1970 about 88 percent of the people were covered by health insurance under compulsory or voluntary programs. More than 25 million people were subject to compulsory insurance. This group included employees, the unemployed who were eligible for unemployment benefits, pensioners, women in certain vocational training fields, such as nurses and teachers, and self-employed part-time workers.

Benefits included complete medical and dental care, free hospitalization up to seventy-eight weeks in a three-year period for the same illness, full maternity care, and full or partial medical care for dependents, depending on the membership group. The scheme is organized through sickness funds on rural, industrial, trade, or occupational bases. Funds are obtained by equal contributions on the part of the employer and the employee, usually amounting to between 6 and 11 percent of the employee's salary, depending on the particular circumstances of the membership.

Accident insurance covers all employed persons including apprentices. It is financed completely by the employers, whose contributions are assessed on the basis of their total payroll and the degree of danger involved in their business. Funds for Industrial Injuries Insurance are based on a company's expenditure for injuries the previous year. Benefits include cash payments of a percentage of the salary, the size and duration of the payments depending on the degree of disability; complete medical care, including rehabilitation; and pension and funeral benefits for the survivors. In the early 1970s accident insurance was administered by more than ninety agencies, among which were industrial, agricultural, and municipal associations, which acted as insurance carriers. They were supervised by the Federal Insurance Office in the Ministry of Labor and Social Affairs.

Old-age, disability, and survivors insurance is organized into several different systems for wage earners, salaried employees, miners, civil servants, self-employed artisans, and self-employed farmers. Old-age pensions are payable after age sixty-five. Disability pensions include supplements for children and complete medical care and rehabilitation for the disabled. Survivors benefits include pensions for orphans under eighteen years of age and for widows or widowers, unless they remarry. Contribution schemes vary among the insured. Manual and nonmanual workers under compulsory programs pay one-half of the required amount, and their employers pay one-half, for a total of 18 percent of the worker's salary. If the worker's salary is below a certain level, the employer may pay the full amount. Self-employed persons under compulsory programs pay the full amount themselves. Various administrative bodies disburse payments, although each is under the supervision of the federal government.

Employees, people in vocational training, and those serving compulsory military duty are eligible for compulsory unemployment insurance. Both the limits of a person's contributions and his benefits were raised in the 1960s. Benefits are based on the previous wages and size of the family of the applicant. This amounts to about 65.5 percent of the person's wages plus the family allowance, if any. Unemployment insurance is available until a person reaches age sixty-five. The system is administered by the Federal Employment Institute through regional and local employment offices. The institution is not a government agency, but it is subject to legal regulations of the Ministry of Labor and Social Affairs. Unemployed workers who are not insured or who have ceased to be insured because of permanent unemployment may, in cases of proven need, be granted assistance for an unlimited period out of federal unemployment relief funds. The basic amount of benefits is usually about 52.5 percent of the applicant's last pay, plus a family allowance. This assistance is also administered by the Federal Employment Institute.

Payment of allowances for children began in 1954 and has since been expanded. Payments are made to families having two or more children, if the family income is not over DM7,200 per year. Funds are subsidized by the federal government. Since 1964 the program has been administered by the Federal Institute for Labor under the supervision of the Ministry of Labor and Social Affairs. Allowances were increased in the 1960s, and in the early 1970s action was being taken to augment benefits further. Children are eligible for the allowances until the age of eighteen. The age limit is extended to twenty-five years if the child is a full-time student or is in a vocational training program.

Since 1945 a number of measures have been enacted for the care of the war-disabled and dispossessed. Medical treatment, welfare, pensions, and employment assistance have been granted to the injured and disabled. Widows and orphans have been included in some programs. In 1952 the Equalization of Burdens Law was established to compensate for losses of homes and possessions. Payments are in the form of maintenance allowances, which are fixed amounts depending on the size of the family, or compensation pensions, which are a percentage of the worth of goods lost, usually at least 4 percent of the loss. In 1969 the average maintenance allowance was DM196 per month. The Equalization of Burdens Law is administered through the equalization authorities of the Federal Equalization Office. Funds are obtained through levies on property, income, and certain financial transactions and are supplemented by federal and state appropriations.

PATTERNS OF LIFE AND LEISURE

The average person lives a life very different from his forebears. The citizen of the Federal Republic of the 1970s is neither particularly industrious nor militaristic. He is, however, more prosperous. Prosperity, the war, and tradition have tended to make older Germans apolitical. The one-time unofficial slogan of the Social Democratic Party *Ohne mich* (Leave Me Out of It), in fact, characterizes one of the major attitudes toward politics in general. The young people of the country are more politically active, having taken to the streets on numerous occasions to protest particular policies. The war left scars of defeat, degradation, and despair. The postwar generation, however, has continued to endorse reparations, and each year a surprisingly large number of young people go to Israel to work and to atone.

Patterns of leisure have responded to the vast improvement in the economic status of the average citizen, who travels more and eats better and more varied foods than at any other time. With affluence, the marks of class are giving way to informality: the informal *du* (you) is gradually replacing the more formal *Sie* (you). Stiff academic titles, such as professor and doctor, no longer command as much respect as they once did. Clothing styles have also followed the worldwide trend toward informality, especially among the youth.

Tourists from the Federal Republic are everywhere—whole tourist areas, such as the Italian Riviera, the Adriatic coast, the Tyrol, and the Dolomites, have taken on a strong Germanic flavor. Domestic travel is simplified by the 2,800 miles (in 1969) of superhighways that carry people to the plays, operas, and nightlife found in the emerging cultural centers of Hamburg, Munich, Frankfurt, Cologne, Düsseldorf, and Stuttgart. These highways also carry festive tourists to the autumn *Karneval* (carnival) in the Rhineland, the *Oktoberfest* (October festival) and *Fasching* (pre-Lenten festival period) in Bavaria, or the carnivals of Berlin.

Foreign travel and the presence of foreign workers have fostered a growing cosmopolitanism in once provincial towns. The traditional meal of sausage, potatoes, and beer has been augmented by foods from other countries. Braunschweig, a plains city in Lower Saxony, for example, now boasts a Turkish, a Yugoslav, an Italian, and three Chinese restaurants.

There is a German joke that, when two Germans meet, they shake hands but, when three meet, they form a club *(Verein)*. This adequately expresses the German penchant for clubs. Although no one knows how many there are in the Federal Republic, the registered number in the larger cities was over 50,000 in 1968. To the traditional businessmen's and workers' associations and sports, student, and drinking clubs, such unique organizations as the beer-coasters collectors, the antibribery association, the association of deaf Catholics, and the corresponding association of deaf Protestants have been added. A club to combat club-forming has even been established.

Sports play a large role as a leisure activity. Skiing, swimming, bicycling, horseback riding, gymnastics, hiking, handball, and tennis are all very popular. The premier sport, however, remains soccer. The game is played by everyone: both amateur and professional teams actively compete throughout the country. In 1974 a crowd of 80,000 avid fans jammed the Olympic stadium in Munich to see a Federal Republic team defeat a team from the Netherlands to become the holders of the World Cup in soccer.

Despite all such activities, however, the average person, according to a 1967 study by the Allensbach Demographic Institute, likes to spend his leisure time at home with his family. The favorite outdoor activity, in fact, remains the traditional *Spaziergang* (family walk). The family dresses for the event and strolls at a "dignified" pace along a traditional route. The promenade ends with coffee and cakes rich with butter and cream taken at a local *Gasthaus* (tavern).

CHAPTER 6

ETHNICITY AND LANGUAGE

In the early 1970s, over 99 percent of the population of the Federal Republic shared the German language and traditions and considered themselves part of a single, though regionally differentiated, ethnic group. The extensive and systematic extermination of non-Teutonic peoples by the Nazis during World War II left the country with no significant ethnic minority. The most important minority in prewar Germany, the Jews, and such lesser groups as the Gypsies were almost completely annihilated or dispersed. Except for a sizable number of temporary foreign workers of varying national origin, the only minority elements of the population in the 1970s were the Danes of Schleswig-Holstein and the few remaining Jews.

In spite of the ethnic homogeneity of the German people, their physical appearance is quite varied. The ancient Teutonic tribes were a diverse people. Thousands of years of intimate contact with almost every major ethnic group that participated in the vast migrations of the pre-Christian and early Christian eras accentuated this diversity. The Aryanism and the Nordic ideal that Nazi theoreticians attempted to implement by the elimination of so-called foreign and inferior elements, therefore, have no validity.

The real foundation of the German nation is its language. It is spoken not only by the vast majority of the population of the Federal Republic but also by several million other people throughout the world. The importance of the German language lies as much in the significance of the literature written in it as in the numbers that speak it. Because of the contribution of Germans in all branches of art, philosophy, and science, German is still required in schools and universities throughout the world in preparation for advanced study.

Germans are proud of their language and the works of literature and philosophy that have been written in it. Pride in its purity has led to several active movements to rid the language of foreign influences. Before and during World War II, the passion for purity bordered on an obsession. In the postwar era, however, it has waned, and borrowings and adaptations of English words are extremely common in the contemporary German vocabulary.

Pride in the formal literary language has in no way affected an equally strong pride in the local dialects. Most Germans use standard German in a formal setting and a dialect for informal communication. German children are generally brought up speaking their dialect at home and with friends and do not learn the formal language until they enter school.

Dialects identify the regional variations among Germans that play such an important part in their attitudes toward each other. In addition, regional differences in temperament are perceived. Although its Roman Catholicism contributes to the regional distinctiveness of Bavaria, religious differences have little effect on regional variations.

THE GERMANS

Ancient Tribes

Germans can be traced back 3,000 years to the Teutonic tribes settled in the glacial hills and lowlands between the Rhine and Oder rivers, in the Danish peninsula, and in southern Sweden. The relatively sparse information about the Teutonic tribes before they were brought into contact with the Romans through the conquests of Julius Caesar in the middle of the first century B.C. is derived mostly from archaeological findings. At the time of the Roman contact some of the tribes were expanding eastward toward the Vistula and others westward beyond the Rhine. Among those who crossed the Rhine, some were known to the Romans as Germani, a name that was widely applied to the rest of the Teutonic peoples and is the origin of the English name for the modern Germans. According to Roman descriptions, the various Teutonic tribes differed considerably both in physical features and in such cultural characteristics as language, religion, and social organization.

In the fourth century A.D., as the Roman Empire began to weaken under the pressure of invading nomadic peoples from Asia, the Teutonic tribes again began to move outward from their original lands. Further unification was undertaken to increase the strength of the expanding Teutons at the expense of their weaker neighbors. The Goths conquered much of the Balkans, invaded Italy, and moved into Spain. The Vandals crossed into northern Africa and controlled much of the Mediterranean, even invading and sacking Rome. The Angles, Saxons, and Jutes from along the North Sea coast, as well as the Danes, conquered the Britons and established themselves in the British Isles. The Franks and the Burgundians moved westward into what is now France, and the Lombards moved into northern Italy.

Between the fifth and ninth centuries, the land vacated by the migrating tribes was occupied by other Germanic tribes, some of which combined in order to expand their tribal domain. Gradually, as these tribes settled down, cleared the forests, became cultivators and herders, and exploited the mineral resources of their new territories, they began to combine into stable political units separated from the neighboring units by wide stretches of uninhabited forest. During the period of stabilization, considerable mixing took place between the Germans and the Celts, Slavs, and other peoples into whose lands they had expanded. By the eighth century several tribes were well established in specific areas, among them the Bavarians, Saxons, Swabians or Alemanni, Frisians, and Thuringians.

Toward the end of the eighth century the Franks, under their leader Charlemagne, became increasingly powerful and assumed an overlordship of the German tribes and other neighboring peoples. Charlemagne promoted the spread of Christianity among the Germans and established the feudal system, but he was unable to unite the tribes into one nation.

Modern Regional Differences and Stereotypes

Time and history produced a German nation as the boundaries between the major tribal groupings became vague and overlapping. Nevertheless, the original cultural and linguistic distinctions of the several groupings are still evident in the Federal Republic and form the basis of a regional differentiation of which Germans are very conscious. A great many Germans, rural and urban, consider themselves Bavarians or Rhinelanders first and Germans second, even if they no longer live in their region of origin.

Although there are many tangible differences between the regional groups—dress, foods, settlement patterns, and architectural styles—the one that is used most often to identify individuals is dialect (see Language, this ch.). City dwellers, who preserve few peculiarities of dress or custom to distinguish them regionally, such as are found in rural areas, still speak distinctive dialects. Some of the larger cities, especially Berlin and Hamburg, have dialects of their own. Germans are alert to dialect differences and are proud of being able to identify them. Much is made of the different modes of speech, and there seems to be a popular impression that in some unexplainable way there is a connection between dialect, temperament, and physical characteristics.

Germans divide the country into regional groups that generally distinguish the Swabians, the Bavarians, the Rhinelanders, and the north Germans, who are often thought of as Prussians, another important regional group located mainly in the German Democratic Republic. Regional distinctions have little to do with political subdivisions or topographical features. Although historical traditions played an important role in establishing regional variations, the traditional religious cleavage between Protestants and Roman Catholics has had an influence only in shaping the distinctive characteristics of the Bavarians.

The most frequently cited difference between regional populations is that of temperament. The Germans have a wealth of impressions about differences in regional temperaments that are expressed in stereotypes. Such stereotypes abound in both serious and popular literature, on the stage, and particularly in the very popular cabaret entertainment (see ch. 9). They are most often used to belittle other kinds of Germans and thereby to reinforce the common feeling in each group. This is also evidenced by differentiating only between one's own group and other

107

Germans without allowing for distinctions among the others. In talking to a foreigner about the distinctive temperament of Bavarians, for instance, a Bavarian differentiated only between Bavarians and Prussians. When asked about Rhinelanders and other Germans, he replied that anyone living north of the Danube is a Prussian.

The importance of regional stereotypes depends not so much on their accurate reflection of a real situation but upon the very fact that Germans believe them. Often regional types in the Federal Republic are included in Germanic populations of neighboring countries. The most common example of this is the grouping of Bavarians with Austrians, who are not highly regarded by north Germans.

The particular point of view is important when considering regional stereotypes because there is so much overlapping of regions and because the boundaries between regions are indefinite. From Munich, Cologne appears to be part of north Germany, whereas in the north it is sometimes referred to as a southern city. Nevertheless, as one German author expressed it: the Germans feel that each area has a quality of its own, differing from the others both in reality and in the minds of the Germans.

Although regionalism still has a strong emotional hold on most Germans and survived the efforts of the Nazi regime to eliminate it, the Germans as a whole have a very strong national spirit. Under the influence of the romantic nationalist movement of the nineteenth century and the chauvinism of the Nazi regime, Germans have been made fully aware of their membership in a distinctly German culture *(Deutschtum)*. Membership in this culture is open to all German-speaking peoples —those living in the Democratic Republic, Austrians, Swiss, and the German minorities in other parts of Europe and in the Americas. It was this feeling of a common national spirit that was used by the Nazis to justify their invasions of Austria, Czechoslovakia, and Poland and to form fifth columns among the German settlers in other parts of Europe and even in the United States. This same national spirit, however, has also made it possible for the Federal Republic to absorb and integrate approximately 8 million Germans expelled from territories ceded to Poland and the Soviet Union after World War II and as many as 3 million refugees from the communist regime in the Democratic Republic.

For a long time the refugees resisted political integration. Refugee organizations aimed to assist the social and economic integration of their members but strove hard to perpetuate the hope of eventual return to their homelands outside Germany. Social and economic integration assisted by the so-called economic miracle, however, gradually pushed the political question into the background until the government of the Federal Republic could afford to accept the eastern boundary of its state and thereby recognize that the homeland of many of its citizens had become foreign soil. Among the older expellees and refugees, fewer and fewer express a desire to return to their former homes. The younger ones, particularly those who have been born in the Federal Republic, consider it their homeland.

ETHNIC GROUPS

The Jews

An estimated 26,000 Jews resided in the Federal Republic and in West Berlin in 1971. The largest Jewish community is in West Berlin and numbers some 5,500. The median age of the German Jews in 1971 was 50.6 years.

The present-day German Jewish population is what remains of about 125,000 Jews who survived the World War II concentration camps or did not emigrate either before or after 1945. Some returned from exile after the war still feeling themselves to be Germans and preferring to live in their homeland. A new dimension was added to the Jewish community during the 1960s by the settlement in Hamburg and Pforzheim of a substantial number of Iranian Jews having a different cultural tradition.

The significance of the Jewish minority is out of all proportion to its present size, because anti-Semitism in recent German history illuminates German attitudes toward themselves and toward other ethnic groups. The volume of material published about Jewish cultural history, Jewish religion, Nazi persecutions, and other aspects of Jewish life since the end of World War II has been astounding. It reflects the German collective feeling of guilt and an effort to prevent anything like the Nazi atrocities from happening again by becoming more open, enlightened, and tolerant.

The Gypsies

Next to the Jews, the Gypsies were a prime target of Nazi extermination during World War II. Because of their nomadic life, both within Germany and across the borders of neighboring states, it was never possible to determine the size of the Gypsy population. Few survived World War II. Those who remain in Germany have lost their sense of ethnic identity, but they are still considered strange and alien by the rest of the population.

The Danes

The Danes are concentrated in Schleswig-Holstein, at the base of the Danish peninsula. Their number is difficult to determine because every census of them seems to be motivated by an effort to prove a point. They have been estimated at anywhere between 5,000 and 100,000, depending on the bias of the reporter.

Those who consider themselves Danes form the only minority in the Federal Republic that harbors irredentist ambitions. The population of Schleswig-Holstein has been mixed for 1,000 years and subject to the hegemony of a number of powers. The northern part of Schleswig was ceded to Denmark in 1920 as the result of a plebiscite. Although many Germans in the ceded territory moved south and many Danes moved north, the population remained mixed.

Since World War II the Danish minority has been disturbed by the large number of German expellees who have been settled in the area. The influx not only has worked an economic hardship on the already poor population but also has changed the ethnic situation to the advantage of the Germans. The minority fear not only that they have lost their chance to be reunited with Denmark but also that they will be absorbed culturally.

In fact most of the Danish minority is being assimilated. They use German commonly in daily communication; they read the German press and watch German television. Intermarriage between Germans and Danes is common. In the *Land* (state; pl., *Länder)* election of 1971, the Danish minority political party polled only 1.3 percent of the total vote (see ch. 12).

The Frisians

On the islands along the North Sea coast and along the shore of Lower Saxony and Schleswig-Holstein live the Frisians, descendants of a seafaring people who have inhabited the northern part of Holland at least since the fifth century B.C. A powerful people during the early centuries of the Christian Era, they engaged in transporting pilgrims and missionaries between Britain and Germany. They lost their power after their defeat by Charlemagne. In the twelfth century A.D. some of the reduced tribes moved eastward into what is present-day Germany and Denmark. The Frisians are fishermen, farmers, and dairymen. In the 1960s they were estimated to number about 20,000.

The mainland Frisians are not very different from the neighboring Lower Saxons, although those living in the more remote areas are independent and suspicious of outside influences. They maintain certain differences in costume, architecture, settlement patterns, and traditions. The main ethnic distinction, however, is the Frisian language, which continues to be used by the group but is being replaced by German. All Frisians speak German, which they are taught in school.

Foreign Workers

The largest non-German group in the population of the Federal Republic in the early 1970s was the more than 2 million foreign workers who left their native lands to seek their fortunes in the booming economy of the Federal Republic. They are generally welcomed as a source of cheap labor to do those jobs that the increasingly affluent and selective German workers no longer desire. In early 1973 the 511,000 Turks constituted by far the largest single group of foreign workers. They were followed in order by 470,000 Yugoslavs; 426,000 Italians; 270,000 Greeks;

184,000 Spaniards; a total of 133,000 French, Dutch, Belgians, and Luxembourgers; and a few thousand Englishmen.

The foreign workers are highly concentrated in certain parts of the country and often form as much as one-half of the work force of an industrial enterprise. A large proportion of them have come with their families and may not return to their homelands until they retire. Under the law, they have the same rights and privileges as German workers, and there have been few incidents of discrimination on the job. In the society at large, however, they are considered aliens and are often made to feel alien. This situation has worsened as the economic boom that attracted them in the first place has slowed down, and many Germans are beginning to look on them as competitors in a shrinking job market.

LANGUAGE

Development of Modern German

Modern German developed over a period of more than 2,000 years from Proto-Germanic, or Common Germanic, the language of the earlier Germanic tribes, which itself had developed slowly from Indo-European. By the early centuries of the Christian Era the German tribes had undoubtedly developed a number of distinct dialects. The major division of the German language, however, came into being slowly between the fourth and eighth centuries A.D. This is the distinction between Low German, spoken by the lowlanders in northern Germany, and High German, spoken by the highlanders in southern Germany. The line dividing the two can still be traced across Germany, running approximately east-west between Aachen on the Belgian border to a point on the border with the Democratic Republic just south of Helmstedt. The dividing line continues across the Democratic Republic.

The differentiation between High and Low German resulted from a change in certain consonants from their original Common Germanic forms, which gradually spread among the highlanders and was generally fixed by the eighth century. The northern lowlanders continued for the most part to use the earlier consonantal sounds.

As further standardization of the language took place, the term *High German* came to be used to refer to the standard written and spoken language. The standard language is called High German because it developed mostly from the highland dialects of southern Germany.

Standardization of the Written Language

The oldest written texts in German that have been preserved appeared in the mid-eighth century A.D. These were a few documents, including religious commentaries, written in local dialects. Latin continued to be used for almost all written communications, which were restricted almost entirely to monasteries and courts.

At about the beginning of the twelfth century, under the impetus of the spirit of chivalry, secular literature began to gain popularity. Bards began to write romances and poems for the courts. Among the best medieval German poets there was a tendency to avoid the strictly local dialects in favor of forms that could be understood in courts in different parts of the German lands.

From the second half of the thirteenth century the domain of the German language expanded greatly. It began to be used along with Latin for administrative and legal documents of the Holy Roman Empire. For a long time scribes wrote in their own dialects but, as documents in the ordinary language became more common and literary contacts between various parts of the German states became more frequent, the need for a unification of the language became more pressing.

Modern German dates from Martin Luther's translation of the Bible into the German vernacular. Luther gave stature to German, which had previously been considered inferior to Latin in religious usage. The dialect of Saxony that he employed in his work was rapidly accepted by all German intellectuals as the literary standard. Few books have ever been so widely read or so highly regarded as a model, in form as well as content, as Luther's Bible. He did not originate modern German but was foremost in spreading it.

The form of standard written German owes much to the grammarians and stylists of the seventeenth century, especially Justus Georg Schottel and Martin Opitz von Boberfeld. During the latter part of the century and in the eighteenth, the language of the educated classes of Saxony, especially the dialect of the city of Meissen, became the norm under the literary dictatorship of Johann Christoph Gottshed, the founder of an academy of poetry in Leipzig. Even the Swiss, who had been particularly resistant to any shift from their own dialects, came to follow it. Great writers of the eighteenth and nineteenth centuries, such as Gotthold Lessing, Johann Wolfgang von Goethe, and Friedrich von Schiller, were to finish the task started by Luther; their contributions to the standardization of the written language made it as easily read in Vienna or Berne as it was in Berlin or Hamburg, and it has remained essentially the same ever since.

Many newspapers, periodicals, and books have traditionally been printed in Gothic characters, known as *Fraktur* in German. For a while the Nazis favored Gothic as distinctively German, but in 1941, in order to propagate German in occupied countries unaccustomed to the Gothic type, newspapers and publishers of books converted to roman type, with the addition of a special symbol for double *s* at the end of a word or after a long vowel. Except for the retention of Gothic in certain aesthetic applications, as in mastheads and captions of newspapers, publishers now use roman type. Some people still use the handwritten form of Gothic script.

Standardization of the Spoken Language

By the late nineteenth century a common language spoken by millions was added to the local dialects. The common language was spread by writers, the schools, the press, and the theater. The development of communication and commerce brought the inhabitants of various regions into frequent contact and furthered the use of a common medium. Even so, before the founding of the empire in 1871, certain German states were concerned with guarding their independence even in linguistic matters and laid down special rules for their schools, so there were striking differences in pronunication even when standard German was followed.

Because dialectical differences were particularly bothersome in the theater, actors made a series of attempts to create a standard pronunciation. The chief credit for accomplishing this is given to Theodor Siebs, who in 1898 presided over a committee of actors, phoneticians and elocutionists, which was to propose a standard pronunciation for use on the stage. The pronunciation advocated in Siebs' treatise, which resulted from the conference, is used not only by actors but also by most schoolteachers and radio announcers. The standard pronunciation is based upon that of edcuated northern Germans, who acquire the standard spoken language with greater care because it is further from their dialects than from those of southerners. For this reason, what is now called High German is associated with the north, although it developed originally mostly from southern dialects.

The expression *Hochdeutsch* (High German) has acquired a significance that has little to do with its geographic origin or history. The standard pronunciation is a prerequisite for high social standing; regardless of family, money, or other qualifications, a person cannot be accepted in professional circles if he cannot speak with the standard High German pronunciation. Poor command of High German, just like a strong regional accent or the use of dialect words, brands a person as poorly educated and therefore low class or as a provincial country bumpkin.

Dialects

The development of a standard spoken language did not cause the decay of dialects, which are still spoken according to the divisions of the country that existed at the end of the Middle Ages. The linguistic areas are vague zones of varying width, in which the passage from one dialect to the other takes place by a series of small changes. There are islands in Low German territory in which High German is the usual speech. In Berlin, for example, the influence of the standard language, spoken by the educated middle class, civil servants, tradesmen, and the like, has made itself felt on the rest of the population, which has contributed its own idiosyncracies of Low German to the distinctive speech of Berlin.

Tribal origins still coincide in some cases with dialects, as shown by careful investigations into Alemannic and Bavarian dialects. The old tribal boundaries were reinforced linguistically if they were along natural barriers and if they were maintained in the political boundaries of medieval times. Many dialect boundaries go back to territorial boundaries established between the thirteenth and seventeenth centuries. Moorland and mountainous forestland have been barriers to the diffusion of dialects; the larger river valleys have been channels of linguistic influences. In lands colonized by scattered settlements, the resulting dialects sometimes show the victory of one dialect, not necessarily that of the earliest settlers, over all the rest.

The dialects are cultivated and preserved. From them the standard language constantly draws new words and idioms. For although the standard language is fixed, the dialects evolve naturally and in time affect the standard. Literatures have developed in all the more important dialects.

The popular classification of dialects corresponds roughly to the scholarly classification; the main dialects are Prussian, Bavarian and Rhinelander, although variations within each of these are recognized. Dialect is the most important and most tangible means of identifying the person's region of origin. Speakers of the most widely separated dialects can have difficulty understanding one another, but most often the gap can be bridged by the use of standard German.

Almost all Germans are bilingual in that they speak both the standard language and their own dialect. A survey in 1968 indicated that two-thirds of the population spoke one of the dialects. The use of dialects, however, is much more common in the south, where 80 percent of the population speak them, than in the north, where only 60 percent do. The influence of radio and television, both of which use standard German rather than local dialects in most programming, is slowly reducing the importance of dialects in daily communication. The greater mobility of the population since World War II and the settling of Germans from other parts of Europe throughout the country have also strengthened the use of the standard language to the disadvantage of dialects.

CHAPTER 7

SOCIAL SYSTEM

The social system of the Federal Republic is still undergoing a long process of change that resulted from the upheaval brought about by twelve years of Nazi rule and the near total collapse of the old system during World War II. In contrast to the traditional social system characterized by rigid class divisions based on family and property, the emerging system is pluralistic and achievement oriented. Status in the new society is based primarily on occupation and earned income. Rigid class barriers no longer stand in the way of social advancement. Traditional thought patterns, however, prevent many from taking full advantage of the opportunities offered by an open society. Such patterns are so ingrained that some working-class parents fail even to consider that, through available educational opportunities, their children might move upward in the social system.

The dramatic changes that have taken place since the end of World War II have been abetted by what is variously called a second industrial revolution or an economic miracle. The economic boom that followed exceptionally rapid recovery from the destruction of war brought with it a shift in the distribution of incomes and in the occupational structure. The number of independent farmers and self-employed small entrepreneurs has been rapidly declining. At the same time, the number of salaried employees in government and private enterprise and the number of skilled industrial workers have been growing rapidly. Personal incomes have risen faster than the cost of living, allowing an improved standard of living for all. Incomes of blue-collar workers have risen more rapidly than those of salaried workers, thereby reducing the social distinctions between them. Nevertheless, even though a university lecturer may earn less than a mechanic, his life-style and interests are different, and he expects to be treated with deference.

The structural changes of the postwar society have been accompanied by changes in values and behavior patterns. These changes, however, are less clear cut than the structural ones.

In fact, considerable ambivalence about traditional and new values is evident. The older generation, in particular, is often torn between the values of their fathers and those of their children. Middle-aged people who grew up during the Hitler era and whose children have no personal recollection of nazism are often torn between the Weimar and pre-Weimar values of their parents and the post-World War II values developed by their children.

In this changing society the family remains a strong and stabilizing institution. It, too, is changing internally, but its basic function of providing security and a sense of identity to the individual has not changed. In fact, this function has been strengthened by the uncertainties and dislocations of modern society. The family is the center where an individual can find refuge from the emotional strains of a changing world.

FAMILY

The Germans are a family-oriented people. Despite the disruptive effects of two major wars and the revolutionary social code of the Nazis, the ideal of the family as a tightly knit social and economic institution still exerts a strong influence on most Germans.

Industrialization and urbanization, which proceeded rapidly during the latter half of the nineteenth century, created significant variations in family structure and customs. Earlier stereotypes based on rural family life lost their applicability in many parts of the country. Many basic elements have remained largely unchanged, however, and the Germans continue to recognize certain common elements as constituting respected family traditions. Since the end of World War II, many families have sought refuge from the confusing and often threatening pressures of a rapidly changing society in a cohesive, introverted family life, in which traditions play an important role.

By the late nineteenth century, urbanization had made the single family household consisting of father and mother and their unmarried children the common basis for family life. As industrialization increased the opportunities for women and young men to support themselves, the formerly overwhelming authority of the father over his wife and children was reduced. The patriarchal tradition has continued, however, to exert a strong influence.

The tradition of the home as an important center of the activities of all family members remains strongly instilled in most Germans. The family spends much of its leisure time in shared activities; such important events as birthdays, name days, marriages, anniversaries, and holidays are family affairs. Sentimental attachments between grown children and their parents are strong and lasting. It is not uncommon for several generations and laterally related families—such as cousins—to gather for important family celebrations.

The Traditional Family

The stereotype of the German family centers in the relationship of the man to his wife and children. The traditional patriarchal relationship was still widespread as late as the early twentieth century, and it is to this period that Germans refer in considering the criteria for the ideal of family life.

The husband was traditionally the unquestioned head of the household. He determined, often without consulting his wife, where the family would live, how it would spend its income, and how the children would be brought up. He was the disciplinarian, the ultimate arbiter of family disputes, and the representative of the family in its dealings with society. He received deferential treatment from both his wife and his children. Although he was expected to consider the well-being of all the members of the family, his decision in all matters was final. His dominating position was given legal sanction in the civil code of the Second Reich, promulgated in 1896.

Women were considered inferior to men socially, intellectually, politically, and—until the promulgation of the Weimar Constitution in 1919—legally. This discrimination was maintained by the differential between the formal education given to boys and that given to girls.

Most women accepted as their chief goal in life making a good marriage, establishing a home, and raising children. Marital unions were based more frequently on mutual respect between the spouses than on romantic love, but the Germans have prided themselves that real affection usually developed as a result of the common bonds incurred in establishing a strong family life.

A wife was by no means powerless in her relations with her husband. In practice, her decisions within the home were law. The wife had "the power of the key" to run the household, to handle the family budget for daily expenses, and to care for the children. In her dealings with her children, she would often use her husband primarily as a threat of punishment or as the final arbiter of disputes.

There was much variation within this general framework, depending particularly upon economic circumstances and upon the personalities of the husband and wife. In the eighteenth and nineteenth centuries, not all wives conformed to the standards of obedient servants to their husbands, and husbands often consulted their wives on various matters.

Children usually remained in the household of their parents until they married, often fairly late in life, and established households of their own. Even mature sons and daughters were treated as minors as long as they lived with their parents; they were forced by custom and the provisions of the Civil Code to yield entirely to the parents' authority. Parents, particularly the father, had the right and the responsibility for the children's well-being, personal property, and relations with society. The children were bound to give their labor for the support of the family, by performing chores, by helping with farmwork, or by working in the father's craft. There was a tendency for sons to apprentice in their father's craft, with the ultimate objective of carrying on the family business. This work was not usually compensated or, if it was, the money was held and controlled by the father until the children left home.

Independence and self-realization were not considered by most parents as values to be passed on to their children. Parents determined the ultimate careers of their children through their responsibility for deciding when the child was in grammar school whether he would prepare for advancement into vocational or academic educational channels. The decision to place a child in vocational school would preclude his continuing his education into a professional career and would destine him for a future as a craftsman, industrial worker, or tradesman. Traditionally, a son followed his father into his business or profession. A daughter was usually educated primarily for marriage and raising a family. The parents also had the legal right to determine a child's religious affiliation until age fourteen.

World War II and Its Aftermath

The preparations for and conducting of the war served to weaken family ties; military and auxiliary service separated husbands and wives and kept children away from their families. The youths were diverted to the purposes of the totalitarian state. The Hitler Youth and the Union of German Girls operated in disregard and even defiance of parental authority; children were encouraged to spy on their parents.

Nazi philosophy rejected feminism as antinational and attempted to counter the trend of the preceding years by exalting the wife as a potential mother and restricting her activities outside the home. But intense war preparations necessitated a reversal of this policy in the employment of many women in industry and commerce. As men were drafted into the armed forces, women were given new responsibilities and thereby regained any importance that they might have lost under the earlier antifeminist propaganda.

The general breakdown of morale at the end of the war weakened parental authority even further in many instances. During the early postwar period there was a sharp increase in juvenile delinquency, particularly among children who were separated from their parents or had lost one or both of them.

The Contemporary Family

At the end of World War II millions of families were without a male head; he had either died in the war or did not return from prison camp for many years. The wife and mother, therefore, were the principal source of economic support and of authority. In a large number of families women and older children had to share with the father the responsibility of earning a living under conditions of extreme economic and social hardship. The result has been a basic change in family relationships. As early as 1951 a German sociologist found that 72 percent of the families he studied considered marriage a partnership of two equals and did not recognize the traditional male prerogative. Other studies since that time have confirmed this change in husband-wife relationships and also found a reduction in parental authority over children.

The changed marital relationship has resulted in a change in the division of labor among members of the family. Almost one-third of the married women in 1970 were employed. As they took on responsibilities that were formerly thought of as belonging to husbands, the husbands, in turn, assumed some of the tasks once defined as in the sole province of women. The difficulty in obtaining servants was another factor in the sharing of household chores by husbands. Among social classes to which domestic help is readily available, however, the stereotyped male-female roles continue to persist.

The standards of paternal authority are still stronger among rural families than in the cities. Rural families are shifting away from this pattern, however, and are experiencing the same social and family problems associated with basic changes that disturbed urban families in the 1920s. As a result of this shift, differences between urban and rural families are steadily decreasing.

The younger generation appears to want the stability of marriage and family. This desire, combined with the prosperity that has existed since the 1950s, has led people to marry at an earlier age than previously. In the early postwar years, most men at time of first marriage were in their late twenties. By the 1970s the median age had dropped to the early twenties. A similarly dramatic change has also taken place in the lowering of the average age of women marrying for the first time.

The birthrate has been declining sharply in the early 1970s mostly because young couples want no more than two children. Even the Roman Catholic population tends to limit families to two or three children, although they are somewhat ambivalent about birth control (see ch. 4).

The divorce rate has been relatively low for a changing and highly complex industrial society. In 1970 it was 1.24 for every 1,000 marriages.

SOCIAL STRATIFICATION

Historical Background

Prewar Germany never experienced a social revolution of the kind that molded many other modern Western European societies. As a result, German social structure has retained remarkable continuity (see ch. 2).

Feudalism

The German feudal system, which developed as a result of the fragmentation of political and economic power after the breakup of Charlemagne's empire in the late ninth century A.D., created two widely separated social classes—the landed aristocracy and the commoners (mostly peasants).

The aristocracy was a numerically small group of hereditary nobles who owed theoretical allegiance to the Holy Roman emperor but were in fact largely independent within their own realms. The German lands disintegrated into hundreds of principalities, duchies, marches, and minor holdings, in each of which the noble ruler was free—within the restraints of custom—to rule his subordinate knights, peasants, servants, and serfs as he saw fit. The rulers maintained private armies, and the more powerful forced their weaker neighbors to pay homage to them in return for protection.

Within the aristocracy, the most powerful nobles were rulers of extensive realms. Seven of the princes were hereditary electors of the Holy Roman emperor, who was chosen from among their ranks. The hierarchy was never strictly observed, however; particularly after the fourteenth century, many members of the lowest order of the hereditary nobility, the knights *(Ritter)*, owed allegiance directly to the emperor. In addition to the hereditary nobility, high church officials—bishops and abbots—were considered part of the aristocracy, organizing their large landholdings as feudal estates. The most powerful bishops shared with the lay princes in the election of the emperor.

Until the twelfth century many peasants owned their own land and were free of allegiance to anyone but the emperor. Civil war and the weakening of the authority of the emperor gradually reduced the poorer free peasants to the status of serfs, tied by feudal obligations to noblemen to whom they turned for protection (see ch. 2). The stronger freemen became knights bound by vassalage to higher nobles but keeping serfs in their own name. Serfdom was by the thirteenth century the base of the German social structure. The serfs were tied to their land and were forced to yield service to their lord and to submit to his authority, which even extended to his right to inflict capital punishment.

The Medieval Cities

In the late Middle Ages, trading centers became important and developed into cities virtually independent of the feudal nobility. They were not large by modern standards, the largest being about 20,000 in population; they were crowded and small in area but possessed considerable wealth, amassed in trade and industry. They often extended their control over the surrounding countryside and formed leagues of cities for defense and control of trade.

The wealth of the cities tended to be concentrated in a few families, who set up hereditary oligarchies that controlled the cities and competed with the landed aristocracy. The rich merchants and financiers of the cities formed a social class of burghers, or citizens, which was next to the nobles and clergy in importance.

The bulk of the population, socially inferior to the small group of wealthy ruling families, was organized into numerous guilds for controlling the various industries and for social and religious purposes. These guilds included masters, journeymen, and apprentices. These three levels were sharply differentiated; promotions from one to another involved fixed examination and ceremonies. A high degree of specialization among the several guilds of a city or town caused interminable disputes about ranking of the occupations. Out of the urban craftsmen was created a class of "small citizens," who had many distinctions among themselves and who considered themselves to be socially superior to the peasantry outside the towns and the casual laborers of the towns.

Despite their wealth, by the time of the Reformation the divided and isolated cities could not cope with the princely power that was pitted against them. Throughout the sixteenth and seventeenth centuries their power declined, and many were incorporated into the increasingly powerful states.

Changing Aristocracy of the Junkers

The rigid class structure associated with the feudal system was perpetuated in the German lands long after it had begun to lose significance elsewhere in Western Europe. The impoverishment of the cities and of the remaining free peasants brought about by the seventeenth-century Thirty Years' War gave the powerful aristocratic landholders an opportunity to strengthen their hold on their vassals. In the southwestern areas, the land was fractionated into almost 2,000 individual states, each owned and completely controlled by a knight. In the eastern areas—the territories that became part of Prussia—petty nobles accrued huge landholdings. These Junkers, whose interests were fostered by the absolutist Prussian rulers, maintained their subject peasants in the depressed status of serfs long after serfdom had been abandoned elsewhere in the West. Their form of feudalism was more repressive than any Germany had known earlier.

The younger sons of the Junker families, who were denied the right to inherit their fathers' role as landowners, became high functionaries of the centralized Prussian state and officers in the elite Prussian Army Corps. Thus, the rigid social hierarchy was transferred from a purely land-based society to one in which the aristocracy was identified with the leadership of a powerful government bureaucracy. The Junkers were able to make the officer corps of the growing Prussian army almost a private preserve. In addition, they were able to restrict access to higher education to their own class, and to gain control of the Prussian bureaucracy and diplomatic corps.

Although membership in a noble family was usually required for acceptance into the upper class until the time of World War I, a few members of the rising intellectual class were socially accepted by the aristocracy; in the seventeenth century and later a few individuals of less than noble birth were able to gain recognition as scholars or artists of the first rank. Gradually, during the late eighteenth and nineteenth centuries, a few marriages between nobles and commoners, especially between impoverished aristocrats and the daughters of wealthy bankers or businessmen, were countenanced, but generally commoner wives were not admitted to the most formal social functions of their noble husbands.

Influence of Nineteenth-Century Industrialization

With the industrialization and urbanization of Germany, wealthy commercial and industrial families developed, who composed an upper middle class along with academicians, artists, untitled army officers, and higher officials. The class exhibited much variation from region to region and according to individual means. But certain complex rules of dress and etiquette were mandatory, along with large domestic establishments, many servants, and lavish entertainment. The class emulated the nobility; in the eastern parts of Germany some Junkers who became industrial capitalists formed a bridge between the upper middle class and the aristocracy. There was some movement from the upper middle class, primarily by marriage, to the aristocracy, and a few newly wealthy members were being recruited from the lower middle class all the time.

An effective device for maintaining class boundaries was the restriction of expensive higher education to the well-to-do, since high school and university education was necessary for admission to the professions and civil service positions. A social gap that transcended most other considerations was maintained between those with a higher education and those without.

Associated with the trade centers and guilds that survived from the Middle Ages were craftsmen and shopkeepers who, along with public officials of lesser ranks, formed a lower middle class. During the nineteenth century the crafts and trades were freed from compulsory guild membership. Factory production and modern capitalism invaded the territory of the craftsmen, who did not usually have the means to compete, and some were forced to become common laborers. Because of the rapid growth of industry and governmental agencies, however, the ranks of the lower middle class were swelled by ever-increasing numbers of lesser officials and white-collar workers.

Movement was possible from the lower middle class to the upper middle class, although full acceptance usually took more than one generation. One way to rise was by getting a higher education, which usually was prohibitively expensive, or by becoming an artist, writer, or composer and attracting the patronage of a wealthy sponsor. Members of the lower middle class were usually very conscious of their social status, particularly in relation to the urban workers and the farmers beneath them. The number of urban workers increased enormously with the great growth of cities that took place in the nineteenth century under the belated influence of the industrial revolution in Germany.

Working conditions were hard, and the life of city workers was often difficult. For most of them, the main object in life was to find and keep employment. Education as a means of advancement for their children was not feasible financially. Most boys were apprenticed to learn a trade at the age of fourteen, after six years or less of formal schooling.

At the beginning of the nineteenth century, two-thirds of the population still lived on the land, largely in a feudal condition. Large numbers moved to the rapidly growing cities during the nineteenth century, and the rural population became a proportionately smaller part of the total population. The decrees emancipating the peasantry in

Prussia in the early 1800s were not fully carried out, particularly in the eastern provinces of Prussia, until after 1918. In Bavaria serfdom was not abolished until 1848, and even then the emancipation was far from complete. There was relatively greater freedom and a greater proportion of landowning farmers in the Rhineland.

The rigidity of this social system undoubtedly contributed to the mechanistic approach of Karl Marx to the question of class warfare. Through his writings the class struggle assumed an important role in shifting the social structure of nineteenth-century Germany. The interests of the workers were represented by the Socialist Labor Party and labor unions, which permitted workers to organize their resentment against the middle class. The aristocracy, wealthy businessmen, and large landowners pooled their interests against the rising proletariat and were able to maintain their strong hold on the government. In the last quarter of the century, Chancellor Otto von Bismarck promulgated a far-reaching public welfare and education program for the workers and peasants to prevent them from taking too aggressive action in their own interests. His policy of opening educational opportunities for all classes spelled the ultimate doom of a rigid social structure.

Social Structure in the Weimar Republic

World War I and the attempted communist revolution of 1918 had little immediate effect on the traditional social structure. The monarchy was abolished and with it the official status of the aristocracy. Positions of leadership, however, were assumed by wealthy businessmen, bureaucrats, and army officers, many of whom were former aristocrats. No far-reaching land reform took place in Germany as it did in many other parts of Europe, so large estates were left intact. On the whole, the upper classes remained aloof from political activity, which was assumed by the middle and working classes. The middle class was quickly alienated by the weaknesses of the Weimar governments and was highly susceptible to the demagogic appeals of nationalist extremists, such as the Nazis. The middle class was also severely hit by the runaway inflation of the early 1920s, which pauperized many of them while leaving the upper classes relatively unharmed. Thus, the Nazis were able to draw much of their original support from the disenchanted middle class.

Nazi Period

Once in power in the early 1930s, the Nazis ignored their goal of creating a uniform German social structure. They maintained a rigid society over which they established a new aristocracy of high Nazi party officials, many of whom had come from the lower classes and had risen to positions of authority solely because of their loyalty to the Nazi cause. No attempt was made to break the economic power of the large landowners or industrialists; indeed, their support, though sometimes reluctantly given, was an important source of Nazi strength. On the whole, the Nazis maintained the traditional social structure, merely superimposing their own aristocracy. They abolished virtually all social organizations—trade unions, private welfare groups, women's and youth movements—and forced the people to join mass organizations under their control.

Post-World War II

The ravages of war left German society in a shambles. The physical and economic hardships faced by the whole population in the period of reconstruction brought about a de facto equality at little more than a marginal level of existence. Some of this downward leveling had already been brought about during the war, but it became quite general in the postwar years.

The expulsion of millions of Germans from former German territories east of the Oder and Neisse rivers and the emigration of large numbers from the communist-held area of eastern Germany added to the dissolution of traditional distinctions of status and privilege. By leaving behind their property and wealth, which were generally the determinants of their social status, these people no longer fitted neatly into one of the established social categories.

The effects of World War II and its aftermath on the social structure of the Federal Republic, therefore, caused a general blurring and even dissolution of the established class distinctions. The restructuring of the society was characterized by a changing attitude toward one's place in the social framework. Formerly most Germans accepted the social status into which they were born and made little effort to change or improve their own position or that of their children. Having lost the security of their former social standing, Germans began to strive for improvement in their economic and social status. The striving was given impetus by the so-called miraculous economic recovery of the 1950s and by the democratic society created by the Federal Republic.

The Emerging Society

There is wide disagreement among sociologists about the structure of post-World War II German society. Some sociologists, notably Helmut Schelsky, see a complete leveling and equalization into a broad middle class through the rise of industrial workers as a group as the result of the economic boom and the loss of status by the former propertied and educated bourgeoisie as a result of the rise into their ranks of the technical and administrative white-collar workers. The large middle class, Schelsky claims, has a uniform life-style and is relatively equal in economic and political status and in social and cultural pattern of behavior. Old hierarchical class distinctions survive only in ideology and in ritual. Other sociologists follow the view of Ralf Dahrendorf, who sees a continuation of a high degree of division into social groups characterized by a particular state of mind, which is similar to the social distinctions of the old society.

Schelsky's thesis can be supported by surveys that indicate the tendency of most Germans, particularly the younger ones, to think of themselves as middle class. Well-paid, high-level executives and

124

government officials, when queried about the matter, placed themselves into the middle rather than the upper class. Most industrial workers also consider themselves middle class rather than lower class or proletarian as they would have before. The high incomes of industrial workers certainly afford them a standard of living at least equal to if not better than that of white-collar workers and many professionals.

In addition to sharing a view of their place in society, most Germans also share what has come to be regarded as the hallmark of modern German society—an emphasis on conspicuous consumption and a quest for status symbols, such as cars and other consumer durables and trips abroad. Within this common "consumer mentality," however, differences in the size and price tag of the goods and services acquired reflect or promote differences in social status. Schelsky himself admits that there are gradations of status within his broad middle class but sees no real barriers between the levels of status.

Dahrendorf agrees, to a point. He sees the boundaries between social strata in contemporary German society as so hazy that it is difficult for an observer to identify the strata clearly. Nevertheless, he sees the existence of differentiated social groups.

The factors determining social status, according to Dahrendorf, are income, education, influence and, to a lesser degree, family background and upbringing. These combine in various ways to determine an individual's social standing. Property in the form of land and buildings is no longer the prime criterion for social standing; instead, a new way of life has been gradually emerging in which style of living is most important, and there are many seeming discrepancies in status. Skilled workers, for instance, often have higher incomes than secondary school teachers who have attained much higher levels of education. A plant manager with a secondary education may earn as much as a university professor or some other highly trained professional. In postwar society, therefore, it is difficult to identify specific social strata and to present a one-dimensional picture of social stratification. On the basis of income, a graphic presentation of the population would be onion shaped; the greatest concentration is in the middle with a narrowing down on both the low-income and high-income sides. A graphic presentation of the distribution of influence and of educational achievement, however, would show the greatest concentration on the bottom levels with a sharp reduction at the top.

Taking the various determinants of status in their most common combinations, Dahrendorf identifies seven main social groups: the elite, the service class, the middle class, the working-class elite, the so-called false middle class, the working class, and the lower class. The groups are not hierarchical but form what Dahrendorf calls "chambers in the edifice of social stratification." The divisions between the groups are not fixed, and each group has within it subgroups with their own peculiar traits as, for instance, the peasants in the middle class or the state officials in the service class. Some occupational groups with a common outlook are divided into several social groups. For example, professionals are included in the elites, the service class, and the middle class. Superimposed on this whole structure of social distinctions are regional differences.

The Elite

The elite constitutes approximately 1 percent of the population and consists of the leaders of the various social institutions—business, politics, the military, education, the churches, law, entertainment, and the mass media. The old aristocracy and the landowning and military elite have disappeared as components of the upper stratum of society. Some of their members have been absorbed by the new elite, but most have taken on business occupations or professions and have become members of the middle classes.

Dahrendorf stresses the pluralistic nature of the top stratum of society and its lack of solidarity and class consciousness. Each component seems to be self-contained, and there is little movement from one to the other and only limited social contact.

Membership in the elite is achieved by reaching the pinnacle of one of the social institutions. Depending on the institution, it requires wealth, education, family background, or a combination of these. Mostly, however, it requires personal achievement. Although members of the elites are usually wealthy, their wealth is a result of having reached the top rather than a prerequisite to it, except possibly in the case of the business elite. The latter consists, for the most part, of the newly rich industrial and business magnates who often flaunt their wealth and social status in conspicuous consumption and high living.

The Middle Classes

Several distinct social groups constitute what can be called the middle classes. Dahrendorf treats each group as a separate class with its own mentality, whereas Schelsky treats them as gradations of one broad social class. The main components of the middle classes are the so-called old middle class of self-employed merchants, tradesmen, small businessmen, and farmers and the new middle class of bureaucrats of all ranks in state and private employment. Two other groups—the highly skilled workers and the growing number of people engaged in various aspects of the service industry—could also be referred to as middle class on the basis of their life-style and outlook, but other factors place them more readily with the working classes.

The new middle class or, as Dahrendorf calls it, the service class is considered by many the most important social group in the new society. It encompasses the whole range of bureaucrats from clerk to company vice president or assistant minister. What gives the group unity is the concept of service to those in power and the idea that they thereby share in the power itself. The group is highly stratified, and the strata are arranged in a hierarchical pyramid. Advancement up the pyramid is dependent on

126

individual effort, personal connections, and proper educational qualifications. Because of dependence on those in power, members of the service class are extremely status conscious. They are often called the original status seekers and take great effort to display the symbols of their status.

The old middle class of self-employed entrepreneurs and landowners has been shrinking in size since World War II as more and more of its members join the ranks of the employed. It has also changed its philosophy from that of laissez-faire to one of increasing dependence on the government for help and protection. As a group, it is extremely conservative in outlook, both in political and economic matters. Since property is no longer a main criterion for social status, the group has lost standing in relation to skilled workers and other employed persons whose income is higher.

Many observers divide the middle class on the basis of income and status into an upper, middle, and lower middle class. The composition of these three groups cuts across the earlier set of groups that are based on a common interest and outlook. Thus, the upper middle class consists of members of the professions, high government officials, high executives in business and industry, and large entrepreneurs whose wealth and influence are sufficient to count them among the elites but are, nevertheless, great. The middle middle class consists of middle-level managers, administrators and government officials, engineers and technical personnel, teachers, middle-level entrepreneurs, and landowners. The lower middle class consists of the lower levels of administrative and managerial personnel and government officials, craftsmen and small tradesmen, skilled workers and foremen, small shopkeepers, and landowners.

There is probably more social contact between members of the same income-and status-based group than among members of the same interest-based group. In social relations, compatibility in education, income, and status may be more important than outlook based solely on occupation.

The Working Classes

Almost two-thirds of the population belong to what may be called the working classes. Dahrendorf distinguishes three groups within this category: the skilled workers, craftsmen, and foremen, whom he calls the working-class elite; the sales clerks, porters, bus drivers, and others employed in service occupations, whom he calls the false middle class; and the mass of industrial workers, whom he calls the working class.

Formerly, a vast gap existed between the working classes and the middle classes. Germans thought of each other in terms of "they" and "us," depending on the segment of society to which they belonged. This was particularly true of the working classes, whose whole concept of society was based on this differentiation. The "they" were thought of as foreign and out of reach by most workers and their position as unattainable. The barrier between the working classes and the middle classes was seen as insurmountable by most workers who, therefore, made little effort to penetrate it themselves or to have their children penetrate it.

The basis of the gap between the two segments of society was education. To be in the middle classes required completion of at least the lower level of secondary schooling, and members of the working classes seldom had more than a primary education. To obtain a secondary education was costly, and few working-class parents could afford it. But even those who could, usually saw little advantage in it and preferred to send their children into some kind of apprenticeship.

Movement from the working classes into the middle classes usually took place by way of Dahrendorf's false middle class. This is the growing mass of lower level service occupations in the expanding service industry. It includes sales clerks, waiters, train and streetcar conductors, drivers of various kinds, mailmen, service station attendants, and others. The members of this group generally consider themselves middle class because they are not manual workers. They are not, however, self-employed as is the old middle class, nor are they part of the bureaucracy as is the new middle class. In addition, few of them have more than a primary school education.

On the way up the social ladder an industrial worker or his child would move into a service occupation and thereby become exposed to the life-style and values of the middle classes. Exposure brought about familiarity and even a desire to emulate or to achieve that higher status. The barrier separating the two classes appeared less insurmountable than to the industrial worker, and parents could see the advantages of a better education for their children. The move from the working classes to the middle classes usually took two generations—one to move from industrial worker into a service occupation and another to move up into the middle classes.

The attitudes that have in the past supported the barrier between the working classes and the middle classes persist to a considerable extent, particularly among the older members of the working classes. Their children and those who have become industrial workers since the end of World War II, however, are less constrained by these attitudes and are willing to take advantage of available opportunities to improve their economic and social status. The increase in real wages for industrial workers has released many working-class families from the uncertainty of poverty, and full employment has relieved them of anxiety about losing their jobs. A result appears to be that the workers are taking on more middle-class values, especially in regard to social advancement for their children.

The economic boom has also opened an alternate avenue into the middle classes through the ranks of the working-class elite. These are the highly skilled workers, craftsmen, and foremen who have always provided the

128

leadership of the working classes. In the past this leadership tended toward radical group ideologies, but under present economic and political conditions it tends toward individual achievement and satisfaction of personal wants. Most skilled workers regard themselves as middle class and assume a middle-class life-style and many middle-class values. Many sociologists also regard them as part of the middle rather than of the working classes.

The main body of the working classes consists of the large number of skilled, semiskilled, and unskilled workers in industry and agriculture. They are differentiated by level of skill and by the nature of their work. According to Dahrendorf and others, however, they continue to exhibit many common traits that group them into one social stratum. Despite great improvement in their standard of living since the 1950s, the majority are still less well off than other social groups. Their patterns of consumption, therefore, differ from those of other groups (see ch. 5). One conspicuous difference is that workers, except for the most highly paid ones, do not travel abroad as do great numbers of their countrymen. They tend to spend their vacations at home with friends and relatives. Another difference often cited by sociologists is the workers' tendency to indulge in immediate consumption or pleasure as the occasion arises rather than to plan for future needs or desires. This last characteristic of the worker mentality is explained by the traditionally precarious economic position of the worker and the need to live from day to day. It is one of the reasons why worker families have been reluctant to invest time and money in the education of their children in order to improve the child's social position.

Mobility

German society since World War II has been described as an extremely mobile society. It has been geographically mobile as a result of the influx of vast numbers of expellees and refugees from the east and the movement of individuals and families within the Federal Republic in response to the labor needs of the economic boom. It has also been socially mobile in that the economic opportunities of the new open society prompted individuals to move from one occupation into another or to increase their qualifications and income within the same occupation, thereby improving their economic and social status. There are, however, limits to this mobility.

A 1969–70 study found that two-thirds of the economically active population were engaged in occupational categories that differed from those of their fathers. This was in marked contrast to the tradition of sons following in their fathers' occupations. Most of this intergenerational mobility was upward into occupations of greater prestige and higher standing. Some, nevertheless, was downward. The downward mobility took place mostly in the highest social groups; members of the aristocracy or other elite groups moved from their elite position into the upper middle-class status of a professional, high government official, or business executive.

The various categories of employees, particularly the new middle class of bureaucrats, attracted a great deal of both upward and downward mobility. The rapid growth of job opportunities in this category together with expanding educational opportunities made it possible for individuals to move into those positions. The greatest upward movement, however, took place into the category of skilled worker from among the semiskilled and unskilled industrial and agricultural workers.

Despite the high rate of mobility, the study found that most of the movement took place only one step at a time, from one occupational category into a related category. Thus, the growing group of bureaucrats attracted children of government officials, officeworkers, and persons in the professions, whereas the growing group of skilled workers attracted children of less skilled workers, farmers, and self-employed tradesmen. This phenomenon has perpetuated the polarization of society into two main groups—the lower segment of blue-collar workers and the upper segment of white-collar workers—following the traditional view of society by the working classes. The study found relatively little mobility between the two main groups, confirming Dahrendorf's claim that traditional attitudes persist and prevent individuals from taking advantage of the opportunities offered by an expanding economy and free, democratic system.

The 1969–70 study of the extent and nature of social mobility in Germany since the beginning of industrialization in the late nineteenth century came to the conclusion that, despite extensive changes in the occupational makeup of society, the rate of mobility and the possibility of upward movement of individuals in the working classes has changed little in the past fifty years. The working classes as a whole have risen in social standing through greatly increased incomes and a consequent higher standard of living. For the individual worker, however, the barrier between the working classes and the middle classes continues to be difficult to penetrate.

The main vehicle for upward social mobility is education. In the Federal Republic educational qualifications are the principal determinant of the actual or attainable social position of an individual. Family background and wealth play an important role in securing high educational qualifications but have little influence in and of themselves. Educational opportunities for all members of the society have greatly improved since the end of World War II through the expansion of the school system and through educational reforms (see ch. 8). The percentage of children attaining a secondary or higher education, however, is still small because of limited facilities, high costs, and the need to pursue a long and narrow educational path from an early age in order to qualify. Children of peasants, working-class parents, and lower middle-class parents are, therefore, at a disadvantage and are poorly represented among students in secondary and higher institutions. Another factor affecting the poor representation of children from lower class families is the persistent failure of most parents from these social groups to see the direct connection between education and the attainment of higher social status. Although they may be anxious to improve their children's social position, their horizon expands only to the next step up in the social ladder, no higher. Thus, the degree of social mobility is very limited in scope, and the upper social strata depend mostly on self-recruitment.

SOCIAL VALUES

German society has been in transition since the beginning of the twentieth century, but the structural changes since World War II have been almost revolutionary. The changes in values and cultural patterns have been slower and have produced a certain ambivalence toward the demands for change and persistent traditional goals and values. The older members of society, those over forty years of age whose formative years were spent under the influence of traditional values, are particularly hard hit by this ambivalence. They tend to cling to the traditional values of their youth but feel the pressure to adopt the newer values of their children.

The traditional German value patterns were based on idealism and service. The ideal individual was disciplined, meticulous, and hard working. He found self-expression through dedicated service to his superiors, to the collectivity of which he was a member, and to the ideal of a German nation. This stereotype of the German national character was widely accepted by Germans themselves as well as by others.

According to most observers, the value patterns of German society in the early 1970s differed widely from the traditional ideal. The difference was most pronounced with respect to the post-World War II generations. The values that guide the behavior of these younger members of society are based on the self-interest and materialism of an affluent, highly industrialized society. These individuals were raised at a time when blind obedience to authority was being questioned from all sides and when a rapidly expanding economy offered vast opportunities for personal advancement and a high standard of living. They dislike and distrust all forms of authority and discipline and feel that they alone are the masters of their fate. High expectations and high ambitions lead them to look at things in terms of quick and easy gratification of their wants and needs rather than in terms of long-range goals and ideals. Their concern is limited to the well-being of their immediate family.

The traditional value ascribed to hard and diligent work is being replaced by a desire for more and more leisure time. Most jobs are seen as lacking personal fulfillment, which is sought either in leisure-time activities or in moonlighting at a more rewarding job. Moonlighting has become a common practice not only in order to find greater satisfaction in work but also in order to earn more money to support the ever-rising expectations of comfort and well-being.

131

The lack of interest in hard work and the loss of pride in good workmanship are seen, in part, as the result of the labor shortage that has plagued the Federal Republic since the 1950s. The demand for labor, particularly skilled labor, has been so high that employers have been willing to tolerate slack work habits and poor quality just to keep their employees from leaving. Workers, for their part, have been showing a certain amount of carelessness as a result of their new affluence and security stemming from the great demand for their services. The slower growth rate of the economy that had become apparent by mid-1974, however, may cause a reassessment of attitudes on the part of both employers and employees as the job market tightens, and job security can no longer be taken for granted.

The outward appearance of self-centeredness, materialism, and conspicuous consumption of an affluent, consumer-oriented society, however, conceals considerable misgivings about the new value system on the part of both old and young. An underlying persistence of traditional values can be seen in the continued use of formal titles as a sign of respect, despite a belief in material achievement as a sign of success. Manual work continues to carry a stigma even though manual workers may earn more than white-collar workers. Hard work and craftsmanship command respect although they may not be pursued as diligently as before.

CHAPTER 8

EDUCATION

The German educational system traditionally has had an excellent reputation for its high standards. The literacy rate has been nearly 100 percent since 1900 and, since World War II, full-time schooling has been compulsory until the age of fifteen in the Federal Republic.

The federal government and the *Land* (state, pl., *Länder*) provide state education through taxation. Private schools, which coexist with the state schools, are financed by private organizations: churches, religious orders, and foundations. Some private schools, however, also are subsidized in part by the state.

The educational system consists essentially of three levels: elementary; general secondary; and higher education. Standard German, also known as High German, is the language of instruction at all levels. At the *Kindergarten* (preelementary) and *Grundschule* (elementary) stages, there is only one form of schooling, and the curriculum is generally uniform. At the age of ten, or upon completion of the *Grundschule*, a child must decide between a general secondary education or a vocational secondary school. This choice not only determines his secondary education but also his possibilities for higher education and ultimately a career or vocation.

Secondary education generally prepares the majority of students for a vocation rather than for higher education. The basic division is between the general secondary schools and the vocational secondary schools. Although there are a few common elements in the curricula, essentially there is little interchange of disciplines between the two forms of schooling. Reforms to reduce this compartmentalization have been introduced, however, and aim at allowing more flexibility and a greater number of interdisciplinary studies.

Most students in higher education are enrolled in colleges, universities, and teacher training institutes. A minority attend art schools or higher technical institutes. The system of higher education is noted for its excellence, but the lack of adequate facilities and staff creates a serious problem of overcrowding. The federal government and the *Länder* have attempted to alleviate this problem through a variety of measures.

HISTORY OF THE EDUCATIONAL SYSTEM

A strong German educational tradition dates from the late fourteenth century when the universities of Heidelberg and Cologne were founded.

An extremely small and self-centered intellectual elite gathered in these universities and in monasteries where they studied the classics; beginning in the fifteenth century an interest in humanism developed. By the seventeenth and eighteenth centuries German universities, which then numbered seventeen, were among the most important centers of learning in Europe.

As early as the beginning of the eighteenth century, many German princes began to provide some kind of formal schooling for the children of the German states. At the time of unification in 1871, education still remained the responsibility of the *Länder*. After unification approximately 90 percent of all children completed eight years of elementary schooling before going on to work. Part-time continuation schools were provided by the state, which enabled children to continue their education while working.

Secondary schools were operated either by local public authorities or by private organizations. Only the socially and economically privileged classes sent their children to these schools, which they attended after completion of a three-year preparatory school. In the secondary schools, children were prepared for professional careers or for entrance into university. The elitism of the secondary school was perpetuated by the high cost of tuition and the length of study, which allowed only a tiny minority to attend.

By the end of the nineteenth century many parents sought better educational and economic opportunities for their children. This attitude led to the establishment of the middle school (*Mittelschule*), which increased presecondary education. Generally, a child would enter the middle school after three years of the elementary school and would then continue in the middle school for six years. An alternative was for the child to attend elementary school for six years and the middle school for three.

During the nineteenth century the universities continued to develop. Although the states supported them financially, they were completely autonomous regarding curriculum and administration. As in the case of secondary education, university education was restricted to a small elite because of the high cost of tuition. The universities had great prestige, and a university education was viewed as the gateway to the professions and to the more desirable positions within the government.

The Weimar Constitution of 1919 stipulated that all children had to attend elementary school for eight years; this elementary education was to be followed by some form of secondary education, either academic or vocational, until the age of eighteen. By 1925 the middle school had become standardized as a six-year school, following the first four years of elementary school. Parents were required by law to determine the kind of school, academic or vocational, the child would enter at ten years of age.

When the Nazis came to power in the 1930s, they seriously undermined the traditional educational system. In 1934 a law was passed that reorganized the entire educational system, bringing all educational matters under the strict control of the Ministry of Science, Education, and Public Instruction. Private and church schools were almost entirely eliminated. The high standards for education were lowered, in part because of governmental policy that held intellectuals in contempt and in part because racial purges eliminated many teachers and students. Teachers' salaries also were extremely low, which caused many to leave the profession.

During the 1930s and 1940s books were rewritten and censored aiming at expounding only Nazi views. The curriculum was designed to instill racism, militarism, and an extreme form of nationalism. In 1937 the *Gymnasium*, which had been the preparatory school for the university, was nearly totally eliminated and replaced with a new form of high school, called the *Oberschule*, which emphasized Nazi ideology. Very few students continued on to higher education; most attended school only during the compulsory period.

The autonomy of German universities was eliminated. Both administrators and professors, previously elected by their fellows, were appointed by the minister of science, education, and public instruction. Professors were carefully screened for both their political views and their racial backgrounds. During the first three years of the Third Reich, 14 percent of all professors were dismissed because of their politics and background. At the same time, enrollment in universities dropped by approximately 50 percent. This decline in attendance resulted not only from the general contempt for education on the part of the government but also from the introduction of two years of compulsory military service and six months of compulsory labor. By 1939 only six German universities were still in existence.

By the end of World War II, German education had reached a low point. The extensive period of Nazi rule had destroyed the once-high educational ideals, and the war itself had demolished the physical facilities. The Allies, occupying the country after the war, dissolved the Nazi educational administration and immediately attempted to instill a democratic spirit in education. Approximately 50 percent of the schools were not fit for use; all texts had to be rewritten; teachers had to be screened to ensure that they had no Nazi leanings; and equipment and supplies, such as paper, pencils, and laboratory equipment, were virtually nonexistent.

Each of the German *Länder* from 1945 to 1949 reflected the policies of the particular occupying power. The Allied Control Council continued to supervise educational affairs in the British, French, and American zones, although educational administration slowly was being returned to the *Länder*. The main basis of the postwar educational system was the same as that of the Weimar Republic. It was viewed as a temporary measure that would later evolve into a more democratic school system. When self-government was granted to the Federal Republic in 1949, a great share of the educational burden shifted to educators in the *Länder*.

The major tasks of the postwar educators were to rewrite texts dealing with the Nazi era, to train new teachers, and to build new school facilities. Although the *Länder* governments recognized the need for a new and uniform interpretation of Nazi history, they were slow in tackling the problem and appeared reluctant initially to deal with such volatile issues as the persecution of the Jews under Hitler. The problem of training new teachers was emphasized, although a teacher shortage remained. The rebuilding of schools was conducted over a long period, and major efforts were made in this direction in the 1950s.

EDUCATIONAL REFORMS

Once the task of reconstruction of school facilities was underway, various reforms were introduced in order to standardize the school system and to introduce into it new elements. In 1953 the Constitution of the German Committee for the Educational System attempted to make the educational system more uniform throughout the *Länder*, and in 1959 the committee published a report on the subject, entitled *General Plan for the Re-organization of the Public School System*. In the 1960s reforms, such as apprentice shops and new methods of instruction in vocational training, were introduced.

In the 1970s even more sweeping reforms were proposed. As the federal government explained: "The desires for improved schooling for children in view of the increasing demands of a workaday world oriented more and more toward science again brought up the questions of curricula and a basically new structuring of the educational system." Fundamental reforms were proposed in a document called *Structural Plans for the Educational System*, which was approved in February of 1970 by the German Council of Education and by the various *Länder* ministers of educational and cultural affairs.

The broad outlines of these reforms, which would extend from kindergarten to institutions of higher education, were: the reorganization of the curricula and an increased emphasis on science, the reorganization of the school structure particularly at the secondary level, the lowering of the school entrance age to five years instead of six, and the extension of compulsory education to ten years rather than nine. The 1970 reforms also were designed to provide for quantitative expansion by increasing facilities and at the same time improving the quality of education by making access to higher education more universal and less elitist.

There has been a great deal of difficulty in implementing the proposed reforms. Because each of the *Länder* is autonomous, it is practically impossible to gain consensus regarding uniformity of the school system. In addition, educators disagree as to whether the entire educational system needs to be restructured or whether changes should be attempted within the existing structure. Moreover, German educators tend to be reluctant to change traditional educational values, which have their roots in the eighteenth and nineteenth centuries. Another major hurdle to be overcome is the huge financial burden that quantitative expansion would impose. In the early 1970s it was anticipated that the proportion of the national budget devoted to education would increase by roughly 300 percent by the mid-1980s. In order to meet these expenses, taxes would have to increase appreciably. Many *Länder* officials have been unwilling to commit themselves to reforms until they are assured of an appropriate amount of funding.

BASIC PRINCIPLES OF EDUCATION

There are three basic principles of the educational system. The foremost principle is to maintain the high quality of education that has served as a model for many other nations, including the Scandinavian countries, some of the Eastern European countries, and the Low Countries, and has also influenced the system in the United States. The second basic principle is that every individual has the right to an education, which is stated in the Basic Law, or constitution, promulgated in 1949. The third essential principle is that the state, in turn, has the right to expect that students going through the system will be prepared for a useful role in society.

Among other principles of education are that full-time education should be compulsory for a period of nine years and that literacy should be as nearly universal as possible. Private schools, maintained generally by churches, private associations, and individuals, are frequently subsidized by the state on the principle that they should coexist with state schools. Although traditionally boys and girls were separated within the school system, there has been a growing trend toward coeducation since World War II. Another important principle of German education is to encourage education in the working, adult population. One government statement declared: "the aim of adult education is to make life interesting . . . to promote adults, in particular, in regard to their working life by information and instruction, to inform them of their tasks as citizens, and to orient them in gaining a critical and intelligent understanding of social and political life."

ADMINISTRATION AND FINANCE

Administration

The overall administrator for education is the minister of education and science, who is at the cabinet level of the government. The ministry is in charge of establishing and maintaining state schools and universities, training teachers, supporting private schools, and funding adult education. The governmental ministry shares responsibilities, however, with the minister of education and cultural affairs of each of the *Länder*. The *Land* minister is in charge of planning, organizing, managing, promoting, and supervising the entire school system of the *Land*. Other duties include: supervising teachers, administering activities of the schools and the various organizations that support them, and supervising boards of education, school committees, and other so-called intermediate bodies at the administrative level. The Commission for Educational Planning ensures that the federal government and the *Länder* cooperate regarding educational policy. This commission also makes long-term plans for educational developments and assesses expenditures.

Although the federal Ministry of Education and Science and the educational ministries of the various *Länder* are the major administrative bodies dealing with education, there are also several ancillary bodies that deal with this subject. Certain federal ministries, such as the Ministry of Agriculture, deal with the administration of appropriate vocational schools. In addition, the German Council of Education, established in 1965, serves as an advisory committee for the entire educational system, with the exception of the universities. It draws up plans regarding the requirements of the educational system, taking into account the needs of society for people trained in specific areas. The Council on Science and the Humanities, established in 1957, is the advisory body for the universities and performs functions similar to the German Council of Education.

The principle of decentralization in administration is rigorously applied throughout the educational system. In this way, despite the fact that the Ministry of Education and Science and the *Länder* administrators have overall control over the system, the administrative body closest to a particular school is the chief administrator of that school. Below the *Länder* authorities are the intermediate bodies, such as district presidents, boards of education in the case of state schools, and religious communities and orders in the case of private schools. Their tasks are to supervise the schools, the teachers, and the activities of other organizations that help maintain the school. Below these intermediate bodies are the so-called lower bodies that include school inspectors, vocational employer organizations, and advisory councils. These bodies generally serve in an advisory capacity rather than as direct supervisors of the system.

Finance

The country places great stress on education and, therefore, gives it strong financial backing. Public education is financed almost entirely through federal, state, and municipal taxes. Parents' associations and industry may also contribute to the educational system on a voluntary basis. Private schools are financed by the organizations to which they belong, such as churches, religious orders, foundations, parents' associations, and private enterprises. At the *Grundschule* level, less than 1 percent of the children attend private schools. At the *Realschule* (formerly the *Mittelschule)* and Gymnasium levels, about 9 and 14 percent, respectively, attend private schools. At the secondary level in vocational training, about 33 percent of the full-time students are in private institutions but the number of part-time private vocational schools is minuscule. Certain approved private schools receive grants-in-aid from the federal government.

The total budget for education is divided three ways: staff expenditures, material expenditures, and general expenditures. The amount expended for the state school system is approximately 7 percent of the total budget of the federal government, the *Länder*, and the districts and communities. By 1985 this total is expected to rise to approximately 22 percent of the budget.

In addition to the basic expenses, there is special encouragement of vocational training and retraining through state allowances. Under the Labor Promotion Act of June 25, 1969, the Federal Institute for Labor gives grants and loans to both children and adults for vocational training. To encourage the vocational retraining of adults who require refresher courses, the Federal Institute for Labor pays living costs of both the individual and family during the period of retraining. This sum usually averages 95 percent of the employee's former income. After retraining, the institute then pays enterprises hiring the retrained person an "initiation allowance." From 1962 to 1971, DM416.5 million (for value of the Deutsche Mark—see Glossary) were spent on vocational training and retraining.

In 1960 total expenses for education were more than DM7 billion, of which the Ministry of Education and Science and the *Länder* ministries expended about DM4.7 billion and the districts, DM2.3 billion. Of these total expenses, DM5 billion were for current expenditures, and almost DM2 billion were for capital expenditures. By 1965 the total for education was almost DM13.6 billion, nearly double the amount spent in 1960. Again the Ministry of Education and Science and the *Länder* ministries paid approximately double the expenditure of the districts. Of the total expenditures, over DM9 billion were current, and about DM4.5 billion were capital. By 1970 the overall total had risen by approximately 66 percent, but the federal and *Länder* expenditures were higher in proportion to the district expenditures than they had been in previous years. Of the total educational expenditures in 1970, over DM16.5 billion were current, and DM5.9 billion were capital.

THE EDUCATIONAL SYSTEM

Kindergarten

Preschool or kindergarten was introduced in Germany in the mid-nineteenth century. Although the institution was exclusively German for many years, it has been adopted by many other countries, including the United States. Kindergartens are sponsored by churches, communities, private enterprises, and parents' groups and are attended by children from three to six years of age. Attendance is voluntary.

The original purpose of the kindergarten was to awaken the child's abilities and interests through participation in games and activities. The word *kindergarten* means "children's garden" or playground. Although kindergartens still tend to deal with the social aspects of the child's development, the government hopes to emphasize the educational aspects to a greater degree in the future. According to a government source, reforms dealing with the kindergarten level "proceed on the assumption that it is precisely the early years of childhood that are decisive for the development of learning and speaking abilities and for the education of creative imagination."

From 1961 to 1971 the number of children attending kindergartens rose by approximately 42 percent (see table 8). The number of places in kindergartens, however, was totally inadequate. In the late 1960s only one child in three was able to attend kindergarten. In order to meet this need, the government's educational reform plan called for an increase in the number of kindergartens.

Elementary Education

After World War I, the *Grundschule*, a four-year basic or elementary school, was established and became compulsory in 1920 (see fig. 9). Children attend from the ages of six to ten. Despite the uniformity of the period of attendance, there is some variety in hours and textbooks, depending on the particular city or *Land*. There was little change in the

Table 8. *Number of Students in the Educational System of the Federal Republic of Germany, 1961 and 1971*

Kind of School	1961	1971
Preschool		
Kindergarten	817,227	1,160,736
Elementary School		
Grundschule	3,096,883	3,600,000
Secondary School (General)		
Hauptschule	2,194,032	2,600,000
Realschule	368,861	851,093
Gymnasium	853,437	1,382,244
Secondary School (Vocational)		
Berufsschule	1,352,463	1,570,270
Berufsfachschule	139,160	208,741
Berufsaufbauschule	n.a.	37,758
Fachoberschule	n.a.	58,973
Advanced Vocational School		
Fachschule	120,051	156,182
Higher Education		
Wissenschaftliche hochschule	239,156	466,044
Kunsthochschule	7,937	12,312
Fachhochschule	n.a.	119,329

n.a.—not available.

Source: Adapted from *Sozialstatistik: Bildungstatistik*, Luxembourg, 1972.

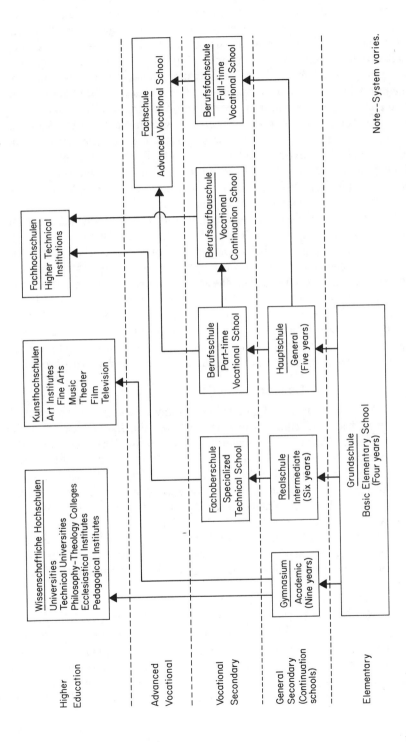

Figure 9. Representative Model of the Educational System in the Federal Republic of Germany

141

number of pupils attending the *Grundschule* in the 1961–71 decade.

When a child finishes his fourth year of the *Grundschule*, he and his parents must make the decision regarding secondary education. Many educators feel that forcing a decision on children at age ten is unrealistic and closes higher educational opportunites for those who develop intellectually during their teen years but whose secondary education does not qualify them for university entrance. The choice also must be concurred in by the child's teachers at the *Grundschule*. Educators, fearing that too much talent has been lost under the rigidly compartmentalized system, have been experimenting with methods of transferring students at various secondary schools into the *Gymnasium*, which is the regular route to university education. West Berlin and Bremen have added two years to the basic *Grundschule* in order to give the student additional time before the decision on whether secondary education will be academic or vocational must be made.

In addition to the loss of talent, many educators and officials view the process of separating pupils into alternate educational channels at the age of ten as preserving the elitism of former German society. In 1973 the minister of science and education, Klaus von Dohnanyi, stated that the decision was more often based on the social origins of children rather than on their real capabilities. The 1970 reforms for the elementary level, which include lowering the entrance age to five and placing greater stress on subject matter, do not directly cope with this problem. The secondary level reforms, however, which aim at making the secondary system more comprehensive and less compartmentalized, could alleviate this problem.

General Secondary Education

There are three forms of general secondary education or continuation schools as they are called: the *Hauptschule*, the *Realschule*, and the *Gymnasium*. There is a great deal of confusion regarding the nomenclature of these schools. Some refer to the *Hauptschule* as the elementary school, and others call it the senior school. The *Realschule* is generally referred to as the intermediate school but is sometimes known as the practical school. The *Gymnasium* is called the senior school by some and the grammar school by others. Terminology, such as elementary, grammar, intermediate, and secondary schooling as used in reference to the German system does not correspond to the same terminology as used in describing the educational system in the United States.

Approximately 50 percent of the children who complete the *Grundschule* go on to the *Hauptschule*. They attend this school for five years, from age ten to fifteen. The curriculum stresses preparation for a vocation, but also includes mathematics, history, geography, German, and sometimes one foreign language. Graduates of this school get a senior school certificate called the *Hauptschulabschluss*. After graduation, they either become apprentices in shops or factories while taking mandatory part-time courses, or they attend some form of full-time vocational school until the age of eighteen.

A much smaller number of *Grundschule* graduates, approximately 20 percent, attend the *Realschule* for a period of six years, or from the age of ten to sixteen. The *Realschule* prepares the student for the middle level of industry and commerce, as well as administrative jobs within the government. The curriculum consists of mathematics, science, German, and two foreign languages; shorthand, typing, and bookkeeping are also stressed. The *Realschule* graduate receives the certificate of *mittlere Reife* (medium maturity) upon completion of his studies. After graduation, a student may either go on to a full-time technical school or continue his education on a part-time basis while serving as an apprentice. Statistically, the number of *Realschule* students increased by 130 percent in the 1961–71 decade. A recent innovation in this area is the *Abendrealschule*, an evening *Realschule*, which gives the graduate the same certificate.

Approximately 30 percent of *Grundschule* graduates go on to the *Gymnasium*. Children attend the *Gymnasium* for nine years, or from the age of ten to nineteen. This kind of school is the main avenue to higher education and eventually to a professional career. There are three specialized branches of the *Gymnasium:* the *altsprachliche* or classical language *Gymnasium*, which includes nine years of Latin and six of Greek; the *neusprachliche* or modern language *Gymnasium*, which emphasizes French, English, Russian, and Spanish; and the *mathematisch-naturwissenschaftliche Gymnasium*, which stresses mathematics and natural science. Among the core subjects in all branches of the *Gymnasium* are German, English, civics, mathematics, and history. In the 1961–71 decade the number of *Gymnasium* students increased by 61 percent.

In order to graduate from the *Gymnasium*, a pupil must pass a very difficult examination, after which he receives the *Abitur*, or diploma. Of the total number of students who enter the *Gymnasium*, fewer than one-half graduate. Students who drop out generally transfer to the *Realschule* or *Hauptschule* or, if they have gone beyond those levels, they enter full-time technical or vocational schools. Nine out of ten students who receive the *Abitur* continue in an institution of higher education, and the others go directly into business or the civil service.

There have been two recent innovations in the *Gymnasium* level that are geared toward making admission to the university more accessible and less elitist than the standard *Gymnasium* route. These are referred to as the second route to education or *der zweite Bildungsweg*. One is called the *Abendgymnasium*, a part-time evening school for people who work. The minimum age for acceptance at this kind of school is nineteen, and the student must either have completed his vocational training or have been employed for three years. The curriculum is similar to the regular *Gymnasium*, emphasizing German, civics, two foreign languages, mathematics, and science. The second school is called the *Studienkolleg*, which is generally affiliated with a university and is primarily for foreign students. Both the *Abendgymnasium* and the *Studienkolleg* grant the *Abitur* or its equivalent.

In recent years, many German educators have felt that the compartmentalization of secondary education has been too restrictive and rigid and has prevented the student from exploring various areas of education. In several of the *Länder*, therefore, a radically new kind of school, called the *Gesamtschule*, has been introduced. It is designed to be a comprehensive school, offering an all-inclusive curriculum for students from six to nineteen who are allowed to pursue whatever course they choose. The 1970 reforms are designed to increase the number of these comprehensive schools and to increase the length of general secondary study by one year and place greater emphasis on science. Some 800 comprehensive schools are planned for construction by 1980.

Vocational Secondary Education

There are several kinds of vocational secondary schools that cater to the vital role that industry and trade play in the country, and there are an increasing number of women in these schools. In 1973 about 39 percent of all apprentices and 62 percent of the total number of students in vocational schools were women. In addition to the full-time secondary vocational schools and the part-time schools, there are evening schools that had an enrollment of 14,000 students in 1972.

The part-time day vocational school, which is generally combined with work and is, therefore, known as the dual system, is called the *Berufsschule*. Students are trained in such fields as mining, industry, housecraft (a combination of nursing and general home care), commerce, agriculture, and horticulture. Approximately 40 percent of the instruction in these schools is devoted to general subjects, which include German, social studies, economics, and religion. Of these general subjects, German receives the greatest emphasis, and the other 60 percent of instruction is in an area of specialization.

The full-time secondary vocational school is the *Berufsfachschule*. The enrollment in the school increased by 50 percent in the 1961–71 decade. This is a specialized vocational school attended by students preparing for a trade or business. There are three main branches of specialization within the school: commerce or business, science and mathematics, and housecraft. Between one-half and three-quarters of the enrolled students study commerce. The commercial course emphasizes business, bookkeeping, clerical work, and typing, as well as German, English, social studies, history, geography, religion, mathematics, and science. The science and mathematics specialization stresses mathematics and so-called technical arithmetic, physics, chemistry, and electrotechnology, as well as German, economics, and social studies. The housecraft specialization emphasizes health care, baby care, nursing, and home economics in addition to English, German, civics, and religion.

Another kind of vocational secondary school, full time or part time, is the *Berufsaufbauschule*. Students who attend this school prepare for higher level jobs or for further schooling. There are five branches or fields of specialization: general technical, industrial technical, clerical and sales, domestic science and social education, and agriculture. Although specialized courses vary according to the field, the usual curriculum is: German, a foreign language, history, community relations, geography, economics, mathematics, physics, chemistry, and industrial management.

The technical secondary school for *Realschule* graduates is the *Fachoberschule*. The period of training in the *Fachoberschule* is two years and terminates in an examination that enables the graduate to go on to a higher technical institute. There are six kinds of *Fachoberschulen*: engineering, economics, domestic science, social studies, design, and ocean navigation. Instruction is divided into three categories: general instruction, specialized instruction, and practical training in a particular field of specialization. The core curriculum for all areas includes German, English, social studies, mathematics, natural sciences, and physical education.

The 1970 reform plans for secondary vocational education are in some ways similar to, and in other ways quite different from, those for general secondary education. A general secondary education will stress science in the future, and secondary vocational education will emphasize a broader base of knowledge. Ultimately, however, these reforms should give the secondary student of both schools a broad-based education and a scientific background.

Advanced Vocational and Technical Education

The Federal Republic places great emphasis on advanced vocational education. As a recent government publication pointed out, "With its rapid technological change, the modern industrial country requires the citizens in the Federal Republic always to be prepared to continue to learn and to adapt themselves to learning a new profession three or four times in the course of their working life. The Federation, the *Länder*, and the communes have made preparations for this development. In the last ten years the State grants . . . for advanced vocational training have roughly doubled." Interest in advanced vocational and technical training has increased not only on the part of the government but on the part of the students as well. The number of students in *Fachschulen* (advanced vocational schools) increased significantly during the 1961–71 decade. In the late 1960s the preference of male students in vocational studies was for mechanical engineering, electrical engineering, and construction engineering.

Graduates of the *Fachschulen* are needed in both the public and private sectors. The public area requires office staff and officials having highly specialized knowledge and skills. In the private domain, trade unions, business firms, commercial organizations, and industry also require graduates. Both the federal and *Länder* governments and other private institutions support these schools. Since 1966 the Federal Institute of Labor, located in Nürnberg, has been responsible for governmental promotion of advanced vocational training. Between 1966 and 1972 the institute spent some DM26 million for this purpose. The federal government and the *Länder*, however, are not the only sponsors of the *Fachschulen*. Chambers of commerce, so-called chambers of handicraft, employers associations, trade unions, and private firms also have spent large amounts of money on these institutes. Data regarding the exact amounts spent by the private sector are not available.

In order to enter the *Fachschule*, a student must be beyond the age of compulsory education and must successfully have concluded his studies at one of the secondary vocational schools and had some vocational experience. Entrants frequently are practical engineers or lower level administrators. The *Fachschule* trains students for a period of at least one year and, upon graduation, they are considered to be medium-level specialists, and may enter such fields as agriculture, industry, and the crafts.

In 1970 *Fachhochschulen* (advanced technical colleges) were developed and accorded the same status as universities and other institutions of higher education. Formerly known as *Höhere Fachschulen* (advanced technical schools) and *Ingenieurschulen* (engineer schools), the *Fachhochschulen* provide advanced technical training in agriculture, economics, engineering, social work, and other fields in which graduates are greatly in demand in the country's burgeoning economy. Courses last for three years, and graduates are eligible for advanced study at universities.

Music and Fine Arts Institutes

The schools of music and the fine arts are known as conservatories and academies, respectively. They are referred to as *Kunsthochschulen* and not only train potential artists but also teachers of the arts. Like university entrants, students must have completed their studies at the *Gymnasium;* but their further education, in contrast to that of university students, is not considered academic. Students are selected on the basis of their artistic talents, and the curriculum is geared to the individual student. Every student must complete eight terms of four years of training. There are eleven academies of art and architecture—the oldest dates from 1662 and the most recent from 1966—and eighteen conservatories of music, all of which were founded in the nineteenth and twentieth centuries.

Teacher Training

The prerequisite for all teacher training institutions is the *Abitur*, or

Gymnasium certificate. Teachers preparing to teach at the *Grundschule* or the *Hauptschule* will train at the *Pädogogische Hochschulen*, or teacher training institutes. Those who will teach at the *Gymnasium*, the *Realschule*, and the various vocational schools attend teacher training courses at the universities. The length of study varies from six semesters or three years for students at the *Pädogogische Hochschule* to eight semesters or four years for students at the universities. In the late 1960s and early 1970s the length of study at the universities was increased to as much as twelve semesters or six years. The curriculum for all potential teachers is highly structured, and the emphasis is on pedagogy, educational philosophy, psychology, and a specialized field of concentration. All academic training, whether at a *Pädogogische Hochschule* or a university, is followed by two years of practical training.

In addition to teacher training for the various levels of elementary and secondary education, there are also specialized institutes for teachers of special education. Teachers of the handicapped train in institutes of therapeutic education called *Heilpädogogische Hochschulen*. Students at these institutes must possess the *Abitur* and must have completed their training at the *Pädogogische Hochschule*. Their training generally lasts for four semesters or two years and is followed by a period of practice teaching.

Teachers of arts and crafts and technical subjects are trained at the *Fachinstituten*. These institutes, unlike the others, do not have university status, and the teachers need only have the *mittlere Reife*, the certificate conferred by the *Realschule*, rather than the *Abitur*. The curriculum includes woodwork, metal work, domestic science, drawing, and physical education. The period of training varies from two to four years, depending on the field of specialization and the rules of the particular *Land*. After passing a final examination, the student practice teaches for one year.

Between 90 and 95 percent of all public school teachers are civil servants, and one-half to two-thirds are women. All teachers must take a first examination to receive civil service status, and at the end of five years they receive tenure as civil servants. Once given tenure, they cannot be dismissed and remain in office until the age of sixty-five, at which time they receive a pension.

Teaching generally is a highly respected profession. This respect is due in part to the length of academic training and in part to the relatively large increases in pay since World War II, which have enhanced the prestige of the profession. Despite all this, however, there is a severe shortage of teachers in the Federal Republic. The *Gymnasium* and various vocational schools are the most severely affected, and science and mathematics are the subjects where the teacher shortage is most acute. In order to counter this problem, the government has imported teachers from other countries. In the early 1970s the government predicted that the teacher shortage would be overcome between 1975 and 1980.

Universities

Universities and technical universities are considered to be the pinnacle of the educational system. There are some forty-four major universities. The oldest is the University of Heidelberg, founded in 1386, and the two most recent are the University of Augsburg and the University of Osrabruch, both established in 1970. In addition, there are twenty-one colleges, excluding the colleges of art and music. There is one general college; two colleges of economics, political science, and public administration; sixteen colleges of philosophy and theology; one college of environmental planning; and one college of technology.

Universities are organized more or less uniformly throughout the *Länder*. At the highest level is the conference of university rectors, which cooperates with the various university and college administrators and with the ministers of culture of each *Land*. Every university has its own rector, who acts as a general administrator. One of the main administrative bodies of the university is the student body, which manages its own affairs—such as location employment for students and providing for cultural arrangements—and also participates in the academic administration of the universities. The degree to which the student body participates in this administration varies widely from one institution to another.

The university student body represents only approximately 10 percent of the age group of the population as a whole that tends to come from the higher strata of society. Most students enter the university directly from the *Gymnasium*, although a small proportion does enter the university from the so-called secondary route to education. Only 10 percent of all university students come form working-class families.

Students generally prefer to study medicine, agriculture, philosophy, history, political science, and law, in that order. Female students prefer the liberal arts, the natural sciences, law, economics, and medicine. Among the subjects selected by women, only the preference toward economics has risen appreciably since 1970.

PROBLEMS OF THE UNIVERSITIES

The university system contains a variety of problems. First among them is the difficulty of admittance to the university itself. Unfortunately for the students, a restriction of numbers clause has been imposed on certain of the preferred fields, such as medicine, pharmacy, psychology, and the natural sciences, primarily because of expanding enrollments and limited staff. The selection process involves the choosing of certain *Abitur* degree students over others. It has been criticized by some German educators on the grounds that computers make the final decision, based on records, grades, and other factors, rather than admission examinations that might better determine the student's aptitude for a particular field.

Another serious problem from the viewpoint of government and

148

education authorities is student activism, which dates from the early 1900s in Germany. Before World War I, students had been actively involved in youth movements, and before World War II, they were active in the Hitler Youth. By the 1950s, however, there was a hiatus in this activist trend, and students tended to be more moderate and conformist. In the 1960s student activism again revived, and students became the vanguard of radical activity. Many were alienated from the older generation, whom they felt had been tainted by nazism, and from what they considered an absence of ideals in their society. As a result of this alienation, many students in the 1960s and early 1970s became attracted to the ideas of Karl Marx, Herbert Marcuse, Ernesto (Che) Guevara, and Mao Tse-tung.

In 1968 there were violent student riots in Frankfurt. In 1969 the radical left began to take over control of student unions throughout the *Länder*. By 1972 the radicals had won control of student parliaments in twelve major universities. They also managed to win seats in the university governing bodies and were, therefore, able to cast vetoes against professors to whom they were ideologically opposed. In early 1974 there were again violent student outbursts in Frankfurt, this time over the issue of student housing.

One of the most serious issues in the universities is severe overcrowding. Between 1961 and 1967 the number of university students increased by approximately 30 percent. By 1973 there were some 36,000 students holding the *Abitur* who could not find places at universities.

Although the federal government and the *Länder* have attempted to deal with the situation, it remained a problem in 1974. Between 1960 and 1970 the number of professors doubled. This did not, however, solve the overcrowding in lecture rooms, seminars, and laboratories. In the same period ten new universities, designed to accommodate 80,000 students, were established in order to reduce some of the overcrowding. Approximately DM1,540 million were spent in these new universities, and in 1970 DM2,000 million were spent on universities. The government planned to spend mearly double that amount, DM3,900 million, per year by 1975.

The most radical solution to the overcrowding was to send students to other countries for further education. This plan was introduced by Christian Schwartz-Schilling, a state deputy from Hesse. He proposed that some 600 American universities that had vacancies accept German students. Although his plan was criticized by many German educators, who alleged that American university standards were inferior to those of German universities, by February of 1974, some 500 students from the Federal Republic had been accepted at American universities in Washington, D. C.; Michigan; Missouri; Washington; and Texas. Most of them have been accepted as sophomores, and twenty students have been admitted to master's and doctoral degree programs. The intended date of enrollment is for the fall of 1975. If the program proves to be successful after a period of five years, as many as 30,000 students would attend American colleges and universities annually.

The costs of enrolling the students in American schools will be borne by the individual *Land* rather than the federal government. The average cost per student was estimated in 1974 to be approximately US$4,750 a year. The main benefits of the program would be the relief from overcrowding in the home universities and the furthering of international understanding through the exchange of students. The major drawback from the perspective of German students is that they would not be allowed to enroll in medical or dental schools.

The government, however, in its 1970 reforms planned to continue university construction and extension of existing facilities. It also intended to reduce the time of study at the level of higher education, which would ease overcrowding to some degree. Among other reforms for higher education were plans to increase the uniformity of curriculum in the various schools of higher education along the lines of secondary education reform. Thus, the universities, technical universities, teacher training institutions, music conservatories and art academies, and advanced vocational schools, despite their respective areas of specialization, would become more comprehensive and less specialized.

OTHER EDUCATION

A variety of *Sonderschulen* (specialized schools) provide for children and adults who have physical, mental, and psychological handicaps. The purpose of the *Sonderschulen* was stated in the Law for the Unification and Organization of the School System of 1964, when the government declared that specialized schools served the function of educating people having physical, mental, or psychological defects who could not be trained within the regular school system.

There are eleven different kinds of *Sonderschulen:* for backward children, for the mentally damaged, for the hard of hearing, for the completely deaf, for the blind, for those with sight deficiencies, for the physically handicapped, for the physically ill, for people with speech defects, for the emotionally disturbed, and for juvenile delinquents. The form of schooling depends both on the facilities in the area and the kind of impediment involved. There are individual classes at both the *Grundschule* and the *Hauptschule*, half-day classes at the special schools, full-day classes at these schools, and boarding schools. There are also teachers who travel from home to home, instructing people who are physically ill. There were 133,087 pupils in the *Sonderschulen* in 1961 compared to 319,400 in 1971. This represents an increase of 140 percent. The reforms of 1970 were designed to increase the number of *Sonderschulen* for the physically handicapped. The precise increase in the number of these schools was not given, nor were schools for other handicapped persons mentioned.

There are also special schools for military personnel that are sponsored by the Bundeswehr (Federal Armed Forces). One government publication stated that the armed forces have become "the vocational school of the nation." Schools for servicemen, however, are not exclusively vocational, and those who have completed compulsory service are allowed to study for academic examinations. If they pass these examinations, they receive either the *mittlere Reife*, the final certificate from the *Realschule* or, in some cases, the *Abitur*.

In the vocational area, the Bundeswehr encourages servicemen to pursue various trades and professions in order for them to resume their vocation or pursue a new one when they return to civilian life. The Bundeswehr has a variety of specialized schools designed for this purpose, that, by 1972, had been attended by some 195,000 servicemen. It also has the Careers Promotion Service, which includes working groups and vocational courses. By 1972 approximately 556,000 servicemen had attended this kind of school. Approximately 55,000 of these men had received highly specialized training in a particular field, enabling them to become master craftsmen or engineers upon return to civilian life.

There are a variety of forms of adult education. As one governmental publication stated, adult education is possible for every person of every age. The goal of adult education, according to the government, is to allow adults to study in special areas, to take examinations, and to prepare for career changes in advance.

The *Länder* have expended a significant amount of money on adult education; in 1961, DM151.1 million; in 1963, DM23.6 million; and in 1966, DM31.5 million. No later data are available on the amount of *Länder* expenditure, although the government stated that the amount has risen considerably in recent years. Adult education also is sponsored by trade unions, farmers' associations, and industrial enterprises. Both academic teachers and vocational instructors take part in adult education programs.

The most common form of adult education is the *Volkshochschule*, or the people's university. These schools generally emphasize advanced vocational training, and approximately 40 percent of all class time is devoted to vocational subjects, although other subjects are also taught. In the late 1960s there were approximately 1,000 *Volkshochschulen* offering approximately 95,000 courses. In the same period some 2 million students attended annually. A greater proportion of women attended the *Volkshochschulen* than did men. In 1968, for example, women comprised 60 percent of the total number of students.

Political education is still another form of adult education and is sponsored by public agencies, political parties, and other organizations and associations that are concerned with raising the political awareness of the people. In 1969 approximately 200,000 people attended political courses, which were held at Europe houses, East-West institutes, political foundations, and at the *Volkshochschulen*.

Among the other forms of adult education are church-related institutions for adults, trade union institutes, correspondence courses, and what is known as the modern method of adult education—using the mass media. Approximately 185,000 women annually attend courses for mothers offered by the Protestant churches, and roughly 80,000 people annually attend Protestant academies. A similar number attend adult education courses sponsored by trade unions. About 250,000 people participate in correspondence courses, and a large proportion of the people watch educational programs on television or listen to courses on the radio.

The reforms of 1970 dealing with adult education were designed to broaden the areas of adult education and at the same time make it possible for people in rural areas to benefit from these programs. One reform that was enacted was the basic studies program, a general course organized by the German Association of Adult Education Institutions. The reforms also were designed to increase the number of courses offered on radio and television and to increase the services provided by mobile libraries. The goal of providing a greater number of mobile libraries has been undertaken by the German Libraries Association.

CHAPTER 9

ARTISTIC AND INTELLECTUAL EXPRESSION

Germans, for a long time, have pictured themselves as a nation of poets and thinkers, and their artistic and intellectual heritage has been highly prized. Artists, writers, composers, scholars, and scientists have always enjoyed high prestige. Germans think in terms of formal art and philosophy, and working people freely use expressions from outstanding literature. Amateur singing clubs, discussion groups, and other similar associations are common in the Federal Republic, but the people think primarily in terms of the formal creative work of the masters rather than folk art. The numerous theaters and concert halls, which abound in every city and town of the Federal Republic, are always well attended. Art and science museums attract large crowds. The appetite for art and knowledge appears to be consistently high.

Germans have made important contributions to every medium of artistic and intellectual expression. For centuries, the country has been a nation of artistic and intellectual giants; men like Martin Luther, Johann Wolfgang von Goethe, Ludwig van Beethoven, Immanuel Kant, Georg Hegel, Karl Marx, and Albert Einstein are masters in the world's heritage of creative genius. It is impossible to consider the history of literature or drama without dealing at length with the works of Goethe, Johann Christoph Friedrich von Schiller, Heinrich Heine, or Thomas Mann. Among the greatest names in music must be included Johann Sebastian Bach, Johannes Brahms, Beethoven, and Richard Wagner. In art Albrecht Dürer and Hans Holbein have made important contributions. In philosophy Gottfried Wilhelm von Leibniz, Kant, Hegel, Friedrich Nietzsche, and Marx are central to any study. Johannes Kepler, Karl Friedrich Gauss, Wilhelm von Humboldt, Wilhelm Conrad Röntgen, and Einstein are but a few of the great contributors to the natural sciences.

Since the Middle Ages, the unity of German intellectual and artistic effort has been defined by language rather than political boundaries. German culture, as part of that of Western Europe, has influenced and been influenced by most of the other countries of the West. From the middle of the eighteenth century to the accession of the Nazis in 1933, Germany's role in Western European music, literature, and philosophy was of paramount significance. Almost all artistic and intellectual traditions were interrupted during the twelve-year era of the Third Reich between 1933 and 1945, when racism and police-state methods

153

drove many of the best artists and intellectuals into exile and checked the development of new talent. Since the end of World War II, the effort has been toward rebuilding the illustrious cultural heritage and reestablishing the creative thread.

HISTORICAL PERSPECTIVE

Philosophy

Major German philosophy began with Albertus Magnus (Albert the Great, 1193–1280), who was regarded as one of the foremost Aristotelians of his day. Like most Germans of his time he was educated outside of Germany in Padua, Bologna, and Paris. Albert held that the fundamental doctrine of Christianity could not be demonstrated by logic and, therefore, must be buttressed by revelation. His attempts to separate theology and philosophy led to his consideration as a major organizing intellect of the Middle Ages.

The Albertists, as his followers were called, came mainly from among the German Dominicans. The two most important of these, Dietrich of Freiberg (ca. 1250–1311) and Meister Eckhart from Hochheim (ca. 1260–1327), emphasized the mystical aspects of Albert's work. Through mysticism, these men and later German mystics (all Dominicans), most notably Johann Tauler (1300–60) and Heinrich Suso or Seuse (ca. 1300–66), sought to offer a higher kind of knowledge beyond natural reason.

The mysticism of the fourteenth century climaxed in the fifteenth-century writings of Nikolaus Krypffs (Nikolaus of Cusa, 1401–64), a cardinal of the church. In *De Docta Ignorantia* (Of Learned Ignorance), Nikolaus reevaluated the place of man and nature in relation to God. He reasoned that God represented the resolution or unification of all opposing attributes and, thus, mystically combined the finite and the infinite into one Being.

Between Nikolaus in the fifteenth century and Leibniz in the seventeenth, the German states were racked by religious strife and the plundering of the Thirty Years' War (1618–48). German universities, which had begun to open in the fourteenth century with the possibility of maintaining a continuous line of discussion and influence, were frequently closed. The issues separating Lutheran, Calvinist, and Roman Catholic philosophers increasingly turned them from German philosophy to theology and politics.

German philosophy was rekindled by Leibniz (1646–1716), who saw all matter as divided into monads or atoms. Each monad held the potential for development through its own inner force. This force was perceived through increasingly complex activity—the chemical reaction of rocks, the vitality of plants, the movement of animals, and the consciousness of man.

Christian Wolff (1679–1754) popularized and systematized this world view by reducing much of Leibniz' philosophy to rational principles. Where Leibniz saw his world as a purposeful whole, which could only have been established by an all-wise God, Wolff placed man in the center of a set of arrangements made for his benefit. Wolff, moreover, was the first philosopher to present an entire philosophic system in German, thereby making it accessible to laymen.

Wolff established the Enlightenment in Germany as a scholastic movement, aimed at domesticating and rationalizing philosophy through the publication of systematic manuals. These manuals, in turn, became teaching instruments in many German universities. Those who followed this tradition, although often not in agreement with Wolff, sought to refine previous work through still newer manuals.

In opposition were the so-called worldly philosophers. Though many of these men occupied university chairs, they maintained the freer and less academic view of Enlightenment philosophy found outside Germany. For them, philosophy was not a doctrine to be propounded but an activity for the clarification of troubling doubts and an instrument for the elevation of the general tone of culture. The most important philosophers of this tradition were Moses Mendelssohn (1729–86) and Gotthold Ephraim Lessing (1729–81).

The influence of the new political ideas of the Enlightenment can best be seen in the work of Christian Thomasius (1655–1728). Thomasius, a contemporary of Wolff, also attempted to plot a man-centered schema of the world. So long as man's acquisitiveness was not brought under the control of a rational principle, that is, law, a constant state of war or competition existed. Thomasius put these beliefs into action by fighting strenuously and successfully against trials for witchcraft.

The great flourish of German Enlightenment philosophy reached its zenith in the writing of Kant (1724–1804). Scientific discovery opened new vistas while raising profound questions about the limits of reason and knowledge. In *The Critique of Pure Reason* (1781), Kant reasoned that the human mind came to conclusions about the natural world as a result of experience. The knowledge of universal truth, however, remained in the realm of "things in themselves" and, as such, was beyond experience. *The Critique of Judgement* (1790) sought to bridge the gap between theoretical reason and the conscience. Religion, within the bounds of reason, equaled morality. A moral law was defined by what Kant termed the "categorical imperative," which guided right and wrong judgment by asking the question "what if everyone did this?"

Although Kant attempted to resolve the philosophical ambiguities of Enlightenment philosophy, he laid bare the problems that Romantic philosophy rose to meet. Romantic philosophers aimed at the construction of a unified system of reason. For some, this unity was thought to be ethical and, for others, aesthetic. These elements can be seen in the writings of Johann Fichte (1762–1841), Friedrich Schelling (1775–1854), and Friedrich Schleiermacher (1768–1834). The greatest of the Romantic era writers, however, was Hegel (1770–1831), who perceived the unity of thought as being logical.

Hegel saw the principle of logic as being dialectical (usually expressed as thesis and antithesis leading to synthesis) and underlying all aspects of the world. Nature, law, history, science, religion, art, and even philosophy itself developed dialectically. Although Hegel's influence during the period on German art, literature, and philosophy was quite extensive, it was his views on state and society that had the greatest effect.

Civil society, according to Hegel, existed because of man's inherent goal of total freedom of spirit. To avoid the clash of self-interests, society demanded that individual liberty merge into public needs. Thus, the state was the true end of man and built itself on the submission of individual rights to the duties of society. Morality was defined by the close adherence to state traditions.

Although these political ideas reinforced the conservative attitude toward the state, Hegel's philosophic method—the dialectic—was adopted by liberals and socialists as proof of the eventual reform of private ownership and the state. The leading figures of these "Young Hegelians," as they were called, were David Friedrich Strauss (1808–74), Bruno Bauer (1809–82), Ludwig Feuerbach (1804–72), Max Stirner (1806–56), Friedrich Vischer (1807–87), and Arnold Ruge (1802–80).

This first generation of followers gave way to a second, exemplified by the teachings of Marx. His work was divided into two broad themes. The first of these traced the development of historical change as caused by changes in what he termed the "modes of production." The stage of development Marx saw about him was industrial capitalism that maintained, by definition, a class of exploiters and a class of exploited. The chief critique of industrial capitalism, *Das Kapital* (1867), is still widely read and has had a great deal of influence on the analysis of society. The second aspect of Marx work was prescriptive. *The Communist Manifesto* (1848) argued that given the evils of capitalism it was necessary to aid the Hegelian negation of capitalism through active participation in its overthrow. This prescription was only adopted by a segment of the rising socialist movement in the last half of the nineteenth century, with obviously mixed results.

Arthur Schopenhauer (1788–1860) revised the Kantian notion of experience (phenomena conditioned by human intelligence) by redefining the will. Will was uncaused activity that expressed itself in man as impulse, instinct, striving, yearning, and craving. The conscious will to live, according to Schopenhauer, was the guiding principle of life. It created struggle, sorrow, and evil in the world, despite the fact that life was itself doomed.

With the progression of natural science, philosophers and scientists-turned-philosophers sought to reassert the Kantian emphasis on experience in the Hegelian logical methodology and became known as New-Kantians (New Idealists). At the same time, discontent with

156

traditional conceptions of truth and knowledge led Nietzsche (1844–1900) to change Schopenhauer's "will to live" to a "will for power." Unlike Schopenhauer, Nietzsche saw this will as essentially good; life that could survive deserved to survive. All things bow to self-assertion, and man must stretch his powers to the limit to become a more powerful kind of person, a "superman." Doctrines of equality must give way to those of an aristocracy composed of these "supermen." Despite Nietzsche's attack on the standard values of his time—Christianity ("a slave morality"), popular education, respectability, the liberal belief in progress, socialism, nationalism, and racism (particularly anti-Semitism)— Nietzsche at once attracted a large following.

Oswald Spengler (1880–1936), in his well-known work *The Decline of the West* (1918–22), accepted Nietszche's triumph of "will for power" in history. For Spengler, however, various historical forms or "culture complexes" maintained a life cycle much like that of plants. The history of any given complex could be predetermined as it proceeded through youth, maturity, and old age. The West was doomed, concluded Spengler, as the final phase of social and moral decay had become self-evident.

The Nazis drew selectively from both Nietzsche and Spengler. While, for example, glorifying Nietzsche's will for power and the "superman," they ignored the condemnation of anti-Semitism. Although Spengler's notion of the inevitable "decline of the West" was contrary to their views, they found support in his declaration that "money can be overthrown and its power abolished only by blood. . . . Life and only life, the quality of blood, the triumph of will, count in history." The regime, too, had its own philosopher, Alfred Rosenberg, whose *Myth of the Twentieth Century* justified the racial and political policy of the Third Reich.

Early in the twentieth century, German philosophers were central to the development of still another current. Phenomenology, as conceived by Edmund Husserl (1859–1938), was the science of all phenomena, both real and conceptual. Phenomena had two representations: appearance and reality. Phenomenology sought to find the difference between these two aspects by discovering the essence or reality of given phenomena. The influence of this endeavor even outside Germany was widespread and profound. Max Scheler (1874–1928) applied the phenomenological approach to ethics and values; Moritz Geiger (1880–1937) applied it to aesthetics; and Martin Heidegger (b. 1889) explored questions of being and made phenomenology central to the existentialist movement in Germany and elsewhere.

During the 1920s, Karl Barth (b. 1886) and Karl Jaspers (1883–1969) recalled the work of the Danish religious philosopher Soren Kierkegaard (1813–55), and each presented what was to become existential analysis. Although there was, and is, no single existentialist position, the philosophy was unified through the view that human nature was determined by the course of life, rather than life by human nature.

German existentialism divided into three areas. The first extended and deepened Nietzsche's criticism of traditional, cultural, and spiritual values and attacked the Hegelian "logical" view of history. This position was best represented by Jaspers. The second trend, represented by Heidegger, emphasized the historicism and psychological analysis of Wilhelm Dilthey while using the phenomenological method of Husserl. Finally, Barth intertwined his own theological themes with those of the Reformation, German spirituality, and medieval mysticism.

Literature

Early German tales derived their heroes from the great Gothic migrations (A.D. 200–600) and the still older mythical heroes of the various German tribes (Wieland, Brünhild, and Siegfried). Written German found its origins in the requirements of proselytization; monks were set to work transcribing Latin texts into Germanic languages by reproducing Germanic sounds in Latin letters. The earliest work in German, in fact, is a Gothic translation of the Bible dating from the middle of the fourth century.

German poetry became fashionable in the twelfth century, particularly in the form of courtly epics. In the short span of thirty years (1190–1220) much of what has had lasting importance in German medieval literature was written—Wolfram von Eschenbach's *Parzifal*, Hartmann von Aue's *Erec*, and Gottfried von Strassburg's *Tristan*. All of these, and most others, display the theme of knightly adventure and chivalry and, more often than not, are copied from a French source.

A contemporary form of epic writing was the *Volksepos* (folk epics), of which the *Nibelungenlied* is the best known. This work, preserved in ten complete and twenty-two incomplete manuscripts, took shape in southeast Germany, ca. 1200. It represented a combination of German myth, history, and magic woven about the central characters of Brünhild and Siegfried.

Much of the lyric poetry of the twelfth and thirteenth centuries was set to music in the form of *Minnesänge* (love songs), and the average lyric poet became composer and performer *(Minnesinger)*. Of all these minstrels, Walther von der Vogelweide (ca. 1170–1230) best represented the lyric qualities of the age and is considered by some to have been the greatest German lyric poet before Goethe.

With the decline of many courts in the period between 1250 and 1500 came a disintegration in the harmony between the court poet and his noble audience. The art of the *Minnesänge* passed from minstrels to organized glee clubs sponsored by various trade guilds and, eventually, to *Singschulen* (singing schools). By the end of the fourteenth century, competition between clubs and schools had become so keen that formal uniform grades of competence were established throughout Germany. The *Meistersinger* was the ultimate grade and signified one who had written one complete song (lyrics and music).

At the end of this period lyrical poetry as represented by the

Minnesänge was dead—presumably destroyed by the *Singschulen*. Epic verse degenerated into prose form, and the court epic became courtly prose romances. The continuity and originality of lyric verse was retained, however, in the popular *Volkslied* (folk song). Another form that enjoyed great popularity in those years was the *Schwank* (anecdote). These were satirical tales often involving ribald themes of adultery built around such characters as the wandering scholar, the wicked old woman, Reynard the fox, and many others.

The invention of movable-type printing in the fifteenth century and the Reformation gave dramatic impetus to German prose literature. Not only did Luther's translation of the Bible into Saxon German and his numerous militant religious tracts find their way into print, but so did those of the Roman Catholic opposition. One Franciscan in particular, Thomas Murner, used a cutting, satirical talent to ridicule Luther in particular and Protestantism in general.

The popularity of the debate and the proliferation of printed arguments had the effect of making Saxon German the standard written language throughout Germany. Pamphlet, *Schwank*, and *Volksbuch* (short story) were the forms through which this new prose language developed. One such *Volksbuch* in 1587 concerned the life of Georg Faust (ca. 1480–1540) and was used by the Lutherans to condemn the godless pursuit of knowledge, power, and pleasure.

The German novel made its appearance in 1554 with the publication of *Knabenspiegel* and *Der Goldfaden* (1557) by Jörg Wickram (1520–62). Later in the century Johann Fischart (1546–90) published novels of polemical Protestantism as well as satires on contemporary German character. Despite these works, the beginning of a truly German literature was forestalled by the Thirty Years' War.

For almost a century after that war, German writing reflected the strong foreign influence of French classical and baroque styles. This influence arose from the constant presence of foreign troops on German soil. What there was of pure German literature tended to be haphazard and occasionally absurd. Even the classic work of the period, *Simplicius Simplicissimus* (1668), a tale of war and fantasy, is modeled after the Spanish picaresque novels popular at the time.

The literature of the German Enlightenment must be seen against the backdrop of the rationalism of the French philosophers and the influence of such British writers as William Shakespeare, Alexander Pope, John Milton, Edward Young, and Laurence Sterne. Domestically, the philosophy of Leibniz, Thomasius, and Wolff and the decline of the church and the rise of an educated middle class brought German literary activity to a peak in the late eighteenth and early nineteenth centuries.

Friedrich Klopstock (1724–1803) combined an enthusiasm for Homer and Vergil with an active Christian faith and an ardent patriotism in setting the form and style of much of modern German poetry. His tendency to substitute Germanic allusion for classical mythology influenced the content of future works and at the same time presented a false notion of German mythology. Christoph Martin Wieland (1733–1813) represented more completely the Enlightenment concept of the poetic calling—literature as a pleasure of the intellect, created for the sake of the community. Lessing (1729–81), a close friend of Moses Mendelssohn, cut a different kind of Enlightenment figure as a critic and rational analyst. His lifelong attempts to infuse deep moral values into a "national" literature are most eloquently stated in his plea for religious and ethnic tolerance in *Nathan der Weise* (1779).

The thread of Enlightenment rationalism that runs through the works of Klopstock, Wieland, Lessing, and Johann W. Gottfried von Herder climaxed in the writings of Goethe (1749–1832), who became Germany's greatest writer and one of the giants of world literature. The young Goethe was the central figure in the *Sturm und Drang* (Storm and Stress) literary movement which, under Herder's influence, rejected all literary, social, and political convention. Goethe's early work is typified by the play *Götz von Berlichingen*, which sought to vindicate the rights of the individual against delegated authority.

Goethe's association with the Grand Ducal Court at Weimar, however, introduced him to the classics of ancient Greece, the ethics of Benedictus de Spinoza and, above all, moderation. His association with Schiller from 1794 to 1805 marked the height of German classicism. Following Kant, Schiller turned to the study of aesthetics and wrote numerous essays and histories. Although like Goethe, Schiller was best remembered as a dramatist, his talent as a poet was conspicuous in the philosophic lyric. His poetry gave expression to his own ideals, spiritual peace, humanitarianism, and the inseparability of beauty, art, and life.

The inertia of classicism carried the influence of Herder, Schiller, and especially Goethe into the Romantic movement in the early nienteenth century. The philosophical reflections of Schleiermacher, Schelling, Hegel, and Schlegel also played a large part in the tone of the age. The Romantics rejected classical rationality in favor of mysticism, drawing their themes from a mixture of medieval German legend, idealized versions of Greek heroics and beauty, pan-German patriotism, and popular philosophy.

The Romantics closely identified with political and social reform, basing their nationalist ideals on German historical and legendary tradition. Of the early group, lyric poets Friedrich Hölderlin (1770–1843) and Friedrich von Hardenberg (Novalis, 1772–98) were the most important. Heinrich von Kleist (1777–1811), Prussia's best known dramatist and poet, was a leader of the patriotic movement against Napoleon Bonaparte and an exponent of German nationalism. The Romantic interest in the German *Volk* (people), moreover, led Jakob and Wilhelm Grimm to publish a collection of German fairy tales in 1812 and 1816.

Goethe, ever open to new stimuli, published the drama *Pandora* (1808) and the novel *Die Wahlverwandtschaften* (1809). Both of these works utilized classical forms but demonstrated the influence of Romantic techniques. Moreover, Goethe's encouragement to the younger writers of the Romantic period earned him their continued respect. His death in 1832, one year after Hegel, coincides with the decline of Romanticism.

The Napoleonic wars of the early 1800s and the abortive revolts of 1848 led to increasing political repression within the German states. Under this shadow, many writers transferred their attention from politics to aesthetics. Others, however, were forced to flee. Heinrich Heine, considered the greatest German lyric poet after Goethe, spent much of his life in self-imposed exile.

In this atmosphere literary realism flourished. For the early realists, realism was a style and a mood. Later writers used narrative prose to mirror the real world. Romantic historical novels gave way to the realistic (and at times exaggerated) historical novels. The poetry of the later period kept close to physical facts, avoiding transcendental themes as well as the lyrical beauty of Heine.

The impact of Marx and Nietzsche on German literature in the late nineteenth and early twentieth centuries was enormous. Marx focus on the plight of the working classes brought literary interest to subjects of class conflict and social welfare. By mocking the values of Christianity, patriotism, and socialism, Nietzsche liberated many writers from tradition. His emphasis on individual assertion led to an individualistic movement in literature. Realism flowed into naturalism; writers deliberately cultivated all aspects of decadence. Gerhart Hauptmann (1862–1946), the most important naturalist writer, emphasized working-class misery and family tragedy in demonstrating man's helplessness in a brutal environment.

Other authors of the time were not as sharp in their characterization of decay. Thomas Mann (1875–1955), for example, used subtle irony to depict the decay of cultural refinement in an apathetic society in *Buddenbrooks* (1901) and society's mental and physical ills in *The Magic Mountain* (1924). Still other writers and poets refused to depict any goals for human existence at all, choosing to represent only what they and much of the artistic world called sense-impressions.

In reaction to naturalism, a group of writers reasserted what they felt to be great timeless values of art and life. Stefan George (1868–1926) devoted his poetic energies to praise of heroic virtues. Rainer Maria Rilke (1875–1926), in contrast to George's stiff imagery, used warm and sensitive symbolism to depict art, religion, love, and death in poetic form.

The Expressionist manner, which dates from 1910, characterized mankind as sustained by the forces of irrationalism. Several major novelists were united by the radical attempt to maintain the force and validity of mystical aspirations in a pragmatic world. Expressionist poetry in the hands of various authors reflected the higher spiritual goals of the time as originally intoned by Rilke.

The revulsion of war produced sobering critiques of the military spirit.

The historical novels of Alfred Neumann (1895–1952) attacked prewar idealist history. Heinrich Mann's (1871–1950) trilogy *Das Kaiserreich* (The Empire) attacked the moral dignity of the "old Germany." Erich Maria Remarque's *All Quiet on the Western Front* (1929) is particularly representative of this period. Hermann Hesse (1877–1962) described both despair and salvation in the face of the world's problems.

The National Socialist German Workers' Party (Nazi Party) government began official control of literature in 1933. Only authors approved by the state could be published. Many writers left Germany, taking the theme of repression with them. Thomas Mann, the greatest of these literary emigrés, wrote in *Doctor Faustus* (1943) of the threat to human values posed by the violence of irrational forces. Other authors, who chose not to leave, sought quietly to preserve their humanity through withdrawal. Still others bowed to the state and wrote works glorifying the new germanic community.

Drama

The polemics of the Reformation fostered the thematic fusion of religious mystery plays with frivolous slapstick carnival comedies. The results were popular plays that either parodied what was seen as the pomp of Rome or defended the church. The ravages of the Thirty Years' War left Germany without cultural centers and consequently no national drama. German writers looked to France, Spain, and Italy for their dramatic forms and content.

Gotthold Ephraim Lessing broke the hold of French classical dramatic style in the mid-eighteenth century. Acting as the house critic of the newly created German National Theater in Hamburg, Lessing promoted the best features of contemporary English (especially Shakespearean) and French drama. He led the way into the *Sturm und Drang* period in literature and drama. The culmination of this movement in drama was the emergence of Goethe and Schiller.

Goethe, the greatest of all German dramatists progressed from the *Sturm und Drang* style of *Götz von Berlichingen* (the first version in 1771 was a historical novel; the second, in 1773, a play) to the classical themes of *Iphigenie auf Tauris* (1787). But the crowning achievement of his genius was the drama *Faust* (1808). For Goethe, the tragic folk-character was motivated not by love of power for pleasure but by a frantic search for knowledge, so compelling that he dealt his soul to the devil to achieve his goal. His pact caused his descent into sin, debauchery, and ultimately death. *Faust* remains one of the greatest dramas of modern literature.

Schiller's dramatic roots were also in *Sturm und Drang. Die Räuber* (The Robbers), 1781, the great revolutionary drama of German literature, denounces the tyranny of state, church, and social custom. Like Goethe, Schiller too moved from the social emphasis of the period to more classical themes; the great dramatic trilogy *Wallenstein* (1798–99) combined elements of Greek tragedy with those of Shakespearean drama. The result was a historical figure molded into a tragic hero.

Drama was the stepchild of the Romantics. The exacting technical demands and active interpretation of life presented, by definition, in drama tended to be disdained by those who sought subjective and passive lyricism. Heinrich von Kleist, the greatest of the Romantic playwrights and an exception to this rule, infused his characters with the excesses of passion, cruelty, patriotism, and fear common to the age.

The foreign influence of Henrik Ibsen, August Strindberg, Emile Zola, Fyodor Dostoyevsky, and Lev Nikolaevich Tolstoy on German literature led in part to the naturalism of late nineteenth-century drama. Hauptmann in particular portrayed the meticulously accurate pictures of decay and degradation common to the naturalist stage. *Die Weber* (The Weavers), 1892, one of his best plays, depicts the rising of the Silesian weavers against the introduction of mechanical looms in the 1840s.

In reaction to the photographic realism found in early twentieth-century drama, a number of playwrights emerged who rejected objectivity altogether. These expressionist dramatists demanded action instead of observation from their audiences. The language of the plays of Carl Sternheim (1878–1942) was terse to the point of explosiveness. Action usually concentrated around a central character acting as the author's spokesman. The genius of the director Max Reinhardt (1873–1943) brought the expressionist theater both artistic and popular success.

Bertholt Brecht (1898–1956) was among the most gifted and original dramatists of the twentieth century. His political vigor (he was a Marxist) was matched by his raciness and poetic vitality. In *Trommeln in der Nacht* (Drums in the Night), 1923, Brecht wove the theme of a returning prisoner-of-war around the Spartacus revolt and political chaos of the post-World War I period. In *Im Dickicht der Stadte* (In the Jungle of the Cities), 1921–24, he grotesquely caricatured the competitive jungle-spirit of modern capitalism, set against an American background. In 1928 Brecht revived an eighteenth-century English play to burlesque modern society as an empire ruled by gangsters. His play was called *The Three Penny Opera* and was his first popular success; it was set to the music of Kurt Weill.

As in other creative endeavors, the suppression of undesirable (in Nazi terms) drama began in 1933. The writers who remained and came to terms with the Nazi artistic formula were referred to as the *Blut und Boden* (Blood and Soil) school, because of their promotion of racism and German expansionism. Their works were of no lasting importance. Other writers left. Brecht left in 1933 and wrote his most convincing dramas in exile.

Science and Scholarship

The foundations of German science were laid by Johannes Kepler (1571–1630). His search for ultimate causes led him to identify the sun with God the Father, with a world based on the principle of perfect numbers, and with part-time employment as an astrologer. Of more lasting importance was his discovery of the laws of planetary motion. His practice of deducing mathematical formulas from general principles, moreover, later became the common methodology of German science.

In 1653 the Leopoldine-Caroline German Academy of Naturalists was founded in Halle. In 1700 the Scientific Society in Berlin (which later became the Royal Academy of Sciences and, still later, the Prussian Academy of Sciences) was founded by Leibniz. These societies served to articulate scientific discovery in Germany with that of the rest of Europe. Leibniz himself invented a differential calculus—independently of Newton—with symbols still in use today.

Theoretically, at least, German science gained independence from religious thought through the writings of Kant. Using mathematics and Newtonian physics, Kant proposed a nebular hypothesis of planetary origins. His views on space-time conceptions, furthermore, established a line of investigation that led to Einstein's theory of relativity. Most importantly, though, Kant established the philosophy of science as a legitimate endeavor.

German science and mathematics assumed a preeminent position in the scientific world of the nineteenth century. An example of German scientific prowess was Alexander von Humboldt's (1769–1859) *Kosmos* (on which he worked for fifty years), which gave a minutely detailed description of all the natural phenomena he observed on his worldwide journeys. This work contained observations on ocean currents, the moon's surface, earthquakes, astronomy, geography, meteorology, plants and plant distribution, and even ethnology. Apart from this, it was Humboldt who first described the electrolytic decomposition of a cell with zinc and silver electrodes when placed in water.

Johannes Müller (1801–58) is credited as the founder of modern physiology because of his study of nervous impulses as well as his influential position with the School of Medicine at the University of Berlin. His students included the leading biologists of the later nineteenth century. Theodor Schwann, for example (1810–82), discovered the enzyme pepsin and advanced his friend Mattias Schleiden's (1804–81) cellular theory of plant life to the animal world. Rudolf Virchow (1821–1902), another student of Müller, used the cellular theory in the explanation of human pathology. Robert Koch (1843–1910), although not a student of Müller, contributed heavily to modern medical bacteriology. He isolated the tubercle and cholera bacillus and discovered the carriers of bubonic plague and sleeping sickness.

Like Müller, the chemists Justus Leibig (1803–73) and Friedrich Wöhler (1800–82) had a decisive influence on the development of their field. Leibig, through fifty years of teaching and research in the fields of organic and biochemistry, left his mark on an entire generation of chemists. His book *Chemistry in Its Application to Agriculture and*

Physiology (1840) promoted the use of chemical rather than natural fertilizers and led to the disappearance of manure piles all over Germany. Wöhler was the first to synthesize urea (1828) from inorganic materials. His work in biochemistry was followed by Emil Fischer (1852–1919), who was awarded the Nobel Prize in chemistry for his investigation of the nature of sugars and purines. Fischer's later research into the nature of amino acids laid the foundations of further exploration into the structure of proteins.

In mathematics Karl Friedrich Gauss (1777–1855) applied his genius to the development of coordinate systems that could be utilized on a non-Euclidean continuum. Georg Riemann's (1826–66) defiance of Euclid's axiom that parallel lines will never intersect established Riemann geometry as a separate investigative route. At the time, these notions were considered theoretical parlor games; later, however, they proved critical to the development of Einstein's theory of relativity. Another German mathematician, Karl Jacobi (1804–51), introduced his theory of numbers in personal letters to Gauss and, in effect, founded the modern German school of mathematics.

The first significant German physicist was Julius Mayer (1814–78), who established the principle of the conservation of energy. Hermann von Helmholtz (1821–94), the inventor of the ophthalmoscope, applied Mayer's principles of energy to the entire range of nature. Together, chemists Robert von Bunsen (1811–99) and Gustav Kirchhoff (1824–87) invented the spectroscope, which led to further explorations into the nature of matter. Heinrich Hertz (1857–94) used primitive means to produce and measure electrical waves traveling at the speed of light. Wilhelm Conrad Röntgen (1845–1923) discovered X-rays by accident in 1895.

In 1900 Max Planck's (1858–1947) formulation of the "quantum of action" (that energy is emitted or absorbed only in the smallest indivisible particles of matter, or quantas, of energy) shook the scientific world. Five years later, Albert Einstein (1879–1955) reinterpreted the concepts of motion, time, and space. His theory of relativity noted the relationship among these properties. A specific aspect of these lawful relationships was that energy has mass and that mass is energy. This postulate provided the theoretical basis for the liberation of atomic energy, which itself took place at the Institute of Chemistry in Berlin-Dahlem. Thirty-four years after the publication of Einstein's theory, Otto Hahn (b. 1879) split the nucleus of a uranium atom by bombarding it with neutrons. Thus began the atomic age.

Epoch-making theoretical developments often led to exaggeration. The English naturalist Charles Darwin published *The Origin of the Species* in 1859, which exerted a strong influence on the German scientific community. Ernst Haeckel (1834–1919), a professor of zoology, used Darwin in propounding his "great law of biogenesis," which noted that the life of an individual was analogous to that of a species. Haeckel's influence continued well into the twentieth century. German academies also became part of the scientific battleground between the mechanists (or materialists), who claimed that the body can be comprehended in mechanical terms, and the vitalists who claimed that a certain "life force" was present in every being. Hans Driesch (1867–1941), for example, a convinced vitalist, saw organic matter governed by a set of "organizing relations" not found in inorganic substances. Another example was Karl Ludwig (1816–95), a physiologist, who laid to rest the vialist notion of blood circulation by demonstrating it to be the result of wholly mechanical forces.

In the nineteenth century, German historical scholarship flourished. Barthold Niebuhr (1776–1831), in particular, used historical criticism in molding contemporary German historicism. His *History of Rome* dealt with collective individualities rather than single individuals. Leopold von Ranke (1795–1886) fused the historical concepts of romanticism with the critical methodology of Friedrich August Wolf (1759–1824) and August Böckh (1785–1867). Ranke sought historical objectivity in portraying the history of the nation-state. Many historians also participated in the drive for unification and afterwards the glorification of the German state.

Still other historians gained prominence. Jacob Burckhardt's *Civilization of the Renaissance in Italy* (1860) is still widely read. Theodor Mommsen's works on Roman history objectively sought to isolate the "primitive cell" of the Roman state that first dominated Italy and then the world. Other historians sought to restore Ranke's ideal of objectivity. German historical scholars also became leaders in classical and middle eastern archaeology and biblical and Semitic studies. Economic history gained a new emphasis in the works of Wilhelm Roscher and Friedrich List.

The social sciences also flowered under the Second Reich and the Weimar Republic. Major works in historical sociology were written by Ferdinand Tonnies, Georg Simmel, Paul Barth, Alfred Weber, and Alfred Vierkandt. Max Weber, an important figure in world sociology, is particularly remembered for his writings on the relation of ideals to social change. The sociology of knowledge *(Wissensoziologie)* propounded by Weber was further developed by Karl Mannheim (1893–1947) in *Ideology and Utopia* (1929).

Germans were also central figures in the establishment of cultural anthropology. Friedrich Katzel (1844–1904), Eduard Hahn (1856–1928), and Adolf Bastian (1826–1905) were prominent in the early development of ethnology. Leo Frobenius (1873–1938) and Fritz Gräbner (1877–1934) formulated what came to be known as the *Kulturkreise* (culture circle) approach. Essentially, this now-discredited view claimed that whole culture complexes spread in ever-widening circles from their places of origin. Remnants of these cultural waves supposedly could be found in the examination of the *Kulturschichten,* or cultural strata, of any given area or peoples.

Germans also made important contributions to political science. Carl Schmitt (b. 1888), for example, sought to broaden the study of law and legal institutions by introducing historical, sociological, and political considerations. Robert Michels' (1876–1936) monograph *Political Parties* developed the principle of oligarchy, noting the tendency of organizations to be run by only a few members.

Germans figured prominently in psychology. Ernst Heinrich Weber and Wilhelm Wundt were main figures in early experimental psychology. Moritz Lazarus and Heymann Steinthal laid the foundations of group psychology. In the 1920s, Wolfgang Kohler, Max Wertheimer, and Kurt Koffka developed configurational, or Gestalt, psychology. These ideas were later extended to the dynamics of motivation by Kurt Lewin.

The continuity of German science was interrupted by Hitler's Third Reich. As in the arts, German scientists and scholars fled before the state. Some scientists, however, such as those concerned with rocket propulsion, stayed in Germany. Those who did not leave suffered from the lack of foreign contact.

Music

Johann Sebastian Bach (1685–1750) fused together the more complex polyphonic music popular in the Netherlands with the simple rhythms of indigenous German music. The essence of Bach's music was stress—the creation and release of tensions created by building on a simple melody using harmonics and counterpoint. He was not only creative but also prolific; he wrote about 300 church cantatas as well as several secular cantatas. In addition to the famous *St. Matthew Passion*, he composed the *Passion According to the Gospel of St. John*, four short masses, the great *Mass in B Minor*, a magnificat, several choral motets, and nearly 400 chorales. Moreover, he wrote numerous and varied harpsichord, organ, orchestral, and chamber music compositions.

Bach's contemporary, German-born composer Georg Friedrich Händel (1685–1759), spent much of his creative life in England writing operas and oratorios. The most famous of his works, the oratorio *Messiah*, was first produced in 1742. This, however, was only one of twenty-seven oratorios and forty-three operas he composed during his lifetime. Händel is also remembered for the "Water Music," composed for the Court of George I of England on the occasion of a royal water party on the Thames River in 1717.

Christoph Willibald von Gluck (1714–87) startled the music world with *Orfeo ed Euridice* in 1762, which was infused with the dramatic sincerity of earlier Italian opera. Such was his contribution that he is sometimes referred to as the father of musical drama. Gluck, together with J.W.A. Stamitz (1717–61) in Mannheim and Bach's son, Karl Phillipp Emanuel Bach (1714–88), consolidated the German style later developed by Franz Josef Haydn in Germany and Wolfgang Amadeus Mozart in Austria.

Haydn (1732–1809) served for thirty years as musical director to the

Hungarian Esterhazy family in Eisenstadt, Hungary. During this time he elaborated upon the sonata form of K.P.E. Bach until he was able to achieve the proper balance between its sections. Haydn was also a prolific composer—seventy-seven string quartets, 125 symphonies, fifty-three piano sonatas and numerous sonatas for violin, trios for piano and strings, oratorios, and the like. His many symphonies, moreover, enlarged the previously narrow confines of the symphonic form.

It was Ludwig van Beethoven (1770–1827), however, who laid the cornerstone of German achievement in the symphony. His use of anticipated stress, delayed resolution of dissonances, and composed silences created new heights of tension. He wrote extensively for piano—then a new instrument—violin, chamber group, and orchestra. Much of what he wrote, particularly his nine symphonies, were masterpieces of thematic development.

The other side of Beethoven—his admiration for Klopstock, Schiller, and Goethe, coupled with a passionate belief in equality—carried over into his music. His opera *Fidelio* deals with the theme of freedom. The third symphony *(Eroica)* hailed Napoleon as a champion of liberty. Upon learning of Napoleon's election as emperor, however, Beethoven trampled the title page in rage. The libretto of the choral movement of the ninth symphony, moreover, was Schiller's *Ode to Joy*.

Beethoven enriched traditional program music with Romantic passion, Carl Maria von Weber (1786–1826) brought the Romantic movement to opera. His themes were drawn from the nationalistic folk melodies and his subjects and characters from medieval German lore. His great opera *Der Freischütz* (1821) was the first operatic work to deal with German peasant life. His orchestration utilized special tones and registers and even the defects of instruments to gain dramatic effect.

After Weber, German opera continued to develop along distinct nationalistic lines. Heinrich Marchner (1795–1861) and Otto Nicolai (1810–49) continued to demonstrate the heavy use of orchestra that differentiated German from Italian opera. This crack grew to canyon proportions with the symphonic opera of Richard Wagner (1813–83).

Wagner attempted to unite the arts into *Musikdrama* where music, poetry, and stagecraft blended into a dramatic whole. A decided nationalist, he used his musical themes to create a national heroic myth that might unify German sentiment. His self-authored libretti revolved around the themes of folklore and romanticized medieval life. His mature works—*The Ring of the Nibelungen* (a series composed of *Das Rheingold, Die Walküre, Siegfried*, and *Götterdämmerung*, completed in 1874), *Tristan und Isolde* (1859), *Die Meistersinger* (1868), and *Parsifal* (1882)—recall motifs of an earlier time.

Concert music continued to explore new avenues in the nineteenth century. Felix Mendelssohn's life (1809–47) was highlighted by his *Overture to A Midsummer Night's Dream*, which he wrote at the age of seventeen, and his last work, the great oratorio *Elijah* (1846). His own influence on the mainstream of music, however, rests in great part on his revival of the works of Bach and Händel, which had long been neglected. Robert Schumann (1810–56) enlarged upon the use of the piano by composing tone poems and piano quintets. His five symphonies demonstrated the appropriate reflection of moods, harmonies, and rhythms of a true craftsman. After Beethoven, however, the symphonic form could do little else but recede. The piano also was the focus for still another nineteenth century figure, Hungarian-born Franz Liszt (1811–86), who was equally influential as a player, teacher, conductor, and composer during his life at Weimar.

Wagner, too, was a controversial figure in concert music. His influence could be discernible in the nine symphonies of Anton Brückner (1824–96), which displayed a Wagnerian wealth of depth and melody. Johannes Brahms (1833–97) symbolized the antithesis of Wagner. His own works combined the polyphony of Bach with the harmonic structure of Beethoven. He wrote the first of his four symphonies late in life, and he recognized the unwieldiness of the song as a symphonic theme (a Wagnerian tendency). In this, as well as in his concerti, overtures, chamber music, and choral music, he remained a traditionalist in the face of popular, but ponderous, romanticism.

Though a disciple of Wagner, Richard Strauss (1864–1949) was unconcerned with ideologies. His early opera sank under Wagnerian pathos, but his later operatic works *Salome* (1905), *Elektra* (1909), and the comedy *Der Rosenkavalier* (1911) were daring, popular successes. *Elektra* marked Strauss' first collaboration with the Austrian librettist Hugo von Hofmannstahl, which continued until the latter's death in 1929.

Strauss' ideological nonchalance in music was matched in politics. Hitler appointed Strauss as president of the Reich's Chamber of Music. In Berlin and Bayreuth, he replaced Bruno Walter and Arturo Toscanini, respectively, as conductor after they had disassociated themselves from the regime. Still, his indifference to national socialist policy caused him to be forced from the presidency of the Chamber of Music.

The German milieu of the early 1900s also produced a counterculture of would-be writers and composers. One such composer to gain prominence from this background was Arnold Schönberg. Although Austrian by birth, Schönberg taught and composed much of his work in Berlin. His major contribution was the establishment of the twelve-tone system based on the twelve-note chromatic scale, which stated that since all notes are of equal importance, no note in a series should be repeated until all twelve notes have appeared. The resulting music was characterized by its atonality and endless variations.

Paul Hindemith (1895–1963) followed Schönberg in providing a theoretical explanation for the composition of modern music by stating that notes have a fixed harmonic relationship. His music was not based on atonality for its own sake but rather on the freeing of tones from tight

169

romantic harmonies or, as once was stated, "the wrong note in the right place." His own work was both extensive and meticulous (he was often accused of "overscrubbing" his pieces). In order to gain popular acceptance of his contemporary music, Hindemith wrote numerous compositions for amateur choirs and instrumentalists. When Hitler declared Hindemith and his music alien and degenerate, Hindemith replied in music. One of his greatest works, the opera *Mathis der Maler* (1938), was a declaration of the independence of art. He spent the war years in the United States, returning to Germany only after Hitler's defeat.

After World War I Berlin became one of the great centers of music in the world. Pianists Arthur Schnabel, Feruccio Busoni, Rudolph Serkin, Vladimir Horowitz; violinists Carl Flesch and Yehudi Menuhin; conductors Erich Kleiber, Bruno Walter, Wilhelm Furtwängler, and Otto Klemperer; composers Franz Schreker, Arnold Schönberg, Alban Berg, and Anton von Webern—are only a few who were in Berlin during the 1920s. Kurt Weill, another major figure particularly identified with this era, studied under Busoni and wrote jazz-inspired "serious" music. His major works were the satiric operas written with Bertholt Brecht. The best known of these, *The Three Penny Opera* (1928), remains a classic in both music and literature.

From 1933 to 1945, music in Germany was mostly an adjunct of Nazi propaganda. Still, some composers continued to produce notable works. Carl Orff's oratorio *Carmina Burana* (1937) combines his own music with a medieval text of Latin and German verse. Werner Egk's first production of *Peer Gynt* in Berlin in 1938 led to the commissioning of a ballet, *Joan of Zarissa*, by the State Opera and its production in 1940.

Architecture

The Romanesque architectural style spread rapidly in Germany with the introduction of Christianity and the crowning of Charlemagne as Holy Roman emperor and remained popular until the end of the thirteenth century. One of the most imposing examples of this style can be found at the cathedral in Aachen, Charlemagne's capital. Its rose windows, rounded arches, low towers, and heavy facade sought to revive the Roman imperial style and led to its use as a model for later churches.

The vigorous and highly original style of the German Romanesque receded slowly before the Gothic influence from France. Romanesque features were gradually replaced by pointed arches, elaborately carved stone pillars, high arched ceilings, flying buttresses, and soaring spires (the spire of the cathedral at Ulm reaches 500 feet) of Gothic architecture. The style continued to copy the French mode until the fifteenth century. The most famous of these "imitative" buildings is the cathedral at Cologne, begun in 1248 and completed in 1880.

The most characteristic Gothic German churches were the *Hallenkirchen*, or hall churches. These were numerous-aisled buildings whose interior gave the impression of a giant hall. Munich's fifteenth-century cathedral is only one of many *Hallenkirchen* remaining. The Federal Republic is unusually rich in medieval buildings, both domestic and civil, dating from the later Gothic and Early Renaissance periods. These are characterized by their timbered construction and steep, enormous roofs, and can still be seen in Nürnberg, Brunswick, and the medieval quarters of other old cities and towns. One of the best preserved of the old walled towns is Rothenburg ob der Tauber.

The multitude of small German states during the Renaissance resulted in a diversity of architectural subtypes in fifteenth- and sixteenth-century Germany. In some buildings the Italian Renaissance form prevailed, and in others it was strongly modified by Gothic elements.

Despite the unparalleled destruction of the Thirty Years' War that brought all building to a halt, examples of German baroque architecture abound. At first the Italian influence dominated, particularly in Bavarian cathedrals. Smaller than the Gothic cathedrals, the baroque churches displayed an extreme ornateness: virtually every inch of wall and ceiling was filled with carved figures and highly colored murals. The Theatine Church in Munich, the Church of the Fourteen Saints near Bamberg, and the Pilgrimage Church in Wies, as well as many palaces and mansions in Berlin and southern Germany, are among the best examples of this style.

In the late eighteenth and early nineteenth centuries Greek and Roman architectural forms reappeared. The Royal Theater and Old Museum in Berlin and Munich's Glytothek Museum were attempts at accurate imitations of classical architectural forms. Romanticism also found its way into nineteenth-century architecture. The Romantic emphasis on the Germanic past led to a reemergence of the Gothic and Romanesque styles in the 1820s. These styles remained popular into the 1860s, by which time they had degenerated into a kind of "gingerbread" Gothic.

Nineteenth-century architecture was characterized by eclecticism. High Renaissance styles were evident in Florentine designs. In Berlin the Reichstag building and the cathedral adopted the style of the Italian baroque. For religious buildings medieval styles were selected, and for townhalls Gothic or German Renaissance modes were widely used.

These popular historical styles were challenged by the rise of expressionism. The movement grew out of the Deutscher Werkbund, an association of manufacturers, architects, artists, and writers founded in 1907, which sought to inject free and expressive forms into architecture.

With the construction of Walter Gropius' model factory at the 1914 Werkbund Exhibition in Cologne, functionalism and a technical aesthetic emerged as a central theme in modern architecture. In 1919 Gropius founded an institution—the Staatliche Bauhaus (National House of Architecture, known as the Bauhaus)—concerned with the synthesis of art, crafts, technology, and architecture. The buildings for the Bauhaus, designed by Gropius, utilized reinforced concrete, extensive glass, and an absence of trimmings in creating a stark and functional effect.

171

During the 1920s the Bauhaus attracted Ludwig Mies van der Rohe (1886–1969) as a teacher. Together with Gropius, Mies van der Rohe influenced the entire world of architecture and made Berlin (and later, Dessau) the mecca of the "international style."

Under the Nazis, the Bauhaus was closed and numerous architects (and many of the major artists of the day) were forced to flee. Others who stayed were allowed only to produce architecture of either a monumental, politically totalitarian classicism—such as the House of German Art (1933) designed by Paul Ludwig Troost—or sentimental nationalist heroic modes as found in the heavy beams, overhanging eaves, and rustic interiors of the Hitler youth hostels in the Black Forest and the Harz Mountains. The only works of any distinction produced during these years were Werner March's Olympic stadium and the traditional buildings of Heinrich Tessenow.

Sculpture

Gothic sculpture made its way into Germany from France in the thirteenth century. In the mid-fifteenth century sculptors continued to bury their figures in the rich decorative folds common to the Gothic style. The emphasis on individual achievement during the late Gothic period led to the popularity of portrait sculpture and carved coats-of-arms. One of the major kinds of sculptured works found in churches of the time were carved and painted winged altarpieces.

Renaissance sculpture was centered primarily in southern Germany. Sculptors produced fountain groups, architectural sculpture, and many small bronzes. They combined many of the traits of the late Gothic period with those of the Renaissance. The great bronze statues of Peter Vischer the Elder (1460–1529), such as those that adorn the tomb of the Emperor Maximilian and St. Sebald's Church, also bear testimony to Renaissance influence.

The turbulent years of the Counter-Reformation and corresponding baroque period in the arts produced only isolated examples of religious art before the mid-seventeenth century. Ecclesiastical architecture in the latter half of the seventeenth century stressed a single, unifying element such as an altar or a dome. In the eighteenth century, southern German rococo churches demonstrated a heavy courtly influence in the execution of interiors. The multiplicity of altars, Madonnas, and church furniture were even used to depict contemporary court figures.

German sculpture was modified by the neoclassical trend of the second half of the eighteenth and early nineteenth centuries. Johann Schadow of Prussia (1764–1850) openly attacked the abstraction and the blind veneration of the perfect human form found in much of classical sculpture. His sense of reality was particularly apparent in the portrait-sculptures of Princess Luise and Princess Friederike. Christian Rauch (1777–1857), also from Prussia, used both pose and facial expression in modeling the warrior and philosopher king, Friedrich the Great. After Schadow and Rauch sculpture tended to lag behind the main artistic currents. The major sculptor in Germany in the late nineteenth century was Adolf von Hildebrand (1846–1921).

At the beginning of the twentieth century the leading German sculptors rejected the idealized human figure and created sculptures with bizarre movements and cracked surfaces. Although they had lagged behind in adopting other trends, sculptors were among the first to adopt expressionism. The romance with the human form also continued into the first half of the twentieth century. Georg Kolbe (1877–1947) used the interaction of tension and repose in the display of beauty and elegance in his figure *The Female Dancer.*

A number of sculptors were associated with the Bauhaus in the 1920s. Oskar Schlemmer (1888–1943), for example, taught sculpture at the Bauhaus while producing the first German iron-wire forms in 1931. This consisted of a stylized figure modeled in circles and curves with a head made of steel.

The Nazis not only found fanatic apostles among second-rate talents but also among respected classical sculptors. The Bauhaus school was well suited to decorate the grandiose public buildings the regime desired. Kolbe's *Youthful Warrior, Athlete in Repose,* and *Revelation* and Fritz Klimsch's elegant nudes were accepted both by the public and the government.

Painting

During the Gothic period, religious sentiment was expressed in the form of illuminated manuscripts and religious panel painting. The rising economic fortunes of the Hanseatic towns led to their commissioning of a variety of these artistic works. Panels painted by North German masters adorned not only the altars of the churches of Hamburg, Lübeck, and other German cities but those of Scandinavian cities as well.

Medieval legacy and individual creativity reached a near perfect union in the works of Albrecht Dürer (1451–1528). His numerous drawings and watercolors demonstrated detailed examinations of his surroundings. His paintings display superb technique and composition. A true "Renaissance man," Dürer published books on fortifications, geometry as it referred to art, and anatomy. His artistic genius, however, lay in engraving. The unparalleled precision and spiritual profundity of his prints stand alone in the history of art.

The transition between medieval and modern painting can be seen in some of Dürer's brilliant contemporaries. Albrecht Altdorfer (1505–38) used traditional landscapes, not as backgrounds, but as dominating images that often dwarf figures in the foreground. Altdorfer was credited with the founding of the European landscape tradition because he created landscapes without figures. Lucas Cranach the Elder (1472–1553), a friend of Martin Luther, produced works whose themes and figures were traditional while their representations were new and imaginative. Angels, for example, became playful rogues. Cranach's ardent support of the Reformation did not stop him from painting altarpieces for Roman Catholic churches, or from seeking commissions for secular works in the Protestant milieu. Matthias Grünewald (1503–28) was particularly known for his altarpiece at Isenheim, which used distortion in the display of tragic violence.

Hans Holbein the Younger (1497–1543) mastered the art of the portrait. He presented his contemporaries with accuracy—self-confident princes, wealthy merchants, reflective philosophers, and fashionable ladies. The growing Protestant aversion to religious painting of any kind forced Holbein to leave for England. The paintings of Lucas Cranach the Younger (1515–86) represented the concession of art to the strong moralizing theme of the Reformation.

The German painters of the baroque and rococo styles were of limited importance. A few painters in the Roman Catholic south achieved some distinction as representatives of the religious baroque, while those of the Protestant north were only followers—not leaders—of the artistic trends emanating from the Netherlands. One of the few painters of note, Adam Elsheimer (1578–1610), was virtually unknown inside his own country.

The decline of the church as a major patron and thematic influence and the corresponding rise of a varied middle class led to the development of numerous themes in the nineteenth century. Neoclassical painting emerged as realistic portrayals of landscapes by such artists as Josef Anton Koch (1768–1839) and his pupil, Friedrich Preller the Elder (1804–78).

Romantic and emotional ideals were expressed through the works of P.O. Runge (1777–1810), whose love of nature led him to produce what he termed "spiritual landscapes." Kaspar David Friedrich (1774–1840) best represented the Romantic movement. To him, man was conceived as a transient figure in the midst of an infinite Nature. The briefness of man's appearance on earth was expressed by Friedrich through the melancholia pervading many of his paintings.

The revolt against this sentimental, poetic conception in Romantic painting paralleled the return to realism in literature. Adolf von Menzel (1815–1905) sought in his landscapes and woodcuts to present things without distortion. Wilhelm Leibl (1844–1900) molded his peasant subjects into the smooth strength reminiscent of Holbein's objective forms. Wilhelm Trübner (1851–1917) followed Leibl's realistic portrayals into the area of landscape painting.

Still, patriotic idealism persisted in the last half of the nineteenth century. Hans Thoma (1839–1924) combined realism and fantasy as he attempted to translate the musical visions of Wagner into graphic art. Monumentality led to the domination of figures over background in the paintings of Arnold Böcklin (1827–1901) and Hans von Marées (1837–87).

German impressionism found early expression in the works of Max

Liebermann (1847–1935). His *Munich Beer Garden* (1883) suggests the influence of the French Impressionists. Max Slevogt (1868–1932) used the technique of the French in portraying exotic animals and plants. Lovis Corinth's (1858–1925) impressionistic style contrasted sharply with his dynamic forms and near-brutal sensuality. In all, however, German impressionism tended toward realism and never achieved the technical skill of the French.

Modern German painting found its origins in the *Jugendstil* (young style) movements of the early twentieth century, which later developed into German expressionism. These new currents found outlets in the antiacademic societies in Berlin, Munich, and Dresden. In Berlin, Norwegian Edvard Munch was a leading figure in the artistic group called Secession. The Dresden circle known as The Bridge, included the painters Emil Nolde (1867–1956) and Max Pechstein (1881–1955). The group called The Blue Rider was founded in Munich by Russian emigré Vasili Kandinsky (1886–1944) and illustrator Alfred Kubin (1887–1959). The group was subsequently joined by Franz Marc (1812–1916) and the Swiss, Paul Klee (1879–1940). The unifying thread tying these groups together was a concern for reducing nature and representation to a minimum, while arbitrarily binding selected objects together in abstract composition.

The Bauhaus became the inspiration for German painting in the 1920s. Kandinsky and Klee taught and wrote about new ways of thinking about plastic form in painting and art in general. In painting Kandinsky reflected his ideas through rational, controlled, and empathetic abstractions, whereas Klee used contrasts of surface and line to depict a pantheist, irrational sensibility. Lyonel Feininger (1871–1955) developed his Cubist principles in architecturally drawn landscapes and seascapes while studying at the Bauhaus. Oskar Schlemmer (1888–1943) continued the line of monumental figure painting while teaching mural workshops.

Dadaism, the broad artistic movement that depicts the antirational simultaneity of life, and surrealism touched German art through the paintings of Raoul Haussman (b. 1886), George Grosz (1893–1959), Kurt Schwitters (1887–1948), Max Ernst, and others. Ernst (b. 1891), or Dada Max as he once called himself, in particular bridged both movements. His paintings were noted for animal and human forms in exquisite colors moving across a surrealistic dreamscape.

With the banning of all nonobjective art as non-German, Germany lost her artists. Kandinsky, Klee, Feininger, Itten, Grosz, and many others left. The plundering of twenty-five German art museums produced the exhibition of "Degenerate Art." In 1939 many precious art treasures were auctioned. Those left—1,004 paintings and 3,825 drawings—were burned in the courtyard of the main firehouse in Berlin.

Films

In 1913 there were only twenty-three film theaters in all of Germany.

The pressures of World War I forced the creation of the government-owned Universum Film Aktiengesellschaft (Universal Film Joint-Stock Company—UFA) to produce propaganda films for the war effort. After the war, the Weimar government sold its predominating interest in UFA to the Deutsche Bank. By 1919 the number of theaters had grown to 245, and UFA had become the major producer of films for the German market.

The demand for films fostered the early production of historical spectacles, such as Ernst Lubitsch's UFA-produced *Madame Du Barry* (starring Ernst Jannings and Pola Negri), *Anne Boleyn*, and *The Loves of Pharaoh*. It also promoted the 1920 production of *The Cabinet of Dr. Caligari*, directed by Robert Wiene and produced by Erich Pommer. The film was intended as an artistic allegory of political authority and was an immediate success. Today it is considered a film classic.

Competition with Hollywood forced the Deutsche Bank to sell its shares in UFA to the Nazi propagandist, Alfred Hugenberg. Despite this shift, UFA did not turn immediately to the production of political films. In 1929 a novel written in 1905 by Heinrich Mann was made into a film. The book, entitled *Professor Unrat*, told the story of the fall of a respectable middle-class schoolteacher resulting from his love for a cabaret singer. The film, *The Blue Angel*, directed by Josef von Sternberg, starred Emil Jannings and the then-unknown Marlene Dietrich. It remains one of the greatest film classics of all time. In 1931 Fritz Lang directed the powerful film *M*, which starred Peter Lorre. The film retold the true story of a child murderer in Düsseldorf who had been responsible for the deaths of twenty-six young boys.

The Nazi rise to power drove many of the most gifted film artists out of Germany. Those who remained produced artless propaganda films that used only "approved" themes. One film that was not artless was Viet Harlan's *Kolberg*—a subtly propagandistic but technically near-perfect work that sought to rouse the flagging spirits of the collapsing Third Reich. Another film of the early 1940s, Helmut Käutner's *Under the Bridge*, used a personal, nonpolitical story to create perhaps the best motion picture of the twelve-year dictatorship.

CULTURAL POLICY IN THE FEDERAL REPUBLIC OF GERMANY

Freedom of expression is specifically guaranteed in the Basic Law (constitution) of 1949. A number of *Land* (state; pl. *Länder*) constitutions further stipulate the promotion of artistic and intellectual development. This support seeks to ensure both the preservation of creative works as well as allowing participation by all who wish. Local communities are even specifically urged by a number of *Land* constitutions to be active promoters of the arts and culture. The result of this policy has been governmental support of such numerous cultural facilities as theaters, opera houses, orchestras, museum collections, libraries, art monuments, and the like.

The administration of cultural policy reflects the decentralized nature of the West German political structure. At the federal level, internal cultural affairs are the responsibility of the Ministry of Interior. In the *Land* governments, the administration of cultural policy lies with the respective ministries of culture. These ministries participate in the Standing Conference, which attends to supraregional cultural policy through a permanent secretariat in Bonn. The *Land* Committee for Arts and Adult Education administers the various departments of the *Land* cultural ministries. Local communities and districts often have special departments for municipal theaters and orchestras. Such central organizations at the federal level as the German Community Assembly (Deutscher Gemindetag) for small communities, the German League of Towns (Deutscher Städtebund) for the smaller towns, the German District Assembly (Deutscher Landkreistag) for local districts, and the German City Assembly (Deutscher Städtetag) for all large cities maintain active cultural committees. The Joint Committee for Cultural Work established by the German City Assembly in 1971, for example, observes and recommends cultural policy.

Individual cultural sectors receive varying degrees of state support. German theater is supported primarily by public funds. In the 1969–70 period there were 185 public theaters in seventy-nine towns and cities, and seventy-four private theaters in twenty-nine towns. Attendance has generally been good. For the same 1969–70 period a total of 22.3 million people attended dramatic performances. All public theaters are subsidized (box office receipts cover only one-fourth of the costs). Most private theaters are also supported by public subsidy. About one-half of the public theaters are financed by local communities, about one-fifth are *Land* theaters; the rest are nationally subsidized. Moreover, the government supports the annual Theater Encounter in Berlin to which eight to ten of the season's best German-language productions are invited.

Musical institutions are not as heavily subsidized. Public support concentrates primarily upon orchestras, which cover only one-half of their own costs. Support is also extended to musical theater and for musical training and education. In 1971 there were about 100 large orchestras (including radio and theater orchestras). Most are municipally supported although some are *Land* orchestras. During the 1969–70 season some 2,000 concerts (not including jazz and rock groups) were given and attended by about 2 million people.

Federal and local support for painting, sculpture, the graphic and related arts, and architecture includes: preservation of old and new artistic works in art museums; art education in public schools and university schools of art; and various kinds of support to individual contemporary artists. The variety and number of state-supported and municipally supported competitions coupled with the extensive purchase of the work of contemporary artists by state-supported institutions

177

provide a degree of subsidy to individual artists (the private art market continues to flourish). The Documenta exhibitions held in Kassel every four or five years are jointly financed by city, state, and federal funds. These exhibitions have sought to document contemporary art.

The federal and state governments seek to avoid any suggestion of intervention or influence in literature. Book production, which tripled between 1951 and 1971, is left entirely to publishers. The state has responsibility for the maintenance of archives, and supports institutions and activities that support the German language. This latter responsibility falls mainly into the hands of the Goethe Institute and such organizations as the German Academy for Language and Poetry in Darmstadt and the Society for the German Language in Wiesbaden. These organizations maintain comprehensive collections of German writings, and support readings by authors, literary symposia, and like.

After the war, filmmaking was once again put into private hands. A voluntary censorship board, sponsored by the film industry itself, reviews all films for moral or religious offense, for antidemocratic tendencies, and for endangerment to relations between the Federal Republic and other countries. In 1952 the *Länder* set up a joint film assessment board, which annually certifies about 10 percent of the films released as being "meritorious" or "particularly meritorious." Between 1950 and 1955 *Land* authorities subsidized film productions. The drop in film attendance in the face of the popularity of television from 817.5 million per year in 1956 to 257.1 million in 1966 led to the establishment of the Federal Office for Film Promotion, which provides funds to the producers of economically viable films. Funds are also given to young directors through the Young German Film Foundation. Despite all efforts, however, motion picture theaters have continued to close. Audiences declined to 167.4 million in 1970. The film industry has been only partly compensated by the rise in films commissioned for television.

Scientific research is supported jointly by the federal government, the *Länder*, the Fritz Thyssen Foundation, and the Donors Society of German Science, whose funds are administered by the German Research Association. The members of the association are drawn from all universities, the academies of science, the Max Planck Society, the German Union of Technical and Scientific Associations, the Society of German Naturalists and Physicians, the Physical-Technical Federal Institute, and the Fraunhofer Society for the Promotion of Applied Research. Particular interest is given toward projects and areas in which the Federal Republic lags internationally. In 1968 West German scientific policy shifted from the task of rebuilding and restoring institutions to one of promoting the application of research projects for economic development and social welfare. The federal government, therefore, has encouraged the development of advanced kinds of reactors able to generate cheap electrical power and has fostered oceanographic and space research.

Museums in the Federal Republic number about 1,400. Perhaps the best known of these are the former Prussian museums in Berlin, the Munich art collections, and such well-known *Land* museums as the Rhenish State Museum in Bonn. Federal funds operate the German Museum of Science and Technology in Munich and the Germanic National Museum in Nürnberg specializing in the German history of art and culture. Other museums have teaching and research services and enjoy the status of scientific institutes; still others deal with the preservation of local monuments and history. In 1970 over 17 million people visited the 700 museums for which accurate statistics are available.

Libraries in the Federal Republic are divided between those of a scientific or technical nature and those that cater to the public. The functions of a national library are served by three major libraries: the German Library in Frankfurt (9.4 million volumes), which is obligated to keep all German-language writings published anywhere; the Library of the Stiftung Preussicher Kulturbesitz (Library of the Institute of Prussian Culture), which specializes in old books and special collections; and the Bavarian State Library in Munich (2.3 million volumes) which specializes in medieval manuscripts. Apart from these, the *Länder* are generally responsible for the maintenance of the library system including most scientific and public libraries.

POSTWAR DEVELOPMENTS

Philosophy

After 1945 philosophy in the Federal Republic continued much as it had before the war. Existentialism based on the philosophic doctrines of the 1920s had attracted a large following in the 1930s during the Great Depression. The bombed-out, occupied country of the post-1945 period also provided fertile ground for a world view that offered salvation through a return to man's innermost being, or *Existenz*. Thus, the popularity of Kierkegaard, Jaspers, and Heidegger continued in postwar Germany.

The doctrines of Christianity reemerged. Joseph Pieper brought the work of Thomas Aquinas back to the mainstream of philosophic thought, Wilhelm Kamlah rediscovered Saint Augustine, and Bernhard Welte attempted an existential interpretation of the texts of Saint Thomas.

The views of Nicolai Hartmann (1882–1950) stood out in the field of philosophy. Hartmann saw a complex reality independent of man. Moreover, unlike the existentialists, Hartmann refused to take any notice of historical situations. There was no sense of crisis pervading his works. Although Hartmann has no real followers today, his perspective was quite influential in the immediate postwar years as a counterbalance to that of Heidegger.

In the early 1950s several philosophers who had fled from the Nazis returned to Germany. Helmuth Plessner, a founder of philosophical anthropology, took a chair at Göttingen. Philosophical anthropology aimed at understanding man's nature through an understanding of how man came to terms with his environment. Behaviorism, medicine, ethnology, and all social sciences, therefore, provided material for study and conjecture.

Ernst Bloch returned first to Leipzig in the German Democratic Republic and later to Tübingen in the Federal Republic. In *Das Prinzip Hoffnung* (1959), Bloch directed his view to the end of history, when man would become capable of salvation. His work was of Marxist origins but drew from Schelling, Fichte, Jewish mysticism, and the existentialism of Kierkegaard.

Max Horkheimer and Theodor Adorno also returned to the Federal Republic in the early 1950s. They had been part of what had been called the Frankfurt School, which also included Jürgen Habermas and Herbert Marcuse. Horkheimer's reflections, contained in numerous sociological and aesthetic essays, aimed at the unmasking of mass media-controlled civilization. Ideas in modern culture were traded as though they were business commodities. Adorno set out to strip ideas of their magic. To him, reality and practice should become the established conceptual definitions in the face of despair.

Although he had returned to the Federal Republic only on lecture tours, the ideas of Marcuse were still very much a part of the contemporary German scene in the late 1960s and early 1970s. The use of violence, said Marcuse, was the right of minorities in their attempts to shatter existing power structures. The influence of the Frankfurt School has been translated into practice through the activism of German students since 1967.

Literature

The themes of war and defeat tended to dominate German literature through the 1950s. Theodor Plievier (1892–1945) used a pseudodocumentary approach in his description of *Stalingrad* (1945). Hermann Kasack (1896–1966) offered a surrealistic picture of the totalitarian state, and Stefan Andreas described the struggle for integrity under the Nazis. Hans Erich Nossack's subject of man as a refugee from catastrophe was extensively explored in his postwar novels.

The end of the war also brought a resurgence of Christian approaches to the problems of modern life in the literature of the Federal Republic. Elisabeth Länggasser (1899–1950) was best known for her novels *Das Unauslöschliche Siegel* (1946) and *Märkische Argonautenfahrt* (1950), which dealt with the religious evaluation of the human condition. Roman Catholic Gertrud von Le Fort presented Christianity as the center of life that should be allowed to enter into all aspects of human endeavor in *Der Kranz der Engel* (The Wreath of Angels), 1946. Religious poetry was also popular. Rudolf Schröder (1878–1962), for example, drew from Lutheran tradition to demonstrate the continuity of Christian humanism despite the war.

Heinrich Böll was one of the first authors to write about the catastrophe of the German defeat. His first novel, *Der Zug War Punktlich* (The Train Was on Time), 1949, presented the experiences of a soldier from the beginning of the war to its end. Since then, Böll has explored newer forms of expression in his collection of short stories *Doktor Murkes Gesammeltes Schweigen* (1958), his ambitious novel *Billard um Halb Zehn* (Billiards at Half Past Nine), 1961, and such other works as *Ende Einer Dienstfahrt* (1966). He was awarded the Nobel Prize for letters in 1972.

The postwar literary movement was given focus by the self-styled Group '47. This loose association of writers, formed in 1947, provided a critical forum for young authors. It was founded by novelist Hans Richter, whose own novel, *Sie Fielen aus Gottes Hand* (1951), documented wartime experiences. One of the better known writers associated with this group, Günter Grass, gained international fame as the author of *Die Blechtrommel* (The Tin Drum) in 1959. This work chronicles the previous thirty years through the eyes of a dwarf street musician. This novel was followed by another major work, *Hundejahre* (The Dog Years), in 1963.

Group '61 was formed in 1961 with the avowed goal of expressing the working-class revolt against an alienating society. Its founder, Max von der Grün (author of *Irrlicht und Feuer* and *Männer in Zwiefacher Nacht)*, revived interest in earlier social criticism and modern industrial society as literary topics. The major writers associated with this movement are Bruno Gluchowski, Josef Reding, Hildegard Wohlgemuth, and Günter Herburger.

The younger poets of the late 1950s and early 1960s rejected the rhetoric of traditional German poetry. Their blunt, often emotionless style, attempted a "new objectivity" in the imagery of man's helplessness in the world. The result was a hybrid style resulting from Romantic realistic precision and bizarre fantasy.

A few writers of the 1960s, influenced by contemporary poetry, renewed earlier literary styles. Klaus Nonnenmann used irony to portray man's hidden greatness. Traditional modes of storytelling reasserted themselves in the stories of Hans Bender, Siegfried Lenz, and others.

Drama

The decade following the war (1945–55) was particularly barren. While theaters recovered quite rapidly, German playwrights were slower to emerge. Much of the drama of the German stage reflected the backlog of foreign plays denied under the Nazis. Thus, the theater of the 1950s reflected an almost "frenzied cosmopolitanism." German works were put behind those of Bernard Shaw, Thornton Wilder, Frederico García Lorca, Jean Paul Sartre, Arthur Miller, Samuel Beckett, and others. Wolfgang Borchert's (1921–47) *Draussen vor der Tür* (1947) was an exception during this postwar period; his play bitterly satirized the effect of the war years on a generation of German youth.

During the middle 1950s a number of plays dealing with the war appeared in the Federal Republic. Claus Hubalek's *Der Hauptmann und Sein Held* (1954), Peter Hirche's *Triumph in Tausend Jahren* (1955), and Lepold Ahlsen's *Philemon und Baucis* (1956) all rejected Nazi Germany and the senselessness of war. Rudolf Hey's political allegory, *Thymian und Drachentod* (1955), parodied the cold war and the divided Germanies.

Two Swiss playwrights, Max Frisch and Friedrich Dürrenmatt, dominated the German stage in the 1960s. Of the two, Frisch seemed the more socially committed: *Biedermann und die Brandstifter* (1957) inveighed against extremism's power over a passive middle class; *Andorra* (1961) dealt profoundly with anti-Semitism; and *Biografie: Ein Spiel* (1967) exposed human relationships in the modern world. Dürrenmatt also argued that scientists can be morally compromised by the truths they discover in his play *Die Physiker* (1962). Many of Dürrenmatt's plays, however, deal with mythical and historical figures, such as *Romulus der Grosse* (1964) and *König Johann*, (1968) and not with social morality.

The theater of the absurd found numerous followers in the Federal Republic in the 1960s. Wolfgang Hildesheimer used his play *Erlanger. Rede über das Absurde Theater* (1960) to describe a parable of life. In essence, the absurd sees the world and life itself as meaningless—a fact that an audience can either lament or find humorous. Elements of the absurd are found in the plays of Hans Michelson and the early plays of Grass.

A second contemporary dramatic trend in the Federal Republic is the Documentary Theater. Following the style and purpose of Brecht, these plays demonstrated how the "real" world can and must be transformed. Rolf Hochhuth's *Der Stellvertreter* (The Deputy), 1963, was the first and perhaps best known of this dramatic form and dealt with the relation of Pope Pius XII to Hitler's massacre of European Jewry. Another of the better known documentary dramas was Paul Weiss *Marat/Sade*, 1962–65, which played the nihilistic Marquis de Sade against the French revolutionary Jean Paul Marat. Grass *Die Plebejer Proben den Aufstand* (The Plebians Rehearse the Uprising), 1966, recapitulates the events of the workers' uprising in East Berlin.

Two other writers, Heinar Kipphardt and Tankred Dorst, have produced notable documentary plays. Kipphardt's *In der Sache J. Robert Oppenheimer* (The Case of J. Robert Oppenheimer), 1964, reviewed the charge of communist sympathies made against the physicist during the 1950s in the United States. Dorst's *Toller* (1968) deals with the short-lived Bavarian Soviet Republic of 1919.

There is a trend in the Federal Republic toward the establishment of more experimental theaters. Many of these theaters have been built as additions to conventional theaters or at universities and seek to promote new, diverse forms of expression. Representative of the experimental theater are the plays *Global Interests* (1972) by Franz Xavier Kroetz, which used social realism to describe the effect of the 1972 Olympic games in Munich on two different people, and Rainer Werner Fassbinder's *Freedom in Bremen* (1972), which dealt with bizarre murder and the psychological drive for freedom.

Science and Scholarship

German science was decimated during the war. An entire generation of scientists between the ages of thirty-five and fifty disappeared, and many others who had remained in Germany throughout the war emigrated afterward. The destruction of many of the Kaiser Wilhelm institutes in Berlin left scientists without research facilities, and occupation statutes forbade the building of new institutions until 1955. The Kaiser Wilhelm Society itself was dissolved in 1947.

In 1948 the Max Planck Society for the Promotion of Science was established. Eighty percent of the society's funding comes from the government, and the remaining 20 percent from private donation. By 1968 the society had enlarged to fifty-two research institutes, 1,750 scientists, and more than 5,000 supporting personnel in centers throughout the Federal Republic. Many of the institutes are headed by leading scientists in their fields. For example, Professor Rheingold von Sengbusch, developer of a new variety of animal feed (a giant mushroom that is large enough to be sliced like a steak) and a feed for fish that causes them to grow at a rapid rate, heads the Max Planck Institute for Cultivated Plant Breeding. Konrad Lorenz, who gained fame in the late 1960s for his work on the behavior of animals in their natural environment, heads the Max Planck Institute for Behavioral Physiology; and several Nobel Prize winners head still other Max Planck institutes.

Participation in areas of nuclear energy, high energy physics, and space research in the Federal Republic has been conducted through active participation in such European organizations as the European Atomic Energy Commission (EURATOM), the European Center for Nuclear Research, the European Space Research Organization, and the European Launcher Development Organization. Scientists from the Max Planck institutes have also advanced fusion research by being the first to hold plasma or ionized gas in the grip of a magnetic field for several hours.

The biological sciences have also progressed. The Max Planck Institute for Cell Chemistry, led by the 1964 Nobel Prize winner, Feodor Lynen, crystallized the fatty acid synthesis. This enzyme material can be used to explore how the body regulates fatty substances and, thereby, aid in the control of hardening of the arteries. The genetics department at the University of Cologne has been active in the field of molecular genetics. Two of its members, Pamela Abel (originally from New Zealand) and Thomas Trautner, discovered in the early 1960s that a complex animal virus could be cultivated on a strain of bacteria.

Although in the Federal Republic scientists have yet to parallel the nineteen Nobel prizes in science associated with the Kaiser Wilhelm Society (1911-47), those that have been awarded give an indication of the trend of research. In physics, awards were given to Walther Bothe (1954) for the invention and the study of the "coincidence method"; Rudolf Mössbauer (1961) for the discovery of the Mössbauer effect; and J. Hans Jensen (1963) for development of the shell model theory of atomic nucleus structure. In chemistry, Herman Staudinger (1953) was awarded the prize for work on macromolecules; Karl Ziegler (1963) for the analysis of the structure and the synthesis of polymers for plastics; and Manfried Eigen (1967) for studies of rapid chemical reactions. In physiology, awards went to Werner Forsmann (1956) and Feodor Lynen (1964) for discoveries concerning heart and circulatory pathology.

Historiography during the first postwar decade dealt with the reformulation of the historical questions of the 1920s. The idealist approach, with its emphasis on German institutions and events, was still applied to the dominant themes of the upward revaluation of the Weimar Republic, the new appraisal of the Treaty of Versailles, and the idealization of Gustav Stresemann. Marxist theories were generally excluded, and contemporary history remained national history. Older historians, such as Hans Rothfels, Gerhard Ritter, and Hans Herzfeld, dominated throughout the 1950s.

In the 1960s a younger generation of historians, led by Theodor Scheider, Werner Conze, Karl Dietrich Erdmann, Otto Brunner, Herman Heimpel, and Gerd Tellenbad, demonstrated newer approaches. Increasing attention has been paid to sociology, to relations between the structure and the programs of political parties and associations, to urban history, and to other aspects of modern industrial society. Papers read at historical conferences in 1967 and 1970 demonstrated an infusion of social science terminology. Nationalism, imperialism, and fascism, for example, are viewed as categories to be used for classification rather than as limited to a particular time and place.

Music

After the war, both Carl Orff and Werner Egk continued to compose. Orff's chief works—*Antigone* (1949), *Trionfi di Afrodite* (1953), *Oedipus der Tyrann* (1959), and *Prometheus* (1968)—displayed a return to primitive dramatic style. Egk's postwar compositions have included several operas and orchestral works. Chief among the latter is *Variations on a Caribbean Theme* first performed in 1960.

Wolfgang Fortner's *Symphony of 1947* represented one of the first attempts of a West German composer to rejoin the international world of composition. The atonality of this work and the twelve-note experimentation of the *Third String Quartet* (1948) showed that Schönberg's influence in German music had not diminished.

Among Fortner's students after the war was Hans Werner Henze. His initial infatuation with Schönberg was present in the tonal, atonal, and twelve-note textures of his opera *König Hirsch* (1956). Since then his compositions have displayed a variety of styles. His opera, *Bassariden* (1966), established Henze as the musical successor to Richard Strauss. Later Henze displayed still newer musical directness in *El Cimmaron* (1970).

Karl Stockhausen has become a leading figure in musical avant-gardism since the war. His compositions are described as "instrumental music in space." His *Groups for Three Orchestras* (1958), for example, was written for three groups of instruments variously placed about a music hall and directed by three different conductors. The interaction of various rhythms and harmonies allows the listener to experience his own time-space relationship. This technique was expanded in *Carré* (1960) through the use of four different orchestras and four choruses.

The postwar period produced other important composers: Karl Hartmann (1905–63) filled the symphonic form with elements of the baroque and expressionism; Günter Bialas was known for his compressed style; and Ernst Papping was widely acclaimed as a church musician and composer. Other composers have emphasized more individualized works away from the avant-garde.

Since 1945 about forty-five new operas have been performed in the Federal Republic. Chief among these was Giselher Klebe's *Die Räuber* (1957). Klebe used the twelve-tone technique in creating dramatic and lyric situations. Another major figure in West German opera is Boris Blacher, whose work is characterized by spontaneity and avant-gardism. Wilhelm Killmayer (1927), a student of Carl Orff, wrote *La Buffonata* using a text by Tankred Dorst. This opera was very popular in the late 1960s.

Architecture

In 1945 Germany lay in ruins. Although creative plans for reconstruction were proposed in the forties and fifties (Hans Scharoun's housing project for Berlin, Hubert Hoffmann's for Magdeburg, Walther Schwagenscheidt's for Emden, and Streb and Trautwein's for the city center of Nürnberg), they were not executed. Residential architecture after the war, despite major schemes undertaken by Sep Ruf and others for Bonn and the Hansa quarter (1957) of Berlin, did not reach the quality evident in the 1920s.

The lack of a dominating German influence during the 1945–55 period led to the acceptance of new ideas from Scandinavia, Switzerland and, particularly, the United States. The latter influence derived from the presence of Walter Gropius and Mies van der Rohe in the United States. Although the first works in the Federal Republic designed by Gropius (1957, an apartment house in West Berlin; and 1960, a residential development plan also in West Berlin) and Mies van der Rohe (1963, Museum of Modern art in West Berlin) came long after the war, their new

American structural style had already been widely imitated. One example, the cloth factory in Blumberg built by Egon Eiermann in 1951, displayed a form demanded by function—a trait emphasized by the two architectural masters, Gropius and Mies van der Rohe.

A younger generation of architects emerged in the late 1950s and early 1960s representing functionalist-constructive austerity similar to that of the 1920s. The designs of Hans Maurer, Helmut Rohde, Herbert Groethuysen, Günter Hünow, and others especially displayed this style. The Thyssen Building in Düsseldorf (1957–60), designed by Helmut Hentrich and Hubert Petschnigg, represented a combination of form and function. The building is divided into three staggered, connecting slabs, thereby breaking away from the anonymous box form of most contemporary skyscrapers.

Church architecture in the fifties and sixties sought to create expressive space. Eiermann's two churches in Pforzheim (1953) and West Berlin (1959–63) demonstrated the important elements of religious architecture: "the accommodation of congregation, space, light, structural concepts and building technique." Gottfried Bohm's Catholic Pilgrims Church in Neviges (1966–68) created a kind of "sculptural architecture."

In the 1960s a number of architects turned away from the sober functionalism of the past and toward new informal and subjective forms and freer, more imaginative designs. Hans Scharoun, one of the leaders in this movement, designed the Berlin Philharmonic Hall (1963) so that the concert hall and foyer display what has been called the "discovery of form from within." The building is among the most important built in the Federal Republic since 1945 and is considered an architectural masterpiece.

Many of the modern theaters built during the 1960s have emphasized simplicity; the most striking of these is at Ingolstadt. The walls are grey exposed concrete, and the foyer lacks accessories. What gives the theater its festive note is the plastic use of functionally determined space.

New building techniques have resulted in new forms of West German architecture. The pavilion of the Federal Republic at the Montreal Expo '67 utilized a hanging roof that could be taken apart and reassembled. A similar idea was used during the 1972 Olympics in Munich. Huge tent-like structures were stretched over various sports areas and became articulated units that blended in with the surrounding landscape.

Sculpture

As in other cultural areas, the continuity of development was interrupted by the dictatorship and war. Gerhard Marcks and Ewald Mataré were among the few outside the classical tradition who seemed to bridge the gap between 1933 and 1945. The former, in his postwar *Chained Prometheus*, used "spatially tectonic compositions" to illustrate order and compactness. Mataré, however, sculpted abstract animal

186

shapes into magical forms.

Younger sculptors have emerged since 1945. Wilhelm Loth used an Expressionist manner in the depiction of the human torso as a part of nature. Fritz Koenig also used the human figure but in diverse themes of human and animal groupings. One of his best known works was *Herds of Cattle and Groups of Riders of Camargue.* Günter Ris utilized unblemished Greek marble in sculpting pure spheroid shapes; he is particularly known for armored figures in exaggerated movements.

Sculpting in metal also became popular in the 1960s. Jochen Hiltmann used the blowtorch in creating forms from molten steel. Another sculptor in steel, Erich Hauser, welded crystalline shapes from sheets of iron. His works give the appearance of solidity, yet display incisions and openings that contradict the continuity of the shape. Norbert Kricke, who also works in steel, is one of the best known of modern German sculptors. His sculpture attempts novel conceptions of space—limitlessness and simultaneous movement.

In the late 1960s German sculpture developed along new lines. These trends have followed new developments in polychromatic materials along with the acceptance of other materials as having artistic value (leather, cardboard, and the like). Kinetic art, or art that incorporates movement, has found expression in the sculpture of Günter Ucker, Otto Piene, and Heinz Mack. Günther Haese used currents of air to propel his sculpture made of watch parts in endless movement. Harry Kramer's sculpture, in contrast, moved under the power of whirring machines.

Attitudes toward shape changed in the late sixties. Reduced forms using the precise cut of industrial design were popular. The cylinders and spheres of Ernst Hermanns and the discs of Kaspar Thomas Lenk are examples of this work. Pop art, or the "new realism," has redefined form in absurd or surrealistic terms. Detlef Birgfeld used torsos (arms, knees) and armor in expressing contemporary world problems. Joseph Beuys used grease and felt-covered objects to create works that rejected the traditional meanings of beauty.

Painting

German painting in the postwar period focused on late expressionism—the art of Paul Klee, Vasili Kandinsky, and others of the Bauhaus school. Abstract painting was influenced by Willi Baumeister (1889–1955), who emerged as one of the Federal Republic's foremost painters when he was director of the Stuttgart Academy. Georg Meistermann, another leader in abstract art, extended his use of color areas in the 1940s and 1950s and attempted to bring abstract forms into religious settings. Other leaders in the postwar period—Hans Trier, Fritz Winter, Ernst Wilhelm Nay—explored new areas of abstract art and the use of color.

In southern Germany more conservative trends were found. Walter Teutsch (1883–1964) used stable forms and colors in the recreation of mythical events. Walter Becker, Otto Dill (1884–1956), Paul Strecher, Adolf Hartmann, and others furthered impressionist and expressionist styles because of the popularity of abstract art.

Since the mid-fifties a younger generation of artists has dominated the scene. Abstraction has been represented in a variety of modes. In collage and decoupage what had been purely abstract structures began to reincorporate representational elements. K.F. Dahmen used rusty iron, rotted rope, torn canvas, and old scraps of writing to express a "poetry of ruin." A 1966 montage used mechanical parts to display the dilemma of man in a mechanized age. Action painting, which portrays uninhibited gesticulation in paint, assumed various forms in the works of younger artists. A quieter form of abstraction was produced in the works of Hans Schreiner, Johannes Schreiter, and Bernd Volke by using contrasts of light and dark, and by varying color key in free formations.

New expressionism also has flourished. In Munich, painters Heinnred Pren, Helmut Sturm, and H.P. Zimmer formed a closely knit group called Spur. Despite individual styles, the group collectively painted a huge hall in the Palazzo Grassi in Venice (1963). Karlsruhe, a less closely knit center of neoexpressionism, boasts Walter Stöher and Horst Antes. The former created extensive fields of pictorial action, and the latter used mythical figures and monsters that, upon close review, threaten the viewer.

Other trends continue to be popular. The new surrealism of Richard Pfenning, Peter Schubert, Horst Janssen, and Edgar Schmandt presupposes expert draftsmanship in the portrayal of what is often grotesque cruelty and perverseness. Pop art developed in the Federal Republic rather late and has not been as popular as other styles. Hans Jurgen Diehl, Werner Berges, and Lambert Wintersberger are leaders in the use of advertising effects and erotic scenes as subject matter. Herbert Schneider used fresh colors and style in his personal variation of pop art in *Panopticon* (1967). Klaus Staudt, Rudolf Kammer, and Roland Helmer are proponents of op art, which uses the manipulation of lines and (or) surface to create a play of light and motion. Still different independent lines of color and contrasts are explored in the art of Peter Bruning, Paul Dreyer, and Rolf Günter Dienst.

Films

Postwar filmmaking began in 1946 with the Helmut Weiss comedy *Sag die Wahrheit*. *In Jenen Tangen,* directed by Helmut Käutner in 1947, told the story of a car and its occupants through the years 1933 to 1945. Harald Braum inaugurated the opening of the Munich Studios in 1947 (90 percent of the film studios were in the Soviet zone) with the film *Zwischen Gestern und Morgen* (Between Yesterday and Tomorrow). The title bore added significance because of the presence of many cast members from the old UFA studios.

The economic instability and competition of Hollywood and French filmmakers made it difficult to find backing immediately after the war. Some first-class works were produced, however, such as R.A. Stemmle's *Berliner Ballade* with Gert Frobe. Even box office successes, such as *Nachtwache* (1949) with its theme of Christian cooperation and the operetta-style film *Schwarzwaldmädel* (1950), occurred only after the 1948 currency reform.

The beginning of the 1950s was marked by the return of two exiles, Peter Lorre and Robert Siodmak, whose films *Der Verlorene* (1951) and *Nachts, Wenn der Teufel Kam* (1952) penetrated the legal insecurity and cynicism under the Third Reich. Several films during the 1950s and early 1960s—*Weg ohne Umkehr* (1953), *Himmel ohne Sterne* (1955), *Swei unter Millionen* (1961), and *Flucht nach Berlin*—dealt with the division of Germany as an obstacle to the fulfillment of personal desires and relationships. Many of the films during these years attempted half-hearted critical appraisals of problems that end, in the majority of cases, in a love story (as in Wolfgang Liebeneiner's *Taiga*).

Bernhard Wicki produced one of the few critical and international successes of the fifties. *Die Brücke* (The Bridge), 1959, tells the story of the senseless death of several young boys defending a bridge during the last hours of the war. Wicki's next film, *Das Wunder des Malachias* (1961), resulted in his receiving the Director's Prize at the Berlin Film Festival.

Various literary works of Thomas Mann, Heinrich Böll, Friedrich Dürrenmatt, Kurt Tucholsky, Carl Zuckmayer, Gerhart Hauptmann, and others have been made into films. Even Shakespeare found his way into German film in Käutner's adaptation of *Hamlet*, called *Der Rest Ist Schweigen* (1959). *Der Junge Törless* (1966), after Austrian Robert Musil's work, offered a picture of the past that parallels the manifestations of modern totalitarianism. This film received the Fipresci Prize at the Cannes Film Festival in 1966.

Since 1966 another generation of young directors has emerged—Peter Schamoni, Franz Spieker, Christian Rischert, Haro Senft, Alexander Kluge, Johannes Schaaf, and Edgar Reitz. Several films by these young directors, for example Haro Senft's *Der Sanfte Laufe* (1967), have received important prizes at major international festivals in Venice, Berlin, and Cannes.

CHAPTER 10

MASS COMMUNICATIONS

A mixture of private and public ownership characterizes the mass media in the Federal Republic. The press, lively and varied, is entirely in private hands. Radio and television, in line with organizational arrangements sponsored by the Western occupying powers at the end of the war, are controlled by public corporations set up on the basis of *Land* (state, pl. *Länder*) divisions rather than federally. The film industry, thoroughly decartelized, is privately owned, but tax advantages and direct subsidies from the *Land* and the federal government have been utilized in an effort to improve its competitive position. Freedom of the media, guaranteed under the constitution, is for the most part effectively sustained, and efforts by the federal government to interfere have been rebuffed by the highest courts.

Daily newspapers, mostly nonpartisan, number over 1,300, compared with more than 1,700 in the United States for a population 3½ times larger. The great majority of the Federal Republic dailies, however, are unable to maintain full publications staffs and print the bulk of their pages from matrices (impressions of set type) supplied by central publishing houses. The lack of a truly national press capital on the model of London or Paris has inhibited the development of national dailies. The weekly newspaper-magazine, typified by *Die Zeit* and *Der Spiegel*, has to some degree filled the gap.

The leading news service is the German Press Agency (Deutsche Presse Agentur—DPA), generally considered to rival the best in Europe or the United States. It is owned cooperatively by the newspaper publishers and the broadcasting companies.

The radio and television services derive most of their operating funds from license fees paid by the owners of radio and television sets. Advertising is held to a minimum, and there are no sponsored programs. Each of the nine regional radio services broadcasts two main programs on amplitude modulation (AM) and frequency modulation (FM) and a third on FM only. Two of the three television programs are produced by the nine regional broadcasting services, while the other is operated by a national public corporation with its headquarters in Mainz.

Two radio stations speak for the Federal Republic in broadcasts abroad. *Deutschlandfunk* (Radio Germany) broadcasts on longwave and mediumwave frequencies to the German Democratic Republic (DDR —see Glossary) as well as to other European audiences. *Deutsche Welle*

(The Voice of Germany) is the shortwave voice of the Federal Republic broadcasting in thirty-three languages around the world. Foreign broadcasting activities from the Federal Republic include the continuing operations of the United States-sponsored Radio Free Europe (RFE) and Radio Liberty, beaming programs to Eastern Europe and the Soviet Union, respectively.

THE ROLE OF THE GOVERNMENT

The postwar framers of the Basic Law, the constitution, for the Federal Republic set forth in Article 5 stringent provisions for the freedom of the press and other media:

Everyone has the right to express and disseminate his opinion freely by speech, writing, and pictures, and to inform himself freely from generally accessible sources. Freedom of the press and freedom of reporting by radio and film are guaranteed. There shall be no censorship.

The sole restraints on this freedom contained in the Basic Law provide that general regulations concerning libel, pornography, and subversion remain applicable to the media. The individual *Länder* also have their own press laws (which cannot, however, contravene Article 5). In general, these require officials to inform the media on matters of public interest, to give journalists the right to refuse to identify sources of information, to require periodicals to print the names of their principal editors, and to grant individuals and organizations that feel they have been treated unfairly in the press the right to request space for reply. The Federal Constitutional Court is the ultimate judge in specific cases of dispute.

On the whole, these provisions of the law, coupled with the jealous regard of the *Länder* for their rights vis-à-vis the federal government, have served to restrain the central authorities from interference with the media. The press freedoms in the Federal Republic are generally considered to be as effectively maintained as anywhere in the Western world.

During the long regime of Chancellor Konrad Adenauer, however, more than a few sharp disputes arose between the media and the federal government, as well as between the *Länder* and Bonn, in regard to control over the media. Adenauer, it is generally agreed, felt a strong personal prejudice against the press; its criticisms of government policies and actions went against the grain of his authoritarian temperament and offended his sense of propriety. From 1952 to 1954 his cabinet proposed a series of measures intended to curb the press. First, the Ministry of Interior drafted a press law designed to ban "newspapers hostile to the state." Then came an effort to establish a Ministry of Information intended to "enlighten" the public in regard to the government's legislative aims, later modified to a proposal to set up a coordinating information committee with much the same objectives. Opposition from the Social Democratic Party (SPD—see Glossary) and the Free Democratic Party (FDP—see Glossary), plus unanimously unfavorable

192

reaction from the press, led to the defeat of all these proposals.

Adenauer was also dissatisfied with arrangements whereby the *Länder* controlled all broadcasting rights, including the increasingly important television channels. Several attempts to pass a federal radio law were defeated, largely as a result of bitter opposition in the *Länder* to any infringement on their rights. In 1959 a draft law was introduced without prior consultation with the radio stations and *Länder* representatives; it would have given the federal government control over a second television network. When this proposal was rejected by the Bundesrat (Federal Council), Adenauer arbitrarily sought to form a private company with the federal government as sole shareholder to operate a second television network, to be financed solely out of advertising revenue. The case was taken to the Federal Constitutional Court, which in February 1961 handed down its widely cited "television decision" to the effect that the federal government had no power, under the Basic Law, to regulate the organization of radio-television broadcasting. Adenauer told the Bundestag (Federal Diet) that the court's judgment, "wrong" though it was, must be obeyed and, therefore, the cabinet had decided "not to concern itself with any further matters connected with television."

In 1962 the celebrated "Spiegel affair" occurred as a culmination of the Adenauer regime's distaste for the strident, muckraking reporting of the newsweekly *Der Spiegel* (see The Press, this ch.). Once again the federal authorities were defeated on an issue that was basically one of freedom of the press. The public uproar over the arrest of newsmen led directly to the departure of the defense minister, Franz-Josef Strauss, and Adenauer announced that he would resign the chancellorship in 1963. To more than one historian of the Adenauer era, the "Spiegel affair" marked the final stage in the decline of Adenauer's prestige; and it remains a watchword, of lasting significance, to the guardians of a free press in the Federal Republic.

A measure of self-censorship of the press, designed to avert government interference, is provided by the German Press Council established in November 1956. The members of the council, ten publishers and ten journalists, are named by the relevant trade associations. Apart from protesting outside encroachments on freedom of the press, the council seeks to "ascertain and deal with defects in the press sphere" and "to guard the press against monopolies and other freedom-endangering business patterns." The council, having no power to compel compliance, relies on its prestige to enforce decisions.

To assist in the gathering of news about government affairs, the Federal Government maintains the Press and Information Office (known as BPA) in the capital city of Bonn. Its primary role is twofold: to make the government aware of domestic and foreign news and views on the country as carried in the mass media; and to keep German and foreign journalists informed in regard to government policies and activities. The most important contact with the journalists is via a press conference held every few days, with government officials invited to appear for questioning by the German correspondents stationed in Bonn.

Some critics have pointed to the easy accessibility of official spokesmen, the abundance of government handouts, and the opulence of official press facilities as factors tending to discourage enterprise and initiative among the Bonn correspondents, domestic and foreign. Such critics note also the absence of any first-rate daily newspaper in Bonn to report critically on government affairs.

THE PRESS

The varied, prolific, and independent press of the Federal Republic is in some respects an outgrowth of Western occupation policies at the end of World War II. No other area of public life was so thoroughly cleansed, in the political sense, as the press and radio. The occupation authorities set up a licensing system in the three Western zones of occupation, which effectively barred the old guard of German journalism; licenses to start up newspapers and periodicals were granted only to persons untainted by Nazi connections. The new press entrepreneurs were thus mostly young, energetic, and liberal minded; by the time the licensing era ended in September 1949, their 140-odd newspapers had a head start on the rest of the field.

Continuous growth through the 1950s and the 1960s resulted in impressive totals for the 1970s: over 1,300 daily newspapers selling about 18 million copies, and some 15,000 periodicals with a circulation exceeding 200 million. Since the mid-1960s, concern has been expressed in regard to increasing tendencies toward an overconcentration of the press, not so much a merging of publications, with consequent disappearance of one or the other, but as a taking over of newspapers and magazines by the larger publishers, albeit with continuing publication. The underlying reasons for this concentration have been primarily economic, with smaller publishers unable to meet growing costs. Axel Springer's press empire, headquartered in Hamburg, with 26 percent of the daily newspaper market in recent years, has given rise to the greatest degree of concern.

Newspapers

The more than 1,300 daily newspapers are produced by some 500 publishing houses. Only about 150 newspapers, however, have a full, independent editorial staff. A large majority are *Kopfblätter* (boiler plate) newspapers printed from matrices supplied by central publishing sources, with a page or so of local news added by the small local staff. The smaller publishers have grouped together to set up joint editorial operations while maintaining individual economic independence. For example, the Editorial Association of German Local Newspapers in Frankfurt issues a common world and national news section for fifty-three publishers in six *Länder*. The larger newspapers are locally oriented as well, in that any one of them may publish ten or more regional editions.

Another significant factor is the independent, nonpartisan character of the majority of newspapers in the Federal Republic. Less than 10 percent are directly sponsored by political parties, and many specify in their mastheads that they are "independent" or "neutral." This constitutes a sharp break not only with the Nazi but with the pre-Hitler period as well: in 1932, 60 percent of all newspapers maintained clear political ties to one party or another.

The process of history has inhibited the rise of a string of national dailies on the British model. Berlin, the former publishing center although never the equivalent of London's Fleet Street, was in no position following the war to regain its former stature. Bonn is totally lacking in the metropolitan stimulus requisite to a national press. Today neither West Berlin nor Bonn produces a single daily of national renown. Almost by default, the North German city of Hamburg has become a sort of press capital (see table 9). It is headquarters for the Springer publications group, producing the tabloid *Bild-Zeitung*, with much the largest circulation among daily newspapers, as well as the more sober and highly regarded *Die Welt*. Hamburg is also headquarters for the DPA, the influential weekly *Der Spiegel*, and the wealthy North German radio-television station, whose main news broadcast "Tagesschau" (Daily Show) is relayed each evening over the nationwide television network.

There are three, or possibly four, daily newspapers that can lay claim to being national in scope, having republic-wide circulation. The tabloid *Bild-Zeitung*, with nine slightly differing regional editions, is the German equivalent of the *New York Daily News*. Photos cover the front and back pages, the emphasis is on sex and sensationalism, and the

Table 9. *Leading Daily Newspapers in the Federal Republic of Germany, 1973*

Newspaper	City	Circulation (in thousands)
Bild-Zeitung	Hamburg	4,365.8
Westdeutsche Allgemeine Zeitung	Essen	657.6
Express*	Cologne	398.7
Rheinische Post	Düsseldorf	383.2
Frankfurter Allgemeine Zeitung	Frankfurt	336.8
Berliner Morgenpost	West Berlin	319.9
Hamburger Morgenpost	Hamburg	315.9
Süddeutsche Zeitung	Munich	311.9
Abendzeitung	--do--	305.3
Hamburger Abendblatt	Hamburg	296.3
BZ	West Berlin	296.1
Die Welt	Hamburg	286.2

*Includes *Düsseldorf Express.*

Source: Adapted from *Editor and Publisher International Year Book*, New York, 1974.

editorial line is basically popular-conservative. *Die Welt,* nearly the direct opposite of *Bild-Zeitung,* is also owned by Springer and centered in Hamburg, with decentralized publication in several cities. Its coverage of national and international news is widely regarded as the best in the country, and its editorial commentary, independent though generally conservative, is thoughtful and serious. The *Frankfurter Allgemeine Zeitung,* politically independent but close to business circles, is a serious conservative newspaper with readers throughout the country. Finally, Munich's *Süddeutsche Zeitung,* probably the outstanding liberal daily, is national in scope but somewhat more regionally oriented than the first three named.

Regional newspapers of stature include the *Frankfurter Rundschau* (circulation, 185,400), the first exclusively German newspaper to start publishing after the war. It is progressive and generally a supporter of the SPD. The *Westdeutsche Allgemeine Zeitung,* centered in Essen but with many localized editions, is undistinguished editorially but enjoys a higher circulation (657,600) than any newspaper except *Bild-Zeitung.*

Very few of the dailies publish a Sunday edition. Enlarged Saturday editions, including special sections and features, are intended to fill the gap. There are a few Sunday newspapers, notably *Bild am Sonntag* and *Welt am Sonntag,* of the Springer group. In 1973 the circulation of the first was 424,000, and of the second, 470,000.

Weekly Newspapers and Other Periodicals

An unusual feature of the press scene is the prominence of the weekly newspaper—actually half magazine and half newspaper—which summarizes, analyzes, and comments on current developments. There are British counterparts, such as the *Economist* and the *New Statesman,* and American newsweeklies, such as *Time* and *Newsweek* that are similar in part; but nowhere else is this sort of publication so dominant. The German weeklies are for the most part more outspokenly political and argumentative than the daily newspapers; some serve as forums for the political parties or religious groups, and others espouse a more widely based ideological stance either to the left or to the right.

Perhaps the best known of the weeklies is *Der Spiegel* (circulation, 890,000), similar to *Time* in its format but far more controversial. Each issue is three times as thick as a copy of *Time.* Although *Der Spiegel* is often sensational and muckraking, its treatment of specific subjects is often near-encyclopedic, and its reporting on political life in the Federal Republic has been highly praised by some Western observers as well as by German readers. The well-known "Spiegel affair" of 1962 led directly to the downfall of defense minister, Franz-Josef Strauss, who had instigated the arrest on treason charges of the publisher, Rudolf Augstein, and several editors, ostensibly for publication of an article on the North Atlantic Treaty Organization (NATO) maneuvers that criticized the performance of the German forces. The subsequent public uproar forced Strauss' resignation, and eventually the treason charges were dismissed by the Federal Supreme Court. This and other incidents of like nature have served to keep *Der Spiegel* in the public eye and have certainly done no harm to its circulation figures.

More sober and dignified by far is the weekly *Die Zeit* (circulation, 260,000), but it too has a record of exposing government errors and fighting for liberal causes, especially in the area of civil rights. Many regard it as the best written and best edited newspaper in the Federal Republic.

Deutsche Zeitung (formerly *Christ und Welt*) is an influential national-conservative, Protestant weekly; *Rheinische Merkur*, also conservative, reflects the views of the Roman Catholic Church hierarchy and the Christian Democratic Union (CDU—see Glossary). The Christian Social Union, which is the Bavarian wing of the CDU, publishes the weekly *Bayern-Kurier* in Munich. The SPD also publishes its own weekly—*Vorwärts*—in Bonn. The *Deutsche National-Zeitung* is a neo-Nazi weekly, to the far right, with a circulation of about 120,000 copies.

The circulation figures of these weekly reviews, except for that of *Der Spiegel*, are dwarfed by the readership totals of the *Illustrierten*, illustrated weeklies lavishly produced in the manner of *Life* and *Look* and emphasizing sex, sin, and sensationalism. The leaders in this field—*Der Stern, Bunte Illustrierte, Neue Revue*, and *Quick*—sell upwards of 1.8 million copies each week. The profile of *Der Stern* differs slightly from the others in that it features highly controversial political exposés along with quantities of flesh and blood.

Well in front in the circulation race among periodicals is *Hör Zu*, the Springer group's television-radio programs weekly, selling 3.8 million copies. Its chief rival, *TV Hören and Sehen*, sells 1.7 million copies. Several women's magazines have circulation totals of over 1 million for their mixture of homemaking and fashion; *Brigitte, Für Sie*, and *Frau im Spiegel* are among the leaders in this field.

Many more narrowly specialized periodicals are published, mostly on a monthly or quarterly basis. Some 2,000 trade periodicals are designed to serve the needs of such specialized areas as industry, commerce, and agriculture. Among some 500 scientific-academic journals, those that cover aspects of medicine and the sciences in particular have in many instances worldwide reputations.

Press Agencies

The leading news service is the German Press Agency (Deutsche Presse Agentur—DPA), founded in 1949 through merger of the three press agencies set up in the Western sectors. Correspondents in all important cities in the Federal Republic and more than sixty countries around the world report their stories to DPA headquarters in Hamburg. The agency is generally considered to rank with the best in the Western world.

DPA is a cooperative venture owned exclusively by the newspaper publishers and broadcasting companies of the Federal Republic. No individual publisher or publishing chain is allowed to contribute more than 1 percent of the basic capitalization, a safeguard against undue influence on the part of more affluent members. The radio-television companies taken together contribute a maximum of 10 percent of the working capital. Members pay a standard charge for service based on the size of the audience. All the seats on the supervisory council are filled by representatives of the mass media, minimizing government influence.

The Associated Press also provides a German wire service that is utilized by some of the bigger dailies. The network previously maintained in the country by United Press International was taken over by DPA in 1971. Reuters of Great Britain and Agence France-Presse also offer services to the media; however, on the basis of an agreement with DPA, Reuters does not provide a news service to the dailies.

Several lesser, strictly domestic agencies provide specialized news services. The Protestant Press Service (Evangelische Pressedienst —EPD) and the Catholic News Agency (Katholische Nachrichten-Agentur—KNA) disseminate news primarily concerned with religious life.

RADIO

To a greater degree than the press, the radio and television in structure and format still reflect decisions made by the occupying powers in the immediate postwar years. The occupation authorities were determined that broadcasting should be free of central government control as well as commercial exploitation. To this end decentralized, nonprofit, public broadcasting organizations were set up for each *Land* or group of *Länder*, and the organizational form followed broadly the model of the British Broadcasting Corporation (BBC). Each autonomous network was headed by a broadcasting council intended to be representative of the community and free of party factionalism. The Basic Law for the Federal Republic, approved in 1949, confirmed the planned independence of broadcasting from government interference by expressly guaranteeing freedom of radio news reporting and by failing to invest the central government with any authority to regulate broadcasting.

In the mid-1970s, despite some regrouping of the *Land* networks and the superimposition of television, organizational arrangements remain basically unaltered. There are nine domestic radio services (North German, Bremen, West German, Hesse, Southwest German, South German, Bavaria, Saarland, and Free Berlin), each administered by a director (*Intendant*) responsible to a broadcasting council and an administrative council composed of representatives of such major civil organizations as trade unions and universities, as well as government and party representatives of the *Land* or *Länder* involved. The nine radio services have formed a public-law consortium, known as the Working Party of Broadcasting Stations under Public Law in the Federal Republic of Germany (Arbeitsgemeinschaft der Öffentlichrechtlichen Rundfunkanstalten der Bundesrepublik Deutschland—ARD), for purposes of program exchange, settling of financial balances, and operation of the first television network.

Revenues for the domestic radios and television are derived primarily from license fees paid by the owners of radios and television sets. The fees—the equivalent of about US$1 monthly for radio and US$2.50 for television—are collected by the post office, which is responsible for the technical operations and transmitting equipment of radio and television. Although the fees are the same nationwide, the amount and distribution are not matters for the federal government. Following suitable deduction for collection costs and technical expenses such as detection of so-called pirate listeners and viewers, the post office channels the remainder to the nine regional broadcasting corporations according to the residence of license holders. Additional revenues are derived by making available limited amounts of radio time for commercial advertising, presented at specified times of the day and embedded in light music or other background programs. Advertising time varies according to financial need, and the North and West German radio services in the more populated areas have been enabled to dispense with it entirely.

The nine domestic radio services follow a similar program pattern: the First Program, on the air twenty-four hours daily; the Second Program, seventeen to nineteen hours daily, both carried on AM and FM; and the Third Program, on FM only for five to seven hours. An effort is made to provide contrast in content between the two generally available programs as well as interplay and alternation between serious commentary and entertainment on each program. Talk and discussion predominate on the Third Program, which also carries special broadcasts for minority groups such as the foreign *Gastarbeiter* (guest workers). Observers are in general agreement that commentary and discussion shows give expression to a wide variety of diverse opinions, with no single political party or social group gaining an undue amount of time to air its views.

In 1960, by a federal act of parliament, two federal public broadcasting corporations were established for the purpose of broadcasting abroad. *Deutschlandfunk*, directed primarily to the Democratic Republic, broadcasts a German-language program around the clock on longwave and mediumwave frequencies. In the evening, it also broadcasts fourteen foreign-language programs plus additional German-language courses for Europe. *Deutsche Welle* is the shortwave broadcasting service of the Federal Republic, carrying programs in thirty-three languages to all parts of the world; relay stations are in Rwanda and Portugal, and another is under construction in Malta. These two federal radio stations are also members of the ARD, the consortium formed by the regional radios.

The radio listener in the Federal Republic has a wide choice of programs, even with an inexpensive radio set. He can usually hear one or two neighboring regional radios as well as the two major programs of his own area. *Deuschlandfunk*, which mostly uses taped material from the regional radios, is also available in many sections of the country. The American and British forces maintain radio networks in the country that especially attract many younger listeners even though the announcements are in English. The United States-managed Radio in the American Sector (RIAS) broadcasts in German primarily for East Berlin but attracts listeners in the West as well. East German broadcasts, whether aimed specifically at the Federal Republic or not, can be heard by many listeners. Radio Moscow broadcasts several hours a day in German, and the Voice of America and the BBC carry programs in German as well. The Saarland has, through special exemption, licensed the powerful commercial station Europa One, which broadcasts primarily in French. From outside Germany, another commercial station, Radio Luxembourg, broadcasts in German for nineteen hours daily, with news on the hour and popular music.

TELEVISION

The television pattern in the Federal Republic developed out of the radio broadcasting arrangements (see Radio, this ch.). When television operations started again in December 1952 (the world's first regular TV program had been inaugurated in Berlin in March 1935), production was firmly in the hands of the radio stations operated by the *Länder*. By 1955 a full interregional network had been formed, with all the regional broadcasting stations participating.

In the mid-1970s there were three channels available to the West German viewer. The First Program, or "German Television" (Deutsches Fernsehen), run by the ARD, is a teamwork operation of the nine regional stations, transmitted nationally over VHF channels. Each of the nine stations produces programs for transmission over the entire network according to a quota system, roughly in proportion to the number of television set licensees in its area. The 1974 breakdown by percent was: West German, 25; North German, 20; Bavaria, 17; Hesse, 8; Free Berlin, 8; South German, 8; Southwest German, 8; Bremen, 3; and Saarland, 3.

The news and political commentary programs are the responsibility of the North German station; they maintain a high reputation for objectivity and fair presentation of a multiplicity of views. Sports programs, widely popular, are the province of the West German station.

The First Program is on the air from 5:00 P.M. until midnight and longer on Saturday and Sunday. The early hours of the evening, from 5:00

P.M. to 8:00 P.M., are mostly devoted to separate regional programs, but at 8:00 P.M. all stations begin to carry the joint program. There is no central studio; one hour of the evening's joint program may emanate from Hamburg, the next from Munich, and so on.

The Second Program (Zweites Deutsches Fernsehen—ZDF) is not the province of the nine regional services; instead, it is produced by a separately established public corporation for television, with headquarters and central studios in Mainz. It grew out of an agreement among the *Länder* in 1961, following Chancellor Adenauer's attempt—widely criticized as arbitrary and undemocratic—to gain federal control of a portion of the radio-television media. In February 1961 the Federal Constitutional Court ruled that radio-television constitutes a "cultural phenomenon" which, insofar as the state may engage in such activities, falls solely within the competence of the *Länder*. Thereupon the *Länder*, which despite their opposition to Adenauer's proposals recognized the need for a separate television channel, proceeded to approve the setting up of the public corporation ZDF, to be financed out of 30 percent of the television receiver license revenues of the nine ARD stations. The officers and members of the controlling bodies of ZDF are selected from the political parties according to their strength in the *Länder*.

The ZDF, which began regular broadcasting in April 1963, is transmitted nationally from Mainz over ultrahigh frequency (UHF) channels only; 96 percent of the country's television sets are equipped to receive its UHF signals. Hours on the air are about the same as those of the First Program, and program plans are coordinated with ARD through a process of consultation. The program makeup of the two networks is not dissimilar, although ZDF devotes a greater proportion of its time to television plays and films; each devotes 20 to 25 percent of its time to news and current events. A joint ARD-ZDF program is televised each morning to the Democratic Republic viewers via transmitters in the eastern part of the Federal Republic; the three-hour telecast consists primarily of repeats from the major network programs.

The Third Program—ARD's second— is operated by the nine *Länder* services individually over UHF channels. Somewhat similar to the Public Broadcasting Service in the United States or to the BBC-TV Second Program, it features educational programming, telecasts for foreign-language minorities, and technical and cultural programs for limited audiences. Each regional service carries its own programs, of varying duration, unlike the national hookup of the First Program.

Like radio broadcasting, television advertising time is strictly limited, and sponsored programs are prohibited. On the First Program, advertising is restricted to five-minute blocks of spot commercials one after the other, presented only during the regional telecasts from 6:00 P.M. to 8:00 P.M., and not to exceed twenty minutes during this two-hour period. ZDF's restrictions on advertising are similar, and in neither instance is the annual advertising income more than supplementary to the major source of income from the licensing fees charged to the owners of television receivers.

Some 17 million television sets and 20 million radios are licensed. Viewers residing on the eastern border are also able to receive East German television programs. Color television was introduced in 1967, and its use continues to expand.

Cooperation between the Federal Republic television networks and other West European television corporations is conducted within the framework of Eurovision. Program exchanges, joint telecasts, and Europe-wide telecasting of major events from sports to politics are frequently arranged. East European stations are sometimes brought in via Intervision, and United States and other networks around the world are occasionally involved as well. An example of this was the worldwide broadcasts of the summer 1972 Olympics.

In the developing countries particularly, there is a growing demand for television material from the Federal Republic and from other Western countries, synchronized in the relevant languages. To service these requirements, the Trans-Tel corporation has been established jointly by the ARD, the ZDF, and the federal government.

FILM

The German film industry, a world leader in the 1920s, was slow in recovering after the war and has not yet regained any real measure of popular or critical acclaim. The main prewar film studios were in East Berlin and were thus permanently lost to the film industry of the Federal Republic. Existing film property, transferred from the famed Universal Film Joint-Stock Company (Universum Film Aktiengesellschaft—UFA) to government ownership during the war, was requisitioned by the Allies as part of the decartelization drive. Veteran filmmakers had either fled the country during the Nazi period or were compromised politically and unable to participate in filmmaking during the occupation period.

Since the late 1940s, fears of creating another huge film monopoly kept the industry divided into a number of small firms, too short of capital to be viable. Just as some of these restrictions were being lifted in the late 1950s, the increasing popularity of television drastically reduced the number of regular filmgoers (there were 167 million film attendances in 1970 against 818 million in 1956) and caused new financial difficulties for the film producers.

The basic fare in the cinemas is still the foreign-made film, with domestic films accounting for only 114 of the 397 new feature films shown in 1969. Yet in 1969, for the first time since the end of the war, more German than American films were shown. Today the film city of Geisel-gasteig in Bavaria is one of the largest studio complexes in Europe.

Government aid has been of increasing help to the industry. An independent film-rating agency set up by the *Länder* awards marks of recommendation that earn a proportionate reduction in the entertainment tax. Since 1968, in accord with a film-promotion law passed by the Bundestag in late 1967, government subsidies have been granted on a merit basis: a filmmaker whose last film won a measure of approval may apply for a subsidy to assist him in producing his next film.

Self-censorship is provided by the film industry's voluntary censorship board (Freiwillige Selbstkontrolle—FSK), composed of representatives of the industry, the public (youth, churches, and labor), and the government. In the early postwar years, the FSK was concerned not only with maintaining the moral proprieties but also with forestalling the showing of scenes that might carry the faintest taint of militarism or neo-nazism. Thus, some critics have charged that the board has served to foster a timid mediocrity among filmmakers. The passage of time has served to liberalize the board's perspective, however, and it has gradually become more permissive both morally and politically.

BOOK PUBLISHING AND LIBRARIES

The German book-publishing industry has a long tradition, dating back to the invention of the printing press by Johannes Gutenberg in the middle of the fifteenth century. The industry suffered great damage during World War II, and the prewar publishing center of Leipzig came under control of the Soviet occupation zone. The licensing regulations applied to newspapers and magazines in the Western zones applied also to book publishing, but recovery was slower for the book trade because of the need for more capital to make a sustained effort in book publishing and because of the higher cost of books that few could afford.

In the mid-1970s Munich led in the production of books, followed closely by West Berlin, Stuttgart, and Frankfurt. In number of titles produced annually, the Federal Republic ranked fifth in the world. In 1969, 35,577 titles were published. Book clubs, which are said to have originated in Germany, deliver a substantial portion of total copies printed to their 5 million members. As elsewhere, the growth of the paperback industry has been phenomenal over the past twenty years.

The International Book Fair held annually at Frankfurt is a major event and is attended by representatives from all over the world. In 1970 the 3,356 exhibitors included 848 German publishers and 2,508 foreign publishers.

German libraries, which suffered enormous losses first from Nazi purges and then from the effects of war, have largely been restored to their former eminence. The loss of the central German Library in Leipzig to the Democratic Republic was a painful one, but the new German Library in Frankfurt, inaugurated in 1946, serves a similar function as a library of public records and a bibliographical center for German-language literature.

Three levels of public libraries have long existed in Germany—Land, municipality, and university. Until the Nazi era their control was in local hands. In 1949 local authority to administer the public libraries was

203

restored, but the federal government assists with small injections of funds where needed and with coordinating efforts to bring the various libraries into a closer mutual relationship.

FOREIGN INFORMATION ACTIVITIES

Foreign broadcasting activities within the borders of the Federal Republic have continued since the immediate postwar period through special agreement between the Federal Republic and the Western powers. The Allied Forces organized broadcasting networks for their own troops at the end of the war, and these activities are still carried on, with the American Armed Forces Network (AFN) the most elaborate. From West Berlin the American-operated RIAS continues to beam programs in German primarily to the Democratic Republic, as it has done since the early days of the occupation. The Voice of America maintains facilities in Munich for its broadcasts in German and other European languages.

Radio Free Europe (RFE) and Radio Liberty, which have their headquarters in Munich, broadcast to Eastern Europe and the Soviet Union, respectively. RFE broadcasts are directed to Bulgaria, Czechoslovakia, Hungary, Poland, and Romania, in the languages of those countries. Radio Liberty broadcasts in Russian and such other Soviet languages as Ukrainian, Armenian, and Turkestani to the peoples of the Soviet Union. These RFE and Radio Liberty broadcasts began in the early postwar period and have continued without a break despite past arguments over their merits and their financing. In October 1973 the president of the United States signed a bill authorizing US$50.2 million for their operations during the fiscal year (FY) 1974. Under the terms of this bill, the radio stations will henceforth be publicly financed and controlled by a newly created United States Board for International Broadcasting.

SECTION II. POLITICAL

CHAPTER 11

GOVERNMENTAL SYSTEM

When the Basic Law (Grundgesetz) of the Federal Republic was ratified in 1949, the occupation of Germany by the Western Allies was technically ended, although certain prerogatives continued to be accorded to the occupying powers under the Occupation Statute until 1952. It was 1955 before full sovereignty was granted to the new republic.

The founders of the republic were constantly mindful of assuring that neither the weaknesses of the Weimar Republic nor the excesses of Hitler's Third Reich be repeated. Consequently, the Basic Law decreed that sovereignty lay with the people, and it established machinery to ensure that fundamental rights could not be arbitrarily abrogated by the government.

Parliamentary and federal principles are combined in the Basic Law. The president serves as head of state; the chancellor and his cabinet make up the government. The legislature is bicameral, composed of the Bundestag (Federal Diet) and the Bundesrat (Federal Council). Through the Bundesrat, the *Länder* (states; sing., *Land*) have a direct voice in the legislative process, as the Bundesrat is composed of members of *Land* governments who are able to articulate *Land* interests at the federal level. Constitutional issues are subject to review by the Federal Constitutional Court (Bundesverfassungsgericht).

Three court structures exist—constitutional, ordinary, and special. Constitutionality of law is determined by the Federal Constitutional Court. Ordinary law, that is, civil and criminal law, falls within the jurisdiction of a four-level system of courts beginning at the local level and ending at the Federal Court of Justice (Bundesgerichtshof). Cases not covered by these courts (that is, cases involving administration, financial affairs, labor, and social security) are relegated to special courts in the *Länder* or at the federal level. Operations of the judicial system are frequently delayed because of innumerable legal proceedings, which are occasioned by the easy access to, and the low cost of, legal aid.

BASIC LAW

After Great Britain, France, and the United States combined their occupation zones in 1948, the occupation authorities instructed the

German administrators of the *Länder* in the Western zones to call a constituent assembly:

> To draft a democratic constitution which will establish for the participating states a governmental structure of federal type which is best adapted to the eventual reestablishment of German unity at present disrupted, and which will protect the rights of the participating states, provide adequate central authority, and contain guarantees of individual rights and freedoms.

The Germans in the three Western zones did not want to be held responsible for perpetuating the division of their country and therefore requested that the constituent assembly be referred to as the Parliamentary Council and that any resultant document establishing governmental principles be called the Basic Law rather than a constitution. The work of the council was to be viewed as a temporary guide until the country was reunited.

Once such concessions were granted, the German administrators called on the *Land* diets to select delegates to the Parliamentary Council on the basis of party strengths within the diets. The sixty-five-member council met in Bonn on September 1, 1948, and chose Konrad Adenauer as chairman. A draft of the Basic Law was approved by the occupation authorities and was adopted by the council on May 8, 1949. The law was ratified by all the *Land* diets except Bavaria's, which objected to the amount of power given the federal government but accepted the jurisdiction of the law. It was promulgated May 22, 1949, and by September the organs of the Federal Republic were in operation in what the Basic Law described as a democratic and social federal state.

The Basic Law drew heavily on the Weimar Constitution of 1919 and on the constitutions that were promulgated in the *Länder* after World War II. Its transitional nature was clearly expressed in the preamble and in Article 146, which stated that "this Basic Law shall cease to be in force on the day on which a constitution adopted by a free decision of the German people comes into force."

To amend the Basic Law a two-thirds vote in both legislative houses is necessary. By 1972 the law had been amended twenty-six times. The Federal Constitutional Court judges the validity of the Basic Law and the constitutionality of amendments and other statutes.

The authors also stressed the break with nazism by introducing an internationalist feature into the Basic Law. The Federal Republic resolved to "serve the peace of the World as an equal partner in a united Europe." Article 24 provided that "the Federation may, by legislation, transfer sovereign powers to international institutions," and "may join a system of mutual collective security," and would subject itself to rules of international law.

Articles 20 through 37 of the Basic Law define the federal character of the government and establish that sovereignty resides in the people. Article 31 specifies that federal law overrides *Land* law. The law defines federal, *Land*, and concurrent authority. It establishes a cabinet form of government and a bicameral legislature. The cabinet is headed by a chancellor, who is responsible to the Bundestag. A system of checks and balances exists among the three branches of government—executive, legislative, and judiciary.

The law outlines the concepts of the social-market economy, or limited free-enterprise system, in broad terms, but trades and professions face some state regulations. The right to own and inherit property is guaranteed, subject to the injunction that property "should serve the public good." Land, natural resources, and means of production may be transferred to public ownership by law and on the payment of legally determined compensation. This provision of Article 15 has never been implemented.

The law delineates the rights of the federal government and the *Länder* to assess taxes and defines the financial relationship between the federal government and the *Länder*. The federal government owns and operates the railroads, roads and waterways, and postal and telecommunications services; a federal bank issues notes and currency. The *Länder* are independent of the federal government in establishing their budgets.

Like the Weimar Constitution, the Basic Law dedicated the German state to the principles that: sovereignty rests with the people; the state is governed by the rule of law; and the maintenance of the individual's freedom and dignity is the highest goal of the state. These concepts are elucidated in the first nineteen articles and "bind the legislature, the executive, and the judiciary as directly enforceable law." These basic rights may not be amended.

Enumerated rights include equality before the law; freedom of speech, assembly, press, and worship; freedom from prejudice based on race, religion, or political beliefs; sanctity of the home and family; the right to form associations; and the right of conscientious objection to military service. Individuals may freely choose their profession, place of work, and training. The government may not infringe upon these rights. A 1968 amendment granted the people the right to resist a person or organization that attempted to overthrow the constitutional system.

EXECUTIVE BRANCH

President

The chief of state is the president of the Federal Republic, who symbolizes the supreme state authority and is, theoretically, above the partisan activities of political parties and factions. His powers are principally formal or ceremonial. He represents the state in its international relations, receiving ambassadors, signing and proclaiming treaties; promulgates the federal laws; appoints and dismisses the chancellor; convenes and dissolves the Bundestag; appoints federal ministers, judges, and military officers, and exercises the power of pardon and reprieve. But he no longer has a direct mandate from the people as did the president of the Weimar Republic, and he has limited authority to act on his own discretion. His powers were deliberately restricted to avoid repetition of the abuses of the Weimar Republic.

The chancellor, who is appointed by the president and who is usually the leader of the strongest political party in the Bundestag, requires the approval of that body. The president appoints ministers and judges on the recommendation of the chancellor; his promulgation of laws passed by the parliament is merely a formality because he cannot veto legislation or indefinitely withhold his signature. A cabinet minister or the chancellor must countersign presidential decrees. In exceptional circumstances the president may act with the approval of the chancellor and the Bundesrat. His right to dissolve the Bundestag is limited by the Basic Law.

The principal initiative the president can take is to delay promulgation of a law by deciding to submit it to the Federal Constitutional Court for judicial review. Once a new government is in office, the president has no constitutional influence over it. He does not attend cabinet meetings. His influence over the chancellor and the Bundestag rests on his personal prestige. If the Bundestag fails to pass legislation that the government considers to be urgent, the cabinet may request that the president, acting jointly with the Bundesrat, declare a legislative emergency. The president, in turn, may exercise a restraining influence by his reluctance to declare an emergency or to dissolve the Bundestag. The president is also able to apply pressure or exert his influence when he confers with the political parties concerning the nomination of a new chancellor.

The president is elected for a five-year term and may be reelected once. The Federal Assembly (Bundesversammlung) exists solely to elect the president. It is composed of over 1,000 delegates, including all the members of the Bundestag plus an equal number of members chosen by the *Land* diets according to proportional representation. The vote is taken without debate. To be elected, a candidate must receive an absolute majority on the first or second ballot or a plurality on the third. The purpose of the indirect election is to choose a candidate who would be acceptable to a broad range of the people and would not be influence by partisan politics.

The president must be at least forty years of age, may not be engaged in commercial activity or hold another salaried office, and must be eligible to vote in general elections. He may be impeached by a two-thirds vote in either the Bundestag or Bundesrat if he has willfully violted the Basic Law or any other federal law. The impeachment trial is heard before the Federal Constitutional Court.

The president is assisted by an administrative staff primarily concerned with matters of protocol and public relations, which is headed by a civil servant having the title of state secretary *(Staatssekretär)*. A vice president is not provided by the Basic Law, which specifies that the president of the Bundesrat shall act as temporary chief of state in the president's absence from the country or if the position should become vacant. If a president should die in office, a successor is to be elected within thirty days of his death.

Chancellor and Cabinet

Executive power rests with the chancellor as head of the government. He is nominated by the president and must receive an absolute majority vote of the Bundestag to be installed in office. A candidate receiving such a majority vote must be appointed by the president. If a majority of the Bundestag cannot agree on a candidate within two weeks of a vacancy, the president has seven days in which he may either appoint a plurality candidate or dissolve the Bundestag and call for new elections to that house. The chancellor is usually the leader of the strongest party in parliament. Although he is elected by and responsible to the Bundestag, he alone is responsible for designing and conducting policy. He outlines his proposed policies to the Bundestag before the vote, which is taken without debate.

A chancellor can be dismissed by the Bundestag only through a constructive vote of no-confidence; that is, the Bundestag must simultaneously vote a chancellor out of office and approve his successor both by absolute majority. If a chancellor submits a motion of confidence to the Bundestag and the house votes against him but does not choose a successor, the chancellor may ask the federal president to dissolve the lower house and call new elections. Barring a vote of no-confidence and majority approval of a successor, the chancellor's term is usually the four-year term of the Bundestag.

The chancellor establishes the general policy of the Federal Republic, but the ministers he selects to assist and advise him in administering the governmental departments may have considerable freedom of action. Ministers are appointed and dismissed by the president on the recommendation of the chancellor. They are usually members of the Bundestag. They are not individually responsible to the Bundestag, but the chancellor is responsible for their actions. The number of ministries varies according to the needs of the times and the policies of the chancellor. In 1974 the newly elected chancellor, Helmut Schmidt, named fifteen ministers (see fig. 10).

The cabinet ministers, who advise the chancellor on policy matters, are aided by state secretaries and the heads of interested agencies or departments. Cabinet meetings are secret and informal; decisions are usually reported as having been unanimous, but there is no doubt that the decision of the chancellor is final.

Ministerial duties range from examining issues and drafting bills to executing directives. Ministers appear in parliament and share actively in molding political decisions. The Bundestag may ask ministers to come to its chamber; likewise, a minister may ask to address the Bundestag.

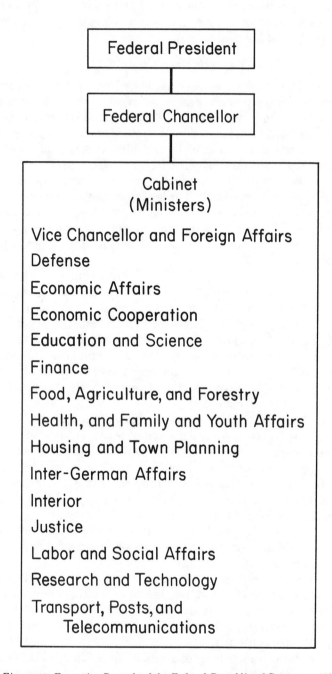

Figure 10. *Executive Branch of the Federal Republic of Germany, 1974*

Ministers enjoy a large degree of autonomy in the administration of their offices, but they usually rely on the permanent bureaucracy, the civil service, which staffs the ministries. The cabinet is organized functionally to handle specific aspects of the federal administrative responsibilities. Because the administration of federal law is delegated largely to the *Land* governments, the federal ministries tend to be small. The most important are foreign affairs, economic affairs, finance, defense, and interior, which includes internal security.

In 1967 the position of parliamentary state secretary was established to aid ministers. Appointment is made by the president on the recommendation of the concerned minister. Candidates must be members of parliament. They share in forming policies, and they present the government's view during formal question periods in parliament.

The chancellor is also assisted by a staff of civil servants known as the Chancellor's Office (Kanzleramt) under the direction of a state secretary who works closely with the chancellor. Also attached to the Chancellor's Office and responsible only to that office are the Press and Information Office and the Federal Intelligence Service.

LEGISLATIVE BRANCH

Bundestag

Bundestag (Federal Diet) deputies are elected for four-year terms. They must be at least twenty-one years of age and eligible to vote. One-half of the deputies are elected by direct vote in single-member districts and one-half by party designation on the basis of proportional representation. The number of deputies representing the ten federal *Länder* gradually increased from 402 in 1949 to 496 in 1973, including twenty-two deputies from West Berlin who have an advisory function only.

Through the procedure of placing party leaders at the head of *Länder* lists, parliament is largely composed of professional politicians and civil servants. In 1969 there were 32.2 percent of the Bundestag members who were such public officials as mayors and county council chairmen. The remainder represented a variety of experience reflecting the backgrounds of the electorate. For example, 9 percent of the delegates were farmers, labor leaders, big businessmen, or professors, among others. Thirty-one women were elected in 1969, and the average age dropped from fifty years to 48.7 years.

The Bundestag makes its own rules of procedure and elects its officers. Deputies are protected by the Basic Law from prosecution for any views they express in the legislature. Their primary duties are to help develop legislation, to elect a chancellor, and to serve as a check on the federal executive.

Party discipline is strong, particularly among the Socialists. Legislative activities are dominated by parliamentary party groups known as *Fraktionen* (sing., *Fraktion*), thereby making it difficult for a deputy to accomplish much outside his party's caucus. Deputies who belong to the same party can form a *Fraktion* if they can align at least fifteen members. These groups hold caucuses to determine positions and to choose spokesmen for major issues in the Bundestag.

The president of the Bundestag is by custom a member of the largest *Fraktion*. He is elected by the members, presides over the sessions and is responsible, with the assistance of a Secretariat, for maintaining order in the Bundestag and for management of its administrative affairs. He has four deputies, called vice presidents, who are elected by the members on the basis of proportional representation among the *Franktionen*.

By use of written questions, which must be signed by at least fifteen deputies, the Bundestag can query the government; and it does so about 400 times during a four-year session. The government is expected to respond within two weeks. A more common inquiry method is the so-called questions for oral answer procedure. According to this system ministers respond to written questions in the Bundestag during an hour set aside as question time.

An important body of the Bundestag is the Council of Elders, which is composed of the Bundestag president, one vice president for each major party, and members of *Fraktionen* in proportion to their strength in the house. Members are chosen by age, not seniority. The council supervises the legislative calendar and distributes committee chairmanships and assignments in proportion to party representation. Consequently chairmanships are shared rather than monopolized by the government party. By agreement, however, the majority party is conceded a majority on all committees.

The major burden of legislative work is borne by committees, which are organized according to governmental departments. In 1969 there were twenty-three, plus one special committee, each having fifteen to twenty-seven members, supported by a staff of civil servants. Membership is proportionate to party strength in the house.

Each committee handles a specific category of legislation and performs some of the preliminary research and investigation that influence the decisions of the assembly. Special investigating committees, formed on demand by at least 25 percent of the house, are called to examine economic and social questions affecting legislation; cases of mismanagement or misconduct; and some criminal and corruption cases. The Permanent Committee serves as a check on the executive when the Bundestag is not in session, but it is not authorized to pass a vote of no-confidence.

Committees are empowered to call before them any member of the government; at the same time the government can voice its viewpoints in committee deliberations. Their meetings are not secret, but few reports of their activity reach the public.

Several reforms were made in Bundestag procedures in 1969. Among the issues were a reassessment of deputies' rights and privileges, particularly concerning their working conditions. Newly elected deputies had suffered inadequate office amenities such as cramped quarters and lacked a professional staff. After the reform they were permitted to hire at least one assistant, and more officials were hired to further help house members. The Council of Elders was granted broader powers and was no longer required to have unanimous votes for decisions. To facilitate parliamentary procedures, the council was entitled to plan its schedule several months in advance as opposed to its previous practice of planning only a few weeks ahead. An attempt was made to bring more spontaneity into Bundestag debates by eliminating the reading of speeches and by establishing time limits for speeches of forty-five minutes for a party spokesman and fifteen minutes for others.

Bundesrat

Land governments choose delegates to the Bundesrat (Federal Council) from among members of the *Land* cabinets, invariably headed by the ministers-president of the *Länder*. The Bundesrat does not have a fixed term, and vacancies are filled as they occur.

The Bundesrat consists of forty-five members, four of whom represent West Berlin and participate on a restricted basis. The forty-one voting seats are distributed among the *Länder* according to population. Each *Land* has a minimum of three seats, but if population exceeds 2 million the allocation rises to four; population of 6 million or more warrants five seats. Bavaria, Lower Saxony, North Rhine-Westphalia, and Baden-Württemberg each have five; Rhineland-Palatinate, Schleswig-Holstein, and Hesse each have four; and Bremen, Hamburg, and Saar each have three. Each *Land* delegation votes as a bloc in accordance with instructions from its government.

The Bundesrat selects its own presiding officer annually from among the ministers-president of the *Länder*. The presiding officer succeeds to the federal presidency if the position falls vacant. Plenary meetings of the Bundesrat are infrequent, short, and orderly, and usually confirm work already done in committee. There are fifteen committees, which are staffed by civil servants and include representatives of all *Länder*. Delegates can attend Bundestag committee meetings, and their requests to speak before Bundestag members must be honored.

In the legislative process, if a Bundesrat vote is required by the Basic Law, the deputies can either approve the bill or do nothing. If they do not act, the bill becomes law in two weeks or, if the house calls the Conference Committee and it votes favorably, the bill becomes law one week after the vote. Coordinating the interests of the *Länder* and the federal government is the primary purpose of the Bundesrat. As guardian of *Länder* interests, it has an absolute veto over legislation affecting relationships with the federal government in administrative, monetary, or territorial matters and over constitutional amendments. For other legislation the Bundesrat has a suspensive veto, which can be overridden by a simple majority of the Bundestag or a two-thirds majority, depending on the vote by which the Bundesrat vetoed the bill.

Legislative Process

A bill may be initiated by the executive, the Bundesrat, or the Bundestag. Most bills, however, originate in an executive department, where they are prepared by a trained staff of civil servants and approved by the cabinet before being submitted to the legislature. Such bills are first sent to the Bundesrat for comment and then to the Bundestag for consideration. The Bundesrat has three weeks to give its opinion. It sends bills to committee, and a report is forwarded to the *Länder* governments, thereby assuring *Länder* consultation. A bill initiated by the Bundesrat is sent to the cabinet, which gives its opinion and then sends it on to the Bundestag. Bills originating in the Bundestag can be voted on by that body without being submitted to outside approval.

In the Bundestag a bill receives three readings. The first consists of brief initial discussion on the floor of the house before the bill is sent to the appropriate committee. Debate at this stage is rare. After a thorough consideration in committee, at which time party positions are upheld, the bill is reported out with recommendations. A second reading on the floor follows, and a detailed debate is held to resolve differences. Often only one spokesman for each party participates. A bill may be sent back to committee or, if the bill is accepted as presented by the committee, the third reading takes place immediately. Otherwise, amendments are printed and, after forty-eight hours, a nominal third reading is followed by the final vote, either by roll call, show of hands, standing vote or, in case of serious doubt, by the deputies leaving the hall and returning through doors marked "yes," "no," and "abstain." Secret ballots are not permitted for bills. If passed—a simple majority vote is needed—the bill goes to the Bundesrat, which may convoke the Conference Committee to seek accord on disagreements. If accepted by both houses the bill goes to the federal president for signature and promulgation. Bills that are not acted on during a session of parliament must begin the cycle anew at the next session.

Besides its legislative role, the Bundesrat also establishes rules for executing *Land* and local programs and participates in electing Federal Constitutional Court judges. Under certain conditions if a deadlock occurs between the Bundestag and the cabinet, the Bundesrat and the federal president can suspend the legislative function of the Bundestag.

JUDICIAL BRANCH

The Basic Law, the Law to Restore Legal Uniformity, and an 1877 law on the structure of the courts form the bases of the Federal Republic court system. Civil and criminal court proceedings are described in procedural codes. A catalogue of norms rather than precedents is used in deciding cases. The Federal Constitutional Court is the highest court in

214

the country. The Federal Court of Justice (Bundesgerichtshof) is the highest of the regular, four-level court system. Lower courts operate in the *Länder* and consist of local courts *(Amtsgerichte)*, regional courts *(Landgerichte)*, and courts of appeal *(Oberlandesgerichte)*.

Local courts are found in most towns. They hear civil and criminal cases, and they may have one or more judges. In minor civil cases and criminal actions local courts have original jurisdiction. Civil cases are heard by a single judge, whereas criminal cases of more than ordinary scope or importance can be heard by a judge and two lay assessors who help decide guilt and punishment.

Regional courts, located in most large cities, are less numerous. These courts have original jurisdiction in civil cases not handled by the local courts and hear appeals from local courts. Such hearings involve complete retrials of the cases, not merely reviews of the laws concerned. Civil cases before the regional courts, whether of original or appellate jurisdiction, are heard by panels of three judges. The court may constitute itself a commercial chamber *(Handelskammer)*, in which case the judge is joined by two commercial judges *(Handelsrichter)* who are merchants or industrialists serving on an honorary basis.

Regional courts have both original and appellate jurisdiction in criminal cases. Original jurisdiction extends from offenses that are beyond the competence of local courts to serious crimes. The number of judges varies. For serious crimes, such as murder, the bench is occupied by three judges and seven lay jurors, who determine legal questions and guilt or innocence. In less serious criminal cases, whether original or appellate, the court consists of three judges and two lay jurors.

Appeals courts have civil and criminal sections, called senates. Each section has several panels of three judges appointed to the court for life by the *Land* minister of justice. The judges review appeals from the regional courts that are subordinate to them. The courts decide points of law; they do not reconsider the entire case. They may confirm or negate a sentence of a lower court or order a retrial by a lower court. They are the final appeals courts for cases originating in local courts and are courts of second instance for regional cases.

The Federal Supreme Court at Karlsruhe is the only court having both original and appellate jurisdiction at the federal level. The Supreme Court has criminal and civil senates, each staffed by five judges chosen for life from among the career judiciary by the minister of justice, who is aided in his choice by a committee of *Land* ministers of justice and Bundestag members. Its appellate jurisdiction applies to serious criminal cases originally decided by regional courts. Appellate jurisdiction in civil cases is likewise limited to cases originating in regional courts. It has original jurisdiction in treason cases.

The Federal Court of Justice is concerned with maintaining legal uniformity in the Federal Republic. It tends, therefore, to base its decisions on precedent, although it is not bound to do so.

A system of special courts exists at the *Land* and federal levels composed of administrative, labor, social security, and finance courts. A high court of review at the federal level is above each type of special court. Administrative courts provide a system for challenging administrative decisions. Questions evolving from *Land* or federal administrative decisions and administrative actions themselves are subject to review if an individual so requests. The Federal Administrative Court is in Berlin.

Labor courts consist of local and appellate courts as well as a high court of review. These tribunals handle cases arising out of disputes between employers and employees over collective contracts, labor laws, and working conditions. They are staffed by professional and lay judges. The Federal Labor Court sits in Kassel.

Cases concerning welfare administration are dealt with by the social security court. The Federal Social Security Court also sits in Kassel. Cases involving taxes and levies are settled by the finance courts, the highest of which is the Federal Finance Court in Munich.

Constitutional courts decide cases involving questions on the Basic Law. The Federal Constitutional Court is concerned with the constitutional review of legislation, disputes between units and levels of government, and complaints about invasion of individual or group rights by agencies of government. It rules on suits by the government to outlaw political parties that are subversive to the constitutional system. It also serves as a court of appeals to determine the outcome of disputed Bundestag elections, although this provision has never been used. If a president is impeached, he is tried in this court. It also determines the acceptability of international law. In these ways it serves as a check on the executive and legislative branches. The twenty-four court justices are senior federal judges and other members of the legal profession. One-half are chosen by a twelve-man commission of the Bundestag and one-half by the Bundesrat, thereby ensuring that one party will not dominate the court. Judges must be over forty years of age. One-third of the judges are appointed for life; the remainder serve eight-year terms, which are staggered to avoid a large turnover of justices at one time. Justices can be reelected but must retire at age sixty-eight.

Personnel of the judicial system include attorneys, prosecutors, and judges. In addition, large staffs of civil servants in administrative capacities are attached to the courts and to the federal or *Land* ministries of justice, under which the courts and prosecutors' offices are organized. These employees are part of the civil service rather than the judicial system, even though many civil servants are trained in the law. Attorneys are not part of the judicial hierarchy, although they may in rare cases be appointed to judicial positions. Prosecuting attorneys represent the *Länder* in preserving law and order; they initiate and prosecute charges against all lawbreakers. Prosecutors' offices are subordinate to the Ministry of Justice and subject to ministry directives and instructions. Within each *Land* is a General Public Prosecutor, who directs the activities of the prosecutors under his jurisdiction. At the top of the hierarchy of prosecutors is the Federal General Prosecutor, who is directly responsible to the minister of justice.

Judicial training usually takes six to seven years. After completing a university law course and passing an examination, which is uniform throughout the country, as aspiring judge undergoes an apprenticeship of 2½ years. A final examination is then given. In the early 1970s attempts were being made to change the system, particularly to shorten the training period to two years.

Judges are formally part of the civil service as employees or appointees of the state, but their independence is ensured both by law and by the practical provision that tenure is not dependent on administrative favor. Federal and *Land* ministers, however, may have considerable influence over promotions. At both levels, judges are appointed by the minister of justice and a committee consisting, in the case of federal appointments, of the *Land* ministers of justice and an equal number of members of the Bundestag and, in the case of *Land* appointments, of members chosen by the *Land* legislature. Judges of special administrative and other courts are appointed in a similar manner except that these courts are organized under ministries other than the Ministry of Justice.

CIVIL SERVICE

The civil service is a large, pervasive, highly trained, professional bureaucracy that exerts a conservative influence on governmental operations. The major divisions are official *(Beamte)*, clerical *(Angestellte)*, and manual *(Arbeiter)* employees. Officials are divided into four classes: ordinary, middle, higher, and highest, ranked according to the complexity of work performed and the degree of responsibility assumed. All classes are represented at the various levels of administration.

One to three years of training and an examination are requisites for the middle and higher grades. Secretaries, inspectors, and lower supervisory personnel are in these ranks. Rigorous training is pursued by those seeking the highest civil service positions. Besides a university degree—usually in law—and an examination, a three-year apprenticeship is required, followed by a general *Land* examination. Promotion from one class to another is rare. Clerical and manual workers are not promoted to official positions because of the nature of their jobs or their lack of education.

STATE AND LOCAL GOVERNMENT

State Government

Länder are responsible for providing the administrative machinery for the execution of federal laws and directives. Legislative authority derives from the residual powers of the the Basic Law according to Article 70: "The states have the power to legislate insofar as this Basic Law does not confer legislative powers on the Federation." Legislation regarding education, religion, and culture is the responsibility of the *Länder*. Mass media, public libraries, theaters, and museums are therefore subject to *Länder* control. *Länder* can also legislate on administrative matters concerning police, water resources, civil service, and health, but decisions must meet federal standards, and they require the authorization of federal authorities. *Land* control over the media was reaffirmed by a court decision in the 1960s. When the federal government attempted to establish a federal television network, the court ruled against the federal government on the basis that setting up stations was the prerogative of the *Länder*.

Land constitutions, which must conform to Basic Law requirements, provide for a governmental structure similar to that of the federal system. Ministers-president and their cabinets fill the executive role. Cabinets are usually small, and their duties are more administrative than legislative. Members are appointed by the ministers-president. Most *Länder* have popularly elected unicameral *Landtage* (legislatures; sing., *Landtag*) whose term is usually four years. Bavaria, the only exception, has a bicameral legislature with the second house known as the Senat. The Senat, however, is not as influential a body as the *Landtag*. Some of the large *Länder* are divided into administrative districts, each having a president appointed by the *Landtag*.

Länder share concurrent legislative authority with the federal government in matters such as civil and criminal law, law enforcement, courts, welfare, war damages and relief, war veterans and survivors, economic policy, scientific research, employment security, social security, health programs, traffic, and highway construction and maintenance. *Land* governments are funded by taxes on real property, inheritance, motor vehicles, beer, and gambling establishments. Federal, *Land*, and local governments share personal income tax and corporation tax revenues. Taxes on goods and services, so-called turnover taxes, are divided among federal and *Land* governments.

Local Government

Local governments are autonomous in local affairs, but most of their activities involve services for federal and *Land* governments. Consequently, local governments are bound by decisions of higher authorities. Within their own realm, the local authorities handle safety, planning, health, and welfare, and sometimes utilities, transportation, and cultural institutions.

Patterns of local government differ. The units of local government are the *Kreis* (county; pl., *Kreise*) and the *Gemeinde* (community; pl., *Gemeinden*). Size and population vary greatly among *Kreise* and *Gemeinden*. A city can also be a *Stadtkreis* (urban district); a rural

218

district is known as a *Landkreis*. Some cities are located within a *Kreis* but are large enough to be granted status separate from it and are known as *kreisfreie Städte*. These have their own autonomous governments for administration of local affairs.

The Basic Law guarantees to all localities freely elected representative assemblies. In most counties the executive official is known as the district president *(Landrat)*, in northwest areas as the senior county director *(Oberkreisdirektor)*, and in towns and cities usually as the mayor *(Bürgermeister)*. *Kreisfreie Städte* and *Landkreise* are headed by an administrative district president *(Regierungspräsident)* who is elected by representative assemblies except in Rhineland-Palatinate, the Saar, parts of Baden-Württemberg, and where he is appointed. A mayor can be directly elected or chosen by city councils. His office ranges from powerful to honorary.

City governments conform to one of three basic types. In Schleswig-Holstein, Lower Saxony, and Hesse each city has an elected city council, which chooses an executive council *(Magistrat)* whose chairman serves as mayor. Executive and legislative authority lie in the executive council. Administrative matters are handled by a city manager who is named by the executive council. The mayor plan prevails in the Rhenish areas and consists of an elected council, presided over by a mayor who dominates the council. The city council system is common in the southern areas and consists of an elected council, presided over by a mayor who is elected by either the council or the people. The council tends to be the dominant factor in this form of government. Some large cities are divided into districts, each of which has its own mayor and other officials, but these municipalities also have an elected assembly and a lord mayor as executive for matters concerning the whole city.

In Bremen and Hamburg, which are cities as well as *Länder*, the legislature is known as the *Bürgerschaft* (literally, citizenry). The *Bürgerschaft* elects the Senat, which in turn chooses the mayor. Mayors oversee the execution of federal and *Land* policies and are accountable to higher authorities.

West Berlin poses special problems. It functions as a self-contained governmental entity, although it accepts and follows decisions laid down for the Federal Republic. As long as it cannot be integrated more closely into the federation, West Berlin will presumably continue to be represented by nonvoting representatives in Bonn. Its own government consists of a lord mayor who, along with a cabinet, is elected by a popular assembly. Subordinate district levels of government duplicate the structure of the city government. District mayors constitute a special council for dealing with common problems.

Intergovernmental Cooperation

The primary duty of the *Länder* is to execute federal legislation. There are several levels of cooperation among the governing units. At the highest level *Länder* have a voice in federal decisionmaking by their representation in the *Bundesrat*. *Land* governments determine how their deputies vote, and the deputies vote as a bloc. To facilitate *Land* and federal cooperation many *Land* agencies have been developed to work closely with the federal government. Joint public policy action is undertaken particularly when *Länder* lack financial resources to execute a program and when the Bonn government does not have full authority to act. Such cooperation has been established in science, education, and urban planning. Partnerships among *Länder* exist for the purpose of legislating uniform policies. One such organization is the Permanent Conference of the *Länder* Ministers of Culture. Special offices and associations have also developed to improve intercity cooperation.

ELECTORAL SYSTEM

A 1970 amendment to the Basic Law lowered the minimum voting age to eighteen years. Common criminals and convicted Nazi war criminals are barred from voting. At age twenty-one a person may be a candidate for office. Candidates on the national and *Land* level are usually named by political parties, but local candidates may be backed by any group of voters, regardless of party affiliation.

By law, elections must take place on Sundays or public holidays. Federal elections for Bundestag deputies occur every four years unless a special election is called. Each voter casts a double ballot—one for a candidate in the voter's district and one for a party list of nominees representing the entire *Land*. Voting districts contain approximately the same number of voters, and necessary redistricting is implemented by the Constituency Boundary Commission.

Deputies are therefore elected by a combination of direct election and proportional representation. The second, or list, vote determines the number of seats a *Land* receives. The total number of seats, 496, is divided equally between district and party list seats. If a party receives at least 5 percent of the party list votes nationally or wins three seats by direct election, it will be represented proportionately in the Bundestag.

Land and local elections are scattered throughout the four-year interim between federal elections. Procedures differ among *Länder*, but national parties become greatly involved in *Land* and local elections because such contests serve as opportunities to test the government's popularity and to express the government's programs and plans. Campaigning may be brief, as in North Rhine-Westphalia in 1966, when the campaign was limited to five days.

CHAPTER 12

POLITICAL DYNAMICS

Political change characterized the Federal Republic from 1969 to 1974. The Social Democratic Party (SPD—see Glossary) became the ruling party in 1969 when it formed a coalition government with the Free Democratic Party (FDP—see Glossary). The newly elected chancellor, Willy Brandt, awakened the people to the need for fresh initiatives in Eastern Europe. Disenchantment developed, however, as some citizens believed their country was not benefiting sufficiently from agreements that had been made, particularly agreements with the German Democratic Republic. Inflation and energy shortages caused dissatisfaction with Brandt's domestic policies. Political activists, especially among young members of his own party, expressed strong disapproval of the SPD program. At times Brandt seemed to be on the verge of resigning. A spy scandal finally resolved the issue, and Brandt resigned in May 1974. His fellow party member and finance minister, Helmut Schmidt, was elected chancellor by the Bundestag (Federal Diet) the same month.

Political parties have a considerable role in the governing process in the Federal Republic. This circumstance developed partly because parties existed before the occupation powers permitted the Germans to establish an independent federal government, and after independence parties became a major source of recruitment for federal officials. In fact, the people regard recruitment of government officials as a party function.

Although numerous parties have been established since 1945, two became dominant, the conservative Christian Democratic Union (CDU—see Glossary) and the socialist-oriented SPD. The SPD was the only direct carryover from a prewar party that gained a sizable following. The organization, although dispersed by the Nazis, was able to regroup, and the depressed state of the postwar economy favored socialist measures for a rapid reconstruction. In 1959 the party made a major shift and dropped its program for a state-controlled economy.

The FDP does not compare numerically with either the CDU or the SPD but has served an important position as a partner in coalition governments. Its position in the political spectrum has shifted from the right to the center. The party stresses individual freedom and free enterprise.

Parties are permitted according to the Basic Law as long as they reflect democratic principles. Only two, a communist party and an extreme right-wing party, have been outlawed as unconstitutional by the Federal

Constitutional Court, although some communist parties have been recognized as legitimate since 1968.

EVENTS FROM 1969 TO 1974

The 1969 election marked a milestone in the history of the Federal Republic. For the first time in the post-World War II era the SPD attained enough Bundestag seats to form a coalition government with the FDP, and the CDU became the opposition party. The new coalition government was composed of the SPD, which held 224 Bundestag seats, and the FDP, which had thirty seats. Willy Brandt, who had served as mayor of West Berlin from 1957 to 1966 and then as vice chancellor and minister of foreign affairs, was elected chancellor. Brandt continued to hold the post of SPD chairman. Gustav Heinemann, an SPD member, had been elected president earlier in 1969. Brandt succeeded in helping the people of the Federal Republic recognize that boundaries established after World War II were unlikely to be changed. Specifically, he signed a treaty with Poland in 1970 that confirmed the Oder-Neisse river line as the boundary between the Democratic Republic and Poland, and he pledged that force would not be used to decide issues (see ch. 13).

Although the chancellor worked to bring about reform in economic, fiscal, educational, and social fields, the most publicized area of his policy was *Ostpolitik* (Eastern Policy), which included improving relations with the Soviet Union, the Democratic Republic, and other Warsaw Pact countries (see ch. 13). Relations with the Democratic Republic were a significant component of this policy. In his State of the Nation address on January 28, 1971, the chancellor spoke of the "necessary effort" to improve relations with the Democratic Republic, but he remained adamant that the Federal Republic would continue to strive for eventual reunification. Brandt stated that no treaty would stop the Federal Republic from seeking a peace that "will allow our nation to recover its unity through free self-determination."

Initially *Ostpolitik* developed considerable momentum. A series of negotiations was carried out between representatives of the Federal Republic and the Democratic Republic in attempts to define the relationship between the two governments. One of the resultant treaties, the Basic Political Treaty, confirmed the existence of two German states, thereby acknowledging the Democratic Republic as a sovereign state. The states agreed to exchange ministers and to cooperate on matters of mutual interest, such as science, telecommunications, and public health.

On the domestic scene Brandt succeeded in bringing about some tax reforms and improved social welfare benefits. Legislation concerning reform of foreign, property, and inheritance taxes was part of an extensive program to be implemented by 1978. Financial aid for families was expanded. The voice of workers in the management of companies —codetermination—was being increased when Brandt resigned. Workers hoped to be on an equal footing with their employers in discussing management issues.

From 1972 to 1974 Brandt's popularity fluctuated. After six of the coalition ministers resigned their posts and the chancellor lost his voting majority in 1972, a special federal election was called for the first time since the founding of the republic. The SPD-FDP coalition returned to power, having attained 54 percent of the vote. Brandt's reelection as chancellor gave him despite some opposition to his foreign policy, a mandate to continue his *Ostpolitik* plans.

In 1973 the Basic Political Treaty was ratified by the Bundestag, and both German states were accepted into the United Nations (UN). As the year drew to a close, however, Brandt faced opposition as a result of the Arab oil embargo, the energy shortage, inflation, party friction, and a resurgence of opposition to *Ostpolitik*. Criticism of the foreign policy stemmed from conservatives who believed that the Democratic Republic was gaining trade and political concessions regarding Berlin, whereas the Federal Republic received only promises concerning improved travel rights. When the Democratic Republic increased the amount of money that travelers from the Federal Republic must exchange upon entering East Berlin, opponents of *Ostpolitik* were further incensed.

Brandt's situation was further complicated by his party's loss of its long-held majority in elections for the Hamburg *Land* (state; pl. *Länder*) legislature in the spring of 1974. Speculations about his resignation appeared in the press, and he resigned on May 6, 1974. The immediate cause was the discovery of an East German spy, Günter Guillaume, who had been serving as Brandt's aide for party affairs and at one time had had access to classified materials. Brandt accepted responsibility for allowing Guillaume to penetrate the government of the Federal Republic. In his resignation announcement the chancellor noted that one reason for his decision was his negligence in allowing Guillaume to retain his position after Brandt had been warned that the aide was under suspicion and that a second reason centered on personal concerns.

The SPD immediately nominated the finance minister, Helmut Schmidt, as chancellor. Schmidt had earlier served as defense minister in Brandt's government and was deputy party leader. He was elected by 267 of the 492 Bundestag deputies' votes that were cast.

At his swearing in on May 16, 1974, the new chancellor stated that he would continue Brandt's foreign policy, but he acknowledged that domestic problems required immediate attention. Schmidt pinpointed specific issues. In hopes of attaining a simplified and just tax system, he would continue Brandt's reform program. Changes in income and wage taxes were among the new chancellor's aims. He also intended to augment codetermination to grant workers a larger voice in determining working and living conditions. Other areas of endeavor would be environmental protection and vocational training.

Political analysts expect Schmidt to stress Western European policies, to support European unity through the European Economic Community (EEC—also known as the Common Market), and to be more United States oriented than Brandt.

Schmidt regrouped an SPD–FDP coalition government but was immediately faced with opposition. Opponents endeavored to widen the rift that was developing between the coalition partners. In June elections in Lower Saxony the SPD lost votes, although it retained a one-man majority in the *Land* legislature.

Heinemann had announced that he would retire as president of the Federal Republic on June 30, 1974, because of his age, seventy-five years. Richard von Weizsäcker was the CDU nominee, and Walter Scheel ran on the FDP ticket in the subsequent election. Scheel, who had served as vice chancellor and foreign minister since 1969 and as party chairman, won the election to the presidency.

POLITICAL ORGANIZATIONS

Christian Democratic Union-Christian Social Union

The Christian Democratic Union (CDU), originating in part from the Center Party of the Second Reich and the Weimar Republic, was founded in 1945. It was intended to be a middle-class party having religious overtones, which have been demonstrated by its support of denominational schools, religious education, and a Christian approach to social issues. A modified free enterprise system and nationalization of basic industries were also part of the party program. Flexibility and vague generalities rather than clear ideological positions have characterized party platforms.

For more than a decade Konrad Adenauer was the binding force behind the CDU. Originally the party's support base came from industrialists and Roman Catholic trade union members, but the base soon spread to include a broader span of management and employee groups, unskilled and unorganized workers, women, nationalists, and conservative Protestants. The party claims a majority of the well-educated Germans, those in the upper echelons of the civil service, and those in professional groups. CDU popularity is also high in northern and southern rural areas. It can therefore be described as a "party of domestic coalitions." Until the 1960s the party faced little effective opposition because the power structures in industry, business, agriculture, the civil service, and the churches were made up of party members of followers. The CDU was equated with the leaders in these fields and in the government. The vagueness of the party platform was partially responsible for drawing together a wide spectrum of the population. A political science professor, Arnold Heidenheimer, believes that another motive for such diverse groups to unite was their fear of being overcome by left-wing parties. In early 1972 membership totaled 331,115.

Funding comes mainly from sources outside the party. Government subsidies are granted to the CDU, as they are to each party that has polled above 2.5 percent of the votes in the previous election.

The party is loosely organized on the *Land*, district, and local levels, except in some regions of North Rhine-Westphalia, where organization is more tightly woven. Every two years each *Land* party congress elects a *Land* party executive committee. Actual party authority emanates from these executive committees rather than from the federal executive committee. For example, *Land* and local party officials have a stronger voice than federal-level party officials in naming Bundestag candidates, as is the case in the other major parties. Delegates to the CDU federal congress are elected from the lower party levels on the basis of party membership and voting strength in the area concerned. They, in turn, elect some officials of the highest body in the party—the federal executive committee—at the annual party congress. Elected officials include a chairman, several deputy chairmen, a general secretary, and a treasurer. It is customary to elect a woman as a deputy chairwoman. In 1973 Helmut Kohl, head of the government of Rhineland-Palatinate, was elected chairman. In addition, the executive committee includes leaders of *Land* party organizations, the chief government and legislative representatives, and the leaders of the party's special interest groups, making a total of about sixty members. Positions on the federal level are more prestigious than powerful.

Interest groups are important to the CDU. Party members usually advance by means of interest group committees. Appointment to a *Land* list is frequently dependent upon one's role in an interest group.

Factions have developed within the party. In the 1960s there was a Gaullist faction, which followed the policies of the French president, Charles de Gaulle, with the exception of his Eastern European policy. The opponents were Atlantic oriented and sought friendship and special relations with the United States and the benefits of its nuclear umbrella. During the late 1960s the party became less concerned about the country's external security, and factions became oriented toward domestic issues. The right wing of the party was linked to conservative business and agricultural interests, and the left wing attached itself to trade union interests.

The CDU is closely associated with the Christian Social Union (Christich-Soziale Union—CSU), which is a continuation of the defunct Bavarian People's Party. The CSU maintains a separate organizational structure from the CDU and elects its own chairman. Franz-Josef Strauss continued to serve in this post in 1974. The two parties usually support the same political policies, although the CSU emphasizes state's rights for Bavaria, its stronghold of support, and is more strongly Roman Catholic oriented than the CDU.

Each of the three major political parties has an organization for people between the ages of eighteen and thirty-five. The CDU–CSU group is named the Young Union (Junge Union—JU). In 1972 the JU claimed about 120,000 members. They choose their own leaders and are financially independent of the CDU–CSU. Of the three major youth groups, the JU has been the most faithful to the party line of the parent organization.

Social Democratic Party

Socialist ideas date from the 1860s and 1870s, when proponents envisioned universally elected governments carrying out programs of state-controlled economy. In October 1945 socialist leaders from prewar days met in Germany to reconstruct a socialist party. Kurt Schumacher, Erich Ollenhauer, and Otto Grotewohl led the party meeting. The record of the socialist party in the Weimar and Hitler periods as a consistent defender of a free society won it followers who saw in it the best security for a democratic renewal. Socialist ideas, therefore, gained popularity after the war. The reorganized SPD took a strong nationalist line.

Schumacher was elected party chairman, and Ollenhauer served as vice chairman in 1945. Schumacher stressed a nationalist line rather than plans for social and economic reform. Criticism of the occupation powers and opposition to the internationalist policy of Konrad Adenauer were undertaken by the SPD leader. There was much disagreement within the party as to the correctness of the Schumacher line, but his personality was forceful enough to forestall modification. He was a leader of genuine moral force and popular appeal, and the loyalty of the party machine guaranteed that more temperate voices would not be heard.

The first blow to the party came in 1946 when the Socialist Unity Party of Germany (Sozialistische Einheitspartei Deutschlands—SED) was formed in the Soviet zone of Germany and headed by Grotewohl. The party was a union of the communist and socialist parties in the Soviet zone. This union weakened the SPD by forcing it to limit its activities and membership recruitment to the Western zones.

In the postwar years the SPD was the only mass party in the Federal Republic but, as prosperity increased, people became more alienated by the Marxist influence on the party and less interested in joining organized groups. By the end of the 1950s the party was unable to increase its membership.

Steps were finally taken to revitalize the party in the late 1950s. Major revisions in the party platform were made at the 1959 party congress at Bad Godesberg. Brandt, Fritz Erler, Heinemann, and Herbert Wehner were instrumental in developing the new program. They demanded that the party cast off its ties with communism, end its antagonism to religion, and accept a free market economy and private ownership of the means of production. The congress adopted the Basic Program, which included a free market economy, regulated private ownership of production, and an end to the antireligious tendencies of the party. The SPD would be a party for all the people rather than for a particular class. Rearmament and membership in the North Atlantic Treaty Organization (NATO) were now acceptable to the party.

The party abandoned its opposition role and adopted a positive attitude in 1961. It emphasized presenting policy alternatives rather than merely opposing programs. The change in the party was successful in attracting new members. Until 1961 support had come mainly from the industrial working classes. Membership fluctuated during the 1960s, and in 1970 the party claimed more than 800,000 members. Among the 1970 recruits nearly 40 percent were workers, and one-third were white-collar employees. Although the party has attracted more middle-class members than previously, this group tends to consist of low-echelon civil servants and people from low social and income groups.

In 1974 the SPD announced revised long-term goals. They included expanding the economy, planning for shortages, planning for urban and environmental development, ensuring full employment, expanding vocational education, and improving health and relief programs.

The SPD has a tightly organized bureaucracy. An executive committee heads the organization and is the center of power. Its thirty or so members include a chairman, a deputy chairman, a secretary general, a treasurer, and some other party faithfuls. Delegates to the party congress, which is held every two years, elect the executive committee. Delegates to the conference are chosen by district committees, which are controlled by local party officials. An eleven-member presidium is responsible for seeing that executive committee decisions are implemented. Members are usually bound to follow formal decisions of the executive committee.

Members contribute to the party coffers according to their incomes. This source and federal subsidies ensure for the SPD more financial stability than the CDU can claim for itself.

In addition to *Land* organizations, there are local, subdistrict, and district organizations, each of which elects its own leaders. District organizations numbered about 8,000 in the late 1960s. Furthermore, there are specialized groups for sports enthusiasts, youth, refugees (people of German origin who were expelled or fled from communist Eastern European countries), and women, among others.

Factionalism exists within the party and is accepted. Until the late 1960s discontent revolved around foreign policy and reunification, but among party regulars there had been no strong pressure for changes. Party leaders could, therefore, make party policy without facing overwhelming opposition.

Since the late 1960s, however, a young left-wing faction has become more vocal. This group, the Young Socialists (Jungsozialisten), whose members are commonly known as Jusos, includes all SPD members under the age of thirty-five, about 250,000 in all, or over one-fourth of the total SPD membership in 1973. Until the mid-1960s the parent organization controlled the Jusos but, as the young people became more strongly opposed to SPD programs, they also became more independent of the SPD. In 1970, however, the Jusos themselves were faced with a divided leadership, which temporarily weakened their faction.

Jusos claim that the SPD is "too bourgeois." In the early 1970s they sought nationalization of the means of production, a communist-socialist front in Western Europe, and an increase of workers' control of industry.

As student support of anarchy in the 1960s shifted to a desire to transform society through organized socialist methods in the 1970s, left-wing university students were often attracted to the SPD through the Jusos. Jusos emphasized holding political and civil administrative positions to accomplish the transformation. Some Jusos are in the SPD secretariat and therefore have some direct influence on the SPD. More often, though, their impractical ideas, such as free streetcar and bus transportation (local economies could not support free transportation), and their blatant attempts to control local party meetings have alienated many older, long-time SPD followers, particularly around university towns.

Heidemarie Wieczorek-Zeul, Jusos chairwoman, has stated that the group will adhere to its program and not be subject to SPD desires. In an April 1974 interview she reiterated that Jusos would resist SPD attempts to discipline them and that, whereas Jusos accepted the SPD party congress program, they did not accept Brandt's government program because it included FDP demands. Jusos were a constant thorn in Brandt's side.

During the first few months of Schmidt's chancellorship, Jusos were more subdued than they had been during the Brandt administration. How successful Schmidt will be in curtailing the activities of the Jusos remains to be seen.

Free Democratic Party

The forerunners of the FDP were liberal parties of the empire and Weimar years. Theodor Heuss was instrumental in founding the FDP in 1945 on a platform of personal freedom and nationalism. The party's strength lies in its role as a balance of power between the CDU and the SPD.

Progressives gained control of the party in 1966. Their party platform fostered institutional reforms, particularly in the fields of justice and education, and sought to end the Hallstein Doctrine by which Bonn refused to have diplomatic relations with any state that recognized the Democratic Republic. The 1960s closed with a leadership struggle within the party between two groups, one that supported a free enterprise system and another that was oriented toward civil rights. Walter Scheel, FDP chairman, led the younger, civil rights-oriented group to success and subsequently shifted the party to the left. One aspect of the shift is that the party began to support negotiations with Eastern European states, particularly with the Democratic Republic. The party thus became more closely aligned with the SPD than with the CDU.

Party support comes from business, industry, and liberal intellectuals. It has made gains among skilled workers, nonmanual workers, and Roman Catholics. It is strongest in North Rhine-Westphalia, Bremen, northern Hesse, Saarbrücken, northern Bavaria, and parts of Baden-Württemberg. In the early 1970s membership was estimated at between 70,000 and 90,000. Financial support comes primarily from outside sources.

Organization is loose, although the FDP does maintain local, district, and *Land* organizations. Most of the power rests with *Land* groups. The party congress meets annually but elects a chairman, his deputies, and a treasurer for two-year terms. Walter Scheel served as chairman from 1968 until his election to the federal presidency in mid-1974, at which time the new foreign minister, Hans-Dietrich Genscher, began serving as acting chairman. The lack of centralization permits FDP Bundestag deputies to act and vote more independently than the Christian Democrats or Social Democrats.

The party's organization for young people is the German Young Democrats (Deutsche Jungdemokraten—DJD), commonly known as Judos. In the early 1970s there were about 25,000 members. Just as the SPD has had trouble with the Jusos, the FDP has had difficulty holding the Judos to the party line. Judos in Bavaria were called upon in 1970 to drop their claim that private ownership of the means of production is dangerous. The next year the FDP disassociated itself from the Judos in Lower Saxony because of the young people's adverse effect on the ability of the FDP to raise money from business groups. The complaint was that the Judos were too socialist. In 1974 the Judos made a new attempt to gain strength by working more closely with the FDP and labor unions.

NATIONAL DEMOCRATIC PARTY

The National Democratic Party of Germany (Nationaldemokratische Partei Deutschlands—NPD) was founded in 1964. Its immediate aim was to unite right-wing groups before the 1965 elections. The party advocates German reunification and the restoration of German land that was lost in World War II. It is strongly nationalist and therefore opposes United States influence in the country and Federal Republic membership in the UN, NATO, and the Common Market because it claims that the Federal Republic is exploited by these organizations. The party also calls for a moral renewal and denounces the moral slackness that it feels is rampant in the country.

Alfred von Thadden led the party until 1971, when Martin Mussnug was elected chairman. The presence of former Nazis among its leaders led to outcries of a Nazi revival, but the party has consistently denied the charges. Members are predominantly young, male, Protestant or nonreligious, urban, and educated. Tradesmen, professionals, independent businessmen, and workers are counted among its members. Because the party appeals to protest voters, there are many temporary followers. In the early 1970s the party claimed about 20,000 members plus numbers of voters who represented a cross section of the electorate and who had previously supported the CDU or the SPD. Government figures, however, differ, as the minister of interior placed party membership at 12,000 in 1974.

By 1965 there were NPD organizations in each *Land*, and the next year the NPD was the fastest growing party in the Federal Republic. In *Land* elections the party received between 5.8 and 9.8 percent of the votes between 1966 and 1968 and was represented in some *Land* diets and in county and town parliaments. Since 1969 it has failed to obtain the requisite 5 percent of the popular vote to achieve Bundestag representation. Support has been declining, partly owing to ineffective *Land* deputies and changes in the economy.

Communist Parties

The Communist Party of Germany (Kommunistische Partei Deutschlands—KPD) was founded in 1918, and its influence increased until, at the peak of its power in 1932, it received 17 percent of the valid vote in the general elections of that year. After Hitler came to power the KPD was declared illegal. In 1945 the party was reconstituted as a legal political party in the four zones of occupied Germany. In the first general elections held in the Federal Republic, the KPD received 5.7 percent of the vote and seated fifteen deputies in the Bundestag. By 1953 the KPD vote had dropped to 2.2 percent and, because the Basic Law requires that any party must obtain at least 5 percent of the total vote in order to be represented in the legislature, no communist deputies were seated in the Bundestag that year. Before the next general elections, the KPD had been outlawed (August 1956), and from that time until the present day it has operated underground. Since the late 1960s the West German Communists have agitated unsuccessfully for reinstatement of the KPD.

In 1967 the ministers of interior of the *Länder* agreed to permit the formation of a new communist party. The next year Kurt Bachmann, who had previously been a KPD member, announced the formation of the new German Communist Party (Deutsche Kommunistische Partei—DKP) and was elected its first president. The party program was carefully worded so as to be acceptable to Basic Law prerequisites. It took a softer line than the KPD. Rather than pressing for an outright dictatorship of the working class, the party intended to place workers in leadership positions in governmental and social affairs. Recognition of the Democratic Republic as a sovereign state, the dissolution of NATO and the Warsaw Pact, a reduction of military strength in central Europe, and the spread of socialism without recourse to coups were among the aims of the party. Principles of peace, higher living standards, improved education, and cultural progress were also set forth. To help implement its program, the DKP has sought the support of Jusos, students, and members of trade unions.

The polling strength of the party has been minimal. Party members have been elected to some local governmental posts, but they have failed to gain sufficient votes for representation on the *Land* or federal level. In the 1972 federal election the party received 0.3 percent of the vote. Membership, though, has been climbing. Between 1972 and 1974 nearly 3,000 people were recruited into the party, bringing the total to 39,000, as listed by the minister of interior in 1974.

There are over 100 other communist groups in the Federal Republic. The largest of these is the radical Marxist-Leninist faction of the KPD, known as the KPD-ML, which advocates a dictatorship of the proletariat and armed revolution. It was founded in 1968 and is led by Ernst Aust. Membership reached 18,000 in 1974, according to the Office for the Protection of the Constitution.

Several communist youth groups have been organized. Among them is the Socialist German Workers Youth, which is affiliated with the DKP. Members numbered about 10,000 in 1972. The Spartakus Marxist Student Union, known as Spartakus, has been gaining popularity at the universities and has an estimated membership of between 2,000 and 3,000. In the early 1970s it was found in about forty universities.

Extraparliamentary Opposition

In the mid-1960s student opposition to authority also formed outside political parties in what has been termed extraparliamentary opposition. The Free University of Berlin was the setting of the first stirrings of unrest in 1965, when demonstrations were held under the motto "What Value Does the State Put On Youth?" Participants in this movement claimed that the government had failed to implement democratic practices in the Federal Republic and to grant minorities a voice in the political system. Part of the student rebellion was directed toward the university system (see ch. 8). Riots at the University of Frankfurt in 1974 centered on housing conditions. Specifically, students opposed the practice of razing apartments to construct office buildings, thereby further limiting an already scarce supply of housing facilities for students.

Professors and intellectuals have also supported the student movement. Widespread coverage by the media has kept the movement in public view. Because the primary commitment of the groups is to freedom of the individual, they will necessarily remain loose knit; they oppose subordinating one individual to another. The groups' demands include limiting political authority, decreasing the powers and functions of the executive branch of government, establishing a neutral state by renouncing the use of internal and external force, and limiting the power of social and economic institutions.

The impact of the extraparliamentary opposition has been limited because of their usually broad, unequivocal demands. They neither suggest alternatives to government proposals nor seem to consider the consequences of their own platforms. Their strength, however, cannot be totally overlooked. A government report in mid-1974 revealed that left-wing extremists held about 44 percent of the seats in student parliaments and about 66 percent of the seats in student committees. Membership in extremist right-wing youth organizations increased from 1,800 in 1972 to 2,000 in 1974.

INTEREST GROUPS

Five major categories of interests have groups to articulate their wishes. The groups represented are business, labor, agriculture, and the two predominant churches—the Roman Catholic Church and the Evangelical Church in Germany. In the late 1960s there were about 1,800 national interest associations and thousands of local and regional groups. Membership frequently overlaps among the organizations. More than 300 groups have enhanced their opportunities for influencing governmental policies by establishing offices in the capital city of Bonn.

The groups have several resources for voicing their demands. Interest spokesmen may confer with members of special government-affiliated bodies whose purpose is to serve interest groups. Interest groups also benefit by virtue of the automatic inclusion of their representatives on the boards of radio and television stations. Cooperation between interest groups and party leaders is based on the mutual support they need to attain their ends. Bundestag deputies who have been affiliated with groups either as members or as sympathizers tend to support the groups' programs. Interest group members serving in the Bundestag gain influence by joining committees, which carry the burden of legislative work. If a group has a national organization, its advisory council works directly with the ministries. In fact, procedural regulations for ministries favor the development of national organizations, as ministers are required to work with national rather than local interest groups.

The most important associations are federated into so-called peak associations (Spitzenverbände)—the major national organizations of interest groups. Special representatives of the interests serve as contacts between the peak associations and governmental bodies. Their influence is apparent in the practice of Bundestag deputies of conferring with peak associations before drafting bills that would affect the associations. Under Adenauer, interest leaders were allowed to bypass intermediaries and go directly to the chancellor.

Employers' interests are not always successfully articulated because of a lack of unity among business organizations. Groups compete with each other rather than joining forces. Furthermore, business lacks broad-based citizen support.

Associations for employers are organized on regional and functional lines. Local and regional chambers of trade and industry and occupational associations exist for employers who hire two or more employees. There are three federated peak associations. They agree that private enterprise should not be subject to government controls, but their potential as pressure groups is not fully realized because they do not band together to support other common goals.

The peak associations are the Diet of German Industry and Commerce (Deutsche Industrie- und Handelstag—DIHT), the Federation of German Employers Association (Bundesvereinigung der Deutschen Arbeitgeberverbände—BDA), and the Federation of German Industry (Bundesverband der Deutschen Industrie—BDI). The DIHT has not been as active in politics as the BDA, which supports political positions that are pertinent to employers. The most powerful peak association is the BDI, which represents all aspects of German industry and nearly all industrial plants. Each federation is independent, but members may belong to more than one, and there are cooperative efforts in matters of concern to all, such as policies regarding taxes, trade, and business regulations.

Most of the labor force is represented by the German Confederation of Trade Unions (Deutscher Gewerkschaftsbund—DGB), which is the foremost federation of trade unions, representing about 82 percent of the country's union membership. Manual workers are members through the national industrial unions that are federated with the DGB. Social Democratic and Christian Democratic unions are also united in this body. In an effort to ease East-West tensions, the DGB took an active role in *Ostpolitik* in 1970. Representatives of the federation demonstrated their support of the policy by meeting with members of East German trade unions in hopes of establishing a cooperative atmosphere. Smaller unions are the German Salaried Employees Union (Deutsche Angestelltengewerkschaft—DAG) and the German Federation of Civil Servants (Deutscher Beamtenbund—DBB).

In early 1973 nearly 7 million people belonged to labor unions. Unions have had adequate financial support to advertise their causes through the mass media. Another factor that is beneficial to labor is the presence of former trade union members in the Bundestag. These deputies promote legislation that is favorable to labor.

Trade unions are particularly interested in obtaining a clear, legal position for collective agreements, rather than depending on voluntary agreements. Social insurance regulations are closely watched by trade unions. Despite the usual practice of contacts between Bundestag deputies and peak associations before writing up legislation affecting the interests of the association, the government has not been noted for consulting union leaders on major economic policies.

Agricultural interests have retained influence through their well-organized associations. The German Farmers League, the League of Agricultural Chambers, and a producers' cooperative association articulate farmers' interests. In the late 1960s most of the 3 million farmers supported these organizations. A key to their success has been cooperation rather than competition among the groups. The German Farmers League has been successful in attaining some of its goals by threatening to shift its voting strength from one party to another and by electing farmers to *Land* and federal legislatures.

The two dominant churches have been successful in influencing cultural and social policy. According to the *Land* constitutions, the clergy are permitted a political role. For example, in Bavaria churchmen sit in the upper house of the *Land* diet. Church representatives establish contacts with the federal government in Bonn. Other resources for articulating interests are pastoral letters and the mass media.

Roman Catholic interests are further articulated through organizations of businessmen, workers, and youth that are geared to church interests and to fostering governmental action suited to church desires. Since the late 1960s, however, church influence regarding such issues as legislation affecting education and support for political candidates has appeared to be declining. This may have been caused by a general decline of church authority that has been felt in many parts of the world, or it may have been a purposeful move on the part of the church to make itself more acceptable to each of the major political parties.

The Evangelical Church in Germany comprises nearly thirty regional churches. Each church retains its autonomy, which makes agreement and cooperation on political issues affecting church interests nearly nonexistent. Church influence is strongest at local and regional levels.

Although the five categories of interest associations represent the majority of interests, they are not the sole avenues of articulation. Interests that do not fall into one of the five major categories have other resources to voice their demands. Urban and rural interests are dealt with by the League of German Cities. The league can lobby for support among members of *Land* governments. Because the Bundesrat (Federal Council) is composed of *Land* officials, interests that arise on a local level, such as those of the league, can receive national attention and support.

POLITICAL VALUES AND ATTITUDES

Several underlying assumptions have influenced the German people's attitude toward politics in general. One view has been that politics is an evil pastime in which the role of subject people is to respond submissively while attempting to fulfill their own interests in nonpolitical pursuits. A second view held that in a hostile world politics is a necessarily pernicious pursuit and the masses are automatically involved in the state's actions. The individual's role is determined by the leaders. A third political philosophy encompassed the tenet that the individual exists for the benefit of the state, which is supreme. These were some of the beliefs that helped imbue Germans with a passive acceptance of authority and, according to Karl Jaspers, respect for government "no matter what kind or how established."

234

The sudden political, economic, and social changes that Germans faced in 1933 and again in 1945 helped them to adapt to postwar conditions. The immediate postwar period, however, also contributed to the people's lack of interest in political affairs. When they compared the miseries of the 1945–47 period with their relative comfort in the 1950s, they were satisfied with the status quo. Also, in seeking to shelve the memory of the occupation, the people pursued material goods rather than political action.

The provisional character of the Federal Republic and the division of the country into two states contributed to a lack of understanding of and feeling for a "German nation." Some felt that the state had become "a mere functional machine" whose primary purpose was to satisfy group interests.

The good life and guarantee of the individual's welfare and the assurance of external security remained preeminent interests of the people in the mid-1970s. The common attitude was that the duty of the state was to provide domestic stability, economic prosperity, and social security. There was little interest in displaying patriotic or national symbols, and polls have demonstrated a lack of pride in political institutions. The black eagle and patriotic songs have a negative symbolism for many because they associate them with Adolf Hitler.

Although 80 to 90 percent of the eligible voters cast ballots in federal elections, few people actively participate in political affairs. In the early 1970s only about 3 percent of the people were members of political parties. About 6 percent of those who voted the SPD ticket were party members, and about 2 or 3 percent of CDU and FDP voters belonged to the parties. The low memberships are due in part to the attitude that parties are primarily bases for recruiting political officials. Even when articulating mass interests, the parties seem distant from grass-roots levels because party officials negotiate with large pressure groups.

In general, politics is viewed as a specialty, a field for experts, but another factor is that government-affiliated positions are not widely sought because the low salary scale is not in keeping with the work involved, particularly at the high levels of employment. Civil service careers are often rejected for higher paying and less arduous employment in private industry. Moreover, a political commentator has written that the generation under thirty years of age shuns the political arena because of a skepticism about formal organizations and collective action. Consequently, fewer than 10 percent of the people participate actively in politics.

CHAPTER 13

FOREIGN RELATIONS

The foreign policy of the Federal Republic in the 1970s continued to have its major roots in the country's location in central Europe and in its post-World War II history. Although constituted as an independent state in 1949, the Federal Republic did not gain full control over its foreign policy until 1955. During those first six years, the Western Allies (occupation authorities) retained a measure of control over foreign affairs. By the time that the new republic gained full sovereignty, it was fully integrated into the Western European and North Atlantic alliances.

Under its first chancellor, Konrad Adenauer, the Federal Republic, after gaining full sovereignty, tried to play an increasingly significant role in the Western alliances and particularly in the economic unions of Western Europe. Adenauer's influence abroad rested to a large extent fully integrated into the Western European and North Atlantic alliances. powerful voice in such supranational bodies as the European Economic Community (EEC, also known as the Common Market) and the European Coal and Steel Community (ECSC). The military position of the Federal Republic as the strongest land power in Western Europe—a position assured as long as French forces were diverted to Algeria —increased its political importance to its allies. Adenauer, however, was cautious and conservative in his use of political power because of the rampant fear among Europeans that German nationalism might again become a threat to the continent.

Until the Bonn agreements of May 1952, which formally anticipated the ending of the occupation, the occupying powers continued to cosign treaties and accords "on behalf of" the Federal Republic. The Bonn agreements, in addition to clearing the way for granting the country further authority over internal and external affairs, charted the main course of its foreign policy for the next two decades, stating that "it is the common aim of the Signatory States to integrate the Federal Republic on a basis of equality within the European Community, itself included in a developing Atlantic Community."

The main thrust of the country's foreign policy remained directed toward the West until Chancellor Willy Brandt introduced his *Ostpolitik* (Eastern Policy) and signed treaties with the Soviet Union and Poland. Brandt carefully ensured that *Westpolitik* (Western Policy)—the country's close ties to Western Europe and the United States—would not be damaged by his initiatives toward the East. By 1973 Brandt, who had won the Nobel Peace Prize for his efforts toward reducing international tensions, could look with pride at the position of the Federal Republic among the nations of the world.

The abrupt political demise of the Brandt administration in 1974 left some uncertainty concerning the country's foreign policy, but by late summer no great changes in direction seemed to be in the offing. Helmut Schmidt, who succeeded Brandt as chancellor, was strongly oriented toward the West but did not seem to be inclined toward scrapping the program of *Ostpolitik*.

HISTORICAL PERSPECTIVE

Some three months after the founding of the Federal Republic on September 20, 1949, Chancellor Adenauer's government established the Foreign Affairs Department. At the express invitation of the Allied High Commission, the department then opened consulates general in Washington, London, and Paris. Thus was inaugurated, with the constraints implicit in the manner in which authority was granted and the level of representation, the modern-day Federal Republic diplomatic service. For the next two years additional attributes of sovereignty were granted piecemeal, as when the Federal Republic was permitted to sign the ECSC treaty in April 1951. In order to join its French, Italian, and Benelux (Belgium, Netherlands, and Luxembourg) partners in giving up of their own free will certain sovereign rights, the Federal Republic had first to be accorded the rights.

The Bonn agreements, linked to the ill-fated treaty establishing the European Defense Community (EDC), had to be superseded when EDC failed to be ratified by the French National Assembly in August 1954. The Paris agreements of October of that year, which went into effect in May 1955, unequivocally made the Federal Republic a sovereign state and a member of the Western European Union (WEU) and the North Atlantic Treaty Organization (NATO). The Foreign Affairs Department, over which Chancellor Adenauer had retained direct control, was raised to the level of a full-fledged ministry in June, and Bonn's diplomatic representation to its United States, British, and French sponsors was raised to the ambassadorial level.

The diplomatic service was recruited and established during the early years of Adenauer's leadership. The strong-willed chancellor believed that policy should be formulated at the top and, therefore, delegated the authority over administrative details and the staffing of the new service. Many senior posts were filled by diplomats who had served the Hitler regime, the principal trained cadre available. Because important diplomatic decisions in the twentieth century are no longer made in embassies, but at the highest levels in the respective capitals, the staffing policy has had little effect on decisionmaking.

The diplomatic training school *(Diplomatenschule)* at Bonn attempts to place less emphasis on etiquette and international jurisprudence and more on political science and economics. The intellectual and social background of the young candidates, however, has consistently tended to be from the upper middle and upper strata of German society. Writing in 1970, Grosser pointed out that of the 584 attachés (male and female) recruited in the first twenty-four competitions, two-thirds had studied only law. Approximately 10 percent were of former noble families, who constituted less than 2 percent of the general population; 27 percent were the sons and daughters of senior officials, who constituted less than 3 percent of the general population; 11.6 percent were the children of clerks who had not had a university education; and 1.9 percent had artisan or working-class parents, who made up about 35 percent of the general population.

Under the Social Democratic Party (SPD—see Glossary) administration of Brandt (1969–74), little was accomplished in the way of modifying the preponderantly upper middle-class background of diplomatic service personnel. Whether SPD Chancellor Schmidt will make changes in diplomatic recruitment remains to be seen. He is regarded as the most assertive leader since Adenauer and somewhat more disposed than his predecessor to involve himself in personnel matters.

BASIC CONTOURS OF FOREIGN POLICY

The fundamental goals of foreign policy have been to regain international respectability, to ensure the security of the truncated fatherland, and to maintain the economic growth that has made the Federal Republic the fourth industrial nation of the world after the United States, the Soviet Union, and Japan. A persisting distant aim—albeit one pursued with varying tactics—is reunification in freedom with the German Democratic Republic.

Until the late 1960s all four objectives were sought officially through exclusive close association with the West. The national security was made to rest squarely on military partnership with the United States and the other members of NATO. The reacquisition of respectability became consonant with economic development. A conscious guiding of the country's industry to satisfy the demands of the developing Common Market of Western Europe gave sustained momentum to the dramatic postwar industrial growth. The search for acceptance in the concert of nations also involved, on the part of political and cultural leaders, an acknowledgment of past Nazi barbarisms and tangible national repentance. This decision to accept moral responsibility for Germany's past, a commitment sought by Chancellor Adenauer, was ultimately approved by the Bundestag (Federal Diet) in March 1953. Even in the mid-1970s, however, a residual anti-German feeling in the West remained concentrated on the Federal Republic—the legatee of Hitler's Third Reich.

Understandably, many believed that the Nazi era should not be allowed to discredit every German quality and cancel every German right; the 1950s and 1960s were marked by efforts to take up the traditions of the Second Reich and the Weimar Republic—though with a strong awareness that certain mistakes should not be repeated and with a growing tendency to question such old idols as Chancellor Otto von Bismarck. Adjuncts of the Ministry of Foreign Affairs, such as the Goethe Institute, have actively supported in all major world areas the objective of reminding others, particularly Europeans and Americans, of Germany's considerable contributions, over the centuries, to the mainstream of Western civilization.

In all European undertakings since Bonn was permitted, in 1955, to assume full control over the Federal Republic's foreign affairs, strong emphasis was placed on West European integration, including Franco-German reconciliation. The assumption, for a time, of the governing Christian Democratic Union (CDU—see Glossary) and ultimately of the opposition SPD as well was that an economically and militarily strong Federal Republic, backed by a strong and cohesive West European community, would hasten the collapse, or withering, of the imposed communist regime in the Democratic Republic.

Since the mid-1960s Bonn has pursued *Ostpolitik* with the intent of establishing a détente with the entire bloc. The new *Ostpolitik* may preserve the possibility of national reunification by slowly overcoming the division of Europe. *Ostpolitik* has, on the whole, received its principal impetus from the Social Democrats. But it is to a measurable degree bipartisan and, despite such setbacks as the Soviet invasion of Czechslovakia in 1968 and the Guillaume affair and resultant resignation of Chancellor Brandt in 1974, should endure concomitantly with the broader East-West détente (see ch. 12).

Ostpolitik, pursued as an adjunct of *Westpolitik*, has its roots in Bismarck's Germany (1871–90). Bismarck, the Iron Chancellor, who forged the Second Reich in the crucibles of three carefully contained European wars, saw Germany's central location as an attribute of future strength in Europe. The need to defend vulnerable borders was met by the maintenance of an army second to none and the development of extensive, closely knit transportation and communications networks. Bismarck urged the kaisers, in the end unsuccessfully, to let the other great and lesser powers have their colonial empires—their so-called places in the sun. Germany, through its highly advanced technology, its abundant natural resources at home, its large dynamic population, and particularly its location, would dominate the continent economically and would thereby remain politically ascendant.

EVOLVING OSTPOLITIK

In the aftermath of World War II, while political parties were still being formed under the patronage of the victor powers, the SPD had at first hoped for some accommodation with their fellow Socialists in the Soviet zone. Representing almost 30 percent of the eldctorate in the Western zones, with prospects of a plurality in all four zones, the SPD regarded reunification as the primary national objective. This could not be accomplished, in the SPD view, by too close an embrace with the Western democracies, economically or politically, nor by permitting an extension of Soviet influence into the Federal Republic. SPD leaders believed in the possibility of a third or intermediate solution, in which socialist governments would be established eventually throughout Eastern and Western Europe. State economic planning, having already gained broad acceptance in postwar Western Europe, need not mean total or even majority public ownership. The developing social democracy in Scandinavia—the so-called middle way, where largely free economies were heavily taxed to support all-pervasive welfare systems—probably served as a model.

Deeply offended by the enforced merging of Eastern zone Social Democrats with the minority Communists in the communist-dominated Socialist Unity Party of Germany (Sozialistische Einheitspartei Deutschlands—SED), the Western Social Democrats nonetheless were willing to sit down with SED representatives to discuss technical arrangements for the holding of free elections in all four zones. They resisted the policy of rearmament in the newly founded Federal Republic, believing neutrality to offer the better chance for an eventual coming together of the Soviet and Western zones.

By the mid-1950s, however, the heavy-handed oppression in Stalinist Eastern Europe convinced most West Germans that an accommodation with the imposed East European regimes could not be reached. Their governments would remain communist dictatorships in the foreseeable future. Furthermore, rearmament not only bound the Federal Republic to NATO, to which it was admitted in 1955, but economic ties, starting in earnest with Marshall Plan aid in 1949 and the ECSC in 1952, had already fastened the reemergent nation firmly to Western Europe and North America. The *Wirtschaftswunder* (economic miracle) was rapidly transforming the Federal Republic from a rubble heap into one of the most prosperous nations in Europe. The broad spectrum of opinion, though moved by the plight of compatriots in the Democratic Republic, became more and more disinclined to do anything to threaten the new prosperity, which clearly stemmed from the Western orientation. Reunification, as an attainable goal, was put off to the distant future.

The Social Democratic leadership came to accept the Federal Republic's attachment to the West—militarily, economically, and politically—by the mid-1950s, and their vote-getting ability was shortly to increase correspondingly. Foreign policy had become bipartisan. When at the Bad Godesberg Party Conference in 1959 they further disencumbered themselves of Marxist ideology and made the SPD a pragmatic workingman's party with clear socioeconomic rather than ideological objectives, they inaugurated a period of growth that was to increase the SPD's share of the vote dramatically in 1961 and to make it the plurality party in 1972.

A major event of 1961—the erection of the Berlin Wall—at first tightened the ties of the Federal Republic with NATO. As in the previous Berlin crises, it was shown once again how dependent on the West the Federal Republic was for survival. But the failure this time of the North Atlantic allies to stand firmly against the East and demand that the barrier be removed had a gradually disenchanting effect. It brought home, over the next three years or so, the realization that the Western powers, notably the United States, would be unwilling to risk a serious confrontation with the Soviet Union to impede the permanent division of Germany. When President John F. Kennedy visited West Berlin in the summer of 1963 after having faced down the Soviets in Cuba several months earlier, his tumultuous welcome was to prove one of the final popular manifestations of exclusive reliance on United States power.

The outcome of the Cuban missile crisis, reinforced in 1964 by Nikita Khrushchev's outster and the more cautious political style adopted by his successors, brought a realization that the Soviets clearly wished to avoid the kind of behavior that might lead to a nuclear confrontation. It was at this juncture that persisting American pressure for offset purchases to balance the costs of keeping troops in the Federal Republic and United States insistence on restricting West German exports to the Soviet Union prompted a gradual shift to greater independence in the political climate of the Federal Republic. Furthermore, United States efforts to reduce American-Soviet tensions, starting with the widely approved nuclear test ban treaty in 1963, tended to awaken fears that the two superpowers could reach some overall accommodation at Germany's expense.

This isolation had been codified in the Hallstein Doctrine, which was to be a touchstone of Federal Republic foreign policy for a decade following its enunciation in 1955. Chancellor Adenauer's state secretary, Walter Hallstein, stated in that year that it was the intent of the Federal Republic to eschew diplomatic relations with any country recognizing the Democratic Republic after the doctrine's promulgation. An exception was made of the Soviet Union, officially because it was one of the victor occupying powers with whom an all-German peace treaty must eventually be negotiated. Bonn, therefore, exchanged ambassadors with Moscow in 1955, marking the only such exchange with a Soviet-bloc country for the next twelve years.

Adenauer departed the political scene in October 1963. During the final months of his chancellorship, his foreign minister, Gerhard Schröder, was already initiating exploratory talks in several East European capitals with a view to establishing or refurbishing trade missions. This early, tentative *Ostpolitik*, encouraged by businessmen looking for markets, had the longer range purpose of penetrating those satellite countries most amenable to Western influence and, through new economic and ultimately political ties, encouraging revisionism and weakening the unity of the Warsaw Pact. By late 1966 it became apparent that Bonn was prepared to overlook the recognition of the Democratic

Republic by the East European states, which were, after all, largely captive to Soviet foreign policy. The exchange of diplomatic missions between the Federal Republic and Romania in January 1967 confirmed this new departure. It also caused Moscow to react. With the strong support of Warsaw and East Berlin, the Soviet Union then undertook to inhibit further eastward probings by the Federal Republic.

The advent of the Grand Coalition government between the Christian Democrats and the Social Democrats in December 1966 brought the Social Democratic mayor of West Berlin, Willy Brandt, to Bonn, as the new vice chancellor and minister of foreign affairs. Approving in principle the eastward demarches of his predecessor, which were about to have a dramatic denouement in Romania, Brandt's *Ostpolitik* was shortly to take a different course. Pushed by external developments, it would not unfold in all its essentials until late 1972 and would constitute the most significant postwar modification of the Federal Republic's foreign policy.

Having just come around to a total commitment to NATO and an integrated Western Europe in 1960, the SPD, through its West Berlin branch, again began shifting ground in the summer of 1963. In July 1963 Egon Bahr, Mayor Brandt's press secretary at that time, responded to the hard fact of the Berlin Wall in a brief speech suggesting "change through closer relations." Drawing on the initiatives of the Kennedy administration—specifically, the official United States contacts in Warsaw with Chinese Communists—Bahr suggested that regular meetings with the Democratic Republic need not entail official recognition. It was apparent that the Democratic Republic would not in the foreseeable future allow free elections and that the Soviets would continue indefinitely to back the regime. An intra-German office could be established where the two German authorities could identify areas—such as the mitigation of hardships caused by the enforced separation of families—where negotiations might be mutually useful.

Mayor Brandt shortly went even further. Since the Democratic Republic had remained adamant for over two years in its refusal to discuss Berlin affairs with the Bonn authorities, he acceded to its demand that any ad hoc talks must take place between East Berlin and the proper West Berlin authorities. The long-standing Bonn contention that West Berlin was an integral part of the Federal Republic was thus undercut, but the Social Democratic government in Berlin believed the humanitarian imperatives outweighed the political. In this stand they had the backing of elite opinion both in Berlin and in the Federal Republic, as reflected in several influential newspapers and periodicals as well as in polls. The prevailing view among the governing Christian Democrats in Bonn, however, was that they would not be blackmailed by East Berlin to trade off political concessions for humanitarian benefits. Despite the consideration of humanitarian alternatives by Chancellor Adenauer, the conservative view prevailed. The political costs, it was felt, would in the long run far outweigh the returns.

The Bahr-Brandt conceptual framework of *Ostpolitik* recognized the overriding element of Soviet consent, as regards both intra-German détente and ultimate reunification and closer relations with Eastern Europe. Nevertheless, when Brandt moved from the West Berlin mayor's office to become foreign minister in the Grand Coalition, he continued his predecessor's efforts to establish relations with East European countries. Thus, a trade mission was established in Czechoslovakia in August 1967, and diplomatic relations were reestablished with Yugoslavia in January 1968 after having been broken in 1957, when Belgrade, in disregard of the Hallstein Doctrine, recognized the Democratic Republic. To the apprehension of the Soviets, relations with the liberalized Alexander Dubcek regime in Prague were moving rapidly toward diplomatic recognition, but the invasion of Czechoslovakia and forceful suppression of Dubcek by the Warsaw Pact countries in August 1968 ended that initiative.

The Bahr-Brandt *Ostpolitik* was once again taken up in October 1969 when Brandt became chancellor in the new Social Democratic government. Recognizing, however, that their earlier effort to improve intra-German relations by so-called little steps was basically unpalatable to the leaders of the Democratic Republic, the architects of *Ostpolitik* concentrated on securing support from Moscow. Only with strong Soviet support could Bonn extract any concessions from East Berlin. The new government of the Federal Republic undertook to reassure Moscow (in implicit contrast to previous efforts to work behind the back of the Soviets) that it would take no further steps in *Ostpolitik* without informing the Soviet Union. The long-pending, controversial nuclear nonproliferation treaty, shelved after the invasion of Czechoslovakia, was signed as an earnest indication of further intentions.

Most impressive to the Soviets was the offer from Bonn, eight days after Brandt was confirmed as chancellor by the Bundestag, to discuss a renunciation-of-force treaty. The offer was preceded by public urgings of Brandt and Bahr that "Germany accept the consequences of defeat" and attempt to build a "European peace order." Enticing to Moscow was the possibility of de facto recognition by Bonn of the Oder-Neisse line as the western boundary of Poland, that is, of the post-World War II territorial status quo. Another achievement that might proceed from the talks was the convening of the Conference on Security and Cooperation in Europe (CSCE)—long desired by the Soviets both to endorse the territorial status quo and to reduce the cohesion of NATO. Through judicious concessions to the Federal Republic and other West European countries, Moscow could conceivably reduce West German dependence on the United States political and military power. A settlement in Europe appealed to Moscow for yet another reason, this one based not so much on its European policy as on its Far Eastern policy. It was in March 1969 that the People's Republic of China (PRC) army units clashed in battle with Soviet units on the Ussuri River. Apprehensive over PRC claims against large tracts of Soviet territory and aware of PRC growing military might, Moscow recognized the advantages to be gained by securing its position in the West.

The talks with the Soviets on the renunciation-of-force treaty got under way in December and were pursued directly by Bahr, now a state secretary in the chancellery, from January to May 1970. Signed in Moscow in August, the treaty recognized pro tempore the territorial status quo, affirming that under no circumstances would any possible future changes be undertaken by force. Even the possibility of future changes had to be stated in a separate letter, not part of the treaty. But the Soviets, in turn, shelved their claim to a special right, as a victor power, to intervene in the affairs of the Federal Republic and agreed to an intensification and improvement of relations between Bonn and Eastern Europe. Federal Republic foreign ministry officials negotiated a similar treaty with the Poles. Signed in Warsaw in December, it accepted Poland's occupation of the former Prussian lands east of the Oder and Neisse rivers. As in the Moscow treaty, the use of force to effect any possible future change was forsworn.

With the Soviet Union and Poland committed to détente, the reluctant Democratic Republic was obliged by Moscow, after much foot dragging, to concede that West Berlin had a special relationship with the Federal Republic and to permit improved access to the Western sector of the city from the Federal Republic. Moscow was induced to support Bonn's efforts by awareness of the well-publicized fact that *Ostpolitik* was hanging on a slender thread in the Bundestag—that without concessions on Berlin there would be no ratification of the Moscow and Warsaw treaties.

After the American, British, French, and Soviet negotiators initialed the Berlin access agreement in September 1971, the two Germanys worked out further agreements on Berlin access and intra-Berlin movement that supplemented the four-power text. The Soviet Union apparently exerted considerable pressure on the Democratic Republic to attain its cooperation and as a quid pro quo imposed a so-called reverse linkage, suggesting that Bonn ratification of the Moscow and Warsaw treaties should be a preliminary to Soviet signature of the Berlin agreement. Christian Democratic opposition to the new *Ostpolitik* mounted, centering on the tacit acceptance of the status quo, that is, the failure to get Moscow explicitly to declare for ultimate German reunification and, to a lesser degree, on the implicit renunciation by Bonn of the German lands east of the Oder and Neisse rivers. After months of bitter debate and intricate parliamentary maneuvering that threatened to bring down the Brandt government, the CDU finally abstained from voting in May 1972, permitting ratification of the Moscow and Warsaw treaties. The negotiation and signing of the Basic Political Treaty between the two Germanys followed rapidly (it was signed in December 1972 and ratified in May 1973), completing the foundation upon which the eastward rapprochement was to rest.

The treaty seemed to reaffirm important concessions from Bonn. It contained only a remote implicit reference to future self-determination in the Democratic Republic and no reference at all to an ultimate peace treaty ending World War II, which would have to tackle the question of a divided Germany. It was a tangible juridical document formalizing the status quo. These concessions were, in fact, the final precondition to Soviet endorsement of the new *Ostpolitik*.

Subsequent events, notably the establishment by the Federal Republic of diplomatic relations with Poland, Czechoslovakia, Bulgaria, and Hungary and the admission of both Germanys to the United Nations (UN), brought the expected pressures on the Democratic Republic. The exchange of permanent diplomatic missions between East Berlin and Bonn in March 1974 marked the culmination of retreat from the Hallstein Doctrine of earlier years, boding well for continuing rapprochement between the two Germanys. The Brandt-Bahr *Ostpolitik* differs from its CDU-sponsored counterpart in that it always recognized the imperative of Soviet consent. Thus, a political understanding with the Soviet Union as well as most, if not all, of Soviet-influenced Eastern Europe was the pillar upon which connections with the Democratic Republic were believed to rest.

These renewed connections, the most visible attainment of over a decade of *Ostpolitik*, would never have been made were it not for the continuing vitality of the Federal Republic's *Westpolitik*. Because of the country's key roles in both NATO and the European Community, it has become a base of formidable economic and impressive military strength. Moscow, therefore, continues to hope for expanded relations. As the leading industrial nation of the Common Market, however, with which it conducts 50 percent of its export trade, the Federal Republic wishes only to strengthen and further integrate the European Community. It is doubtful that foreseeable Soviet blandishments would persuade the people of the Federal Republic to seek a reduction in their NATO role—especially in the strength of the United States forces stationed on their soil (see ch. 17). As Chancellor Brandt stated in January 1970, "the Federal Republic . . . is no wanderer between two worlds." After two sessions of the CSCE, first convened in July 1973, he was moved to note again that the continued success of Bonn stems from the Federal Republic's "firm anchorage in the West."

WESTPOLITIK

Relations with the United States

As the Federal Republic's generous benefactor in the early days of economic recovery and the guarantor of its security for over a quarter of a century, the United States remains the number one ally. Despite the inevitable irritants caused by the protracted stationing on German soil of

American troops, few are anxious to see them go. To Bonn and the average citizen of the Federal Republic the American soldiers are the visible bona fides of the United States commitment to defend the Federal Republic and West Berlin from Soviet aggression. The informed public has generally acquiesced in the purchase of increasing amounts of American military goods and services as a means of offsetting the dollar costs of maintaining these forces in Germany. On United States insistence, the proportion of the costs thus offset by Bonn finally amounted to 100 percent in early 1974.

In part to help ensure continued friendship and support, in part to ensure competitive prices for their own exports, and perhaps in some measure as an expression of national gratitude, the Federal Republic has cooperated closely to help the United States solve its balance-of-payments deficits, occasionally at some cost to itself. The Federal Republic's dependence on the United States for its security continues to be the keystone in the relations between the two countries, and all responsible political formations recognize that it was essentially American generosity, albeit pragmatic generosity, that launched the country's sensational economic recovery.

In 1948, while the Soviet army continued to dismantle and ship to the homeland much of what was left of the industrial plant in their occupation zone of the vanquished Third Reich, the British and the Americans persuaded France to curtail and then stop the practice in its zone. The three Western powers then eased many of the economic restrictions imposed by the four victor powers three years earlier. The government of the newly formed Federal Republic established itself in Bonn in September 1949 and three months later accepted the first allotment of Marshall Plan funds. Over the next three years a massive inflow of United States investment capital combined with German industry to accomplish the *Wirtschaftswunder.* By 1953 rebuilt and bustling cities were rapidly transforming the desolate postwar landscape. The Federal Republic reentered the world market with such highly competitive goods as Volkswagen automobiles, Telefunken radios and phonographs, and Vögtlander cameras and by the mid-1950s enjoyed a favorable trade balance.

Although the eventual accession to NATO of the Federal Republic, entailing German rearmament and West European military cooperation, had to be a matter for the Europeans to decide, much of the forward thrust had come from Washington. Because the political absorption of Eastern Europe into the Soviet bloc signaled by the Czechoslovakian coup and Berlin blockade of 1948 and the aggressive intent of international communism made clear by the invasion of the Republic of Korea (South Korea), the United States saw the need of transforming the Western-occupied part of Germany from a weak, defeated pariah to a bastion of the free world in Europe. The United States secretary of state met with the British foreign secretary and French foreign minister in

New York in September 1950 to work out a joint declaration on Germany. The Tripartite Foreign Ministers Conference declared the Federal Republic of Germany, as the only freely elected authority in Germany, to be its sole legally constituted government. It further stipulated that the United States, Great Britain, and France would regard an attack upon the Federal Republic or West Berlin as an attack upon themselves. In 1954 the Basic Law was amended to permit rearmament, and in May 1955 the Paris agreements went into effect, making the Federal Republic a fully sovereign state and a member of NATO and the Western European Union (WEU). WEU, composed of the continental NATO powers plus the United Kingdom, became the monitor of German rearmament.

The next contribution of Washington to the Federal Republic's military rehabilitation dealt with nuclear arms. After one major reformulation and several minor ones, United States-British nonproliferative nuclear sharing evolved as a broadly based compromise. Recognizing that most European countries would be against German possession of nuclear weapons, President Kennedy in 1962 launched the concept of the Multilateral Nuclear Force (MLF). In its first planning stage, beyond which it scarcely evolved, naval ships of mixed NATO crews were to be armed with nuclear missiles. The French were lukewarm at best, but the British were willing to give MLF a try; the Germans were optimistic. Soon, however, the impracticability, the fundamental unwieldiness, and the tactical vulnerability of the scheme became apparent to all, and it ended in 1965. It was replaced the next year by the eleven-member Nuclear Defense Affairs Committee (NDAC), including all NATO states except France, Iceland, Portugal, and Luxembourg, all of whom opted out, and the functional distillation of NDAC, the seven-member Nuclear Planning Group (NPG). The latter, composed of the United States, the United Kingdom, the Federal Republic, Italy, and three rotating members of NDAC, actually plans NATO nuclear targeting that is supplemental to the American, British, and French national strategic schemes.

By the late 1960s the enhanced self-confidence of the Federal Republic, engendered by its membership in the NPG, was somewhat compromised by strong United States backing of the unpopular nuclear nonproliferation treaty. Opposed by most Christian Democrats, the treaty was believed to contain many dangers, including the permanent consignment of the Federal Republic to an inferior status, difficulties for its extensive peaceful nuclear activities, and even fears that the treaty would provide the Soviets with a pretext for interfering in its internal affairs. Painstaking efforts by the treaty's negotiators, notably the United States, succeeded in reducing some of the opposition by taking Federal Republic objections into account, but the opposition rebounded with the invasion of Czechoslovakia under the Warsaw Pact. Only the advent of a Social Democratic government accompanied by Chancellor Brandt's renewed *Ostpolitik* brought about its signature by Bonn in late 1969.

248

In the meantime an economically resurgent Federal Republic had become the third industrial nation of the world, a rank maintained from the early 1960s until overtaken by Japan in 1973. Now an important power in its own right, the country conducted a *Westpolitik* that was, on the whole, reasonable and forthcoming. Its strong support of United States policy from 1963 through 1966—the period of Ludwig Erhard's chancellorship—almost ended the rapprochement between France and the Federal Republic so assiduously constructed by Adenauer. Subsequent administrations continued to favor the United States as the principal ally but, on the whole, proved somewhat more solicitous of French sensibilities. As the Common Market grew in strength, Bonn saw to United States interests where it could. It staunchly supported British admittance against French opposition throughout the 1960s and was particularly helpful during the interminable negotiations on the Kennedy round mutual tariff reductions.

Bonn tried to help the United States overcome its balance-of-payments deficits in a number of ways; the increase in offset purchases, which were still negotiated annually in the 1960s, were only the most publicized. The Grand Coalition government of Kurt Georg Kiesinger, for example, concluded two agreements providing for large-scale purchases of United States bonds. During the 1973 crisis of the dollar, Bonn bought up US$600 million in one week, paid for in strong Deutsche Marks. When Washington subsequently devalued by 10 percent, Bonn accepted the 10-percent loss, fueling its own inflation. Mild self-interest, of course, dictated that a stable, strong American dollar would help keep West German exports competitively priced. Such exports, however, accounted for no more than 8 percent of the total.

The Federal Republic has, on the whole, mainained a liberal policy toward foreign investment. As American investment became extensive, amounting to US$1.1 billion by December 1966, it gave rise to domestic criticism, especially of takeovers of Federal Republic enterprises and the extent of United States influence in the petroleum and electronics sectors. In January 1968 an embargo was imposed on new direct United States capital investments. But the subsequent brief decline in input and the repercussions on the economy brought about a reconsideration. Restrictions were again eased, and by December 1972 American investment amounted to US$4.1 billion. In early 1974 both countries reciprocally lifted most remaining restrictions on investments.

In the late 1960s Federal Republic officials were becoming increasingly sensitive regarding the migration of German scientists and engineers to foreign countries, principally to the United States. The American economic recession in the early 1970s, and the attendant surfeit of highly trained technicians, has eased this problem.

Bonn has tended to be a dependable ally of the United States not only in NATO and the European Community but notably, since 1973, in the UN. Although initially skeptical of United States-Soviet rapprochement and fearful that such arrangements as the nuclear nonproliferation treaty might not take adequate account of the interests of the Federal Republic, it has frequently rallied to a semi-isolated United States under international attack. The most striking example occurred during the Vietnamese involvement. The Erhard government staunchly supported the United States role as a courageous containment of the aggressive expansionism of world communism. Under increasing domestic pressure as the war dragged on, Kiesinger and Brandt backed away from such forthright support, but they never attacked the policy, and their occasional criticism remained muted with professions of understanding for the difficulty of the United States position.

Relations with France and the European Community

If most of the informed opinion in the emergent Federal Republic promptly recognized the primacy of United States friendship and support, the ruling Christian Democrats early felt the need for rapprochement with France—the historic continental adversary. Chancellor Adenauer saw German rehabilitation in terms of an economically and politically integrated Western Europe. In occasional interludes of historic fantasy, the usually pragmatic Adenauer spoke of a resurrected Carolingian state. A close Franco-German association would have to undergird such a scheme.

During the early years of restored nationhood there were still too many impediments to rapprochement. The French government, strongly backed by a Germanophobe public opinion, was doing its best to wrest the Saar from the Federal Republic, and the French occupation zone suffered under the harsh policies of the occupiers. In addition, the French veto in the four-power Allied Control Council defeated early attempts to establish any central German authority.

Until the outbreak of the Korean War, France was to prove incapable of fully recognizing the Soviet threat, believing its future security to depend entirely on a rigidly contained, divided Germany. Having suffered invasion across its vulnerable northeast frontier three times in seventy years, France was determined to create a buffer zone along the left bank of the Rhine. Any future sovereignty of a central German state would not be permitted over this large area. As late as early 1948 some French leaders were still hoping for an accommodation with the Soviet Union, the natural ally against a resurgent Germany. It was not surprising that France obstructed several initiatives of its partners in the Allied Control Council—all looking to the enhancement of central German authority to facilitate rehabilitation. When Great Britain and the United States integrated the economies of their two zones, France refused to go along.

A concession to French as well as to Benelux sensibilities was the Brussels Treaty of March 1948—a fifty-year alliance between France, the United Kingdom, and the Benelux countries against armed attack in

Europe. Germany was acknowledged as an enduring possible menace in the preamble of the treaty. Article 4, however, which provided for automatic military aid if any of the parties should be the object of an armed attack in Europe, did not specify the potential aggressor. The seizure of power by Soviet-backed Communists in Prague the previous month was already suggesting that aggression could come from another quarter.

The London agreements of June 1948, however, which launched the new Federal Republic, and the Occupation Statute of April 1949, outlining the still close limits of its independence, rejected major elements of the policy desired by France. The Rhineland was not given any special status to ensure its perpetual demilitarization; the industry of the Ruhr remained completely in German hands; and a centralized government with police, legislative, and tax-raising powers was established in Bonn. The French felt forced to go along, although the London agreements were ratified in the National Assembly by the slim majority of 300 against 286. Belatedly recognizing the Soviet expansionist menace, French leaders saw the need of strong ties with their Western partners.

Unable to neutralize the Rhineland, to bring the industrial Ruhr under international control, or to attach the Saar with its coal to Lorraine with its iron, French planners began focusing in earnest on European integration as the remaining means of eliminating any military threat from a resurgent Germany while rationalizing the economies of Western Europe. Already during the war years Jean Monnet, an associate of Charles de Gaulle during World War II and a member of his government after France's liberation, had drawn up the plans for France's postwar technological renovation. These were shortly extended to include the concept of economic rationalization in cooperation with neighboring states. By 1948, in collaboration with Foreign Minister Robert Schuman, Monnet had devised the European Coal and Steel Community (ECSC), calling for a coal, iron ore, and steel manufacturing common market between France, the Federal Republic, Italy, and the Benelux countries. Ratified by the respective parliaments, the ECSC went into effect in 1952. Immediately successful and giving a marked boost to European recovery—already primed by Marshall Plan aid—this pooling of economic resources boded well for further integration.

The invasion of South Korea by Soviet-equipped armies from the north convinced the NATO allies that Western Europe was in imminent danger from massive Soviet forces poised in Eastern Europe. United States pressure for the prompt creation of twelve West German divisions brought the French counterproposal—the Pleven Plan—for the creation of an integrated European army, to include at the outset soldiers of the continental Brussels Treaty nations, plus Italy and the Federal Republic. The separate national units would be fused at the lowest feasible level, presumably platoon or company, and the West German troops would perform essentially auxiliary roles under close supervision. Lengthy negotiations between the military commanders produced the European Defense Community (EDC) treaty in May 1952. It was agreed that an effective military force could only be created if the fusion took place at or near the division level and that West German troops should have a coequal role, thus reasserting, in effect, the essentials of the United States scheme of 1950. Still, the French, pressured by the United States and other NATO powers and abandoned by the British who had at first expressed aversion to West German rearmament, now seemed amenable.

Public opinion in France, however, while for the most part attracted to the growing economic and even political integration of Europe, was as yet unprepared for German rearmament. Under the able leadership of Pierre Mendes-France, the French government, which had labored hard in "building a fence around the tree of German rearmament," tried to persuade the public that the mechanisms of EDC, just like those of ECSC in its sphere, would provide adequate safeguards. But in the summer of 1954, notwithstanding the Soviet threat, the thought of rearming Germany under whatever safeguards was still ahead of its emotional time frame. The EDC treaty had been ratified by the Federal Republic (March 1953), the Netherlands (July 1953), Belgium (November 1953), and Luxembourg (April 1954). Ratification by the Italian parliament was imminent when it was rejected by the French National Assembly in August 1954.

United States Secretary of State John Foster Dulles threatened France with an "agonizing reappraisal" of the nature of the American commitment to Europe's defense. The French government, nonetheless, felt obliged to seek further guarantees that German rearmament would be contained. Primarily, the French could not accept Great Britain's position, as expressed by Prime Minister Winston Churchill, that the United Kingdom was with, but not of, Europe and insisted on a British commitment to the defense of the continent. This basic demand was essentially met in the London and Paris agreements of October, which led to the creation of the WEU. Under the WEU arrangement, all five Brussels Treaty nations plus the Federal Republic and Italy would have part of their military forces earmarked for NATO, these forces to be under national commanders but subject to the orders of the NATO theater commander, who in turn is subordinate to the Supreme Allied Commander Europe (SACEUR). The arming of the Federal Republic, which had renounced (after the defeat of EDC) the manufacture on its territory of any atomic, biological, or chemical weapons, long-range or guided missiles, large warships, or bomber aircraft, would take place under WEU supervision with the United Kingdom as a participating member. The Paris agreements, making the Federal Republic a fully sovereign state and a member of WEU and NATO, were promptly ratified by the respective parliaments and went into effect in May 1955.

Next on the agenda for a coalescing Western Europe was the extension of ECSC to a common market embracing all industrial and agricultural production. With the signing and ratification by the respective parliaments in 1957 of the Treaty of Rome, which associated the six ECSC countries into the Common Market and established the European Atomic Energy Community (EURATOM), Chancellor Adenauer saw his dream of a Carolingian "Little Europe" begin to materialize. He seized the opportunity for an accelerated Franco-German rapprochement. The possibility for such rapprochement was markedly enhanced by de Gaulle's accession to power in France in 1958, the first year of the Common Market's implementation. The French president came to appreciate and share the European views of Adenauer. There also developed a strong personal affinity between the two.

The traditional antipathy of most French for the Germans had yet to be overcome, but rapprochement was given a marked boost by the immediately successful Common Market and a resultant surge in transborder tourist travel. When so prestigious and nationalist a leader as de Gaulle obviously shared the German desire for improved relations, most of the remaining diehards gave in. The rapid rehabilitation of Germans in the esteem of the French may be seen in public opinion surveys and a sampling of the media from 1954 through 1963. The Franco-German Treaty of Friendship and Cooperation of the latter year enjoyed instant popular support in both countries.

Although the treaty officially confirmed the existence of a new era of Franco-German understanding and the intent to build a more integrated Europe, the strategy and modalities had yet to be worked out. To Adenauer the periodic high-level intergovernmental conferences the treaty envisaged would facilitate an even more intimate political, cultural, and military cooperation. But such cooperation had to be consonant with the aims of the other Common Market partners and with NATO. The aged chancellor particularly hoped that the closer political cooperation would encourage the development of the European political institutions anticipated by the Treaty of Rome. He was censured by Europe-minded statesmen for an apparent unawareness of how intimidating a special Franco-German relationship appeared to the other Common Market countries. Despite the strong personal rapport with de Gaulle and a shared apprehension of socialist power and intentions, he failed to fathom the French president's ultimate aspirations.

For de Gaulle, Franco-German amity was but a building block, albeit an important one, in his grand design for France and Europe. This design was not to brook any submersion of the "French personality" in a politically united Europe. He wished, rather, to slow and even arrest political integration, to eliminate supranationalism. Through the tightening economic ties within the Common Market and the enhanced political cooperation with Bonn, he would harness and better control within "Little Europe" the growing industrial might of the Federal Republic.

France could offer the Federal Republic, in addition to diplomatic support, military cooperation up to, and perhaps eventually including, nuclear weapons. Ultimately, he foresaw a loose confederation of European states acknowledging France's leadership, if not hegemony, that would assist in the dissolution of the East and West blocs. The confederation would have formidable economic power, challenging that of the United States, and could, if astutely managed, be a most effective third force that would end bipolarism. Once there was no more cold war division of the world, the West Europeans would look eastward, resolved to bring about détente, entente and, finally, mutual cooperation. De Gaulle eventually professed to believe in the possibility of a loosely confederated Europe "from the Atlantic to the Urals."

Such a grand design would not have appealed to Adenauer, who was a staunch West European. When the retired ninety-one-year-old chancellor died in early 1967, the contagious prointegration sentiment among the Common Market countries seemed to have run its course. While blaming his successor, Erhard, for the new difficulty with the French, Adenauer may well have wondered why de Gaulle had not taken more decisive action when the moment had been propitious.

De Gaulle recognized that, while working toward his broader goals, he would have to depend upon the guarantee afforded by the United States military presence in the Federal Republic and elsewhere in Europe for some time to come. But United States power, however vital, must influence to the minimal degree feasible the political evolution of Europe. This was a cardinal reason for his rejection of British membership in the Common Market from 1963 on. The United Kingdom's special defense ties with the United States appeared to him as an intolerable restraint on the freedom of action of the Europe he envisaged. Additionally, in the 1960s the British could well have been a potential competitor for leadership.

Chancellor Adenauer had signed the Franco-German treaty in June 1963 and retired, at eighty-seven years of age, in October. He was succeeded by Minister of Economic Affairs Ludwig Erhard, who may have seen more clearly where Gaullist policy was headed but who, in any event, lacked Adenauer's capacity for dealing with de Gaulle. Erhard was also a firm friend of the United States and an advocate of British entry into the Common Market. Within the Common Market there were long, often acrimonious disputes with France over a unified grain price. Accord was finally achieved in December 1964, and common agricultural prices were to go into effect in July 1967. But efforts of the Germans, Italians, and Benelux countries to get French agreement on democratizing the Common Market decisionmaking process were unsuccessful, and in July 1965 the French started a seven-month boycott of the Common Market.

With the advent of the Grand Coalition government in December 1966, both Kiesinger and Brandt gave high priority to arresting the deterioration in relations between France and the Federal Republic. A more independent stance was also adopted in dealing with Washington, but Bonn displayed scant interest in tentative French schemes for military cooperation that aimed at a dilution of United States influence in NATO. The militarily vulnerable Federal Republic needed American troops and the nuclear umbrella for the foreseeable future. The periodic high-level talks provided for in the 1963 treaty were reinvigorated, however, and relations improved until May 1968, when grave internal disorders in France obliged de Gaulle to sharply reorder priorities, again souring relations in the Common Market, particularly with the Federal Republic.

Georges Pompidou was elected as France's new president in June 1969. He proved sufficiently anxious to repair the damage to hint at the possibility of French concessions in the Common Market. He was aided in his peacemaking efforts by having been dropped as prime minister by de Gaulle in July 1968. He was therefore out of office during the low ebb in Franco-German relations. Although Pompidou no longer spoke of a special relationship with the Federal Republic, recognizing that the personal relationship between de Gaulle and Adenauer had been unique, he called for an exemplary association. His foreign minister, Maurice Schumann, amplified this formulation by calling close Franco-German ties the "cornerstone of the European edifice."

When Chancellor Brandt's government assumed power in the Federal Republic in October, it too was anxious for a restoration of cordial relations. A series of courtesy visits to Paris by Bonn officials underlined their desire to dispel possible French doubts about the new socialist government. Brandt was particularly anxious to avoid French opposition to the renewed *Ostpolitik* he was immediately contemplating.

An improved climate rapidly came about, aided by mutual recognition of the Federal Republic's formidable economic strength. The groundwork was laid for close cooperation at The Hague summit of December 1969. Here, French demands were met for a final settlement among the six Common Market countries of the question of agricultural financing and for an agreed common negotiating position before opening talks with applicant states, notably including the United Kingdom. The French then committed themselves—though not in the official communiqué—to prepare for such negotiations in 1970. The Hague summit conference restored movement in the Common Market, now referred to as the European Community since the merger in 1967 of its institutions with those of EURATOM and the ECSC. This movement was to continue unabated until the crisis in late 1973 brought on by the Arab oil embargo. In mid-1971 Prime Minister Edward Heath of the United Kingdom met Pompidou in Paris for a historic summit meeting that seemed to signal the end of years of bitterness engendered by de Gaulle's vetoes of British accession. In June 1971 the six countries reached accord on the terms of British entry, and the British Parliament approved this action in October. The United Kingdom, accompanied by Denmark and Ireland, joined the European Community in January 1973.

The ultimate French acquiescence in British entry, after years of solitary opposition in the smaller community of six, was not just the fruit of France's desire for renewed Franco-German amity. The burgeoning industrial might of the Federal Republic had so surpassed expectations that the United Kingdom was needed by France as a counterpoise against possible Federal Republic preeminence in the European Community.

RELATIONS WITH THE MIDDLE EAST

Bonn's relations with the Middle East countries have long been complicated by its so-called moral debt to Israel. In 1952 the Bundestag voted to deliver to the nascent Jewish state goods and credits valued at the equivalent of US$862 million over a period of twelve to fourteen years. The commitment was fulfilled in its entirety by March 1966. Bonn also undertook secret arms aid to Israel; when this aid was discovered in 1965, it led to a breach in diplomatic ties with ten of the thirteen Arab states. Already accustomed to economic aid from the Federal Republic, however, none of these states risked calling the Hallstein Doctrine into force by recognizing the Democratic Republic. They permitted Bonn to retain consular representation, and existing aid programs were carried forward. A climate of gradual rapprochement was once again disrupted by the 1967 Arab-Israeli war. The sympathy for Israel expressed in the media and by prominent Germans offended the Arabs but, since only Jordan had again normalized diplomatic relations and had no intentions of disrupting them anew, no significant direct actions were taken against the Federal Republic.

The Democratic Republic scored an important breakthrough in 1969 by gaining recognition in quick succession from Iraq, Sudan, and Syria. Bonn, in line with its developing *Ostpolitik*, however, had already eased its stand against third-country recognition of the Democratic Republic, and no serious consequences followed. By the time of the 1973 Arab-Israeli war, full relations had been restored between the Federal Republic and Egypt, Libya, Tunisia, Algeria, Sudan, and the Arab Republic of Yemen.

In the aftermath of that war and the accompanying Arab oil embargo, Bonn felt compelled ultimately to adopt a less pro-Israel, more balanced stance. By February 1974 Bonn publicly went along with the European Community resolution that any Middle East settlement must take into account the more pressing Arab claims, notably those of the Palestinians.

Of significance for the future was Chancellor Schmidt's designation, in May 1974, of Hans-Jurgen Wischnewski as parliamentary state secretary. During the Brandt administration, Wischnewski, then minister of economic cooperation, had been highly successful in selling industrial plants to the Arab nations. Largely because of his efforts, the Federal Republic was the only nation enjoying a balance-of-trade surplus with the Arab states, notwithstanding the dramatic increase in the price of Arab crude oil. Notwithstanding an increasingly vigorous policy toward the Arab states, the Federal Republic in mid-1974 remained steadfast in its essential moral commitments to Israel—a position apparently accepted by the Arabs. An embargo on West German arms shipments to the entire Middle East continued, however.

INTERNATIONAL ORGANIZATIONS

The Federal Republic has participated in all the common postwar efforts aimed at closer political, economic, and defense cooperation among the Western European countries. The Federal Republic is a charter member of the ECSC, launched in 1952, and in 1955 its accession by the Paris agreements to the WEU and NATO provided for the integration of the Federal Republic defense with that of its West European neighbors. WEU, as a coordinating and supervisory agency, composed of France, the United Kingdom, Benelux, Italy, and the Federal Republic, placed certain controls on the latter's rearmament and weapons manufacture. The Paris agreements also granted essential sovereignty to the Federal Republic, reserving to the three Western Allies only those powers affecting the security and operations of their armed forces, and prerogatives involving Berlin's status and that of Germany as a whole, including reunification and a peace settlement. The Federal Republic was one of the eleven NATO nations that in 1966 formed the Nuclear Defense Affairs Committee (NDAC) and its seven-member Nuclear Planning Group (NPG).

In 1957 the Federal Republic signed the Treaty of Rome and thereby became a member of the Common Market and of EURATOM, both of which were formally launched in January 1958. The executive commissions and institutions of the EEC, EURATOM, and ECSC were merged in 1967 to form the European Community. Because of the division of Germany, the Federal Republic was not formally admitted as a member of the UN until September 1973, at which time it was accorded, as was the Democratic Republic, the status of a regular member. Bonn has long had membership in the UN specialized agencies, however, and had been represented on their boards. It also belongs to the Organization for Economic Cooperation and Development (OECD) and the coordinating and guidance group for the aid programs of OECD members, the Development Aid Committee (DAC).

During the decade of the 1960s, Bonn energetically extended aid to less developed countries, notably in South Asia, Africa, and the Middle East. In 1967 Federal Republic developmental aid programs were exceeded only by those of France in percentage of national income allocated to foreign aid, that is, 1.3 percent for the Federal Republic and 1.6 percent for France. Until the early 1970s the Federal Republic's expenditures continued to exceed comfortably the 1 percent of its national income judged an adequate outlay by the OECD. Since 1971 it has been forced to cut back somewhat but continues to meet the 1-percent minimum outlay.

About half of this aid is disbursed through multilateral agreements under the direction of the UN specialized agencies and the OECD. In 1966 a ten-year advanced planning program was inaugurated. Such planning commits bilateral as well as multilateral efforts in experimental programs (such as birth control), while technical assistance, long preferred by the Germans, is now emphasized even more than in the past.

Notably in the bilateral efforts, the Federal Republic has been criticized for exacting relatively hard loan terms and for tying aid to the purchase of Federal Republic goods. Here the hardheaded German businessmen tend to practice their art in a traditional manner. This rugged free enterprise in the less developed world seems compensated for, in a humanist sense, by the scope and fairness of most West German programs and by such special efforts as the German Development Service (Deutsche Entwicklungsdienst—DED). The DED, a kind of peace corps, was founded in 1963 and had placed some 500 workers by the end of the decade. DED members generally work on Bonn's technical assistance projects and are carefully chosen, and each must be fully qualified in some particular activity, such as crafts, industry, medicine, commerce, or social work.

SECTION III. ECONOMIC

CHAPTER 14

CHARACTER AND STRUCTURE OF THE ECONOMY

In mid-1974 the economy of the Federal Republic was among the strongest in a world beset by material shortages, inflation, and monetary instability. Strict official control measures succeeded in containing the rate of inflation well below the levels reached in other countries. Exports and export surpluses continued to grow despite the relatively high value of the Deutsche Mark on foreign exchange markets. The Federal Republic's external position was sufficiently strong to enable it to offer substantial financial aid to an economically troubled partner in the European Community.

The anti-inflationary policy of the government, however, drastically reduced the rate of economic growth in 1974 and, together with the world oil crisis, adversely affected important sectors of industry. Unemployment, although low by international standards, reached levels not experienced in more than a decade. Nevertheless, labor pressed for and obtained increases in wages that exceeded the growth in productivity. The government, however, refused to provide direct relief to enterprises in distress on the ground that such a policy would conflict with the basic principles of the free, competitive economy. The government held the view that the current economic difficulties should be allowed to bring about needed structural adjustments.

The country's economic performance, particularly the strength of its export sector, baffled foreign observers. Despite that performance, the unsettled world economic and political conditions beclouded the future course of the Federal Republic's economic development.

STRUCTURE AND GROWTH

In the 1960–73 period the gross domestic product (GDP), which in the Federal Republic is virtually identical with the gross national product (GNP), more than tripled at current prices to a level of DM926.5 billion (for value of the Deutsche Mark—see Glossary), or DM22,300 per working person. The annual rate of growth averaged 7.7 percent but varied within a range of 6.5 to 13.4 percent, except in 1967 when it fell to only 1 percent. The average growth rate for the twelve years excluding 1967 was 9.7 percent. The largest increase in the volume of generated

GDP occurred in the services sector and construction; the least advance was made in agriculture and mining. As a consequence the structure of GDP changed significantly during the period.

The growth of GDP in 1974 was officially expected to reach no more than 2 percent, compared to 11.6 percent in 1973. This slowdown of the economy was caused largely by anti-inflationary measures of the government, which had particularly severe repercussions in the construction industry, but also by the adverse effects of the 1973 oil crisis on the automotive industry and the decline in textile production as a result of foreign competition. A partial relaxation of anti-inflationary policies, however, and the possibility of the introduction of selective reflationary measures to boost the economy were reported toward the end of August 1974.

The anti-inflation program of May 1973 was successful in limiting the rise in consumer prices to 7.2 percent in that year and to an anticipated 7 to 8 percent in 1974. These rates were reported to be less than half the inflation rates suffered by some of the Federal Republic's major competitors. The success in restraining price inflation, however, was paid for in part through a rise in unemployment to almost 200,000 workers, or 2.2 percent of the labor force (which includes more than 2 million foreign workers). This level of unemployment, which is very high by Federal Republic standards and the highest since 1960, may explain the reported intention of the government to revitalize economic growth.

The growth of GDP in real terms, as measured in prices of 1963, was substantially slower from 1960 through 1970, the last year for which comparable data are available; it amounted to 61 percent, as compared to 127 percent in current prices. The difference was accounted for by a price inflation of about 41 percent during the period. The rise in prices differed substantially from sector to sector; it was 10 percent in agriculture and 17.3 percent in mining, power production, and water distribution but 67.2 percent in construction and 82.2 percent in services. Price inflation amounted to 27.8 percent in manufacturing and 38.8 percent in trade, transport, and communications.

Manufacturing has been by far the most important sector of the economy; in most years of the 1960–72 period it generated about 42 percent of GDP, and in only two of the years did it contribute less than 41 percent. Despite their increased contribution to GDP in absolute terms, agriculture and mining declined in relative importance; in 1972 these sectors generated only 2.9 and 3.6 percent of GDP, respectively. The GDP contribution by trade, transport, and communications declined by 2 percentage points to 17.6 percent, while the GDP generated by other private and public services rose from 20.2 to 27 percent of the total.

Significant changes occurred in the distribution and use of GNP in the 1960–73 period. The share of income from employment increased, while the proportion of property and entrepreneurial income—and the government's share in this income—declined. Whereas depreciation absorbed a rising fraction of GNP, excise taxes accounted for a declining proportion. There was little change over the period in the proportion of total GNP devoted to consumption, but the government's share of consumption increased. A declining portion of government consumption was devoted to defense. Gross capital formation absorbed about one-fourth of GNP, fluctuating annually within a narrow range; somewhat more than half the investment was devoted to building construction. Net exports accounted for a fraction of GNP each year.

CONSTITUTIONAL BASIS OF ECONOMY

The Basic Law of the Federal Republic prescribes no specific form of economic organization and provides little guidance for the resolution of concrete problems involved in shaping the economy. The Federal Constitutional Court has repeatedly emphasized the neutrality of the Basic Law in matters of economic policy. The government has interpreted this neutrality not as a disregard for basic structural problems but as a decision in principle to leave the responsibility for economic policy to democratically legitimized legislation. The economic order was not to be constitutionally fixed once and for all but was to be left to the discretion of changing parliamentary majorities. Decisions concerning economic policy must be made by the parliament and not by the constitutional court.

The Basic Law, however, circumscribed the political latitude of parliament in the economic sphere through the prescribed distribution of powers within the federal state, legal and democratic principles, social directives, and specific grants of basic legal rights. Several provisions of the Basic Law clearly established the responsibility of the state to attain and preserve social justice. For this reason economic policy has always been equated with social policy.

Nevertheless, the totality of constitutional provisions bearing on the economy has no great normative force and requires a great deal of concrete elaboration. This elaboration is primarily the function of lawmakers, whose freedom to make economic policy decisions provides ample room for legislation; the laws cannot be defended on constitutional grounds but must be justified in political terms.

The Basic Law guarantees the right to private property and freedom of economic initiative to all citizens, provided that rights of others are respected and that the constitutional and moral codes are adhered to. Any legislative limitation of individual freedom must therefore be justified on grounds of public welfare. This applies, for instance, to any transfer of land, natural resources, or capital assets from private to public ownership (subject to appropriate compensation) and to all market and price regulations that significantly curtail entrepreneurial freedom. Official regulation of economic activity must leave to private initiative adequate scope for self-regulating development. The constitutional provision that grants broad economic legislative powers to parliament also guarantees fundamental rights of contract and economic initiative for the protection of individual citizens. Thus, for instance, public authority may not eliminate the autonomy of private enterprise in order to establish a highly centralized system of binding plan directives.

ECONOMIC POLICY

The economic policies of the Federal Republic have been based on the concept of a social market economy, which was developed by a group of German scholars after World War II. The basic principle underlying the social market economy was that political freedom and maximum public welfare could be ensured only through free competition in an open market. Free competition, however, could not be expected to thrive under conditions of complete enterprise freedom—generally known as laissez-faire—which might lead to harmful concentrations of economic power and to economic instability. A duty therefore devolved upon the government to establish and maintain a free competitive order through the promulgation of broad economic policies that would provide guidance for economic activity.

The aims of the social market economy, which are embodied in the government's economic policy, include the stability of prices, full employment, equilibrium in foreign trade, orderly economic growth, and a just distribution of the national product. These aims are to be attained with as little governmental interference in the economic process as is necessary to maintain free and fair competition. The concept of the social market economy has not been applied to agriculture and transportation, where freedom of competition is considered to be economically and socially impracticable. Agricultural production, marketing, and prices have been determined by comprehensive governmental support programs consistent with the Common Agricultural Policy of the European Community (see ch. 15).

The need to follow the overall economic development closely in order to anticipate problems and to be in a position to meet unexpected difficulties effectively led, in 1963, to the creation of the Council of Experts for the Evaluation of Overall Economic Development. The task of this council is to determine through appropriate research how equilibrium can best be maintained in the framework of the market economy. Members of the council are appointed by the president of the Federal Republic on the recommendation of the government; they may not themselves promote economic policies. The work of the council is carried out with the aid of research institutes and universities. The government is obliged to respond to the recommendations of the council and thereby to make its policies public.

Competition Policy

To ensure competition, the Law Against Restrictions of Competition (Cartel Act) was passed in 1957 after seven years of intensive debate.

Labeled as the basic law of the social market economy, the Cartel Act forbade contracts and secret understandings to influence marketing conditions by restricting competition. The government's policy did not contemplate the introduction of perfect competition as it exists in theory. The government recognized that certain imperfections in the dynamic market process had to be accepted, if only for the reason that higher profits enabled oligopolistic enterprises better to finance research and development.

For various reasons, not the least of which was to give entrepreneurs sufficient incentive for a rapid reconstruction of the war-ravaged economy, the Cartel Act was not strictly enforced. An increasing number of enterprise mergers and growing domination of the market by large corporations, however, led the government in the fall of 1971 to propose an amendment strengthening the Cartel Act. The amendment provided for preventive controls over mergers of large corporations and for improved supervision to guard against abuses by enterprises dominating the market. At the same time the draft amendment sought to facilitate cooperation among small and medium-sized business enterprises in the interest of greater efficiency and greater competitive strength.

Strong opposition to new controls over corporations delayed legislative consideration and enactment of the proposed measure. In January 1973 the chancellor welcomed an agreement by the coalition partners to resubmit the draft law to the Bundestag (Federal Diet) and promised the government's cooperation in broadening and strengthening the proposed legislation (see ch. 11). In mid-1974 a new antitrust law had not yet been enacted. In the spring of that year, however, the Cartel Office took energetic action against what the government believed to be unjustified price increases by major concerns in the petroleum, automotive, and pharmaceutical fields.

In the context of European Community discussions during that period on a common energy policy, the Federal Republic opposed the institution of central controls over the energy industry. It remained committed to a policy of free competition within the framework of governmental regulations. The commitment to a free market economy was forcefully reaffirmed by the government in mid-1974, when it rejected an urgent appeal for aid from the economically depressed automobile industry. On that occasion the state secretary was reported to have remarked that there was no way for the government to help industry because the free market economy prevailed equally in good and in bad times.

Monetary and Fiscal Policy

Proponents of the social market economy held the view that maintenance of a competitive order and of orderly economic growth required above all stability of the currency. A stable currency, they thought, would eliminate the danger of recurring business cycles. Monetary policy was therefore regarded as the most important instrument of economic guidance and intervention by the state. Memories of runaway inflation in two postwar periods also contributed to establishing price stability as the primary objective of economic policy.

The Federal Bank Act of 1957 assigned responsibility for monetary policy to the country's central bank—the German Federal Bank—which was established as a legally independent institution not subject to government direction in monetary matters. The same law, however, obliged the bank to support the general economic policies of the government, without prejudice to its own responsibility for safeguarding the currency. Cooperation between the bank and the government was provided for mainly in the form of mutual consultations and participation in policy discussions. The ambiguity of the legal provisions and of the distinction between government policy and government directives provided opportunities for conflicts of policy between the central bank and the government.

The means available to the central bank for carrying out its monetary policy include the authority to alter the discount rate on loans to commercial banks and to change the level of currency reserves against their deposits that banks must maintain at the central bank. The central bank may also buy and sell government securities in the open market and may ask the government to require the social security system to deposit a portion of its liquid reserves in the central bank.

Until 1967 fiscal policy could not be used as a means toward achieving economic stability. The Basic Law required that estimates of federal budgetary receipts and expenditures be balanced annually and set a limit on government borrowing. Loans could be obtained by the government only from the central bank and were restricted to financing expenditure for productive purposes. Budgetary autonomy of the *Länder* (states; sing., *Land*) and local communities, whose combined budgets substantially exceeded the federal budget, also constituted a major obstacle to the pursuit of a consistent fiscal policy.

According to a study published by the Organization for Economic Cooperation and Development, legal restrictions did not, in practice, prevent either substantial deficits or surpluses from arising in the implementation of the federal budgets. Because of experiences with budgetary mismanagement in earlier periods, however, parliament, government, and public opinion strongly opposed deficit financing and rejected the use of budgetary policy as an instrument for countering cyclical business fluctuations.

The economic boom and subsequent recession of the mid-1960s demonstrated that monetary policy alone could not be relied upon to ensure stability of the economy. That experience also brought the recognition that protection of the currency could not remain the sole preoccupation of the central bank and that the bank must share with the government responsibility for policies concerning economic growth and the control of business cycles. In June 1967 this recognition culminated in

264

the enactment of the Law for the Promotion of Stability and Growth of the Economy and of a constitutional amendment to accommodate the new legislation.

The stabilization law required federal and *Land* authorities to take into account the equilibrium requirements of the national economy in all their economic and financial policy measures. The law defined economic equilibrium as the stability of the price level, maintenance of high employment, and equilibrium in the balance of payments, accompanied by a steady and appropriate rate of economic growth. In contrast to established custom, it empowered the government to use fiscal measures in carrying out its economic stabilization policy.

Although the independence of *Land* and community budgets was preserved, the federal government was granted the right to freeze federal and *Land* budgetary funds up to 3 percent of the preceding year's receipts in a so-called business-cycle-leveling reserve account at the central bank when deemed necessary to restrain expansionary tendencies. These reserves could subsequently be released to counter a decline in economic activity. For the same reason the government was also authorized to propose the imposition by law of limits on borrowing by all levels of government. The federal government, however, has no direct means for influencing the size and nature of *Land* and local budgets and must rely on persuasion to enlist cooperation with its fiscal policies.

Other tools for fiscal management provided by the stabilization law include the right of the government to raise or lower personal and corporate income taxes; levy temporary surcharges on these incomes during periods of economic boom and subsequently disburse receipts from this source to stimulate the economy in periods of slowdown; grant investment premiums or raise investment taxes; and raise or lower depreciation allowances. Advice to the government on business cycle management is given by the Council on Business Cycles, composed of high-level federal, *Land*, and local officials.

In dealing with external threats to the stability of the economy, the government must first try to develop protective economic measures at home. In the event that domestic measures alone prove inadequate, the government must exhaust all possibilities of international cooperation. Only after these measures have been exhausted may the government have recourse to such means legally at its command as altering the exchange rate, introducing flexible exchange rates, and changing the level of turnover taxes on exports and imports. All of these measures have been used at one time or another. Administrative measures, including the limitation of capital exports and restrictions on investment and deposits by foreigners, may also be used but require authorization by the Commission of the European Community.

The stabilization law accentuated the need for close cooperation between the central bank and the government, by placing upon the government responsibility for stabilizing the price level. This provision

265

necessarily implied authority for the government to participate in the formulation of monetary policy and the stabilization of the currency. No definite division of responsibility between the bank and the government was achieved at least until mid-1972, when the bank, in response to widespread public interest, published a statement on this subject in its regular monthly report. The stabilization law also failed to provide any guidelines for the coordination of monetary and fiscal policies.

Wage Policy

The right to determine wage scales is legally reserved to employers' organizations and the labor unions through mutual negotiation; the government may not interfere directly in the wage-setting process. With a view to eliminating possibilities of conflict between wage policy and official business cycle policy, the stabilization law authorized the government to issue quantitative guidelines for coordinated action involving the official budgets, employers' organizations, and labor unions. Such concerted action has been sought through frequent consultations by the government with representatives of employers and the unions. These meetings have not been limited to discussions of wage policies but have also addressed important long-term problems concerning the level of employment, investment and price policies of enterprises, competition policy, administrative price changes, and the distribution of income and property. In this way important segments of society have been associated with official economic planning. The government, however, remains solely responsible for the adopted policies.

Economic Planning

Meaningful guidance of the economy necessarily implies a need for forward-looking planning. In the postwar Federal Republic economic planning was generally proscribed on the ground that it conflicted with the principles of the social market economy; it was widely feared that planning would eventually lead to a centrally directed socialist system. By the time the stabilization law was drafted, however, sufficient support had been gained for the idea that purposeful overall guidance of the economy was essential to attain rational economic development. The change in public opinion was attributed by the finance minister to the experience gained in the recession of 1966 and 1967 and the success of official policy in combating it.

When passed, the stabilization law therefore contained a provision for planning that required that annual budgets be formulated in the framework of a five-year financial plan based on a projection of the economic development over that period. The main purpose of the legal provision was to allow the purposeful use of the budget as an instrument for combating economic fluctuations by contracting budgetary expenditures in periods of rising economic activity and expanding outlays in periods of economic decline. With necessary adjustments to reflect changed economic conditions the plan, generally known as the medium-term plan, is moved forward annually by dropping the first year of the plan period and adding a new year at the end. The first medium-term plan published by the Ministry of Finance covered the years 1967 through 1971. In addition to the financial plan the government must submit to parliament an annual economic report that also includes a statement of its economic policy objectives for the coming year.

The financial plan reflects the policy aims of the government; it must reconcile the political will with the economic potential and financial imperatives. This requires the determination of specific priorities and the elimination of less essential or less desirable objectives. The selection of priorities by the government inevitably arouses acclaim or condemnation by sections of the public depending upon their particular interests. Such a one-sided approach leads to an erroneous evaluation of the financial plan, according to the minister of finance. To arrive at a correct judgment about the plan and the official decisions it reflects, the minister suggested, it is necessary to know the entire work. To this end the new plan is published annually to give every politically minded citizen the opportunity to inform himself about the aims and intentions of the government. The government hopes thereby to gain understanding for its policy and support for the policy's implementation.

Coordination of fiscal policies between the federal, *Land*, and local governments for purposes of medium-term planning is worked out by the Financial Planning Council. Members of the council include the minister of finance, who acts as chairman; the minister of economy; finance ministers or senators of the *Länder;* and four representatives of local governments. The council is not empowered to make binding decisions but is limited to making recommendations. Successful coordination therefore depends to a large extent upon the willingness of the council members and their constituent bodies to follow the recommendations of the council and to formulate their budgets accordingly.

At least until 1973 effective coordination of budgets presented major difficulties because of disparities in structure, differences in the timing of budgetary formulation, and discrepancies in the underlying economic assumptions. As long ago as 1968 the Financial Planning Council recommended a uniform budget format for adoption by all jurisdictions, but the recommendation had not been fully acted upon by 1973. Participation by local communities in the planning process was to be made mandatory by law effective January 1, 1974. In the preceding three years they were required by decrees of the *Länder* to formulate financial plans in accordance with a prescribed pattern.

In its middle-term report for 1973 to 1977 the government pointed out that the relatively low and declining share of the federal budget in total public expenditures—43.2 percent in 1972—constituted a major obstacle to consistent and effective fiscal planning for the purpose of countering cyclical business fluctuations, inasmuch as the government had no control over expenditures by *Land* and community authorities. The problem would be compounded and the stabilization program jeopardized, the government held, by a proposed further reallocation of tax revenues to these authorities, because it would lead to increased outlays by the *Länder* and communities and would force the federal government to meet its obligations by deficit financing. In this context the government suggested that *Land* and community authorities should be made to bear a greater share of responsibility for stabilization policy.

Economic Democracy

The social content of the government's economic policy has been expressed mainly in democratic control of industry through worker participation in management and in the promotion of property accumulation by workers below a specified income level. Codetermination, as worker participation in management is officially called, was given legal sanction in 1952. Property accumulation has been encouraged mainly through various tax concessions to savers. Many large companies, however, have voluntarily enabled their workers to purchase shares at favorable prices.

Codetermination operates on three different levels. The works council, elected directly by the entire labor force, participates on an equal basis with enterprise management at the shop level in decisions concerning personnel, wage scales and fringe benefits, working-hour schedules, and other matters of a social and economic nature. At the top management level, workers elect one-third of the supervisory board's members in all stock companies with more than 500 employees and half the members in all mining enterprises. Workers' representatives need not necessarily be employees of the company on whose board they sit, but only 15 percent of the supervisory boards include outsiders. A labor director is also included in the executive committee as a full-fledged member with responsibility and authority extending beyond the primary function of personnel administration. The labor director is appointed by the supervisory board from a slate of trade union members agreed to by representatives of the company's employees and the national union. The director may not be removed from office against the wishes of a majority of workers' representatives.

Codetermination at the supervisory board level was reported to have worked out successfully in the coal-mining industry, where labor and stockholders have equal representation. A rise in productivity and a reduction in the labor force were attained without undue hardship to displaced workers, because of measures that made transition to other occupations relatively painless. In other industries, however, the minority status of worker representatives on the boards precluded any significant influence of labor on the companies' business policies.

The role of workers in management at the shop level was enhanced by law in 1972. Draft legislation, however, to introduce parity of labor with stockholders in representation on supervisory boards of about 660 of the largest companies outside mining met with strong industry opposition and little support from the junior partner of the ruling political coalition. A similarly unfavorable reception was given the proposal to require companies with taxable annual profits in excess of DM400,000—about 27,000 in number—to surrender for the benefit of workers up to 10 percent of their annual net profits, in shares or in cash. These funds would be invested in centrally administered trusts on behalf of all employees below a certain—reported to be fairly high—income level. The yield from these trusts is expected to reach about DM5 billion per year; it would be distributed to qualified workers at the rate of DM212 per year. Accumulated funds could also be used for investment in socially useful projects. The eventual fate of these codetermination and property accumulation proposals was uncertain in mid-1974.

An important measure of social justice is to take effect on January 1, 1975, with the introduction of an income tax reform aimed mainly at equalizing the tax burden by providing tax relief to lower and middle income groups. The tax measure was initially conceived in 1971, but resistance to parts of it by the parliamentary opposition delayed the enactment of the legislation. The reform has been officially estimated to entail an annual revenue loss of DM13 billion for the federal and *Land* budgets.

LABOR

In 1972 the economically active population in the Federal Republic numbered 24.5 million people, almost two-thirds of whom were male. Almost half these people were engaged in industry, including construction, but little more than 7 percent were active in agriculture. The remainder were divided between trade and transportation, 18 percent, and services, 26 percent. Men outnumbered women in all branches other than agriculture, where the proportion of men toward the end of 1971 was 49 percent. The largest ratio of men to women—three to one—was in industry, the lowest in services—53 to 47 percent. In the 1962–72 period the number of economically active people had declined by 1 percent, and a significant shift from agriculture into services had taken place. In 1970, 12.1 million of the 26.5 million economically active people—about 46 percent—were classified as workers, that is, hired individuals working for wages.

Until the erection of the Berlin Wall in 1961, the labor force had been largely augmented by the influx of refugees from the German Democratic Republic. More than 6 million workers were reported to have been added to the labor force from this source. By 1960, however, the domestic labor force no longer sufficed to support the rapid expansion of the economy, and a policy of recruiting foreign labor was adopted. The number of foreign workers increased rapidly; it more than doubled between 1968 and 1972, when it reached a level of 2.3 million, and rose to 2.6 million in

1973. The largest contingents of foreign workers, in order of magnitude, came from Turkey, Yugoslavia, and Italy, followed, on a somewhat lower scale, by Greece and Spain.

In 1973 foreign workers constituted about 11 percent of the labor force. They were heavily concentrated, however, both by type of employment and in geographic location. Almost 35 percent worked in the iron and steel and metalworking industries, 28 percent were engaged in manufacturing, and 18 percent were employed in construction. More than half the foreign workers were located in about 4 percent of the country's territory. Their proportion in the labor force was reported to reach as much as 20 percent in Frankfurt and 25 percent in Stuttgart.

Although the original intention was to rotate foreign labor so that individual workers would remain in the country only a year or two, almost one-third of the workers in 1973 had already stayed more than four years, and over 25 percent had worked for more than seven years. More than 60 percent of the foreign workers were reported to have expressed the desire to remain in the country permanently. The absorption of so many mostly unskilled foreign workers posed serious economic and social problems. Rising unemployment associated with the government's anti-inflationary policy and the international oil crisis put an end to foreign labor recruitment in November 1973.

Workers in the Federal Republic are organized in sixteen industry-wide trade unions affiliated with the Federation of German Trade Unions. Aside from the strictly industrial field, these unions also embrace workers in agriculture and forestry; education and science; art; trade, banking, and insurance; food handling and catering; public services and transport; and the postal service. In addition to the workers' unions, there are also the union of white-collar workers, the German Federation of Civil Servants, and the Postal Union. Membership in trade unions is not obligatory. In 1972 the Federation of German Trade Unions had a membership of about 7 million, or somewhat more than half the total number of workers. The other union organizations had a total membership of more than 1.2 million.

The size of the trade unions—the metalworkers' union counts 2.4 million members—and their disciplined behavior has earned for them a position of power and respect in the labor field. They participate as equals with employers' organizations in the process of collective bargaining. The ultimate union weapon in a labor dispute—the strike—is subject to strict and binding restrictions imposed by the federation, and unauthorized strikes that breach existing labor contracts are punishable by heavy, court-imposed indemnity payments to employers.

The incidence of strikes and the attendant loss of worktime have been relatively low in comparison with those of other industrialized countries, particularly before 1969. In 1971, 2.6 million workdays were lost through strikes involving about 330,000 workers and 624 plants. More than half the strikers returned to work in less than seven days, and no strike lasted longer than twenty-four days. In 1972 only 66,000 workdays were lost through strikes of 23,000 workers against fifty-four plants.

The threat of strike action increased in the early 1970s, as workers began to demand a greater share of the returns from the expanding economy and progressive inflation, albeit low by international standards, threatened to reduce their income. In February 1974, after prolonged unfruitful negotiations, the civil service employees' union went on strike to support its demand for a 15-percent pay increase against the government's offer of 9 percent. The strike was settled three days later by a compromise that raised wages by 12.5 percent. This settlement was expected to have repercussions on other pending wage negotiations and ensure what the government considered to be inflationary wage increases. A study by the European Community of wage increases in 1973 found the average rise in workers' pay in the Federal Republic to have been 12 percent, compared to a 6-percent increase in output per worker. This level of wage increase was lowest among the community members.

The real income of workers has risen steadily. In the 1962–73 period hourly wage rates increased by 135 percent, gross hourly earnings rose by 144 percent, but the cost of living advanced only 47 percent. Gross hourly earnings in real terms thus increased by 66 percent, a rate close to the growth rate of real GDP during that period.

THE BUDGET

The public sector is of considerable importance to the country's economy. In the 1962–72 period the combined annual budgetary outlays of the federal, Land, and local authorities were equivalent to 30 percent of the GNP. During the same period the overall budget increased more than twofold to DM233.5 billion in revenues and DM252.3 billion in expenditures. A further increase to DM273.5 billion in receipts and DM282.6 billion in expenditures was estimated for 1973. Except for 1969, when the overall budget had a DM2.5 billion surplus, annual expenditures exceeded revenues by DM1.6 billion to DM18.9 billion. The share of federal outlays in total budgetary expenditures declined from 47 percent in 1962 to 43.2 percent in 1972.

In principle, the Land and community authorities enjoy full financial autonomy within limits specified by the constitution and the law. Activities not specifically allocated by the constitution to the federal government fall within the province of the Länder and local governments. The expenditure patterns of the different levels of government reflect this division of responsibility. The federal budget covers all, or virtually all, costs of defense, social security, and foreign affairs. It also provides from two-thirds to three-fourths of the funds for food, agriculture, and forests; veterans and refugees; and scientific research outside the universities. These items account for about 60 percent of the federal budget. The Länder and community budgets bear virtually the entire burden of costs for schools, community services, health, sports,

271

and the support of art, culture, and the churches. They also cover the bulk of the costs for family welfare, housing and urban development, transport and communication, energy, and water supply.

In addition to its regular budget, the federal government administers through specialized institutions the Equalization of Burdens Fund, used to compensate war victims, and the European Recovery Program Fund, designed to repay economic aid received under the Marshall Plan after World War II. The size of these funds declined from 6 percent of the federal budget in 1965 to 3 percent in 1971.

The *Länder* and communities are legally free to decide about expenditures in their fields of activity, but only the federal government, with minor exceptions, can legislate in the field of taxation. Aside from local trade and real estate taxes, where the communities may determine the rates of taxation, and some other minor local taxes, changes in taxation at all government levels depend upon action by federal authorities. Tax legislation affecting the *Länder* requires approval by the Bundesrat (Federal Council). Tax administration, however, including the collection of taxes, is primarily a function of the *Länder*.

Revenues

The tax system includes a wide range of direct and indirect taxes, which are subject to frequent revisions. An official classification of taxes in 1974 listed six different categories and forty-six separate kinds of taxes, excluding miscellaneous community taxes. The most important of these in revenue yield are the progressive personal and corporate income tax and taxes on trade turnover; together these taxes account for two-thirds of total tax receipts including customs duties. The income tax yield increased from 38.3 percent of total tax revenue in 1967 to 43.1 percent in 1972 and an estimated 46.7 percent in 1974. At least until January 1975 incomes of up to DM24,000 were exempt from tax, and the highest rate at which income was taxed was 53 percent.

Proceeds from most taxes are allocated to specific levels of government, but tax sharing is practiced in the case of income, turnover, and local trade taxes. The share of the federal government in income taxes was raised from 38 to 39 percent in 1964, then lowered to 37 percent in 1967 and 35 percent in 1969. Thereafter, under a budgetary reform effective in January 1970, a permanent distribution scheme was established under which both the federal and *Land* governments receive 50 percent of the corporate and 43 percent of the personal income taxes, while the remaining 14 percent of personal income taxes is allocated to the communities. The communities, in turn, must turn over 40 percent of their trade tax receipts to the federal and *Land* governments.

The distribution of turnover taxes has been left flexible as a means for meeting the legal requirement to equalize the ratio of receipts to expenditures in the federal and *Land* budgets, a function that had previously been performed by the income tax. The distribution is reviewed biannually, and agreed adjustments are formalized by law. Under this scheme the federal government received 70 percent of the turnover taxes in 1970 and 1971. Subsequent negotiations between the federal and *Land* governments reduced the federal share to 65 percent for 1972 and 1973. In addition the federal government was persuaded to make grants of DM550 million in both years to financially weak *Länder*, including Bavaria, Lower Saxony, Rhineland-Palatinate, Schleswig-Holstein, and the Saar. This tax reallocation was made despite the federal government's position that raising the tax share of *Länder* seriously complicated its task of fighting inflation.

For 1974 the *Länder* demanded a further increase in the tax share. In an effort to put tax sharing on a sounder basis, a working party was formed in May 1973 under the chairmanship of the federal chancellor. Members of the working group are the federal ministers of economic affairs and of finance and the minister-presidents of Baden-Württemberg, Lower Saxony, North Rhine-Westphalia, and Schleswig-Holstein. Information on the discussions and conclusions of the working group was not available in August 1974.

Expenditures

In the 1961–71 period total budgetary outlays of all government levels more than doubled, from DM95.3 billion to DM225.4 billion. At the same time the structure of outlays changed significantly. The proportion of expenditures for defense declined while that for public safety increased. The expenditure shares of universities and research, public schools, health, sports, recreation, and public transport rose substantially, while the proportion of outlays for social security, housing, urban and rural development, and energy declined. All categories of outlays, however, increased in absolute terms; the increases ranged from fivefold for universities and research to two-thirds for housing and urban development. On a per capita basis the rise in expenditures was only slightly lower.

Official statistics on the distribution of budgetary expenditures fail to include about one-fourth of the outlays. These outlays cover such items as the cost of government administration, foreign aid, contributions to the European Community, interest payments, subsidies and loans to the railroad and post office, and financial assistance to some of the poorer states and to West Berlin.

Budget Formulation

The fiscal year coincides with the calendar year. During the first half of the year preceding the budget year, the minister of finance formulates the federal budget proposal for presentation to the cabinet in July, based on expenditure estimates submitted to him by the various federal ministries and estimated revenues. The finance minister has the right to adjust the ministries' expenditure estimates, but his own draft budget may be modified against his will only by a majority of the cabinet including the federal chancellor. The agreed federal government budget must be submitted to the Bundestag before October 1.

Both houses of parliament and their budget committees discuss the draft budget and any proposed amendments. Differences between the two houses are debated and reconciled in a mediation committee; if this committee fails to reach an agreement, the Bundestag makes the final decision by majority vote. Parliament, however, has only limited possibilities of changing the government's revenue and expenditure estimates, and a decision by either house to increase expenditures requires the federal government's approval. If agreement on a budget is not reached before the beginning of the new budget year, the government may continue spending for some time within defined limits. Supplementary budgets may be presented at any time; they are handled in the same manner as the regular annual budget. Most of the *Länder* have adopted budgetary procedures substantially similar to those followed in the preparation of the federal budget.

CURRENCY

The currency unit of the Federal Republic is the Deutsche Mark (DM), divided into 100 pfennigs. The Deutsche Mark is freely convertible and ranks among the strongest currencies of the world. There are no reserve requirements of gold or foreign exchange for the national currency.

The fifth revaluation of the Deutsche Mark in less than four years established its official value in June 1973 at DM1 equal to 0.310580 Special Drawing Right (SDR). The SDR is an international unit of account used by the International Monetary Fund; it is equivalent to the value of US$1 before August 15, 1971, or 888.6706 milligrams of fine gold. The gold content of the Deutsche Mark was thus set at 276.003 milligrams. In the meantime the theoretical gold content of US$1 was reduced to 736.6617 milligrams, so that the official parity value of DM1 became equal to US$0.3747, or US$1 equal to DM2.67 (rounded to the nearest pfennig), compared to the rate of DM4.00 that prevailed until October 1969.

Under the Smithsonian Agreement concerning international exchange rates, reached by major Western trading nations in Washington in December 1971, currencies, including the Deutsche Mark, were allowed to fluctuate within margins of 2.25 percent on either side of the parity rate. In April 1972, however, the Federal Republic in common with other European Community countries narrowed the range of fluctuation between their own currencies to a maximum of 2.25 percent, or 1.125 percent up or down. The Scandinavian countries were included in this agreement. The wider range was maintained against other currencies, including the United States dollar.

About a year later, after another devaluation of the United States dollar in February 1973, the Federal Republic announced that the maximum margin of 2.25 percent would be maintained only against the currencies of France, Belgium, Luxembourg, the Netherlands, Denmark, Norway, and Sweden. France was eliminated from this arrangement when it floated the franc in January 1974. As a result of the currency float, the dollar-Deutsche Mark rate fluctuated by as much as 12 percent in a three-month period and by 15 percent over nine months. At the end of August 1974 US$1 equaled DM2.66, compared to DM2.47 one year earlier.

The country's net holdings of gold and foreign exchange increased from the equivalent of DM45.9 billion at the end of 1967 to DM110 billion in March 1974. This increase was brought about by persistent export-generated balance-of-payments surpluses, despite repeated revaluations of the currency and a substantial rise in the cost of imported materials and fuels.

Gold may be owned and traded without restriction, except that a license is required for imports from Rhodesia. Restrictions on trade are few and apply mainly to trade in strategic commodities, trade with communist countries and Rhodesia, imports of coal, and imports of agricultural products under European Community regulations. Payments for imported goods and services are free even in the case of restricted trade transactions. Measures to restrict capital flows have been used and modified from time to time in efforts to control domestic inflationary tendencies.

BANKING

The banking system of the Federal Republic comprises a variety of private and public financial institutions. Any individual or group of persons may enter the banking business, provided that they comply with the requirements of the 1961 credit system law. In 1973 as many as 6,892 banking institutions with 36,393 branches were active in the credit field. Virtually all legal forms of business organization were represented among the banks, such as corporations, joint stock companies, cooperatives, various types of partnership, and single proprietorships.

Public banking institutions include the country's central bank, municipal savings banks and their reserve banks, and such specialized institutions as the Credit Institute for Reconstruction and the Equalization of Burdens Bank. There is also an extensive network of postal savings banks under the supervision of the federal government; these banks make long-term loans mainly to public authorities.

In its present form, the German Federal Bank dates from 1957, when it was established through reorganization of the Bank of the German States, which had functioned on an interim basis after World War II. The bank is legally independent of the government but is obliged to cooperate with it in matters of financial and general economic policies. The government holds the bank's capital stock, and the president of the Federal Republic appoints the members of its directorate for periods of eight years. The administrative functions of the bank are carried out through central bank offices in each of the ten *Länder* and West Berlin.

The central bank has the exclusive right to issue bank notes. Its main function is the promotion and enforcement of a monetary policy that will ensure economic stability. To this end it has various means at its disposal to regulate the availability of credit and the financial liquidity of the banking system. The central bank has the power to vary the rediscount rate on commercial paper presented to it and to set limits on the amount of such paper it is prepared to rediscount at any given time. Control over the rediscount volume is exercised through rediscount quotas based on the banks' capital structure and reserves and differentiated according to type of financial institutions. The quotas may be raised or lowered to expand or contract the supply of credit. Commercial banks may also borrow from the central bank within prescribed limits on the security of bonds or commercial paper. Advances secured by bonds usually carry a higher interest charge.

Between January 1959 and June 1973 the rediscount rate was changed thirty times; individual rates remained in effect for periods ranging from only four weeks to almost two years. Rediscount rates, which also apply to cash advances, ranged between 2.75 and 7.5 percent. Rates for advances secured by bonds ranged from 3.75 to 9.5 percent. Until September 1969 the difference between the two rates was a uniform 1 percent; thereafter the spread ranged between 1 and 2 percent. Special advances on the security of bonds made in the winter of 1973 and the spring of 1974 carried an interest rate of 13 percent.

The central bank exercises control over minimum legal reserve requirements that commercial banks and other financial institutions must maintain against deposits. By varying the reserve requirements the central bank can directly influence the ability of the banks to extend credit. The central bank has made frequent use of this power in its efforts to stabilize the price level after 1967.

Through purchase and sale of securities on the open market the central bank can influence the supply of liquid funds in the banking system. Securities traded by the central bank include bills and bonds of the Treasury and medium-term notes of the federal and *Land* governments, the federal railroads, and the federal post office. Prime bankers' acceptances and bonds traded on the official stock exchange may also be included in open market operations.

The central bank has no independent means to curb borrowing abroad by banks and industrial enterprises or to stem inflows of foreign capital and speculative funds, all of which tend to have an inflationary effect through the expansion of the domestic money supply. In an effort to control the influx of foreign funds, the central bank and the federal government jointly introduced a law, effective January 1972, that requires interest-free cash deposits to be made with the central bank against certain kinds of foreign borrowing.

In July of that year the cash deposit requirement was raised from 40 to

50 percent of the liabilities incurred abroad, and the amount of borrowing exempt from the deposit requirement was reduced from DM2 million to DM500,000. At the same time the sale of domestic bonds, bills of exchange, and noninterest-bearing treasury bonds to nonresidents was made subject to government authorization. In January 1973 the DM500,000 allowance under the cash deposit requirement was further reduced to DM50,000, and the obligation to obtain government authorization was extended to cover sales of all types of securities, arrangements for foreign loans or credits, and the supply of capital equipment to production units in the Federal Republic by nonresidents.

A virtual stagnation of industrial growth in the second half of 1973 and expectations of a very low rate of economic growth in 1974 led to a relaxation of the restrictions on capital inflows effective January 31, 1974. The requirement for prior authorization was lifted for all transactions other than the sale to nonresidents of certain types of bonds, the cash deposit on foreign borrowing was reduced to 20 percent, and the deposit-free allowance was raised to DM100,000.

Municipally owned savings banks are generally small, having assets of less than DM50 million, but some of them rank among the largest financial institutions in the country. Savings banks usually accept both savings and short-term deposits. The volume of savings has grown substantially, in part as a result of premiums for saving offered by the government to lower and middle income groups. Traditionally, savings banks have made loans for local housing, small business, and municipal projects and have invested a portion of their funds in *Land* and federal bonds. Gradually they have expanded their field of operations by making loans to medium-sized firms, including industrial concerns, and by investing in corporate securities. In mid-1974 about 70 percent of the savings banks' outstanding loans were classified as long-term obligations, and 21 percent were listed as short-term. The remaining 9 percent were medium-term loans.

Twelve central savings banks serve as clearinghouses and reserve banks for the municipal savings banks. They are moving increasingly in the direction of providing a full range of commercial bank services, including foreign exchange transactions. Through merger with two other regional banks one of the central savings banks became the second largest of the country's banking institutions, with assets of DM29 billion in 1970. The central savings banks have acquired importance in the international banking field by placing or underwriting loans, investing in foreign banks and industrial enterprises, and participating in international investment trusts. They are also becoming increasingly active in international business mergers and takeovers. The facilities of the central savings banks make it possible for the local savings banks to provide for their customers a complete line of commercial banking services.

The Credit Institute for Reconstruction, capitalized in equal parts by the federal and *Land* governments, was originally created to handle the

European Recovery Program Fund. In part, it continues its original function of economic reconstruction by granting medium- and long-term credits for approved projects that other credit agencies are unwilling to finance. Its main current task is to provide long-term credits for exports, to both domestic exporters and foreign buyers. Special attention is given to trade with developing countries. Aside from its credit function, the institute is responsible for handling all loans granted to developing countries under the development aid program. The institute receives operating funds from the European Recovery Program Fund, through the sale of debenture bonds, and in the form of loans from the federal government. It may also obtain financial support from the German Federal Bank and from other financial institutions at home and abroad.

There are other specialized public credit institutions that use resources obtained from two special federal government funds and from the capital market. These include the Industrial Credit Bank, which makes short- and medium-term loans to medium-sized industrial and trade enterprises; the Equalization of Burdens Bank, whose main function is to provide loan assistance for industrial development in problem areas; and the Berlin Industrial Bank, which helps finance industrial establishments in West Berlin.

Banks in the private sector may legally operate on the principle of universal banking, which allows each bank to carry out all kinds of financial transactions and to deal with all kinds of customer. Commercial banks, though dealing mainly in short-term credit, have progressively moved into the fields of savings accounts and medium- and long-term loans. Some of the largest commercial banks have also diversified their lending operations to include mortgage loans, installment credit, and small personal loans. The three largest commercial banks operating on a national scale are the Deutsche Bank, the Dresdner Bank, and the Commerzbank. Their combined assets totaled about DM75 billion in 1970. The large banks have also entered the field of international banking, largely through participation in multinational banking organizations. In 1973 almost one-third of the business volume and profits of the Deutsche Bank originated in foreign operations.

Specialized mortgage banks, both public and private, finance housing construction and municipal development. Whereas activities of the public banks are restricted to specific areas and financing tasks, no such restrictions apply to the private mortgage banks. All mortgage banks acquire funds through the sale of long-term mortgage bonds. These banks constitute the main source of long-term credit in the country. In mid-1971 they accounted for 30 percent of such credit compared to 13 percent for the commercial banks. Most of the private mortgage banks are under the control of large commercial banks.

In December 1971 previously independently operating agricultural and trades credit cooperatives were united for a trial period of five years in the Federal Union of People's and Raiffeisen Banks. The union was formed to eliminate friction between the two credit groups, reduce operating costs, and increase competitive strength, particularly in relation to the postal savings system. At the time of its organization the new union had a membership of about 6,400 credit cooperatives with 18,900 field offices. With its combined assets of DM145 billion, the union ranked as the third largest banking group in the country, after the savings banks and the commercial banks.

Banks exercise a substantial influence over business policies of enterprises. They are able to do so not only in their role as creditors but also on the basis of substantial stock ownership and stock management for individual investors. The bank's equity in business enterprises in the late 1960s was officially estimated at DM3 billion in nominal value, or 6 percent of the total capitalization of all share companies. At the end of 1972 the Berlin Industrial Bank alone owned shares in West Berlin enterprises valued at more than DM23 million. Their equity participation enables the banks to place directors on the boards of many companies and thus participate directly in the process of decisionmaking. The influence of the banks is further enhanced through the medium of interlocking directorships.

The government is aware of the problems posed by the pervasiveness of the banks' influence over enterprises and of the difficulty of eliminating possible conflicts of interest through legislation. An example of such legislation is provided by the law concerning capital stock issues, a provision of which seeks to protect the interests of stock owners by preventing banks from voting stock that they manage under general power of attorney contrary to the wishes of the owners.

FOREIGN TRADE AND PAYMENTS

Merchandise Trade

Foreign trade has been of growing importance to the Federal Republic. The value of annual exports, which equaled about 15 percent of GNP during the first half of the 1960s, rose to the equivalent of more than 19 percent of GNP by 1973. Net exports have absorbed from 2.4 to 2.8 percent of GNP per year. In the 1960–73 period exports rose 3.7 times to DM178.4 billion, while imports increased 3.4 times to DM145.4 billion. The balance of merchandise trade was positive throughout the period.

Because of the relatively small domestic market, major industries are largely export oriented, and exports have helped cushion recessionary tendencies in periods of slack domestic demand. Imports are essential to provide materials for industry and food supplies for the population. The steady rise in exports and trade surpluses was achieved despite the unsettled world monetary situation and repeated revaluations of the Deutsche Mark, to the amazement of foreign observers. There is a wide divergence of views concerning the reasons for the success of the country's export performance, and no persuasive explanation of this phenomenon has been offered.

About four-fifths of the foreign trade volume has been generated in trade with other Western industrialized nations, particularly countries of the European Community and the European Free Trade Association (EFTA). In 1972 European Community countries supplied about 49 percent of imports and absorbed 40 percent of exports; comparable figures for the enlarged community in 1973 were 52 and 47 percent, respectively. After the shift in European regional organization, the trade share of EFTA was reduced to about 9 percent of imports and less than 16 percent of exports. Trade with the Democratic Republic, though important politically, accounts for only 2 percent of exports and a smaller proportion of imports.

Trade with the United States and Canada constituted about 10 percent of total trade, and an equal share was accounted for by other industrialized countries, including Yugoslavia, South Africa, Japan, Australia, and New Zealand. The proportion of trade with developing countries declined from 1969 to 1972 and constituted about 15 percent of imports and 11 percent of exports in the latter year. Imports originated mainly in Asia and Africa, while exports were destined primarily for Asia and South America. Trade with communist countries, excluding the Democratic Republic, remained below 5 percent of total trade. Some economists have considered the high concentration of foreign trade a weakness, because it made exports vulnerable to the adverse effects of economic recession in any one of the major trading partner countries.

Although the same categories of goods are included in both imports and exports, exports contain a much larger proportion of industrial products and of more highly processed goods. In 1972 industrial products constituted 79 percent of imports but fully 95 percent of exports. Comparable figures for final end-use products were 38 and 69 percent, respectively, but the proportions of finished products for industrial use were about equal. The share of industrial raw materials and of food was about five times larger in imports than in exports. Almost half the exports consisted of machinery and transport equipment, including automobiles. Other important export items included chemicals, iron and steel, and paper and paper products.

Balance of Payments

The overall balance of payments of the Federal Republic from 1960 through 1973 was positive in nine of the fourteen years, including the last four. The cumulative balance for the entire period was DM87.2 billion. The current account was negative only in 1962 and 1965; the capital account was negative in seven years and positive in seven, including the last four years of the period. The cumulative totals of these accounts for the entire period were DM53.7 billion and DM8.3 billion, respectively. Unclassified items, including errors and omissions, made up the DM25.2 billion remainder of the overall balance.

The current account includes the balances of trade, services, and transfers. The merchandise trade balance was positive each year; after a sharp decline to DM1.2 billion in 1965, it rose to DM33 billion in 1973. In the first five months of 1974, despite disruptive developments in world trade and payments, the trade balance rose at an even faster rate, by DM22.7 billion. The total trade surplus from 1960 through May 1974 amounted to DM195 billion.

Transfer payments, including private and official remittances abroad, rose from DM3.5 billion in 1960 to DM15.9 billion in 1973. Private transfers, up to 90 percent of which consisted of remittances by foreign workers, constituted less than half the total transfers in the second half of the 1960s but more than three-fifths in the four years of the 1970s. Official transfers consisted mainly of indemnification payments, contributions to international organizations, mainly the European Community, and pensions to annuitants residing abroad.

The balance of services was positive in six years and negative in eight. Income items in the services account included receipts from transport, foreign military agencies, and in some years from investments. The single major expenditure item was for travel of Federal Republic citizens abroad. Other significant expenditure items included commissions, advertising, and trade fairs; licenses and patents; and miscellaneous other services. For the entire fourteen-year period the balance of services had a deficit of DM8.6 billion.

CHAPTER 15

AGRICULTURE

Employing almost 7 percent of the economically active population and producing a steadily rising farm output, agriculture contributed only 2.9 percent to the gross domestic product (GDP) in 1973, the lowest contribution on record. Although crop yields were among the highest in the world, the small size and fragmentation of farms caused costs to be high in relation to competitors within the free trade area of the European Community. Agriculture provided only about two-thirds of the country's needs out of domestic resources; together with production based on imported livestock feed, domestic farm output covered three-fourths of the country's requirements.

The precarious economic position of farms and farming and a determination to avoid social dislocation through massive out-migration from rural areas led the government at an early stage to pursue a policy of active economic support for agriculture. The support was provided through a multiplicity of programs in such areas as farm structure, production, marketing, prices, cooperation, and social security. The ultimate aim was to obtain income parity for agriculture based on scientifically operated, viable modern farms and on small part-time farms worked by their owners in conjunction with nonagricultural occupations.

The national agricultural support policy was integrated into the country's broader regional economic development policy. All policy measures were made subject to policy directives issued by the supreme authorities of the European Community. The diversity of interests among member countries necessitated often prolonged negotiations and compromises on vital issues. Although membership in the European Community placed constraints on farm support activities of individual countries, the government of the Federal Republic of Germany firmly believed that closer European Community cooperation in other economic fields would also help solve some of the problems of agriculture.

The extent of the government's involvement in agriculture was illustrated by the magnitude of expenditures for farm policy measures. In the fiscal year (FY) 1973 these expenditures were equivalent to one-fourth of agriculture's contribution to the GDP.

CLIMATE AND SOILS

The Federal Republic lies in the temperate climatic zone and is subject

283

to frequent changes in weather. Winds are predominantly from the west. Precipitation occurs throughout the year. Average annual precipitation measures from less than twenty to almost twenty-eight inches in the northern lowlands, from twenty-eight to fifty-nine inches in the central uplands, and up to seventy-eight inches or more in the alpine region. Daily and seasonal fluctuations in temperature are moderate, and there is little variation in average temperatures throughout the country. Average January temperatures, the lowest of the year, range from about 27°F to 35°F in the lowlands and fall to 21°F at the highest elevations in the mountains. Average July temperatures range from 61°F to 68°F in the lowlands and are slightly higher than the upper limit in the protected mountain valleys. The highest temperatures occur in the lowlands of the upper Rhine Valley.

The country has a variety of soil types, most of which are of low fertility. They range from podzols—highly leached, acid clay and sandy soils, poor in plant nutrients and underlain by a highly compacted layer known as hard pan—to relatively rich brown loess soils of varying quality. Podzols predominate in the northern lowland; they are best suited for pastureland. Loess soils occur mainly at the southern edge of the lowland and in the central upland, particularly around Hannover, in the upper Rhine Valley, and in the valley of the Main River. In other areas the soil pattern is too complex to allow generalization. Despite the generally low natural fertility of most soils, much of the land responds well to good management and has become highly productive after generations of intelligent use.

Overall, natural conditions are not particularly favorable for agriculture. A relatively late onset of spring and summer limits the possibilities for growing crops that require warm temperatures; favorable climatic conditions are found only in the coastal regions and in the central plains and valleys. Almost two-thirds of the country's land area is hilly or mountainous; this condition places narrow limits both on land use and on the organization of individual farms. Many of the country's districts, comprising about 37 percent of the agricultural land, have been officially designated as naturally disadvantaged. Their distribution among the *Länder* (states; sing., *Land*) is uneven; they comprise almost 35 percent of the farmland in Bavaria and 17 percent in Lower Saxony but less than 6 percent in Hesse and little more than 1 percent in the Saar. Steep slopes are gradually being converted to pastures or woodlands.

Poorer soils are used to produce less demanding crops, such as rye, oats, and potatoes. Land in the more favored climatic and soil regions is devoted mainly to the production of wheat, malting barley, sugar beets, and alfalfa. These regions include the Mainz plain, the Köln basin, the northern slopes of the Mittelgebirge, parts of Bavaria, the Main-Neckar region, small areas of the northern marshes, and portions of the Baltic coast.

LAND USE

In 1973 agricultural land in use comprised 13.5 million hectares (one hectare equals 2.47 acres), or 54 percent of the country's area. Arable land constituted 56 percent of the farmland; meadows and pastures accounted for 40 percent; and the balance of 4 percent was devoted to vineyards, orchards, kitchen gardens, and nurseries. Only 29 percent of the agricultural land was used to produce crops for direct human consumption; 71 percent of the land was devoted to the production of feed for livestock.

In the 1960–73 period the area of agricultural land actually in use declined by 837,000 hectares, or 5.9 percent, but the ratio of arable land to grassland remained stable. Agricultural authorities expect a further decline of more than 700,000 hectares by 1980. The area of abandoned and unused farmland totaled 272,000 hectares in 1973 and was expected to reach 500,000 hectares by 1980. The government and various research institutes have been searching for ways to use this wasteland for socially desirable purposes.

The largest areas of farmland were in Bavaria (3.7 million hectares) and in Lower Saxony (2.9 million hectares). North Rhine-Westphalia, Baden-Württemberg and Schleswig-Holstein also had extensive agricultural areas, ranging from 1.9 million to 1.2 million hectares. The proportion of farmland to total area was largest in Schleswig-Holstein (74 percent) and Lower Saxony (61 percent). These *Länder* also ranked first and second in agriculture's contribution to the GDP.

Although Bavaria had the largest agricultural area, it ranked fourth in the ratios of farmland to total area and farm output to GDP. Third place with regard to these ratios was held by North Rhine-Westphalia and Rhineland-Palatinate respectively. The proportion of arable land to total agricultural area in the various *Länder* deviated little from the general average of 56 percent; it ranged from 53 to 57 percent except in Rhineland-Palatinate, where it reached 61 percent.

Most of the arable land has been used for the production of grains and root crops. A significant shift in hectarage from labor-intensive root crops to grains took place in the 1960–72 period. While the proportion of arable land occupied by grains increased from 61 to 70 percent, the proportion devoted to root crops declined from 23 to 15 percent. The balance of the arable hectarage in 1972 was divided among fodder crops other than beets, 11 percent; industrial crops, such as rape, tobacco, flax, hemp, poppies, and mustard, 2 percent; vegetables and berries, 1 percent; and pulses and fallow, 1 percent.

In 1972 wheat and barley each occupied about 30 percent of the grain area; rye and oats accounted for somewhat more than 15 percent each. Corn for grain occupied slightly more than 2 percent of the grain hectarage, and mixed grains made up the balance of 7 percent. Whereas the wheat area had been steadily expanding, the area of rye had declined. Compared to the three-year average for 1959 through 1961, the 1972 wheat hectarage was 18 percent larger and that of rye 35 percent smaller. During the same period the area of corn for grain increased eighteenfold, the area of barley more than doubled, and the hectarage of oats rose by 6 percent.

Potatoes accounted for 44 percent of the root crop area in 1972, and the remainder was almost equally divided between sugar beets and fodder beets. Since the 1959–61 period the areas of potatoes and fodder beets declined by 51 and 30 percent, respectively. The area of sugar beets, however, expanded by 18 percent in response to high government support prices for this crop.

ORGANIZATION

Number and Size of Farms

Despite a steady reduction in the number of farms and a corresponding increase in farm size since World War II, small, fragmented family farms predominate in agriculture. In the 1960–72 period the number of farms declined by an annual average of 39,800 units, or 3 percent, while the average size of farms rose from 8.1 to 11.2 hectares. Throughout that period the decline involved farms smaller than fifteen hectares, while the number of larger farms increased for the country as a whole. In 1972, however, Schleswig-Holstein, Lower Saxony, North Rhine-Westphalia, and the Saar also experienced a decline in the number of farms in the size group of fifteen to less than twenty-five hectares, the first such decline in the post-World War II period. Agricultural authorities anticipate a further decline of 36 percent in the number of farms to about 790,000 units by 1980.

The number of farms smaller than fifteen hectares declined by 41 percent; the reduction of individual size groups in the various *Länder* ranged from 12.6 percent for farms of ten to fifteen hectares in Bavaria and Baden-Württemberg to 70.6 percent for farms of one to two hectares in the Saar. The number of farms thirty hectares and larger rose by 39 percent; it doubled in Hesse and Baden-Württemberg and tripled in Rhineland-Palatinate.

In 1972 there were 1.1 million farms having 0.5 hectare or more of agricultural land; their average size was 11.2 hectares. One-fourth of the farms were smaller than two hectares; they contained little more than 2 percent of the land. On the other end of the scale, farms of fifty or more hectares constituted only 2 percent of all farms, but they contained 14 percent of the farmland; their average size was close to eighty hectares.

The greatest concentration of small farms is in the east-central and southwestern portions of the country; the proportion of large farms is greatest in the northern lowland. In 1972 more than half the farms in Hesse, Rhineland-Palatinate, Baden-Württemberg, and Saar were smaller than five hectares, and the proportion of farms under ten hectares in size ranged from 70 percent in Hesse to 80 percent in the Saar. By contrast, 33 percent of the farms in Schleswig-Holstein and 16 percent of the farms in Lower Saxony had thirty hectares of agricultural land or more.

Many farms have been operated on a part-time basis by owners who derive a major portion of their income from nonagricultural occupations. In 1972, 500,000 part-time farms constituted 45 percent of all farms half a hectare in size and larger; they contained 1.5 million hectares, or 12 percent of the agricultural area. In addition there were 185,000 farms with almost 1.6 million hectares of land that were dependent upon outside sources of income. Only 39 percent of the farms subsisted on farm income alone.

Part-time farming is often a transitional step toward abandoning agriculture altogether, but it has also become a permanent pattern for many farmers. This method of farming has been stimulated by the decentralization of industry that spread industrial plants throughout most of the country, with the notable exception of Schleswig-Holstein. The proximity of industrial employment opportunities has enabled many small farmers to remain on their farms rather than move to towns. This development has been in line with official policy, which seeks to avoid the depopulation of rural areas. Most part-time farmers, however, doubt that their children will remain on the farm.

Farm Organizations

Farmers in the Federal Republic are organized in a number of cooperative associations for the promotion of their general welfare and economic interests. The total membership of farm cooperatives in 1971 was officially reported to have been 5.4 million, or almost twice the number of people active in agriculture, because many farmers belong to more than one association. About 14,000 local cooperatives were federated on a regional and national basis in the German Farmers' Association and the German Cooperative and Raiffeisen Association. Both associations are members of the International Federation of Agricultural Producers (IFAP) and the Council for European Agriculture (CEA).

The German Farmers' Association comprises fifteen regional associations, which represent more than 1 million farms, and several interregional professional bodies, including the German Farm Women's Association, the Federation of German Agricultural and Forestry Employers' Unions, the Central Association of German Fruit and Vegetable Growers, the Working Group of German Livestock Breeders, the Working Group of German Forest Land Owners, and the German Wine Producers' Association. The association does not limit itself to economic matters but seeks to improve all aspects of rural living. The German Farmers' Association, with particularly strong branches in

Bavaria and Lower Saxony, was reported to have used its political power successfully for the benefit of farmers. The association is affiliated with the Committee of Professional Agricultural Organizations (COPA) of the European Community in Brussels and has thus been in a position to influence farm policy decisions on the European Community level.

The German Cooperative and Raiffeisen Association was formed in 1971 for a trial period of five years through the amalgamation of the rural German Raiffeisen Association and the German Cooperative Federation of small tradesmen. The announced purpose of this union was the better protection of the common interests of the country's middle class. At the time of its formation the German Cooperative and Raiffeisen Association had a membership of 16,000 cooperative associations with 6.8 million individual members.

The association included 6,400 credit cooperatives with 18,900 offices and total assets of DM145 billion (for value of the Deutsche Mark—see Glossary). This credit organization ranked third in size in the Federal Republic banking system, after savings banks and commercial banks. About 10,800 rural commodity associations, including 4,300 credit cooperatives also engaged in commodity trade, had a trade turnover of DM32 billion (net of turnover tax) in 1971, about 45 percent of the total agricultural trade turnover. Another 1,860 farm cooperatives were engaged in a variety of activities, including the joint use of farm machinery; the provision of electricity, water supply, and cold-storage facilities; fodder drying, range management, and livestock breeding; and the distillation of potatoes for alcohol and the production of starch.

With a view to achieving a better quantitative and qualitative adjustment between the supply of farm products and the requirements of the market and to strengthening the bargaining position of farmers in dealing with economically powerful buyer and food processor groups, legislation was enacted in 1969 to permit the organization of producer associations and their federations on a commodity basis. The associations must receive government approval.

In order to secure approval, association members are obliged to meet prescribed standards of production and quality and to sell their produce through the association. Financial incentives for the formation of marketing associations are provided by the government in the form of start-up grants for a period of three years, investment aid for the associations and their federations for a period of five years, and investment aid to buyers of produce who enter into long-term contracts with the associations.

By December 1973, 657 local and twelve regional producer associations had been officially recognized, and 109 local and eighteen regional associations were awaiting government approval. A national federation had been established in 1971 under the name of the Central Marketing Association of the German Agricultural, Forestry, and Food Economy. The largest number of producer associations was formed among producers of wine, quality grains, and slaughter livestock. Although some consolidation of production and improvements in quality and marketing methods were achieved in a few areas, the economic importance of the producer associations remained small relative to the total volume of farm produce sales.

FARM LABOR AND PRODUCTIVITY

Employment

The decline in the number of farms was paralleled by a large reduction in agricultural employment. In the 1960–72 period the number of gainfully employed people who derived the major part of their income from agriculture fell from 3.4 million to 1.8 million, or from 13.2 to 6.8 percent of the gainfully employed population. A further reduction in the number of those gainfully employed in agriculture to 1.7 million in 1973, or 6.6 percent of all gainfully employed people, was officially estimated in that year.

In FY 1972, 2.8 million people were engaged in farmwork either full- or part-time. Fewer than 7 percent of this number were hired workers. About 60 percent of the family and hired workers were employed full-time. Women predominated among full-time family and part-time hired workers, where they constituted 61 and 65 percent, respectively. The total labor input in agricultural production for the market was estimated in that year at 1.3 million man-years in terms of the output of an adult worker between the ages of sixteen and sixty-five, which is used statistically as the standard labor unit. Labor input per 100 hectares ranged from twenty-five labor units on farms of two to five hectares to only two labor units on farms of fifty hectares and larger.

The low and declining proportion of hired labor in the agricultural labor force resulted from the disproportionate rise in farm labor wages compared to prices for farm products. In the nine-year period ending in mid-1970, wages increased by 83 percent while farm prices rose by only 14 percent. The continuing replacement of human labor by machines brought about a steep rise in the agricultural labor productivity.

Productivity

Adequate information on productivity in agriculture is not available. Statistics published in the *1973 Agricultural Report* concerning value added per person economically active in agriculture and in other sectors of the economy cited preliminary 1971 figures of DM8,295 and DM22,621, respectively, in current prices. Accordingly, productivity in agriculture was only 37 percent of the productivity level in the rest of the economy. The report pointed out, however, that productivity in agriculture was really higher, because the cited value per person was based on a labor force that included a large proportion of part-time workers and also because the labor force figure used in the computation was inflated, a fact that was revealed by the census of 1970. In subsequently published statistics the number of gainfully employed people in agriculture in 1971 was reduced by 129,000.

The *1974 Agricultural Report* published adjusted value-added data per economically active person of DM8,790 in agriculture and DM22,975 in all other economic sectors. Productivity in agriculture was thus 38.3 percent of the productivity level in the rest of the economy; it rose to 40 percent in 1972. Both reports indicated that productivity in terms of value added in current prices had grown more slowly in agriculture during the 1960–71 period than outside it.

The 1974 report presented two additional comparisons of sectoral productivity. In terms of value added in current prices, productivity of DM15,439 per agricultural labor unit in FY 1973 was 58 percent of the productivity level per economically active person outside agriculture; the figure was officially estimated to have reached DM17,000 in FY 1974. In this context it must be noted that the data are not strictly comparable, because part-time employment also exists outside agriculture, and the average number of work hours per week is higher in agriculture than in other sectors of the economy.

Based on the contribution to GDP per labor unit in agriculture, in prices of FY 1964, and per economically active person in other sectors, in prices of 1962, productivity per farm labor unit in FY 1973 was 72 percent of the productivity level in the rest of the economy. On this basis the average annual growth rate of productivity in the FY 1965–73 period was 7.8 percent in agriculture and 4.1 percent in other sectors. This comparison suffers from the additional defect of differences in valuation. The difference in the rates of productivity growth in current and in constant prices is due to the more rapid rise of prices for nonagricultural output.

INVESTMENT AND CREDIT

Investment

Net investment in agriculture declined substantially in the FY 1967–73 period. Gross investment during that period ranged between DM4.6 billion in FY 1968 and DM5.8 billion in FY 1973 and averaged DM5.1 billion per year. Annual depreciation of assets, however, rose steadily from DM3.2 billion to DM4.9 billion, so that the annual volume of net investment, in current prices, declined from DM2.2 billion to less than DM200 million in FY 1972 but recovered to DM900 million in the next year.

Investment data in real terms have not been published. During the period under discussion investment costs had risen by 9 percent for farm buildings and tractors, 25 percent for farm machinery, and 47 percent for one-family homes. Net investment in real terms therefore declined substantially more than the published data indicate.

The distribution of gross investment by investment purpose changed significantly during the period. Investment in buildings declined from about one-third to one-fourth of the total while investment in machines and equipment rose from about two-thirds to three-quarters. Small amounts ranging from DM29 million to DM38 million were invested annually in permanent crops. Annual changes in livestock herds ranged from a reduction of DM294 million to an increase of DM347 million.

Investment in farm machinery brought about a rapid rise in the number and draft power of tractors, grain combines, and other farm equipment. In the 1960–70 period the number of tractors increased by 57 percent to more than 1.2 million units. The increase in tractor draft power, however, was much larger, because the number of the smallest tractors declined by one-fourth while the number of tractors with twenty-five to thirty-four horsepower increased 2.5 times and that of tractor units of thirty-five or more horsepower rose more than elevenfold. The number of grain combines increased from 68,000 units in 1961 to 160,000 in 1970; during the same period the number of milking machines rose from 345,000 tto 519,000 units.

Much of the farm machinery has been inefficiently used, because many farms are too small to operate the equipment to its full capacity. In an effort to minimize the economic loss involved and to reduce farm production costs, the government has encouraged the joint use of machinery by several farmers and the formation of specialized machinery rings. About 38,000 machinery associations were reported in existence in 1970, 22,000 of which were located in the three *Länder* of Bavaria, Lower Saxony, and Hesse. There were also 478 machinery rings—more formal, government-sponsored kinds of associations—most of which were located in Bavaria and Lower Saxony. In 1972, 144 machinery rings had a volume of business large enough to justify the employment of a full-time manager. These rings had almost 49,000 members with total landholdings of not quite 1.2 million hectares. Information on the machinery inventory of the rings is not available. In 1970 about 13,000 tractors were owned jointly by more than one farm, by cooperatives, or by enterprises operating on a contract basis.

Credit

The amount of debt outstanding in agriculture doubled in the 1963–73 period to a level of DM32.7 billion. During that period the proportion of long-term credits rose from 34 to 49 percent while the share of short-term credits declined from 35 to 22 percent of the total. At the same time medium-term credits declined from 23 to 15 percent while the amount of rents and share payments due increased from 8 to 14 percent. The change in the ratios of loan maturities was reflected in a reduction of the amounts repayable each year from 25 to about 20 percent of the outstanding credits. The absolute volume of annual repayment obligations, however, rose by 72 percent to a level of DM6.8 billion in 1973. The interest rate rose quite steadily from an average of 5.4 percent in FY 1963 to 6.8 in FY 1973.

AGRICULTURAL POLICY

In common with other industrially advanced nations, the Federal Republic has had to provide protection and support for agriculture in order to ensure essential food production and an adequate farm income. Experience over a period of two decades led the government to conclude that problems of agriculture and rural life could not be resolved in isolation by a policy narrowly limited to the agricultural sector. Since the late 1960s, therefore, agricultural policy has been more closely linked with the complex of general economic, regional, social, and educational policies.

As stated in 1974, the government's agricultural and food policy has four basic aims. In the domestic field they include the improvement of rural living conditions and equal participation by the rural population in the general rise of incomes and well-being; provision of high-quality food products for the population at reasonable prices; and conservation, restoration, and development of natural resources and the environment. In the foreign field the policy calls for a contribution to the solution of world agricultural and food problems and for an improvement in foreign agricultural relations. A schematic presentation of the policy aims listed twenty-six subsidiary goals and eighty-one specific action targets.

Measures for the realization of the policy aims have been grouped into eleven programs and five interprogram activity areas. Measures concerned with the structure of agriculture, production, marketing, and prices have had the most direct impact on agricultural development. Since the mid-1960s government measures in support of agriculture have had to be increasingly adapted to regulations issued by the European Community in the context of the community's Common Agricultural Policy. Full compliance with these regulations has been required since the spring of 1973. The government is aware that individual objectives in the different areas of its agricultural policy may not be compatible and that resolution of conflicting claims may necessitate at times difficult political decisions.

Structural policy has been advanced through the improvement of rural living conditions; development of infrastructure, such as roads and water supply; resettlement; promotion of labor mobility and land consolidation; and farm modernization. Other measures in the field of structural reform have included the raising of farm income through better organization of farm activities and the creation of nonagricultural employment opportunities that have enabled many farmers to combine occupations and sources of income. Provision of special retirement benefits for older farmers who agree to relinquish their land has been an important aspect of the structural program.

In the area of production, marketing, and price policy, the adopted measures include the promotion of greater productivity, in part through cooperation among farmers; a more widespread introduction of contract farming; and raising the agricultural price level through selective price increases, in the light of general income and cost developments and in the framework of overall economic requirements. The measures also contemplate market stabilization through the abolition and prevention of surpluses and through the formation of price relationships justified by market conditions; elimination of competitive distortions in the European Community; strengthening the position of producers in domestic and foreign markets; and compensation to farmers for losses due to exchange fluctuations.

Other measures are intended to expand social security coverage for farmers; eliminate social hardships arising from the reorganization of agriculture; and reduce the tax load on farms and farmers' cooperatives. Provisions are also to be made to afford equal educational opportunities for the rural population and adjust school curricula to changing needs; expand the agricultural extension service; and improve opportunities and facilities for the retraining of farmers.

FARM INCOME

The Agricultural Law passed in 1955 established the principle of income parity for farmers with comparable occupational groups outside agriculture. In practice the average wage of industrial workers covered by the social security system, excluding miners, has been used for purposes of comparison. Under a provision of the law, comprehensive, detailed reports on agricultural developments, with a focus on farm income, have been submitted annually by the government to the Bundestag.

Available data indicate that the goal of income parity has been attained, in a sense, on an overall basis. A survey of families earning annual incomes of up to DM10,000 in 1969 disclosed that the average net monthly farm family income of DM1,819 was 24 percent higher than the comparable income of nonagricultural families. The survey also revealed that the proportion of farm families with annual incomes of DM,2,500 to DM10,000 was second only to that of self-employed professionals and tradesmen and was superior to that of civil servants and of white- and blue-collar workers. Farm income in 1969, however, was reported to have been above average, and farm families were larger, on the average, than urban families.

Farm family income includes substantial earnings from nonagricultural pursuits, and there is a wide spread in incomes among individual farms. Income from farming alone has been well below the parity level, and the gap between it and nonfarm income has been widening.

In 1970 the share of nonagricultural earnings in farm income was 31 percent on full-time farms (through work of family members), 46 percent on farms worked part-time, and 83 percent on farms operated as subsidiary enterprises. In the same year the net family income of full-time farmers was 24 percent lower than the income of part-time farmers and 15 percent below the income of subsidiary farm operators. Wide disparities in incomes also result from differences in the type, size, and location of farms and in the technical and managerial competence of individual farmers.

In FY 1972 in each of several farm groups, grouped according to type and size, 25 percent of the farms at the bottom of the income scale attained a gross income per labor unit only one-fourth the size of the income in the upper 25 percent of the farms. The spread between the lowest and the highest labor unit income for all farms was from DM5,594 to DM38,431; it was still wider in terms of net income per labor unit. The income spread between farms in individual *Länder* is greater than the general average and continues to widen.

In early 1974 it was not yet possible to determine whether or to what extent part-time farmers could attain the income level actually achieved without separating their families, overworking their wives, or sacrificing the education of their children. It was officially concluded, however, that in general the income situation of adequately trained or retrained part-time farmers who had secured steady work in a nonagricultural occupation was superior to that of their nonfarm coworkers. On the other hand, the social and economic position of individuals whose predominant occupation consisted in working on a farm with limited income potential and who had no opportunity for nonagricultural work was often unsatisfactory. This situation was most pronounced in central mountainous areas at substantial distances from industrial sites.

For agriculture as a whole, the average gross farm income per labor unit in FY 1972 was DM15,927, compared to average gross wages of DM16,239 for nonagricultural workers. Farm income was expected to increase by 10 to 14 percent in FY 1973, and the gap between farm income and industrial wages was expected to narrow. In general, farm income per labor unit has been above average in Schleswig-Holstein, Lower Saxony, and North Rhine-Westphalia and below average in the southern *Länder*.

STRUCTURAL REFORM

The small size and fragmentation of farms constitute major obstacles to efficient agricultural production because they preclude the optimum use of manpower and modern technology. Structural reform of agriculture aimed at enlarging and modernizing farms has therefore been considered a key element in the achievement of higher farm incomes. The integrated reform program has included the consolidation of farm plots and farms; relocation of farmsteads outside existing villages; replacement of obsolete, and construction of new, farm buildings and housing; and construction of farm roads and water control systems. Special provisions were made to encourage the retirement of older farmers, to compensate farmers for surrendering their land or leasing it on a long-term basis, and to assist younger farmers remaining on the land to meet the high cost of expansion and modernization.

In 1973 structural reform measures were modified to conform to new guidelines issued by the European Community Council in April 1972. This change was expected to receive council approval and qualify the Federal Republic for contributions from European Community funds to the extent of 25 percent of the cost of the program. These costs have been financed by the federal government and the governments of the *Länder* in a ratio of 60 to 40 percent; the European Community contribution was to be apportioned among them in the same ratio. The change in regulations created practical difficulties in the execution of some assistance programs. Particular problems were posed by differences in the definition of the term *agriculture* and by limitations on investment aid for hog raising.

Land Consolidation

Land consolidation has proceeded at a slow pace. High land prices, legal and fiscal provisions affecting land ownership, transfer, and lease, and the reluctance of farmers to relinquish their landholdings have constituted major obstacles to the execution of the land consolidation program. A serious problem has also been posed by the rapid progress of agricultural technology in countries of the European Community, as a result of which farms that had been consolidated only ten years earlier may no longer be large enough to withstand foreign competition.

In the 1960–72 period 3.7 million hectares of farmland were earmarked for consolidation under the integrated program, but a smaller area was actually consolidated; information on the magnitude of this area was not available in mid-1974. During the same period 39,000 hectares were voluntarily exchanged among farmers with financial assistance from the government. As of January 1968, 5.9 million hectares remained to be included in the consolidation program for the first time, and 2.8 million hectares of previously consolidated land needed to be realigned in the light of more modern requirements. In the five years 1968 through 1972 an average of 286,000 hectares was brought under the consolidation program annually, including voluntarily exchanged land. At that rate it would require thirty more years to complete the task, provided that all land included in the program were actually consolidated.

The cost of land consolidation in the 1968–72 period averaged DM804 million per year and DM2,850 per hectare. The federal government bore 37 percent of this cost; the balance was covered by grants from the *Länder*, contributions by third persons, the farmers' own funds, and loans.

Farm Modernization

Under the new European Community regulations, government aid for farm modernization must be limited to full-time farmers with demonstrated professional ability, including the keeping of farm accounts, who have a workable plan to make their farms viable in a maximum period of six years. The standard of viability has been defined as the equivalence between farm income per labor unit and the average nonagricultural wage income in the same region, along with an adequate interest return on invested capital. In exceptional cases the income of a farm in the modernization program may be augmented by a 10-percent government grant during the developmental period. A qualified foreign observer reported that relatively few farmers could meet this standard of eligibility.

In the Federal Republic the time span for attaining viability was fixed at four years. For purposes of eligibility the required basic income level was set at a countrywide average of DM17,300 per labor unit in April 1973, with a range of DM13,500 to DM19,200 in twenty-seven designated regions. To receive aid farmers also had to demonstrate a potential to increase farm income by an average of 3.5 percent per year. A farmer who applied for aid in 1973, therefore, had to prove his ability to obtain by 1977 an income per labor unit of DM15,500 to DM22,000, depending upon the location of his farm.

The eligibility provision for farm modernization aid was amended in December 1973 with an effective date of January 1, 1974. Based on a general rise in nonfarm labor income of about 8.5 percent during the year, the required basic farm income level was increased to an average of DM18,800, and the expected annual income increase for those receiving aid in 1974 was lowered to 2 percent per year. Farmers who received aid in 1974 were expected to attain a labor unit income in 1978 of DM15,900 to DM22,600, depending on the region. The number of farms scheduled to receive modernization aid was 11,920 in 1973 and 10,071 in 1974.

Modernization aid to farmers consists mainly of an interest subsidy of up to 5 percent for investment capital loans, with the exception of loans for the purchase of land and animals other than cattle and sheep. The subsidy may not lower the interest cost to the farmer below 3 percent. Government guarantees may be given for loans to farmers who lack adequate collateral. Farms that undertake to specialize in the production of beef, veal, lamb, and mutton to the extent of at least 50 percent of sales at the end of the development period may obtain special grants for a period of three years. These grants were fixed at DM165 per hectare for the first year and DM110 and DM55 for the second and third years.

Outside the European Community-approved program, farmers who do not qualify for modernization aid because of the inadequate growth potential of their farms and who lack opportunities for outside employment may receive limited investment assistance for the purchase of machinery and building maintenance. An interest subsidy of up to 5 percent may be granted on 85 percent of the approved investment loan volume, generally limited to DM35,000 for livestock farms and DM30,000 for other kinds of farms. Assistance of this nature was scheduled to be granted to 2,200 farmers in 1973 and 1,550 farmers in 1974. Most of these farms were located in the three southern *Länder*. Guidelines for expanded aid to farms in mountainous and naturally disadvantaged areas were agreed upon by the European Community Council in November 1973 and were expected to be promulgated in 1974. Difficult problems, however, remained to be resolved concerning the joint financing of the program and the designation of areas entitled to aid.

PRODUCTION

Total farm output in FY 1973 amounted to DM43.6 billion; over a ten-year period it had increased at an average annual rate of 4.6 percent in current prices. In physical terms, however, the annual increase in output was only 2.7 percent; the difference was accounted for by an annual rise of 1.9 percent in the price of farm products. Throughout the ten-year period livestock products constituted about 70 percent of the output, and crops made up the balance of 30 percent. Pork, milk, and beef predominated in livestock production, and grains, flowers and ornamental shrubs, and fruits led in crop production. These products accounted for about 85 and 60 percent of the livestock and crop output, respectively.

Farm output based on domestic resources covers only about two-thirds of the country's requirements. Including food produced with imported livestock feed, the degree of self-sufficiency is about three-fourths. The largest deficits are in fresh fruits, vegetables, and wine. Production of milk and butter has exceeded consumption. Self-sufficiency in sugar was believed to have been attained with the 1973 crop of sugar beets. The Federal Republic is among the largest importers of agricultural commodities in the world.

Crops

Grain production in 1973 reached the record level of 21.1 million tons. Major changes in the crop production pattern took place in the 1959–72 period (see table 10). Whereas the average annual output of grains increased by 32 percent from the 1959–61 period to the 1970–72 period, production of bread grains rose by only 6.8 percent while the production of feed grains increased by 63.5 percent. Production of corn during that period rose thirtyfold, and the output of barley increased by 88 percent. While wheat production increased by 23.6 percent, production of rye declined by 15.5 percent. During the same period potato production declined by one-third while the output of sugar beets rose by 42.5 percent. These trends reflected the decline in popular consumption of bread products, particularly those made of rye flour, and the rise in the consumption of meat products and sugar.

In the production of fodder crops, a substantial shift occurred from clover and alfalfa to corn for silage and green feed. Production of these grasses declined by 38 and 40 percent while the production of corn rose

Table 10. Area and Production of Principal Crops in the Federal Republic of
Germany, 1959–61 and 1970–72 Averages and 1972

Crop	Area (in thousands of hectares)*			Production (in thousands of metric tons)		
	1959-61 Average	1970-72 Average	1972	1959-61 Average	1970-72 Average	1972
Wheat	1,378	1,555	1,626	4,508	5,570	6,608
Rye	1,308	858	843	3,397	2,871	2,917
Barley	684	1,510	1,549	2,929	5,508	5,997
Oats	760	823	808	2,043	2,803	2,888
Mixed grains	453	390	359	1,219	1,288	1,270
Corn	6	111	118	19	555	563
Total grain	4,589	5,247	5,303	14,115	18,595	20,243
Potatoes	1,023	551	503	22,920	15,488	15,038
Sugar beets	280	316	331	9,916	14,131	14,656
Fodder beets	445	333	312	22,993	29,403	27,811
Corn (green)	44	238	285	1,494	10,186	12,396
Hay						
Clover	493	276	257	3,388	2,099	1,983
Alfalfa	153	88	83	1,154	695	655
Rotation meadow	160	148	136	954	1,011	966
Permanent meadow	n.a.	4006	3,971	20,381	27,050	27,444

n.a.—not available.
*One hectare equals 2.47 acres.

Source: Adapted from *Statistisches Jahrbuch für die Bundesrepublik Deutschland, 1962,*
Wiesbaden, pp. 183–185; and *Statistisches Jahrbuch für die Bundesrepublik
Deutschland, 1973,* Wiesbaden, 1973, pp. 172–173.

almost sevenfold. During the same period the output of fodder beets
increased by 28 percent.

Future crop production is officially expected to continue the trend of
expanding grain output, with a predominant rise in the production of feed
grains and a stronger emphasis on quality improvement. Further
expansion of rape production is also considered likely.

Much of the rise in crop production was achieved through increases in
yields per hectare, which ranged from 23.6 percent for summer barley to
89.3 percent for fodder beets; advances in the yields of hay crops were
substantially lower. Rising yields also kept production losses relatively
lower than hectarage reduction for a number of crops. In the case of
fodder beets a sizable increase in output was actually achieved despite a
reduction in the crop area.

Higher yields were attained very largely through increased fertilizer
and lime inputs. Fertilizer use in terms of plant nutrients rose by 66
percent from FY 1961 to FY 1971, while the application of lime increased
by 45 percent. The increase in fertilizer use was largest for nitrogen, 93
percent, intermediate for phosphates, 49 percent; and lowest for potash,
29 percent. The Federal Republic is one of the leading countries in

consumption of fertilizers per hectare; in the European Community it is surpassed only by the Netherlands, Belgium, and Luxembourg.

Livestock and Livestock Products

In the 1960–72 period the numbers of hogs, cattle other than cows, chickens, and turkeys increased, but other kinds of livestock and poultry declined in numbers. The decline was largest for goats and horses and smallest for cows (see table 11). The cow herd had been quite stable at 5.8 million to 5.9 million head until 1969 but declined in the next three years, in part as a result of a government-sponsored slaughter program in 1970 to reduce surpluses of milk and butter. An increase of 2.1 percent in the number of cows, however, was reported to have taken place from mid-1972 to mid-1973.

The quality of livestock and yields of livestock products were reported to have improved markedly through government-supported breeding programs, better veterinary services and disease controls, more advanced feeding practices, and government controls over additives to livestock feeds. Stricter regulation of feed production and distribution was contemplated by the government in early 1974 as a health protection measure for the population and livestock. The annual milk yield per cow rose from 3.4 tons in 1960 to 3.9 tons in 1972.

Meat production, excluding poultry, increased by 39 percent in the 1960–72 period. While the output of pork and beef rose by 49 and 31 percent, respectively, production of veal, lamb, mutton, goat, and horse meat declined (see table 12). Considering the large increase in poultry numbers, production of poultry meat must also have risen substantially.

Table 11. Livestock in the Federal Republic of Germany,
December 1960 and December 1972
(in thousands)

	1960	1972
Hogs	15,775	20,028
Brood sows	(1,499)	(2,058)
Cattle	12,867	14,122
Cows	(5,854)	(5,453)
Sheep	1,035	908
Goats	325	40
Horses	710	283
Chickens	60,034	99,712
Layers	n.a.	(60,689)
Other poultry	3,437	2,462
Beehives	1,416	945

n.a.—not available.

Source: Adapted from *Statistisches Jahrbuch für die Bundesrepublik Deutschland, 1962,* Wiesbaden, pp. 193–194; and *Statistisches Jahrbuch für die Bundesrepublik Deutschland, 1973,* Wiesbaden, 1973, pp. 180–181.

Table 12. Output of Livestock Products in the Federal Republic of Germany, 1960 and 1972
(in thousands of metric tons)

Product	1960	1972
Pork	1,805	2,683
Beef	829	1,085
Veal	97	69
Other[1]	35	15
Total domestic livestock	2,766	3,852
Poultry	n.a.	208
Milk	19,250	21,490
Butter	406	489
Eggs[2]	n.a.	1,340

n.a.—not available.
[1]Lamb, mutton, goat, and horsemeat.
[2]In millions of dozens.
Source: Adapted from *Statistisches Jahrbuch für die Bundesrepublik Deutschland, 1962*, Wiesbaden, pp. 195–196; and *Statistisches Jahrbuch für die Bundesrepublik Deutschland, 1973*, Wiesbaden, 1973, pp. 182–183.

The volume of pork production in 1972 was 2.5 times as high as beef output.

Milk production of 21.5 million tons in 1972 was 11.6 percent above the 1960 level. More than four-fifths of the output has usually moved into commercial channels, where the bulk has been processed into butter, cheese, and condensed and dried milk. Butter production reached an average annual volume of 505,000 tons in the 1966–69 period but declined thereafter and was about 20 percent higher in 1972 than in 1960. Because of the government's high support price for milk, based on its farm incomes policy, milk and, consequently, butter production has been in surplus for a number of years. In July 1970 butter stocks amounted to 122,000 tons; they were reduced to 36,000 tons by the end of 1971 through various government programs of subsidized distribution and export at lowered prices, with substantial losses. Curtailment or cessation of subsidized distribution after 1971 brought the butter stocks up to 111,000 tons at the end of 1972 and caused a further rise in the milk surplus in 1973.

FORESTS

In 1972 forests occupied an area of 7.2 million hectares, 151,000 hectares of which were not commercially exploited. The state owned 31 percent of the forests; communities, 25 percent; and private individuals, 44 percent. Coniferous trees covered 68 percent of the forest area, and deciduous trees accounted for the balance. The forest area was divided among 1.2 million farms and forest enterprises. Forty-five percent of the forestland was scattered among holdings of less than two hectares. The largest 1,074 holdings averaged about 2,630 hectares. The forest area is expected to expand in the future through afforestation of marginal land that will be withdrawn from agricultural use.

A storm in the fall of 1972 caused severe damage to the timber stands, felling more than 15 million cubic meters (53 million cubic feet) of commercial timber. This volume was equivalent to about three-fifths of the timber harvest planned for 1973. Urgent measures were taken by the federal government to salvage the fallen timber and to provide financial assistance to affected private owners, although forest management was usually the responsibility of *Länder*.

Various forest improvement measures are in progress under provisions of the 1973 law for improvement of the agrarian structure. Inferior tree stands are to be replaced by superior varieties. The program emphasizes the expansion of deciduous and mixed tree stands. In the northern storm-damaged region where pines have predominated, large areas are to be replanted with oaks. Pines are also to be increasingly replaced by Douglas fir.

In early 1974 a draft law was under study by parliament that was intended to modify existing regulations concerning forests in the light of environmental needs. The law was intended to provide a legal basis on the federal level for the promotion of forestry and establish a balance between the public interest and the private concerns of forest owners. A federal law was also deemed necessary for the purpose of coordinating national forestry policies within the European Community.

Domestic production of timber has not been fully adequate to meet the country's needs. Both in 1972 and in 1973 about 4.3 million cubic meters (15 million cubic feet) of lumber were imported, the equivalent of 45 percent of domestic lumber production. Demand for lumber in these years, however, was reported to be unusually high because of a strong building boom.

CHAPTER 16

INDUSTRY

Industry is the dominant sector of the economy of the Federal Republic; over the years it has generated more than half the country's gross domestic product (GDP). In mid-1974 industry was in the process of adaptation to drastically changed economic conditions marked by sharply rising production costs, a tight credit situation, increased international monetary instability, and ruinous trade deficits in other member countries of the European Community. These conditions posed a threat to industry's export potential and thereby endangered the economic health of the country, which relies upon exports to pay for massive imports of materials and fuels. Exports constituted a fifth of industry's total sales in 1972; thereafter its dependence on exports was heightened by the shrinkage of the domestic market as a result of anti-inflation measures introduced by the government.

Not all branches of industry succeeded in making a satisfactory adjustment. While the chemical, steel, and paper industries, benefiting from a strong worldwide demand, were able to increase their output and sales in the first quarter of 1974 above the comparable levels in 1973, the automobile and construction industires suffered a severe decline in activity accompanied by reduced earnings and partial unemployment. In several industrial branches, particularly in machine building, small, financially insecure enterprises went bankrupt and were absorbed by larger and stronger concerns, thus continuing the trend toward business concentration and rising control of the market by giant and, in some cases, multinational industrial corporations.

Although the position of the country's industry, as well as the entire economy, compared favorably with conditions in most other countries of the European Community and the industrialized West, the industrial community felt uneasy about future prospects because of the uncertainties that were inherent in the disturbed world economic situation. The misgivings, however, did not deter the major industrial companies from taking energetic measures to safeguard and expand their economic interests, including the expansion of direct investments abroad.

STRUCTURE AND GROWTH

Industry, including handicrafts and construction, has been the dominant sector of the economy. In the 1960–72 period it contributed more than one-half of the GDP annually; about 11 percent of the GDP was generated in handicraft shops. Manufacturing accounted for more than three-fourths but not quite four-fifths of industry's GDP contribution. The proportion of construction in industrial GDP rose during the period while the shares of mining and energy production declined.

Machine building, including the production of transport equipment, has been the major branch of manufacturing, contributing 20 percent of manufacturing GDP in 1960 and 23.6 percent in 1970. In the latter year it was followed, in order of importance, by industries producing electric and electronic equipment, chemicals, food products and tobacco, and metals and metal products. The relatively minor branches, contributing from 9.8 to 3.9 percent of manufacturing GDP, included the manufacture of wood products, paper, and printing; ceramics and glass; textiles; and leather and clothing. In the 1960–70 period the structure of manufacturing was altered through greater relative advances in the production of machines and transport equipment, electric and electronic equipment, chemicals, and wood products, paper, and printing.

In the 1960–72 period industry grew at an average annual rate of 5.2 percent. The growth pattern was uneven; advances of 11.8 and 13 percent in 1968 and 1969 followed a rise of only 1.8 percent and a decline of 2.4 percent in the business recession years of 1966 and 1967. In other years the growth rates ranged from 6.3 percent in 1961 to 1.8 percent in 1971.

Among the four major industry subdivisions, the largest gain was made by the public sector of the energy industry. The annual increase in the production and distribution of electric power and gas was 8.4 percent; it was somewhat higher for electricity and lower for gas.

Mining suffered a decline of 3.4 percent over this period. This average concealed a more than threefold rise in oil and natural gas production and simultaneous declines of 22.4 and 65.5 percent in the production of coal and iron ores. During the same year output of potash and rock salt rose by 40 percent, and the production of nonferrous ores increased by 10 percent.

Manufacturing advanced at an average annual rate of 5.4 percent, or slightly faster than industry as a whole. The most rapid advance in this sector—6.4 percent—was made by industries producing raw and processed materials for industrial use. The slowest growth was attained in food and tobacco processing. Growth rates of industries producing investment and consumer goods other than processed foods was about midway between the two extremes. Construction activity expanded at an annual rate of 5 percent.

ORGANIZATION

Small industrial establishments predominate in numbers, but production is highly concentrated in large enterprises. A census of industry and handicrafts in 1967 listed 558,960 enterprises with a total gross output volume of DM572.2 billion (for value of the Deutsche Mark—see Glossary). Eighty percent of the enterprises had fewer than ten employees and accounted for only 9 percent of the output. On the other end of the scale, 1,094 enterprises with 1,000 or more employees, constituting less than 0.2 percent of the total number, produced 43.5 percent of the output. Almost two-thirds of the total output was produced by the 1.2 percent of all enterprises that had 200 or more employees. The average annual net output per enterprise ranged from DM59,250 for the smallest to DM124 million for the largest. There was a decline in the number of enterprises and an increase in their average size in the intercensus period of 1962 to 1967. This trend continued to the early 1970s.

In general, the largest enterprises in terms of capitalization, employment, and sales are concentrated in oil refining, mining, metallurgy, and in the production of chemicals, motor vehicles, and aircraft. Small enterprises predominate in woodworking and in consumer goods industries producing such items as leather and leather goods, clothing, musical instruments, toys, jewelry, and sports equipment. Handicraft shops play an important part in the consumer goods field and, to some extent, work as subcontractors for larger industrial firms.

Aside from individual ownership and simple partnership, the predominant form of industrial business organization is the joint-stock company (*Aktiengesellschaft*—A.G.). In 1972 there were about 32,800 such industrial companies with a total nominal capital of DM78 billion. All but 1,100 of them were companies with limited liability, closely akin to corporations in the United States. Limited liability companies were generally much smaller; they had an average capitalization of DM1 million compared with DM42.6 million for the other stock companies. A number of enterprises in the industrial machinery, motor vehicle, steel, chemical, and electric equipment industries are among the largest in the world.

REGIONAL DISTRIBUTION

The government's regional development policy brought about the establishment of industrial enterprises in all *Länder* (states; sing., *Land*). The intensity of industrialization in the several *Länder*, however, has been uneven because of such factors as earlier industrial development, differences in natural and labor resources, and proximity to transportation and markets.

North Rhine-Westphalia is by far the most industrialized of the *Länder*, with about one-third of employment and sales in manufacturing and mining in 1972. Next in order of importance in that year, but on a significantly lower scale, were Baden-Württemberg and Bavaria. Excluding the city-state of Bremen, the Saar and Schleswig-Holstein ranked lowest with regard to both employment and sales. In terms of the proportion of industrial employment to total population, however, Baden-Württemberg held first place, followed by North Rhine-Westphalia and the Saar. Whereas this ratio ranged from 17.1 percent in the leading *Land* to 10.8 percent in Lower Saxony and averaged 13.5 percent for the country as a whole, it was only 7.4 percent in Schleswig-Holstein.

The highest concentration of industry is in the Ruhr district, an area of about 1,500 square miles in the west-central part of North Rhine-Westphalia, on the Rhine River. The Ruhr includes several towns, the largest of which are Essen and Dortmund, and the world's biggest inland port at Duisburg. In this area are coal mining, electric power and gas production, ferrous and nonferrous metallurgy, oil refineries and chemical works, metalworking and machine-building plants, and plants producing electrical, transport, and optical equipment.

Adjoining the Ruhr are the commercial and industrial city of Düsseldorf; the commercial and manufacturing city of Cologne; the industrial towns of Wuppertal, Solingen, and Remscheid; the chemical center of Leverkusen; and the textile centers of Krefeld and Mönchen-Gladbach. Together, the Ruhr and the adjoining areas form what is one of the most important industrial regions in Europe, if not the most important.

Raw Materials and Fuels

The Federal Republic is among the world's largest producers of coal and lignite, potash, and rock salt but is deficient in most other mineral resources for industrial use. Apart from minerals for the building materials industry, mining also provides barites, crude oil and natural gas, and ores of iron, lead, and zinc. Hard coal, potash, salt, and barites have been mined in quantities large enough to allow significant exports. Lignite production has been supplemented by imports from the German Democratic Republic. Other mined products cover only a fraction of needs—7 percent in the case of crude oil—and there are no resources of phosphates and asbestos or of ores for such essential metals as aluminum, copper, nickel, tin, chrome, manganese, molybdenum, tungsten, vanadium, titanium, platinum, and uranium. These deficiencies necessitate a heavy reliance on imports. In 1970 the Federal Republic's foreign trade in fuels and minerals had a deficit of almost DM14 billion.

The heavy dependence upon imported raw materials is perceived as a serious problem, in that industry must rely upon essential supplies from countries whose ability or willingness to deliver are often uncertain. The uncertainty is compounded by the political instability prevailing in many of the developing countries that are important exporters of raw materials.

Coal and Lignite

Hard coal deposits are located mainly in the Ruhr—the largest coalfield in Europe—and in the Saar. Measured reserves of hard coal were estimated at 70 billion tons in 1967, a volume sufficient for more than 600 years at the 1972 rate of extraction. Because of competition from petroleum and, to a lesser extent, from cheaper imported coal, production of hard coal declined from a post-World War II peak of 152 million tons in 1956 to 102.5 million tons in 1972. The volume of cleaned, marketable coal in that year was only 60 million tons. In 1972 coking coal from the Ruhr was reported to have cost DM16 per ton more than coal from competing sources.

Continuation of hard coal mining was made possible by a variety of measures introduced by the federal government. One of these measures consisted in the concentration and rationalization of coal mines in the Ruhr and their reorganization into a single corporation. This process brought about a substantial rise in labor productivity; output of hard coal per worker-hour increased by 75 percent in the 1962–72 period. In 1973 the coal industry was officially reported to have been foremost in Europe in technological equipment and output per man. Other measures included import duties on coal; limitation of coal imports from sources outside the European Community to 5.5 million tons per year; price equalization subsidies; freight subsidies on coal transport; and a fuel oil tax.

Concentration and rationalization of mines were promoted by premiums for mine closings and by tax incentives. At the same time subsidies were granted for coal exports. Special measures were also taken to protect coal miners against undue hardship from structural adaptation. Costs of the coal industry conversion program were covered largely by federal funds; coal-mining *Länder* contributed one-third of the cost of many support measures.

Lignite deposits lie in the southern portion of the northern lowland; in the Vorgebirge area southwest of Cologne; and, to a lesser extent, in the Hesse depression, in Bavaria, and near the city of Helmstedt, east of Hannover. Measured reserves of lignite were reported as 62 billion tons in 1967, 5 billion tons of which were suitable for surface mining. Lignite has been mined primarily in the region of Cologne, in open pits to depths of several hundred feet by means of huge excavators and very little labor. Because of its high water content and, consequently, excessive transport costs, lignite has been used mainly near the site of the mines as fuel for thermoelectric power plants and as raw material by chemical plants producing synthetic nitrates and oils. Small quantities have been converted into briquettes for domestic heating use. Annual production of lignite has been in the neighborhood of 100,000 tons.

Crude Oil and Natural Gas

Deposits of crude oil are located in the northern lowland. The major exploited fields are near the Ems River; north of the city of Hannover; and in the region of Kiel on the coast of Schleswig-Holstein. Reserves in these fields, recoverable with currently used methods, were estimated at about 80 million tons in 1971. Annual production of crude oil declined from about 8 million tons in the late 1960s to 7.1 million tons in 1972.

Natural gas has also been found in the northern lowland. In the 1960s the main area of exploitation was at the estuary of the Ems River. Total reserves of natural gas in 1971 were variously estimated at about 400 billion and 500 billion cubic yards. Production of natural gas has been rising rapidly: from 1.8 billion cubic yards in 1964 to 15.7 billion in 1970 and 22.4 billion in 1972. To meet domestic requirements, natural gas has also been imported from the Netherlands and, to an increasing extent, from the Soviet Union.

Iron and Steel

Iron ore has been mined in the southwestern portion of Lower Saxony and the Westerwald region of Hesse. Most of the remaining ore is of low quality, with an iron content of only 25 to 37 percent. Because the mines are small and located at relatively long distances from the metallurgical industry in the Ruhr, costs of extraction and transportation have been high. Domestic production, therefore, has not been able to compete with higher grade ores imported from Sweden, Brazil, and the Lorraine Province of France. As a consequence the output of iron ore declined from a peak of 18.7 million tons in 1960 to 6.1 million tons in 1972. In that year domestic ore production in terms of iron content was, at most, equivalent to 8 percent of imports.

The iron and steel industry is located in the Ruhr and the nearby Rhine area. Production of pig iron and ferroalloys and of crude steel reached 33.9 million and 45.3 million tons, respectively, in 1969. By 1971, a year of slackened economic growth, output of these metals declined to 30 million and 40.3 million tons, respectively, but recovered to 32 million and 43.7 million tons in 1972. Compared with the output in the 1964–67 period, the average annual production in the 1968–72 period was 19 percent higher for pig iron and ferroalloys and 18 percent higher for crude steel. Production of steel was reported to have reached a record level of 49.5 million tons in 1973, mainly in response to heavy foreign demand.

Production of rolled steel products followed the general trend of the raw metals; it amounted to 32.3 million tons in 1970, declined to 28.7 million tons in 1971, and recovered to 31.1 million tons in 1972. About 40 percent of the output consisted of tinplate and sheet steel. Other major items of output included steel rods, wire, hot-rolled band steel, and seamless steel tubes.

Most of the steel output has been used by domestic industry, but the Federal Republic has had a consistent surplus in its foreign trade in steel. The favorable trade balance in steel reached more than US$1 billion in 1967 and was only slightly less than that figure in 1971. The average annual steel trade surplus in the years 1966 through 1971 was US$826 million. Yet a well-known London financial paper reported in October 1972 that for the first time in its history the Federal Republic's steel trade balance had been in deficit for a year. No confirmation of this report was found by mid-1974.

Potash

Potash deposits and mines are located in Lower Saxony, Hesse, and Baden-Württemberg. They are estimated to contain from 1.8 billion to 3.6 billion tons of pure potash. Production of crude potash in the 1960–72 period increased from about 19 million to 23 million tons; the marketable pure potash content of the mined salts reached 2.4 million tons in 1971 and 1972. Virtually all the potash is used in the production of fertilizers. About 45 percent of the potash output has been exported, mostly in the form of fertilizers.

ENERGY

Electricity

At the end of 1971 the installed electric generating capacity amounted to 53.6 million kilowatts. Two-thirds of the capacity was in public power plants; the remainder was in power plants of industrial enterprises, except for 1.6 percent of capacity operated by the railroads. Because some equipment is usually idled by maintenance and repairs, the actually available capacity was 8 percent lower than installed capacity. Total installed capacity toward the end of 1973 was officially reported to have been about 60 million kilowatts.

Thermoelectric plants were in the overwhelming majority. Only about 9 percent of the generating capacity was in hydroelectric plants because of the dearth of usable water resources. Plants constituting 56 percent of capacity were designed to use hard coal as fuel, and 17 percent of capacity was based on lignite fuel. The remaining plants used oil, gas, and miscellaneous other fuels. There was a significant difference in the pattern of power plants in the public and industrial sectors. In general industrial power plants relied more on hard coal, oil, and gas and less on water power, lignite, and miscellaneous fuels. Water power is less dependable than fuels because of fluctuations in supply due to weather conditions.

In the 1960–71 period electric generating capacity had virtually doubled, and the utilization of available capacity had increased by 12.3 percent. The largest proportional increase in generating capacity occurred in oil-and gas-burning power plants; the lowest proportional rise took place in hydroelectric capacity. The expansion was most rapid in railroad-operated plants and slowest in power plants owned by industry. Expansion of public power plants was somewhat faster than the average for all plants.

Production of electricity in 1971 reached almost 250 billion kilowatt-hours, or 123 percent more than output in 1960. This volume was supplemented by net imports of 6.6 billion kilowatt-hours. About 10 percent of the total supply was consumed by the electric power industry or lost in transmission. The major electricity consumers and their shares of the remaining net supply included industry, 60 percent; residences, 20.4 percent; and trade and handicrafts, 9 percent. Only 3.4 percent of the net supply was used in transport, and 2.2 percent was consumed in agriculture. Other unidentified consumers accounted for the remaining 5 percent of the electricity supply; this category presumably included street lighting. Whereas industry's share of electricity had declined from 72.4 percent in 1960, the shares of other consumers, excluding transport, had increased; the largest gain was made by the use of electricity in residences.

Energy Policy

The Federal Republic's total requirements for primary energy have been rising at virtually the same rate as the country's gross national product (GNP), and this relationship is expected to continue in the future. The provision of an adequate energy supply has therefore been considered of utmost importance to continued economic growth.

The structure of primary energy consumption changed drastically after the mid-1950s. In the 1957-72 period the proportion of energy derived from coal and lignite declined from 84.7 to 32.3 percent, while the share of crude oil rose from 11 to 55.4 percent, and the share of natural gas increased from 0.3 to 8.6 percent. By 1972 nuclear energy was providing 0.9 percent of the supply, a share that was roughly equivalent to the decline in the proportion of hydroelectric energy. The change in the structure of energy consumption entailed a sharp increase in the dependence upon foreign supplies from 11 percent in 1957 to 55 percent in 1972.

On October 3, 1973, three days before the outbreak of war in the Middle East and the consequent oil embargo by Arab states, the Federal Republic government announced a comprehensive energy policy that was intended to ensure a dependable energy supply to cover the country's rapidly growing needs for the middle and long term, at the lowest possible economic cost and with proper regard for the protection of the environment. The major aims of the policy concerning primary energy sources included the reduction of risks involved in the dependence upon imported crude oil; rapid expansion of the use of natural gas, nuclear energy, and lignite; and reliance on hard coal to the extent necessary from the viewpoint of specific energy needs and overall economic considerations. The proportion of crude oil in the total energy supply was nevertheless to remain fairly stable—54 percent in 1980 and 1985, compared to 55.4 percent in 1972 and an estimated 57 percent in 1975.

The energy policy was to be carried out in collaboration with the domestic energy industry, the international oil companies, and the European Community. It also envisaged the need for much closer cooperation with energy-producing states and with major energy consumers outside the European Community, particularly Japan, the United States, and the Soviet Union.

In the area of foreign crude oil, the government announced its readiness to assist in the economic development of oil-exporting countries, in return for the shipment of oil, and to enter into long-term agreements that would balance and safeguard the interests of both parties. With regard to the domestic oil industry, the government's plan proposed a closer grouping of the oil companies, so as to enable them to participate more effectively in the activities of the newly formed organization created for the purpose of exploring for oil and promoting investment projects in developing countries. A first experiment in this kind of activity, supported by a DM575 million conditionally repayable government loan, was said to have laid a good foundation for the successful continuation of the program. Nevertheless, the government found that the program required much closer coordination among the participating companies, more efficient organization of the work, and a stronger entrepreneurial drive.

To ensure the availability of an adequate tanker tonnage for the transport of oil, the government offered an additional subsidy of DM150 million to the shipbuilding industry. Provision was also made to guard against the effects of a temporary disruption of the foreign oil supply by raising mandatory reserve quotas for producers and importers, undertaking to establish a substantial federal government oil reserve, and introducing legislation that would empower the government to control the production and distribution of oil and oil products in the event of an energy crisis.

For some time before the adoption of the new energy policy, the federal and *Land* governments had politically and financially supported the efforts of the domestic natural gas industry to obtain foreign gas supplies for the home market. Contracts for natural gas were concluded with the Netherlands, the Soviet Union, and Norway, and contract negotiations were under way with Algeria. Under the new policy the government undertook to provide additional support for the exploitation of new discoveries in more remote areas, mainly through credit guarantees for equipment provided to foreign countries against repayment in natural gas.

On the domestic scene the government emphasized the need to exhaust all possibilities for discovering new natural gas deposits and offered to support systematic seismic exploration at great depths and deep drilling at promising sites. For environmental reasons natural gas was to be reserved mainly for residential use. Its use by electric power stations was to be limited to the technically unavoidable level.

The development of nuclear energy for the production of electricity was given high priority. Of the estimated 90 million kilowatts additional generating capacity that would be needed by 1985 (at a cost of more than DM70 billion), as much as 40 million to 50 million kilowatts were to be based on nuclear energy. Through participation in three international nuclear programs, the Federal Republic was able to create a competent nuclear reactor industry, which had strongly emphasized the public safety factor in its construction work. Further research into the safety aspects of nuclear energy power plants was to receive government support.

Attainment of the nuclear energy program presupposes a reduction in the construction time of power plants from the usual time span of six to eight years and the assurance of an adequate nuclear fuel supply. With regard to the former problem, the government proposed to take appropriate measures in cooperation with the industry to improve the organization of work and speed up construction, with priority consideration for public safety and the environment.

As to nuclear fuel, needed supplies would be secured almost entirely under contracts with the United States Atomic Energy Commission, at least until 1980. At the same time, however, the Federal Republic will continue its cooperation with Great Britain and the Netherlands in the development of the centrifuge uranium enrichment process. This work is expected to result in the creation of facilities that would provide the bulk of the country's requirements for enriched uranium by 1985. A revised fourth atomic energy program for the years 1973 through 1977, including provisions for government financing, was scheduled to be issued shortly after the announcement of the new energy policy.

Lignite has been considered to be a competitive and environmentally desirable fuel for power plants. Its use for this purpose was to be increased by 23 percent by 1980. Maintenance of lignite consumption at that level beyond 1980 would necessitate opening new deposits. The government favored the development of new mines without damage to the environment.

In order to ensure a domestic market for hard coal, the government set coal consumption goals for the electric power and iron and steel industries. The government will continue to subsidize the price of hard coal to these industries (the rate was DM15 per ton in 1974) and will also continue the export subsidy up to a volume of 15 million tons per year under a provision of European Community regulations. At the same time the government decided against abolishing or curtailing the annual coal import quota of 5.5 million tons from outside the European Community, because such a step would adversely affect the supply of the northern coast area.

Despite the noncompetitive cost of hard coal, the government considered its continued use essential not only as a safety factor in the energy supply but also for social and regional policy reasons, as long as costs did not rise to an economically prohibitive level. The government's plan for hard coal was formulated for a five-year period to 1978, when coal output should be stabilized at 83 million tons per year. The coal industry was called upon to ensure this level of output at an acceptable cost through further rationalization of production and the fullest utilization of all available resources. Financial support for these measures was to be provided by the government in various forms up to specified levels.

Provision was also made in the new energy program for continued research into all essential aspects of energy, including nuclear fusion, gasification of coal, utilization of such new sources as solar and geothermal energy, and improved technologies for the production and distribution of electricity. The cost of the entire energy program to 1978, in addition to previously undertaken energy measures for that period, was estimated at an annual average of DM600 million.

The oil boycott failed to produce any serious economic disruption in the country, even though it caused temporary inconvenience to the motoring public and created difficulties for the automobile industry, with the exception of Daimler Benz, manufacturer of the Mercedes-Benz. Despite the subsequent steep increase in the price of imported oil, the Federal Republic's trade balance continued to accumulate substantial surpluses, in sharp contrast to the experience in other European countries and Japan, and its rate of inflation was also lowest.

The oil crisis, however, spurred the government's efforts to translate its energy policy into concrete action. Thwarted by two major European states in its desire for a common European Community approach to the oil problem in concert with other major oil consumers, the Federal Republic intensified its bilateral negotiations with Iran, Algeria, the Soviet Union, and other oil-producing countries for long-term contractual deliveries of oil and gas in return for assistance in industrial development.

At the end of May 1974 projects under negotiation included the construction of a 25-million-ton oil refinery in Iran at a projected cost of DM2 billion; a trilateral deal involving Iran and the Soviet Union for the delivery of more than 13 billion cubic yards of natural gas per year; and a contract with Algeria for annual purchases of 8.5 billion cubic yards of natural gas in return for a DM85 million loan toward the construction of a natural gas terminal near Arzev. In May 1974 a long-term loan of DM6 million was granted to Burma for the construction of a gas liquefying plant and the purchase of spare parts and other supplies. Exploratory discussions were held with Libya and Saudi Arabia, which were to be continued in 1974, aimed at the conclusion of contracts for the exchange of oil and gas against industrial technology. The Federal Republic, however, was seeking firm guarantees for the security of its investments before entering into binding agreements. Its actual investment in these various countries was relatively small by mid-1974.

As a result of the oil embargo, the government placed greater emphasis on the exploitation of domestic coal resources, and larger sums than planned were allocated for intensified research. In early January 1974 a DM1.5 billion coal research program to 1977 was authorized. Some DM616 million of this sum were earmarked for the development of improved methods of obtaining gas and oil from coal. About half that amount was allocated to research on methods to raise productivity in the coal mines, and another DM74 million was to be used on technology for improved methods of prospecting for oil and gas. The government's financial support of the program was to include DM800 million in federal funds and DM150 million from North Rhine-Westphalia, the *Land* where most coal pits are located.

In the spring of 1974 one of the largest Federal Republic steel producers was negotiating with a United States firm for development of a coal mine in Virginia that would produce high-grade coking coal in about three or four years. The concern was also investigating similar possibilities in other major coal-producing countries and was urging the government to relax the restriction on coal imports as an alternative to rising subsidy payments for domestic coal.

Toward the end of 1973 five Federal Republic companies, with the approval of the Commission of the European Community, entered into a long-term uranium enrichment contract with the Soviet Union. The agreement covered 700 tons of uranium—a fraction of total needs—at a price that was believed to be somewhat below the price paid for uranium from the United States. A foreign observer remarked at the time that the agreement may eventually provide an alternative to the high-priced supply obtained under a long-term contract from the United States.

In February 1974 eight leading industrial and research organizations entered into an agreement to pool their efforts to extract gas from coal and lignite by means of high-temperature nuclear reactors. This development program was planned to 1982 at an estimated cost of DM1.45 billion. The group hoped to obtain federal and *Land* financial aid for the project. They tentatively and cautiously estimated that success of the program might reduce the country's dependence on oil to between 30 and 35 percent of total energy needs in the late 1980s, compared to a level of more than 50 percent originally planned by the government in its energy program.

LABOR

In 1972 industry, including artisan shops, employed close to 13.1 million people, half the number employed in the economy. More than 80 percent of those employed in industry worked in manufacturing. Construction provided employment for 15.6 percent of the work force, while mining and energy production employed only 2.5 and 1.4 percent, respectively. About 11 percent of the people employed in industry worked in enterprises with fewer than ten employees.

Total industrial employment fluctuated within a range of 6 percent during the ten-year period of 1963 through 1972. From a level of 13.1 million in 1963 it rose to 13.3 million in 1965; declined to 12.4 million in 1967; recovered subsequently to the highest level of 13.2 million in 1970; and declined to below 13.1 million in 1972. The pattern of change differed substantially among major industry sectors. In mining and energy production there was a steady decline for a total loss of one-third of the workers in each sector. In construction the number of workers declined by 8 percent until 1967 and then stabilized at slightly more than 2 million. Only in manufacturing was the number of workers higher in all years after 1963 except in 1967 and 1968. The highest level of employment in this sector—10.6 million people—was reached in 1970; in the next two years it declined to 10.5 million.

The machine-building industry has been the largest single employer in the manufacturing sector. In 1970 it had more than 1.3 million workers, or 13.3 percent of the total number. Electric and electronic equipment construction was a close second with a work force of more than 1.1 million people. The textile, clothing, and leather and shoe industries together occupied more than 1.2 million workers. Other important manufacturing employers and the proportions of the work force they employed included the woodworking and wood-processing industries, 10.4 percent; chemical and allied industries, 9.6 percent; food, beverages, and tobacco processing, 9.5 percent; metals and metalworking, 9 percent; and motor vehicles, 7.9 percent.

The structure of employment in manufacturing changed significantly in the 1963–71 period. In the production of chemicals and rubber and of machinery and metal products employment rose quite steadily by a total of more than one-fifth. In the basic metals and electric machinery industries the number of workers increased by almost one-tenth, after some initial declines in the intervening years. In printing and publishing employment rose 25 percent until 1970 but declined sharply in the next year to a level only 7 percent higher than it had been in 1963. All other manufacturing industries experienced declines in employment, ranging from 2 percent in woodworking and wood processing to 27 percent in the production of nonmetallic mineral products, mainly glass, ceramics, and building materials.

In 1971 and 1972 about 48 percent of total employment in manufacturing enterprises with ten or more employees and more than half the white-collar and technical personnel were concentrated in the production of investment goods. About half that number was employed in the production of consumer goods other than processed foods. Production of basic and processed materials for industrial use was a close third in terms of employment, with about 22 percent of those employed, and the food, beverage, and tobacco industries absorbed only a little more than 6 percent of the manufacturing labor force.

In the 1960–72 period production of investment goods made the greatest gains in employment. The labor force in that branch rose by 27 percent, including an increase of 71 percent in the number of white-collar and technical personnel. The corresponding increases in all other branches of production were only 2 percent and 40 percent, respectively. The lowest employment gains were made in the production of materials and industrial consumer goods.

Labor productivity rose substantially in the 1962–72 period. For industry, excluding energy production and building construction, the increase amounted to 76 percent per hour of total employment and 90.7 percent per hour of blue-collar employment. The corresponding average annual rates of increase were 5.9 and 6.7 percent, respectively. An exceptionally high rate of increase in productivity—about 21 perecent per year—was attained in the newly introduced extraction of crude oil and natural gas. Relatively high rates were also attained in chemicals, oil refining, and tobacco processing. The lowest productivity advance was made in several branches of the food industry, in individual branches of metalworking, and in the manufacture of shoes.

Industrial wages have been rising steadily. In 1972 the average gross hourly wage for workers was DM7.42. The average wage of DM7.89 for male workers was substantially higher than the DM5.53 wage for female workers. The highest hourly earnings prevailed in printing and oil refining. Substantially higher than average wages were also earned in energy production, the automobile and chemical industries, metalworking, and construction. The lowest hourly earnings prevailed in the leather, textile, clothing, and woodworking industries.

In the 1962–72 period gross hourly wages of industrial workers more than doubled, while productivity per worker-hour rose 91 percent. Until 1968 the wage increase was slightly lower than the rise in productivity, 47 as against 50 percent. The situation changed drastically, however, in the subsequent years, when a 56-percent rise in hourly wage was accompanied by a productivity increase of only 27 percent.

In 1972 roughly 15 percent of the industrial labor force consisted of foreign workers, whose number in industry approached 1.9 million. About 44 percent of these workers were employed in metallurgy; 30 percent were occupied in other branches of manufacturing; and 22 percent were active in construction. Only 4 percent of the foreign industrial labor force were engaged in mining, but that percentage represented 77,000 workers. The ban on recruitment of foreign workers from countries outside the European Community, imposed in November 1973 in the context of the oil crisis, led to complaints of manpower shortages by the Ruhr coal-mining concern, which was called upon to increase production under the revised long-term energy program.

INVESTMENT

Information on industrial investment is tenuous, in part because legal provisions prevent the collection of data from enterprises with fewer than fifty employees, except for the census years 1962 and 1967. Published data cover establishments with twenty or more employees; those for enterprises with twenty to forty-nine employees represent official estimates. Investment by establishments with fewer than twenty employees was reported on the basis of census data to have constituted 9.7 percent of total investment in 1962 and 9.8 percent in 1967.

Comparability of the investment data suffers because some, but not all, include a variable investment tax imposed by the government under its economic stabilization program. In 1973 this tax amounted to 11 percent of investment.

With some fluctuations related to the business cycle, annual gross investment by industrial establishments with twenty or more employees, excluding the electricity and gas industries, increased from DM27.8 billion in 1962 to DM45.1 billion in 1970. Including investment by small enterprises in the proportions reported for 1962 and 1967, investment in 1970 was about DM50 billion. Investment in energy production and distribution rose from DM4.5 billion in 1965 to DM5.3 billion in 1970 and DM7.3 billion in 1971. In 1970, therefore, the last year for which relatively complete data were officially reported, total gross investment in industry amounted to somewhat more than DM55 billion. Depreciation was maintained at a level in excess of 40 percent of gross investment.

The bulk of investment by establishments employing twenty or more people was channeled into manufacturing, and the share of manufacturing in the annual investment volume rose from 71.7 percent in 1962 to 80.3 percent in 1970. At the same time the proportion of investment devoted to mining and construction declined by one-half and one-third, respectively. While total annual investment in the 1962–70 period increased by about 72 percent, it rose by 92 percent in manufacturing, 53 percent in construction, and 16 percent in energy production. Investment in mining, by contrast, declined by 27 percent; in 1970 it accounted for only 2 percent of the total, compared to 7.1 percent for construction and 10.6 percent for energy production.

In the manufacturing sector, the chemical industry consistently received the largest and most rapidly growing share of investment; in the 1962–70 period its share rose from 12.2 percent to 16.9 percent (it had reached 18.5 percent in 1966), and the annual investment volume increased 2.7 times. Other major investment targets in manufacturing, with annual investment shares fluctuating between roughly 8.5 and 12 percent, included industries producing machinery, motor vehicles, electric and electronic equipment, and processed foods and beverages. Annual investment in the motor vehicle and electric and electronic industries doubled during the period. The proportion of investment channeled into the iron and steel industry declined from 10.1 percent in 1962 to 5.1 percent in 1969 and 6.4 percent in 1970. Together, the listed industries received about 60 percent of the annual investment in manufacturing.

Investment has been financed primarily with funds out of the firms' own resources, through reinvestment of undistributed earnings and depreciation reserves. The share of these funds in total investment financing amounted to 76.5 percent in 1973 and slightly less in 1972.

The capital market has played a minor role in investment financing. New stock issues by all kinds of businesses, at market value, amounted to only DM1.7 billion in 1968 and in 1969 and averaged DM2.5 billion in the 1970–72 period. New industrial stock issues in 1972 were reported to have totaled less than DM685 million at par value and less than DM1.5 billion at market value. Stocks are usually purchased by insurance companies and other institutional investors. The public at large is reluctant to invest in stocks because of unfortunate experiences in the aftermath of World War II and subsequent currency reforms.

Bonds are another form of securities used to raise investment capital. Most bond issues are subscribed by one major underwriting syndicate that is composed of commercial and central savings banks, including the largest credit institutions in the country. External financing may also be obtained by borrowing from financial institutions of the government.

The preferred source of outside financing has been in the form of bank loans; banks provided 78 percent of new credits taken up by industry in 1971 and 58 percent in 1972. This tradition created problems for industry in 1973, when the government tightened credit controls in its fight against inflation. Because of industry's generally poor profit performance in 1972, following upon two years of major investment outlays after the recession of 1967, internal sources of investment funds were depleted, and greater recourse had to be taken to borrowing. Because of the shortage of liquid funds caused by the credit restrictions, banks could only cover less than half the credit requirements. This situation forced the postponement of many investment projects and necessitated increased borrowing from abroad.

Many smaller firms were unable to survive the credit squeeze and were either forced out of business or absorbed by larger concerns. This was particularly true in the machine-building industry, where the great majority of firms were undercapitalized family enterprises employing fewer than 200 workers and heavily dependent on bank credits. The domestic credit stringency, however, did not adversely affect the financially strong, larger concerns and groups of companies that have far greater access to domestic and foreign sources of finance on easier terms. These companies were able to maintain a remarkably high level of exports which, in the first quarter of 1974, produced an even larger trade surplus than the year before.

Because of the large-scale foreign investment losses after two world wars, Federal Republic companies were reluctant to expand their production activities beyond the country's borders until the early or mid-1960s. A trend toward establishing production facilities abroad began under the influence of rising labor costs. This trend was reinforced in the late 1960s and early 1970s by the growing labor shortage and wage inflation and by industry's fears that the repeated upward revaluation of the Deutsche Mark would result in a loss of export markets. Another element in this context was the desire of companies to take advantage of the expansion possibilities in developing countries.

Direct foreign investment in the 1961–71 period was reported to have increased from 8 to 18 percent of exports. These figures imply a sixfold rise in foreign investment during the period. A further strong impetus to investment abroad was provided by the changed world oil situation at the end of 1973, which gave rise to industrial development projects in oil- and gas-producing countries in exchange for an assured supply of these vital products.

SECTION IV. NATIONAL SECURITY

CHAPTER 17

THE ARMED FORCES

The Bundeswehr (Federal Armed Forces) of the Federal Republic in 1974 numbered approximately 475,000 men, of whom about 70 percent were in the army, 20 percent in the air force, and 10 percent in the navy. The army was organized into thirty-three brigades, its basic combat units. All of the brigades have North Atlantic Treaty Organization (NATO) assignments, fulfilling the twelve-division NATO commitment of the Bundeswehr. The air force's striking arm consisted of twenty-six squadrons of modern combat aircraft. All of these squadrons, plus the air force's missiles and most of its miscellaneous aircraft, were also committed to NATO. Naval forces consisted of approximately 320 ships. A small territorial army for rear area defense was the only major part of the regular armed forces under national control and not committed to NATO.

Army and air force units were trained and equipped to match on an equal basis the best of those in the Warsaw Pact forces to the east. The navy was relatively small, designed for action only in the vicinity of the northern sea coasts. It had no surface ships larger than destroyers and no long-range submarines.

Regular German armed forces were prohibited after World War II, and the modern Bundeswehr was not authorized until 1954. It has never been accepted enthusiastically by the people of the country, who could look back upon defeat in World War I and a far more disastrous defeat in World War II. The people also suspect that a major war involving the new forces would be one in which German territory would be the scene of an encounter—possibly not of the Federal Republic's choosing—between major alliances, in which its role would not be decisive, and from which there would be little to be gained.

In addition, the period during which the Bundeswehr was developed and expanded was one in which the rights and freedoms of the individual received great emphasis. The discipline of military life appeared to some to be incompatible with popular concepts of individual freedom. Men of serving age also felt the lack of public support, and many entered the service reluctantly. As a result, military leaders have had to work hard to make service life as acceptable and worthwhile as possible while retaining the discipline required in a combat organization.

The Bundeswehr has been under undisputed civilian control. Administration and command have been executed through the federal chancellor and the minister of defense, but the parliament has control of the military budget and also maintains close liaison with the service organization and with service personnel. Although both the executive branch and the parliament deal more intimately with the military establishment and have more authority over it than was the case before the establishment of the Bundeswehr, soldiers and officers in the services have retained their traditional apolitical character. Tradition is partially responsible for their reluctance to become involved in politics. The general negative attitude of the public toward armaments is also a factor. In any event, there is no military lobby associated with the parliament, and there have been very few instances where military spokesmen have attempted publicly or by personal contact to influence parliamentary action.

HISTORICAL BACKGROUND

The reputation for excellence that the German armed forces have had for more than a century can be attributed in large part to the legendary Prussian General Staff. This staff created the forces that were first fully recognized when they easily and decisively overran France in 1870 and 1871. The concepts and practices of the Prussian military establishment and leaders were retained when the German states were united after that war, and almost fifty years later all three services of the German forces performed remarkably well in a losing cause during World War I.

Provisions of the Treaty of Versailles after World War I were calculated to prevent German armed forces from again becoming a menace to the neighboring states. Some of the restrictions were evaded, and Adolf Hitler in 1934 reintroduced military conscription, and in 1936 he publicly repudiated the Treaty of Versailles altogether.

By 1939, when World War II broke out, Germany had a fifty-one-division army, the strongest and best equipped air force in the world, and an impressive navy. In the spring of 1940 these forces attacked and destroyed the armies of France in about one month. Hitler's *Blitzkrieg* (lightning warfare) used highly mobile ground armies with air forces in close support and exhibited a capability that had never before been seen.

Germany was unable to secure a peace, however. Long fighting with the Soviet Union in the east wore down its armies, and inability to get at the forces of the United Kingdom and the United States gave those countries time to develop armies with striking power similar to that of Germany. When they were mobilized, the Allies' manpower resources and industrial capacities were far greater than those of Germany. Allied bomber aircraft became a constant harassment, forced a portion of the country's war-supporting industries to relocate, and necessitated the remaining at home of equipment and personnel that were badly needed at the front lines.

The situation for Germany had been hopeless from the time that Soviet forces were able to take the initiative and go on the offensive in the east; once the Western Allies had established themselves in France, the outcome of the war was in no doubt whatsoever. Hitler, however, would not seek peace. The inevitable result was that his armed force was decimated, Germany was completely overrun, and vast amounts of housing and most of the country's industrial enterprises were destroyed.

In spite of the fact that the ultimate outcome had not been in doubt, the war had not been easy for the Allies and, when they met in 1945 at Potsdam, a suburb of Berlin, they decreed total disarmament for Germany. At that time their primary concern was the possible resurgence of German militancy. No formal peace agreement followed the Potsdam meetings, however. Before a peace could be worked out, the victorious Allies had separated into two camps, and the cold war between them had set in. As events turned out, total German disarmament was more acceptable to the German people than it became, very shortly, to the Allies who imposed it.

The Federal Republic was invited to enter the Western European Union (WEU) and NATO in 1955. The new alliances' terms retained some controls over the rearmament of the Federal Republic, but they reversed the character of the Federal Republic's relationship with the Western European nations and the United States. The Federal Republic was now a partner in the Western alliance against the Soviet Union.

The WEU consisted of the Federal Republic, the United Kingdom, France, Belgium, Luxembourg, the Netherlands, and Italy. Its charter called for automatic mutual cooperation against an aggressor. The NATO charter prepared about a year later was less binding on its fifteen members, although the deployment of the international NATO forces and their common exercises are calculated to ensure an automatic and cooperative reaction to an aggressor force.

Upon entering NATO, the Federal Republic promised its new allies to raise, train, and equip twelve divisions of ground forces and roughly comparable air and naval forces. The Basic Law of May 23, 1949, which serves as the Federal Republic's constitution, had little to say about national defense. It provided compensation for victims of World War II and stated that no one should be compelled to serve as an armed combatant against his conscience. The 1949 law was amended in March 1954, to authorize for the first time the creation of regular armed services. In accordance with the amended Basic Law, legislation on compulsory military service was passed in 1956. The first law provided for drafting 10,000 men each quarter of the year.

The Bundeswehr grew steadily from 15,000 men in 1954 to about 435,000 in 1964. The basic organization programmed for the Bundeswehr was established and in operation by that time, although manning of some units was meager. Growth to the 1974 strength of 475,000 was achieved irregularly after 1964. During the first three years of NATO's existence, the Federal Republic contributed approximately as much of its defense appropriations to the support of its allies' forces as to its own, although the greatest amount of such support was contributed during 1955. During that year less than 15 percent of the country's defense money was spent on its own forces. By 1958, however, the Federal Republic's forces had grown to the point that they consumed more than 90 percent of the defense budget. Assistance to other forces remained relatively low until 1973.

Even after the first draft law was enacted, whether or not to acquire a professional all-volunteer army or to raise the force by conscription was argued at length. In support of a volunteer force, it was argued that a complex modern army demanded professionals and that conscripts serving for short periods of active duty were costly and could never become adequately trained. A professional military establishment, however, could become a self-sufficient, independent force—a state within a state—and if the political situation in the country changed in an undesirable direction, such a force could be used unscrupulously. As matters developed, however, the decision reached was determined by unrelated economic factors. Prosperity returned to the land and, with jobs and good wages for nearly everyone, conscription was required in order to raise the number of men needed.

There was also much early debate on nuclear weapons. Much of the discussion was undoubtedly premature, as the country would not have been permitted either to produce or possess the weapons or to have the capability to employ unilaterally those that might be deployed with its forces. Arguments as to whether nuclear weapons should be permitted on the country's soil, however, were valid. It was arguable that the presence of such weapons would probably guarantee the use of similar weapons against the country in a conflict in which any nuclear weapons were used. It was decided by both major political parties, with some difference in detail, that they should be maintained for their deterrent effect, so long as opposing Warsaw Pact forces not only had nuclear weapons but were deploying a considerable superiority in conventional forces and weapons on or relatively near the Federal Republic's borders.

ORGANIZATION AND MISSION

The federal chancellor is the individual directly charged with responsibility for the country's defense. He delegates much of the responsibility to the minister of defense, who commands the forces during peacetime and who in 1974 was one of the seventeen members of the cabinet. In time of war or extreme emergency, defined as a state of defense by the parliament, command is reassumed by the federal chancellor.

The minister of defense is a civilian, as each of his predecessors in the Federal Republic has been. The principle that the minister of defense is a civilian is so firmly established that a departure from it would probably be considered of great significance.

The president of the Federal Republic is titular head of the armed forces but has no command authority over them and no responsibility for their organization or performance. At the apex of the military establishment is an armed forces staff headed by the general inspector of the armed forces. His is the highest military position in the defense establishment. The highest ranking position in each of the regular services—the inspectors of the army, navy, and air force—are also the chiefs of staff of the respective services.

Defense policy and basic defense planning are the responsibility of the Federal Security Council, which is a special committee within the cabinet presided over by the chancellor. The council also coordinates the implementation of its plans and policy.

Apart from the formally established lines of control by the executive branch over the armed forces and the responsibility of the Bundestag (Federal Diet) for the defense budget, the Bundestag debates defense policy and monitors morale and conditions of service. Its relations with the armed forces include member visits to military units and military installations and regular contacts through its defense ombudsman. It is in the parliamentary arena, incidentally, that the parties in opposition to the government gain access to defense information and details that are not made public.

During much of the period since 1954, the issue of defense having been unpopular with the public, the leaders of both the party in power and the opposition have supported the military establishment more loyally than their constituents. It has, nonetheless, been difficult to provide finances for the Bundeswehr sufficient to maintain its personnel and equipment at the strength achieved by the late 1960s. Personnel and equipment costs have increased rapidly.

According to Article 87 of the Basic Law, the sole mission of the Bundeswehr is defense. It is in existence only to deter, in conjunction with the armed forces of its allies, a potential enemy from the use of military forces in central Europe. The tactical mission of the forces is to defend the territory of the Federal Republic in the event of an invasion by an enemy. The army is charged with repelling the enemy's ground forces. The air force is to provide support to the ground forces, aerial defense, and reconnaissance. The navy's task is to defend the country's coastal area and to combat enemy naval forces in the North and Baltic seas.

All major defensive units are committed to act in cooperation with NATO forces in the area. The NATO mission, as it relates directly to the Federal Republic, is to present an aggressor with a mixed international force having an integrated command and organizational structure. Since 1969 this force has been committed to the policy of holding nuclear weapons back initially and committing them only in extreme necessity and then only in limited and selective fashion. No use of the Bundeswehr's major combat units beyond that of their NATO commitment is envisaged. Smaller detachments could be used to support the police and the government in the event of serious riots or internal disorder or to assist local agencies during a major disaster or catastrophe.

Army

The army has three corps commands, and its thirty-three brigades include thirteen armored, twelve mechanized infantry, two mountain, three airborne, and three that are described only as fighter brigades. Three separate armored regiments were being formed in the early 1970s, to become a part of the NATO command forces when manned, equipped, and trained.

The same units are also described, usually in relation to their NATO assignments, as twelve divisions. Four of the divisions are classified as armored, and six as mechanized infantry. The basic army unit, however, is the brigade, and variations in unit structures account for the fact that only ten of the twelve divisions can be classified specifically as armored or infantry. In addition to the brigades, the army had two separate tank regiments and fifteen surface-to-surface missile battalions.

The territorial army, which is not integrated within the NATO organization, consists of nine geographical commands with home defense, communication, engineer, police, and civil defense support units, all of which are charged with the support of NATO units by covering the area to the rear of the combat forces and by protecting vital installations. The territorial army numbered about 30,000 men in the early 1970s. According to its directives, it was established to relieve the regular armed forces of "duties that are not compatible with combat mobility." The functions performed by the territorial army do not require the large amounts of heavy tanks, artillery, and other equipment that are maintained in the major combat units.

About 500,000 men who have had prior military service are maintained as trained reserves and are subject to immediate recall to active service. Privates are held in the reserve forces to age thirty-five, noncommissioned officers to age forty-five, and officers to age sixty.

According to information available in mid-1973, at that time the army numbered about 334,000 men, 183,500 of whom were conscripts. Its major equipment included about 3,250 tanks, 7,000 armored personnel carriers, 1,100 tank destroyers, 850 medium and 300 heavy artillery pieces, 200 multiple rocket launchers, 105 surface-to-surface missile launchers, and 467 helicopters.

Full-strength armored divisions have 14,500 men organized into five tank, four infantry, one reconnaissance, and four artillery battalions. If fully equipped, the armored division has 300 tanks supported by tank destroyers, heavy and medium-caliber artillery guns, mortars, multiple rocket launchers, and surface-to-surface missile launchers. All of the tanks are in the medium category and may be either the American Patton or the Leopard. The newer, German-made Leopard carries a heavier gun than the Patton.

Mechanized divisions run slightly larger than the armored and are authorized 15,500 men. The typical mechanized division is little different from an armored unit and has four tank, five infantry, one reconnaissance, and four artillery battalions. Not only are there very small organizational differences between the armored and mechanized divisions, the differences in major equipment items are even less. The mechanized division has 250 tanks, forty-one tank destroyers, sixteen heavy and thirty-six medium artillery pieces, thirty-six mortars, sixteen multiple rocket launchers, and four surface-to-surface missile launchers. Its major equipment is thus identical with that of the armored division, except that it has fifty fewer tanks and twenty-four more mortars.

Navy

In 1973 the navy had about 37,000 men, including those in its air arm, 9,500 of whom are conscripts. Its 320 vessels included eleven destroyers, eight fast frigates, thirty-eight fast patrol boats, sixty-one minesweepers, two landing ships and twenty-two smaller landing craft, twelve submarines, twelve combat support ships, and five utility vessels. The naval air arm had four squadrons equipped with American-built fighter-bombers, two squadrons of maritime reconnaissance aircraft, and about forty helicopters and light liaison aircraft. Its fighter-bomber squadrons had eighteen aircraft each, and the reconnaissance squadrons twelve each.

None of the navy's ships, submarines, or aircraft are designed for long-distance or open-ocean operation. Their mission since World War II has been to defend the coastal area and to counter any enemy naval activities near the shore in the North and Baltic seas. The destroyers are a miscellaneous group. The four oldest were built in the United States during World War II. Four were built in the Federal Republic between 1960 and 1963. The three newest were built in the United Kingdom during the late 1960s. Those built in the United States are small, displacing about 2,100 tons; the postwar models displace an average of about 3,350 tons.

With a few exceptions, all the frigates, escorts, corvettes, minesweepers, and torpedo boats were built in the Federal Republic. Two of the older frigates were British built; a few of the support ships and two landing ships were built in the United States. The landing craft were built in the Federal Republic but are similar to American types.

The minesweepers are small vessels that include three types. Inshore types are the smallest, displacing an average of about 190 tons. The so-called fast minesweepers displace about 200 tons. Coastal types are larger but displace less than 375 tons. Minesweeping and minelaying operations would be limited to the river estuaries and shipping lanes near the coast.

Although the newer submarines are classed as medium oceangoing types, none of them could range into the middle Atlantic to destroy shipping as did the German U-boat fleets during both world wars. The newer classes displace about 500 tons. Older ones displace about two-thirds as much and are classed as coastal submarines. All of them have been built in the Federal Republic since World War II.

In an emergency the navy could double its personnel strength on short notice. It has 35,000 trained reserves who are liable to immediate recall.

Air Force

The air force has more than 100,000 men, about one-third of whom are conscripts. Of its 1,800 aircraft, two-thirds are jet, and approximately 450 are first-line combat models. Combat planes are organized into twenty-six fighter, fighter-bomber, and reconnaissance squadrons; four transport squadrons; and four helicopter squadrons. The twenty-six squadrons with higher performance aircraft include four that are trained primarily for reconnaissance, four for aerial interception only, six exclusively fighter-bomber, and four that could perform in both fighter-bomber and interceptor roles. Eight of the squadrons can combine ground attack with reconnaissance missions.

The air force also has sizable missile units. These are organized into two wings of thirty-six surface missile launchers each and nearly 450 surface-to-air missile launchers. The surface-to-surface missiles are short-range types, and the surface-to-air missiles are for aircraft interception only.

The air force has an altogether tactical and defensive mission. It has no long-range strategic capability. The surface-to-surface missiles and fighter-bomber aircraft could strike any kind of target, but their range is short, and it is unlikely that they would be used except to assist in an overall mission that would be undertaken by a combination of all the regular armed services.

MANPOWER, SUPPORT, AND CONDITIONS OF SERVICE

Manpower

Approximately 420,000 young men reached draft age (nineteen) in 1973. The number will rise for the next decade, reaching more than 500,000 during the early 1980s. After about 1985 it will drop to under 400,000 when the effects of the low birthrates of the late 1960s and early 1970s are felt (see ch. 4). A large percentage of those arriving at draft age are physically fit and are qualified for military service in all other respects.

The estimated male population of the country at the end of 1971 was approximately 29.3 million; that of the males in the working-age group between fifteen and sixty-five years was approximately 18.9 million. The 230,000 men serving mandatory duty tours in 1972 constituted about 0.8 percent of the country's male population and 1.2 percent of the men in the working-age group. The total armed forces strength—approximately 475,000—constituted 1.6 percent of the total male population and 2.5 percent of the males of working age.

In order to maintain force strengths at 1973 levels with the same percentage of conscripts, it will be necessary to draft approximately 200,000 men annually, or about 60 percent of those in the annual nineteen-year-old age-group who are physically fit. This is a considerable increase over those required in 1972 and earlier; on January 1, 1973, the conscript tour of duty was reduced from eighteen to an average of fifteen months. Various factors other than physical condition add to the numbers of those who may be deferred, and authorities estimated that the group from which they could draw in 1974 would include only some 240,000 men. Over 80 percent of this smaller group, therefore, could anticipate being called into the armed forces.

Service Obligation

A 1954 amendment to the Basic Law states that all males except those in West Berlin are subject to conscription for military service between the ages of eighteen and thirty-five. Exemptions and deferments are granted to university students and apprentices in certain professions. Conscientious objectors are not called into the regular military forces but may be required to serve the country in some substitute capacity. There were 27,000 conscientious objectors in 1971.

In spite of the opportunities for deferments, those called are intelligent, have technological aptitude, are in good physical condition, and are accustomed to discipline. They fit readily into the military organization and respond quickly to basic training and technical courses.

Although the conscription system was instituted because it alone could provide the required number of properly qualified men, it is conceded to have had other favorable side effects. It has provided the services themselves with a manpower reserve from which they are able to recruit noncommissioned officers and long-service career soldiers. The generally high quality of conscripted personnel also enables the forces to keep pace with the changing society of the country, particularly in the areas in which society is progressing rapidly. The system is also considered by most officials to be of benefit to the country at large. Conscripts acquire training that is of value to society as well as to themselves when they return to civilian life. The great majority of conscripts serve their tours cooperatively and without serious disciplinary problems.

Morale and Conditions of Service

The post-World War II armed forces leaders have been faced with a variety of problems, not the least of which have been attracting personnel and determining the degree of control to exert over them in the changed atmosphere. In this atmosphere, the public has been reluctant to have a military establishment, and those who were forced to serve have been divided in their attitude toward military discipline and in the degree of responsibility they have to the armed services.

Part of the problem stems from the difficulty the older generation has encountered in explaining the attitude of the nation toward Hitler and Hitlerism in the 1930s. Parents, and schoolteachers of the parents' generation, have tended to avoid the issue insofar as possible, and it has occurred to them that the armed forces would be an excellent vehicle for the teaching of democracy. There is also a persisting memory of the terrible defeat in World War II. The resulting public attitude has been expressed as hostility to military things in general and has been manifest in a reluctance to support forces or to budget for their maintenance. Whereas time might ordinarily have been expected to erase much of this attitude, fatigue from the generation of cold war that followed World War II has tended to hold the armed forces in a status of low, or at least limited, public favor.

The Federal Republic is also experiencing the condition wherein patriotic dedication to the state and nation, as the highest value and worthy of the utmost in sacrifice, is being questioned. Service to such an ideal is considered by some people as insufficient motivation to join the armed forces. Furthermore, a continuing threat to the state, having been lived with for so long in a condition of cold war, has come to mean relatively little. As a consequence, in the eyes of a sizable segment of the society, the armed forces are at best a necessary evil, or they are considered to have become superfluous.

Military leaders have considered the subject of training their personnel in democratic principles carefully, and they are concerned over the public's attitude toward military discipline, but they have resisted pressures to relax discipline to an extent that would, in their opinion, endanger their ability to command or render the forces less capable of performing a military mission. In this light, they have stated as a basic objective "to create, not a democratic army, but an army to serve a democratic society." In this context, the forces are trained to serve their democratic government and to respect its laws and international laws.

Rights of the individual soldiers are, however, guaranteed by legislation enacted in 1956, usually referred to as the Soldiers Act. Among other things, the act specifies that, before derogatory statements about an individual soldier are entered in his personal file, he must have a hearing. If the hearing does not dispose of the problem and the remarks are still to be entered in his file, his comments about them must also be included. The act further provides for committees to represent the various ranks on personal and welfare matters. These committees are elected by the troops, by secret ballot, and have access to commanding officers to discuss individual or group problems or to present suggestions on other than purely military matters.

Whether or not members of the armed forces should consider themselves NATO troops or, in a more restricted context, German soldiers, is the subject of considerable debate. Few observers claim that more than a handful of the troops would refer to themselves as NATO soldiers; nearly all would think of themselves as serving primarily their own country. Those considering the matter seriously, however, understand that the country's own forces are altogether inadequate to defend it in a major war and that their status within the NATO alliance is a necessary one. Instilling a degree of alliance team spirit is one of the objectives of the training program.

Provisions for exempting conscientious objectors are spelled out in detail in federal law. Applicants for exemption on grounds of conscience are screened by special committees and, if their claims are considered valid, are permitted to serve the country in some alternative fashion.

The parliament's defense ombudsman attempts to assist the services as they grapple with their social problems. He makes an effort to remove or reduce the causes of friction and is a point of liaison between factions having differing interests or opposing approaches to common problems. He is responsible for safeguarding the individual rights of service personnel, in particular those of the conscripts.

The ombudsman also ensures the application of the principle of "inner guidance," which is a concept written into the Basic Law establishing the forces, by which the soldier is charged to defend his country according to his conscience rather than through blind loyalty. The principle is intended to make each soldier a citizen in uniform responsible in final analysis to his fellow citizens.

The ombudsman visits any unit or station he chooses, without prior notice. His visits are usually initiated by requests from members of parliament or by complaints from the troops. His office receives some 5,000 complaints, petitions, or reports annually. The ombudsman, however, serves in a dual capacity in which he stands between the state, which demands obedience, and the individual, who is entitled to certain rights and a degree of freedom.

The forces' commanders initially looked upon the ombudsman with suspicion or hostility, but they have learned to cooperate with the office and not infrequently find that it has worked to their advantage. The annual ombudsman report to the parliament has come to be a comprehensive assessment of the problems of the armed forces in general, as well as of the troops as individuals.

Training

Basic objectives of the training program are to acquire fundamental combat effectiveness and to develop motivation among service personnel toward a conscientious performance of their duties. The problem, however, that confronts those who formulate the various forces' training programs is to strike a balance between peacetime training that is acceptable to the country's society and preparing the men for battle. Training programs aim at giving the men technical competence useful to the military establishment and at instilling the discipline required in combat situations. At the same time the programs attempt to create duty tasks that are meaningful and satisfying, that take into account the personal desires of the trainees, and that make the individual of greater value to society when he returns to civilian status.

Military leaders are exploring social programs that may be undertaken by the armed forces in addition to more conventional military training. Preferably such programs would use the technical resources, mobile capabilities, and the like of the forces and would be adaptable to the forces' personnel and leadership structures. Assistance in environmental protection programs is being considered, among other programs, as an extension of the range of such tasks.

Basic training and small unit exercises are carried out regularly and on a continuing basis. Larger exercises and field maneuvers are conducted less frequently than commanders think is desirable, largely because of the dense population of the country and the lack of suitable space. Some joint exercises are carried out in France and the United Kingdom. The air force uses an advanced training airfield in Portugal, and all of its pilots receive some early flight training in the United States.

Noncommissioned officer training varies with the period of the individual's enlistment. Under a program introduced in 1973, those who volunteer to serve eight years are eligible for fifteen months of specialized training; those who volunteer for twelve years may receive up to thirty-three months. Long-term enlistees—those who volunteer to serve from twelve to fifteen years or more—receive the thirty-three months of training that relates to their military specialty and are also entitled to receive three years of vocational advancement training after they have completed their military service. The costs of the training and provisions for the individual's living expenses during that three years are provided by the Bundeswehr.

Those concerned with officer training are confronted with the problems that have arisen as the conflicting attitudes of the society have been carried into the military establishment. They have, however, rejected the view that the military should diverge from society, holding itself aloof from its conflicts. Their reasoning is partly that an isolated military establishment is a potential threat to society and partly that the advanced technology necessary both to the military and to the industrial society has brought about a situation wherein much that is military is difficult to distinguish from much that is civilian. This includes not only military equipment and its use but also the risks of war.

The military itself feels that it must pursue a careful balance between civilianizing its officer cadre and developing a professional group with a group identity and a code of compatible conduct and behavior in order to ensure disciplined and coordinated action under duress. Thought and effort are being applied to avoid the creation of a military subculture or a separate, exclusive military community.

The services prepare most of their young officers for an early specialized assignment with a line or combat unit. Career officers, however, advance from their initial squadron or regimental duties to staff work or to positions that are either politically related or that are performed in a fashion resembling other managerial and professional work. Such assignments call for more general education. Early career schooling is aimed at instilling certain professional standards and emphasizing managerial techniques and such military aptitudes as the ability to cope with emergencies and to maintain flexibility under conditions likely to generate panic and chaos.

Much of an officer's advanced education may be acquired during his military duty. Limited service officers, whose careers are normally limited to between four and ten years, need to have only ten years of prior schooling. Upon entry into the service they receive an initial 2½ or three years of technical and military training, most of it while serving in line officer assignments. Upon completion of the initial training program, they are qualified for command assignments at the company, squadron, or regimental level. There is provision for a percentage of the short-term limited service officers to attain university degrees and become longer term or career officers on completion of ten years of service.

Those who volunteer originally as career officers or twelve-year limited service officers must have university entrance level secondary educations upon entry into the service. They then receive four years of military training or specialist study at university level. In typical career progression, such an officer then serves an average of about seven years in regimental level military assignments, during which he attends short-term schools, seminars, and the like. At mid-career—according to his ability, reputation, and personal inclinations—the officer has an opportunity to acquire further education. In some cases this consists of short periods of schooling spread over several years. It may also consist of a three-year separation from routine service assignments for attendance at advanced schools.

Typical career officers have ten years of active duty in staff assignments or in senior command positions before retirement after twenty-five years of service. Those who advance to the general officer ranks and the most responsible positions remain on active duty for longer periods.

Career officers are classified as specialists or generalists. Specialists receive more intensive training in some equipment or weapon system or even in a professional field, such as law or medicine. Generalists usually have a specialty, but they have a general educational background, and more of their training is in subjects less immediately related to their specialist field.

By the time they are selected for staff positions, officers are required to have a university level education in some area of leadership or technical specialty and enough familiarity with other subjects to aid in decision-making. Generalists among them may have less specific technical backgrounds and must have a minimum familiarity in a much broader area. Their general educational requirements are higher and include studies in the political sciences. Officers earmarked for diplomatic assignments, positions within NATO, or exchange duty involving work with other country forces, are required to have all of the generalist staff officer background.

After about twenty years of dependence upon civilian universities, most of which were reluctant to offer courses expressly for the purpose of training military personnel, career officer colleges, or military academies, have been established in Hamburg and Munich. They accepted their first 600 students in late 1973, but the two schools will have a capacity for 4,600 students by 1976, when their curricula will be complete, and there will be students at all class levels. The five-year program includes fifteen months of basic military training, which is accomplished in regular service units, followed by three years in the Bundeswehr college. Because students are on active military duty and get only the usual military leave time, they can be given three semesters' work in a year. The degree they receive upon graduation is, therefore, the equivalent of that given at the end of four-year degree courses in other universities.

Logistics

There is a continuing effort to keep military expenditures to a minimum. The services do not get as much new matériel as they consider necessary and are required to retain in use much that they consider overdue for replacement. By most standards, however, they are well equipped, and most of what they have is of good quality and is maintained in good condition.

Infantry weapons, including the Leopard main battle tank, artillery rocket launchers, and conventional ammunition, are produced domestically. Local shipyards can build all types of naval vessels now in use or that are contemplated. Some combat aircraft are produced under license, but no new high-performance aircraft have been designed in the Federal Republic.

The Federal Republic's experience with the aerospace industry has illustrated the country's industrial potential, but it has also pointed up the difficulties that accompany the development and marketing of complex weapon systems. Initial development of the industry was accomplished during the mid-1950s. After about five years it secured the license rights to manufacture the Italian G–91 and the American F–104 aircraft. Both are high-performance fighters or fighter-bombers. These programs, plus small joint-manufacture agreements with both the United States and

334

France, gave the industry enough work to expand upon. By the mid-1960s, however, the major programs had been completed, and further work seemed to depend upon increased military appropriations or upon the development and discovery of a new market for new designs. It has been comparatively easy to produce new designs but very difficult to penetrate the world market. Also, international projects have been fiercely competed for by the participating nations with the result that the interested governments and the pressures they have generated have meant greater problems in the political area than there have been in engineering and production.

The result for the early 1970s has been a dimming of the brighter plans of the industry. It has experienced no difficulties that are not, in varying degrees, affecting aerospace industries throughout the world, however, and many observers believe that the Federal Republic's industry is effectively manned and properly managed and has the plant and equipment required to be among the world's most competitive if there should be a resurgence in the demand for its products.

The WEU determines the stock levels of major weapons and ammunition that may be accumulated in the Bundeswehr and makes inspections periodically to ensure that they are not exceeded. Manufacture of nuclear, chemical, and biological weapons and missiles having ranges in excess of twenty miles is prohibited.

Medicine

Service personnel are provided preventive medical attention, clinical care, and hospitalization when required. The medical service is also responsible for sanitation in living quarters, kitchens, and all other places where unsanitary conditions could be a hazard to health. The importance attached to the office of inspector of medical and health affairs is shown by his being one of four members of the Military Command Council; its other members are the inspectors of the army, navy, and air force, the services' highest ranking positions.

It has been difficult for the Bundeswehr to compete with civilian medical facilities in acquiring medical officers. In 1974 the forces had fewer than 1,100 physicians and dentists and fell short by nearly 50 percent of being able to recruit a sufficient number of civilian doctors to serve in military hospitals.

Career medical officers enter the service as doctors, but they receive specialized military medical training at an armed forces medical college. The amount of training in a strictly medical specialization (such as surgery, internal medicine, or orthopedics) to which a medical officer is entitled while serving in the armed forces depends upon the number of years he has volunteered to remain in the military. Those on two years of duty in place of a tour as a conscript receive little or none; career officers may become fully qualified in some medical specialty. About 30 percent of the medical officers in 1973 were serving long-term tours. Most of them had attended medical college with the aid of Bundeswehr scholarships, for which they were obligated to serve eight years or more in the armed forces.

Medical facilities are made available to the civilian population during an emergency or in any situation where military mobile equipment and transportable facilities may be needed. There are permanent rescue centers at Ulm, Koblenz, and Hamburg that have rescue helicopters and emergency vehicles. Three other military hospitals provide emergency ambulance services. Medical units have given blood and medical supplies, provided medical services at mass events, and attempted to cooperate wherever possible with civilian hospitals.

Military Justice

The national penal code includes a section called the military penal code, which deals with those offenses that are purely military in character. There are also military disciplinary courts whose panels —other than the judges—are composed of military personnel.

Unit commanders also have the authority to impose disciplinary detention or disciplinary fines. Revisions of the military disciplinary laws in 1972 have given company and regimental commanders more latitude for reprimand and disciplinary action than they have had since the formation of the Bundeswehr and a similar increase in measures they can take to reward men for unusual performance. They may impose up to seven days of detention for breaches of regulations; they may give citations for outstanding performance; and they may accompany the citations with extra days of leave time. A company commander is able to grant a maximum of five days of extra leave; a regimental commander may grant as much as two weeks.

About 107,500 minor crimes, requiring what are classed as ordinary disciplinary measures, were committed by about 72,500 servicemen in 1972. The most frequently committed minor crimes were unauthorized absence from the unit or failure to report for work. The punishment in about 45,000 of the cases consisted of small fines; in 33,000 it consisted of confinement to barracks. The remainder were reprimanded, given extra work, or deprived of some privilege.

Only about 500 people were found guilty of more serious crimes by military disciplinary courts. A majority of these cases involved long unauthorized absences or desertion from the military unit. About one-half of the sentences in these cases included a reduction in pay. The most frequently committed of the offenses that are defined in general criminal laws and tried in civilian courts are those involving property damage and bodily harm resulting from negligence or drunkenness, committed most frequently while driving private automobiles.

Uniforms, Insignia, and Ranks

The service uniform is worn for most social and recreational activities and for general duty. Dress uniforms are available for formal occasions, and fatigue or special uniforms are worn for combat training, heavy work, or in dirty working conditions.

The army's service uniform consists of a light-gray, single-breasted coat and darker gray trousers, worn with a light-gray shirt, black tie, and black shoes. Most units wear garrison caps, but paratroops, armored troops, and motorized infantrymen wear berets. Officers' coat collars are trimmed with a braided piping—gold for general officers, silver for others.

Summer uniforms are less frequently worn but occur in a greater variety. One kind has color and styling similar to those of the winter uniforms, but it is made of lighter weight material. A second kind has a light-tan coat and trousers. A third, which is usually worn only on social occasions, has a white coat and dark-gray trousers.

Navy uniforms have traditional dark-blue double-breasted coats and matching trousers for winter and the usual summer whites. The air forces wear a medium-blue coat and trousers and a light-blue shirt, dark-blue tie, and black shoes.

Rank insignia is worn on shoulder boards, shoulder loops, the upper arm, or the lower sleeve. Army arms and services have different identifying colored backgrounds on collar tabs. General officers of the army and air force have red cloth collar tabs with gold leaf ornamentation. There are four general ranks that are identified by the number—from one to four—of gold-colored diamond-shaped pips worn on shoulder boards. Army generals have a gray shoulder board with gold piping bordered with red. Air force generals' boards are similar but have a blue background. Field rank officers (major, lieutenant colonel, and colonel) wear silver piping and silver pips. Lower ranking officers wear silver pips but no piping. The army and air force use the same number of ranks as there are in the United States services, and rank names translate to the same titles.

The navy has an officer rank of commodore, which is the lowest star rank and is between the captain and rear admiral. All other ranks, titles for rank, and rank insignia are the same as those in the United States Navy. The ensign rank insignia—on the lower sleeve or shoulder board—has one wide stripe. Half and full stripes are added with increasing rank until the captain has four full stripes. The commodore has an extra wide admiral stripe with one half stripe. The rear admiral has an extra wide stripe plus one full stripe. The vice admiral and admiral have two and three full stripes, respectively, in addition to the wide admiral stripe.

FOREIGN MILITARY RELATIONS

Although the Soviet Union maintains a numerically greater force in the German Democratic Republic, a larger number of countries maintain sizable forces in the Federal Republic than is the case anywhere else in the world. Of the military personnel and major combat units stationed in the country, less than one-half are those of the Federal Republic. Approximately the same is true of major weapons and equipment. Less than one-half of the main battle tanks and less than one-third of the combat aircraft in the country belong to the Federal Republic.

In 1973 the United States forces in the country numbered about 205,000 men. Most of them manned two armored and two mechanized divisions, two armored cavalry regiments, and one mechanized brigade plus air force contingents. United States equipment included 2,100 main battle tanks and 230 aircraft.

British forces in the country totaled about 55,000. They manned two armored divisions and had 600 main battle tanks and 130 tactical aircraft. Canada maintained a relatively token force of 3,000 men in one mechanized brigade. This force had about thirty tanks and fifty combat aircraft.

Belgium and the Netherlands share borders with the Federal Republic and, inasmuch as their national armies are committed to the same force, the side of the border on which their forces were maintained was, in large degree, irrelevant. All major combat units in Belgium's 65,000-man army and the Netherlands' 72,000-man army are integrated into the NATO force, but only some 25,000 men from their combined total have been maintained in the Federal Republic. Belgium's total force assigned to the NATO mission in the area included a mechanized division and an armored brigade and had 300 tanks and 140 aircraft. That of the Netherlands included two armored and four mechanized brigades and had 450 tanks and 140 aircraft.

France also maintained 58,000 troops in the Federal Republic, primarily in two mechanized divisions. Major weapons included 325 main battle tanks and 500 aircraft. The French situation was unique in that, although its forces were in the Federal Republic, they were not a part of the NATO force, nor were they cooperating with the forces of the Federal Republic.

The Federal Republic's contribution to the maintainance of the NATO forces is, after that of the United States, relatively high. A large portion of its 1973 military budget went to support NATO-committed forces. The French and British have total defense budgets approximately three-fourths as large as that of the Federal Republic, and a much lower percentage goes to the support of forces committed to NATO.

In April 1974 the Federal Republic and the United States reached an agreement by which the Federal Republic was to provide about US$2.2 billion toward the support of the United States forces in the country for the two-year period between July 1973 and July 1975. A similar agreement to apply after July 1975 would presumably take into account changes in the strength of American forces in the country and fundamental changes in the economic conditions of the two countries.

The limitations on the production of heavy weapons that were imposed upon the Germans after World War II initially made the Bundeswehr dependent upon its allies for some of its combat aircraft, fighting ships, tanks, and artillery. The desirability of using common equipment for complex electronic communications systems has also resulted in the use of much American equipment or equipment of American design, primarily because large amounts of it were available at the time that the NATO forces were first integrated.

THE MILITARY ESTABLISHMENT AND THE NATIONAL ECONOMY

The defense budget for 1972 amounted to approximately DM25.7 billion (for value of the Deutsche Mark—see Glossary), which was 23.7 percent of the federal budget and 2.9 percent of the country's gross national product (GNP). This amounted to a per capita expenditure for defense of DM397. Another DM5.8 billion was charged against the defense budget for financial assistance to West Berlin. If this amount is included, per capita cost of defense was DM493, and defense expenditures were 3.6 percent of the GNP.

Defense expenditures have risen steadily from about DM3.6 billion in 1954 at an average annual rate of about 9 percent. The time of greatest increase occurred just after the Berlin crisis of 1961. Increases were very small between 1963 and 1970 but were greater during the early 1970s as the Federal Republic increased its share of the support of NATO forces in north-central Europe.

The 9-percent average increase in defense expenditures was more than matched, however, by the increase in GNP, which grew by more than 10 percent annually. During a more recent five-year period, from 1968 through 1972, military expenditures increased at an annual rate of 10.7 percent, and the GNP at 13 percent. During this period inflation averaged 4.2 percent annually. This indicated that there was real, as opposed to paper, growth of the economy; that the increase in the outlay for defense was greater than needed merely to keep pace with the inflation costs; and also that the GNP has generally continued to increase at a more rapid rate than the outlay for the military establishment. The statistics are misleading to some extent, however, as the costs of sophisticated military equipment have risen much faster than those of most basic products in the economy.

The comparative statistics do indicate with probable accuracy that the 1972 armed forces, with their 475,000 men and impressive inventory of modern weapons and equipment, are a proportionally smaller burden upon the population than were the smaller armed forces of the 1950s. As of 1972, therefore, the armed forces had not been a continually increasing burden upon the country's economy.

Analyses of the situation since 1972 are incomplete, and all the effects of the changes that have occurred as the values of the world's currencies have been adjusted in relation to each other during the early 1970s may not have been felt. If the Federal Republic assumes a larger portion of the cost of the NATO forces stationed in the country, if the country's currency holds or increases its 1973 status in relation to other world currencies, and if the Federal Republic's economy has completed its period of rapid expansion, the relative costs of the armed forces upon the country may be appreciably increased during the mid-1970s.

During the four-year period 1968 to 1972, when the Federal Republic's defense expenditure amounted to 3.7 percent of its GNP, the average for NATO countries (excluding the United States) was 3.3 percent. During the same period the Warsaw Pact countries (excluding the Soviet Union) spent 3.4 percent of GNP for defense.

The effect of the loss of the country's manpower to the armed forces can also be subject to various analyses. The conscripts called into the service each year include a large number who would otherwise be unskilled laborers, a segment of the population that has for many years been in short supply. Some of these unskilled persons acquire a marketable skill during their service tours. Officials see the initial draft of unskilled laborers as a loss to the economy but, in apparent contradiction, they see the acquisition of a skill by some of these same persons as a gain, not only to the individual, but to the country.

The forces cooperate with many local agencies during all kinds of disaster situations—floods, fires, accidents, windstorms, and emergencies in the mountains and at sea. During 1972, for example, the army provided nearly 200,000 man-hours and used about 1,500 vehicles, plus helicopters, mobile kitchens, cranes, pontoon bridges, electric power generators, pumps, and other special equipment during various emergencies. Some 11,000 army men were involved. The air force and navy conducted search and rescue operations for missing or crashed aircraft and ships in distress and to assist persons in danger.

CHAPTER 18
PUBLIC ORDER

The Federal Republic inherited a tradition of maintaining good police forces and of having those forces perform an unusually large share of local government functions. The tradition was well established by the time the country was united in 1871, and it was continued through the days of the German Empire, the Weimar Republic, and—with many abuses of the system—during the Third Reich.

The federal Ministry of Interior is responsible for protecting the state and its institutions from threats during an uprising, riot, or in any circumstance considered likely to undermine the constitutional order. The ministry's Office for the Protection of the Constitution is concerned with countering subversion, espionage, and sabotage.

Routine police functions affecting the daily lives of the population are performed as far as possible by police units controlled by the *Land* (state; pl., *Länder*). *Land* ministries of interior administer local, communal, and municipal forces, the criminal police, and even the paramilitary Emergency Police. Consignment of maximum possible police authority at the *Land* level has been the established practice since 1871, at which time the states that united into the post-1871 German Empire were reluctant to lose any more than necessary of their former autonomy. Restructuring the country's institutions after World War II was accomplished while the memories of the Third Reich police state—when all police agencies were brought under the control of Adolf Hitler's central government—were still vivid. There was near unanimous agreement among the people, the Allied military occupation authorities, and the leaders of the newly established government that control of police forces should again be decentralized insofar as possible.

The border police, who have an essentially national mission—as do the railroad, river, shipping, and postal police—are controlled at the federal level. The federal government also maintains a criminal police office that deals with criminal activities affecting more than one *Land*, the entire country, or directed against the federal government; and it serves as the coordinating point for disseminating information among all appropriate national and international police agencies. The office maintains the best criminal laboratory in the country.

Authorities believe that an overwhelming majority of the people feel a sense of revulsion against violence as it is practiced by extremist political groups and that the possibility of a successful attempt to overthrow the

341

government or the country's institutions by violence is extremely slight. They are concerned, however, at the size and number of extremist groups and at the potential that they have for disruption and for undermining popular confidence in the capability of the government to maintain order.

The rights of the individual are carefully spelled out in the law, and the system has been designed to keep the courts free from influence and bias. The first objective of a criminal trial and the sentencing of a convicted person is to rehabilitate the offender and restore him to society. Three levels of courts below the federal level have jurisdiction in criminal cases—two courts of first instance and the *Länder* courts of appeal. The high federal court at Karlsruhe is the court of final appeal in ordinary criminal cases. It also has original jurisdiction in cases having to do with treason or high crimes relating strictly to federal institutions or officials.

HISTORICAL BACKGROUND

When the German states united in 1871, the states retained control of their local police forces. The newly organized central government had only a few special police units, none of which were involved in the daily affairs of the people.

Between 1918 and 1933, during the Weimar Republic, the same structure was retained, although the central government defrayed a portion of police force expenses. It was persuaded to do so inasmuch as the police were charged with enforcing federal laws. Even during this unstable period the police retained their highly efficient and incorruptible reputation, although they were described as militaristic in attitude and authoritarian in bearing.

During the Third Reich, Hitler placed all police under central control, reorganizing existing forces and creating special new police agencies that were better suited to carrying out some of the less attractive practices of his regime. The existing police were reorganized into the uniformed, or regular, police (Ordnungspolizei—ORPO) and the Security Police (Sicherheitspolizei—SIPO). Both were placed under the Third Reich's Ministry of Interior. The ORPO included the local city and town police (Schutzpolizei—SCHUPO); the rural area gendarmerie; the road-patrolling motorized gendarmerie; water, fire, air raid warning, and auxiliary police; and the administrative police offices that were responsible for enforcing welfare, health, building codes, and other such regulations and that attended to various records-keeping and clerical functions.

The SIPO was the more powerful organization; its members could demand cooperating action from any ORPO officer of the same rank. It incorporated the Criminal Investigation Police (Kriminalpolizei) and the uniformed Border Police (Grenzpolizei). The SIPO also included the newly created Secret State Police (Geheime Staatspolizei—Gestapo).

Two more organizations with primarily police or internal security

342

functions and with combined strengths of about 50,000 men were established by Hitler in 1933. These were the National Socialist German Workers' Party's (Nazi Party) Storm Troops (Sturmabteilung) and the Elite Guard (Schutzstaffel—SS). The Storm Troops, the SS, and the Gestapo were internationally notorious during the 1930s and in World War II. The Gestapo was protected from what were termed "outside influences," that is, from the supervision of the courts or other agencies that might have acted on behalf of people it apprehended. The Gestapo used inspection of mails and search without warrant and authorized its own taps on telephone and telegraph circuits. People apprehended by these or other means could be held in "protective custody." This could mean confinement for indefinite periods in concentration camps that were also built and operated by the Gestapo. Late in World War II the SS was expanded to some ten times its prewar strength, and its units —considered more reliable and more willing to fight to their deaths than regular army troops—fought as regular army units.

Tradition from the days of the empire and the Weimar Republic, the unsavory reputation of the centralized forces of the Third Reich, and the reluctance of the occupying powers after World War II to permit the restoration of anything reminiscent of a police state—including centrally controlled military, paramilitary, or police forces—led to the reforming of the Federal Republic's police at the *Land* level. Although several police organizations functioning at the federal level have been formed since 1951, they have been kept as small as possible and have been held strictly accountable to civilian authorities to ensure that they could not exercise irresponsible power.

The first action restoring local police in the Federal Republic was taken in September 1949. At that time the Western occupation forces' Allied High Commission instructed the *Länder* that the police were not to assume the character of a paramilitary organization or to be centralized in a way that would permit them to become a threat to the democratic government or to the occupying forces. The functions of the new police were to maintain public order and safety, to keep local administrative records, to prevent crime, and to bring offenders to justice. Personnel strength and arms were not to exceed whatever would be authorized by local elected governments, and local authorizations were to be subject to reductions by the Allied High Commission. No merger of the police forces of more than one *Land* was to be permitted.

Some of the early restrictions were lifted within two years, when the border and emergency police forces were authorized. Both of those organizations were created to deal with situations that were national rather than local in scope or character and whose operations could not reasonably be restricted to the limited area of one *Land*. In 1974 a large majority of police personnel were in local or *Land* forces, but the border police and several criminal investigation, special security, and other special police agencies have been organized on a national basis. Emergency police units were organized by *Länder*, but they were equipped and prepared to serve across *Land* borders when requested.

INTERNAL SECURITY

Local Police

Local police forces are organized on a *Land* basis, and they have retained the mission and tasks given them in 1949. They include those that perform in urban and rural areas and may be variously referred to as municipal, communal, or state police. Where the cities have their own municipal forces, they may be separately organized, but they are nevertheless an integral part of the *Land* forces and are subject to the regulations of the *Land* Ministry of Interior.

Police in the various *Länder* have different colored uniforms, but they are sufficiently similar in styling that all are readily identifiable, and even the fact that there are different colors frequently goes unnoticed. For normal duty all have open-neck jackets, with matching shirts, ties, and trousers. Rainwear, heavy overcoats, and boots are worn according to weather conditions. Green is the color worn by a majority of the forces; West Berlin and Lower Saxony have worn blue-gray; Hamburg, navy blue; and Bremen, black. Most wear caps with stiff peaks; Bavaria's soft peaked caps have been the only exception. All forces carry pistols and billy clubs.

Each *Land* has a police school and a basic course that lasts for about twelve months. Upon completion of this course, young policemen go to an Emergency Police unit for perhaps two years of additional schooling and on-the-job and weapons training. They then take up duties in a city or other local force.

The *Länder* also have varying numbers of specialized police schools. In the mid-1960s, for example, North Rhine-Westphalia divided its specialist training programs among three schools, in addition to the twelve-month basic training school. One was a school for driving, vehicle maintenance, police communications, small arms, first aid, and photography. Another school was expressly for dog handlers. A third school provided a twenty-two-week promotion course offering public law, the penal code, traffic regulations, criminology, overall police responsibilities, and the psychology, politics, and ethics applicable to police duties. Successful graduates were promoted to the rank of police corporal; they could advance thereafter without additional examinations.

Candidates for higher police officer positions from all *Länder* attend the police college at Hiltrup, North Rhine-Westphalia. The college has separate courses for general police officers and for detectives of the criminal police. Both offer police tactics, police law, the penal code, police history and administration, psychology, criminology, and public servant,

344

civil, and traffic law. The detectives get an additional course in criminalistics, and their courses in psychology and criminology delve more deeply into those subjects.

The college admits only those candidates who appear to have well-rounded qualifications for a successful police career. It also has a course for police officers having fifteen years or more experience; they receive a course designed to fit them for top-level assignments. The college's research department specializes in criminology and in ways to improve the effectiveness of police forces.

Policemen can join labor or trade unions but cannot legally go on strike. Of the three that most police personnel affiliate with, one union is exclusively for policemen; one is for all public servants; and the third is for workers in transportation and traffic services.

Criminal Police

All *Länder* have Criminal Police (Kriminalpolizei) attached to their local police forces. Personnel in these units do not work in uniform and, depending upon the risk entailed in the particular work they may be engaged in, they may or may not carry weapons. The Criminal Police do most of the detective, crime laboratory, and crime prevention work—all that can be done without calling on federal agencies. They have a tradition for thorough, painstaking, and generally excellent performance. Although they required complete reorganization after World War II, as a group the postwar units appear to have regained the competence expected of them, and they are generally respected by the public.

Emergency Police

The Emergency Police (also called Standby Police or Alert Police) has a strength of just under 20,000 men. Although it is nearly always referred to as a force, it is organized on a *Land* basis and would be more accurately described as nearly a dozen separate forces. There are, however, links to the central government in that the federal Ministry of Interior furnishes its arms, and there is an inspector general of the Emergency Police within that federal ministry. His inspections of the various forces help to ensure uniform standards and high levels of capability among them.

The *Länder* finance the force and provide the clothing, housing, salaries, all support other than weapons, and some specialized transportation and communications equipment. Emergency Police personnel live in barracks and, in contrast to the communal or municipal police, their mission is regional rather than local.

The mission of the force is to assist the local police, to control local disturbances, and to participate in relief and rescue work in the event of a disaster. If requested by neighboring authorities, its units may cross *Land* lines to assist in an emergency situation—a natural disaster or a riot—greater than the forces of a single *Land* could manage. In a serious emergency situation, the federal Ministry of Interior could assume control of the Emergency Police, and its commands would override those of the *Länder*. The Emergency Police have special equipment, above and beyond that of local police forces, enabling them to get to and deal with a wide variety of situations. They are less heavily armed, however, than the border police.

In addition to their operating duties, the Emergency Police provide practical police training for the personnel in local police organizations. A recruit to the municipal force in Munich, for example, spends a period of perhaps one year in basic training, after which he spends about two years with a contingent of the Bavarian Emergency Police. During those two years he receives more classroom instruction and weapons familiarization and, more important, a great deal of on-the-job practical police experience.

Most of the force's personnel serve voluntarily, although it is not clear what proportion of volunteers would select the duty in preference to other occupations if it were not an alternative to obligatory service in one of the regular armed services. A voluntary tour of duty in the Emergency Police is three years, however, as opposed to a mandatory tour of as little as fifteen months in the Bundeswehr (Federal Armed Forces).

Federal Border Police

The Federal Border Police (Bundesgrenzschutz) organization was established in 1951. It was formed earlier than the Emergency Police and was the first national police force to be permitted by the post-World War II occupation authorities. A force of 30,000 men had been authorized in 1950 to ensure the security of the eastern border and frontier region.

At the time that the Federal Border Police were authorized, the Western Allies and the Soviet Union had returned much of the administration of their respective post-World War II occupation zones to the German people. The emerging states, however, remained as strictly separate as the two major zonal areas had been before. Realization that normal transit across the federal borders would be unlikely for many years made many people decide to relocate if they were dissatisfied. Most of the movement was from east to west.

It was considered important to have a competent force to deal with possible border incidents, and it was appreciated that such incidents could take on undue seriousness if North Atlantic Treaty Organization (NATO) forces became involved. It was decided, therefore, that a police force, rather than a military one, was needed, even though that police force might appear to resemble an army more closely. It became apparent to the government that the Federal Border Police would be the first involved in the event of a surprise military attack from the east. Legislation in 1965 amended the law creating the Federal Border Police to ensure any of them that might be taken prisoner protection under The

Hague Rules of Land Warfare and the Geneva conventions. In the event of armed conflicts, the border police would become a part of the Federal Republic's Bundeswehr.

The Federal Border Police are responsible to the federal Ministry of Interior. Unlike local police of the *Länder* and to a greater degree than the Emergency Police, border policemen are organized into a military kind of organization; they are also quartered in military barracks. Headquarters of the four commands are located in the four *Länder* sharing a border with the German Democratic Republic. The Southern Command's headquarters is at Munich; the Mid-German is at Kassel; the Northern is at Hannover; and the Coastal is at Kiel.

Unit equipment and unit training are on the order of a well-armed and highly mobile light infantry outfit. Special units have helicopters; others have patrol ships to police the northern sea frontier. The Federal Border Police coast guard units were abolished when the federal navy was formed in 1956 but were recreated in 1964.

Regular units are equipped with automatic rifles and machine guns, tear gas, hand grenades and grenade throwers, antitank weapons, and armored personnel carriers. All personnel have side arms.

Personnel strength of the Federal Border Police in 1972 was about 18,000, about 1,000 of whom were in the organization's Individual Service. The main units of the force are responsible for security in a nineteen-mile (thirty-kilometer) strip along the eastern border of the country and are charged with prevention of illegal entry into or exit from the Federal Republic. They are not subject to routine duties that would interfere with their being available to deal with organized and mass attempts to cross the border or with riots and uprisings that could be fomented as a part of such attempts. This being the case, they are useful in other riot or mass disorder situations and may be called upon to operate outside the border strip. In March 1974, for example, the mayor of Frankfurt appealed for assistance when the city was threatened with a riot. A demonstration by 4,000 people had been approved by the city, but the legitimate demonstrators were joined by groups described as anarchists, Trotskyites, a motorcycle gang, and a group known locally as the Frankfurt Heavy Mob. In this situation the mayor was provided a contingent of Federal Border Police.

Field units are organized on the military model into regiments, battalions, and companies. Policemen in the field units have rank titles similar to those in the Bundeswehr. They wear green uniforms. Most units are positioned along the border with the Democratic Republic; there are a few adjacent to Czechoslovakia and Austria; and there are three in the vicinity of Bonn. Those near Bonn provide guards for certain federal institutions, state occasions, high government officials, and foreign guests. Other personnel are in the management headquarters at Koblenz, the force's school at Lübeck, and the four field headquarters.

347

Travelers usually encounter customs officials or the Federal Border Police's Individual Service personnel and ordinarily have no dealings with regular units of the Federal Border Police. The Individual Service mans border posts at the seventy-nine busiest crossing points that are located all around the country's perimeter, where they are responsible for customs and passport control. Individual Service personnel wear dark-blue uniforms.

Federal Criminal Office

The federal government maintains a central criminal agency in Wiesbaden, on the Rhine River west of Frankfurt. The agency collects and evaluates information and particulars for combating major crimes. It deals only with criminal activities that are national or international in scope unless *Land* authorities request assistance. The office maintains a federal forensic laboratory and coordinates the exchange of criminal information between the various *Land* police forces. To facilitate the latter task, the office maintains national criminal statistics and records, including a register of recidivists, with fingerprint and other information on major criminals. It also acts as the Federal Republic's reporting and contact center for the International Criminal Police Organization (INTERPOL), the agency that provides and coordinates useful information in its field of interest for criminal police agencies in approximately ninety countries.

Other Law Enforcement Agencies

German police have traditionally carried out functions and administrative duties that are not handled by police forces elsewhere. In addition to the enforcement of laws and the maintenance of public order, they have supervised safety and health standards and carried out governmental legislation or executive edicts that require regulation or monitoring action at the local level. In the early 1970s a number of such groups or agencies existed. Their personnel were usually seen in uniform, sometimes carrying side arms.

Among the group of miscellaneous police organizations are railroad, river, shipping, air traffic, customs, forestry, and post office police, factory guards, and firefighters. Railroad Police work exclusively with the railroad lines, stations, and other railroad property, to protect the installations and cargo and passenger traffic. River Police maintain the navigable inland waterways, both canals and rivers, in a condition considered safe for shipping. Shipping Police are responsible for security of waterway traffic. Tradition is so ingrained that air safety and air traffic controllers are frequently termed Air Police; customs personnel, Customs Police; and foresters and game wardens, Forest Police. Forest Police are organized under the *Land* ministries of food, agriculture, and forestry. Customs Police are under the federal Ministry of Finance. Railroad Police are under the federal Ministry of Transport, Posts, and

348

Telecommunications. Fire Police include both volunteers and professionals. Personnel in all of these agencies have the authority to enforce the regulations applicable in their fields.

CIVIL DEFENSE

Civil defense functions are defined in federal statutes, and the countrywide organization is directed by the federal Ministry of Interior's Federal Office for the Protection of the Civil Population and the Federal Association for Self-Defense. The 1949 Basic Law gives the federal government exclusive authority to legislate in civil defense matters, but it was 1957 before the first such law was enacted. A package of seven more laws was passed in 1965. Four of the 1965 safeguarding acts are still in force—those that relate to food, water, transport, and the economy —but the Self-Protection Act has been repealed, and the Shelter Construction Act and the Civilian Protection Corps Act have been suspended. The costs of implementing the last three acts were considered exorbitant by the parliament.

The original 1957 legislation defined four civil defense functions: maintenance of the functioning of the state; protection of the civilian population; maintenance of essential emergency supplies, principally food; and support of the armed forces. Among the measures for protecting the civilian population are an alarm and warning system, sanitation measures, construction of shelters, instructions for self-defense, and provisions for protection of cultural treasures. Ancillary equipment and services are maintained for protection against disasters. Plans have also been drawn up for emergency action in the veterinary, communications, civil welfare, refugee, and rescue areas and for protection against the results of radiological, biological, and chemical contamination.

Civil defense officials will be able to call upon numerous existing organizations and groups, not established primarily for civil defense work, in the event of a serious emergency. Both rural volunteer and urban professional fire brigades would be committed to civil defense work, along with other such emergency services as the German Red Cross and various welfare organizations.

Funding for civil defense programs has always had low priority. As a result, the staffs that have been set up are mostly on a part-time and volunteer basis, and almost all work has been of a planning nature. Little time or money has been available for exercises, for training, or for stockpiling emergency supplies. Authorities believe, however, that most of the people are still vividly aware of the country's bitter wartime experiences and that their cooperation in an emergency would be at a level that would result in effective civil defense efforts in spite of the lack of a continuing training and exercise program.

In 1968 what is frequently called the Emergency Constitution was drafted. It provides for the prerequisite measures that would have to be taken in a national emergency, allowing for a quicker reaction and orientation of early defensive efforts and adding to the measures that can be taken in a disaster situation. It also ensures a continuity of parliamentary control during an emergency.

CRIMINAL JUSTICE

It is fundamental to the Federal Republic's law that no act is punishable unless its criminality was laid down in the law before the act was committed and that the administration of justice is accomplished by judges whose independence is as nearly guaranteed as the country's policymakers have known how to assure it. Minor criminal cases come before local courts *(Amtsgerichte)*. More serious cases and first appeals from lower courts are heard by regional courts *(Landgerichte)*. Appeal courts *(Oberlandesgerichte)* are the final recourse for cases that originate in the local courts, and they are the courts of second instance for cases that originate in the regional courts. The Federal Court of Justice at Karlsruhe is the court of last resort in regular criminal, as well as civil, cases (see ch. 11).

The criminal code is basically that which existed in the late nineteenth and early twentieth centuries, important parts of which were suspended during the Hitler years. Most of the modifications to the code since World War II have been minor. A proposal to merge local and regional courts to form a single court of first instance was being studied during the mid-1970s.

Judges are appointed for life or until voluntary retirement and, according to the law, cannot be transferred against their will. They are subject only to the law and to their own consciences. Preparation for their office, however, is extensive, and it is rare that an individual can become a judge before he is twenty-eight years of age. He must have a university degree and complete about 3½ years of a law curriculum, after which he takes the First Juristic Government Examination, sometimes called the junior barrister examination. He then must practice law for three years—in the courts, in public prosecutors' offices, or in private legal practice. Then he is eligible to take the Second Juristic Government Examination. Passing it successfully permits a lawyer to be appointed to a position as a judge, although for several years he probably serves as an assistant to a more senior judge.

The individual who runs afoul of the law is well protected by provisions of the law. As a suspect he may refuse to talk to police and, if he does talk, he may retract what he has said to them when tried in court. The law prevents police from interfering with an individual's free will through rough treatment, fatigue, injury, drugs, torture, deceit, or hypnosis. Only the force required to capture or restrain him is authorized. He may contest in court any measure that is seen to encroach upon his rights. Limitations on his freedom may also be only as defined in the law. He may not be held in custody beyond the end of the day following his arrest without a court decision. Some person, named by the suspect, must be notified if he is to be held beyond that time. If he is found guilty, he may be punished only once for a single crime.

Police records of a case are turned over to the prosecutor in all criminal trials, and evidence accumulated by the police is admissible in court without being presented at that time by those who collected it. As a result, police are only rarely required to testify in court.

There are occasional highly critical articles in local periodicals when the administration of justice breaks down or when there are enough instances in which the system does not work according to the loftier principles set down in the law. Much of the problem is caused by delays in criminal investigation, preparation of the case by the prosecutors, and getting a prepared case to trial.

Some 50,000 people are arrested annually for misdemeanors or more serious crimes for which a prison sentence is a possibility. About one-third of those arrested and held in custody are either acquitted or receive court sentences of less than the time they have already been detained. The numbers who receive sentences exactly the same as the period they have already been remanded is probably much higher than can be attributed to coincidence. The average time between arrest and trial for those remanded is more than two months and, although most do not spend that long in pretrial custody, the average figure results from the considerable number who are imprisoned for one year and the few who may be imprisoned for two years or more, awaiting trial.

Rehabilitation is the single stated objective of a prison sentence, but the spirit of the law has not permeated the entire prison system. A number of prison officials continue to view the rehabilitation of their inmates as less of a mandate than separating them from society or punishing them for their infractions of the rules of society. There is encouragement for this view, in appearance at least, because prisons get the minimum budget allocation, and frequently facilities desirable in rehabilitation programs are not available. Prisons and prison conditions get little attention and little publicity. Except for relatives and acquaintances of inmates, the public tends to forget the prison population.

A juvenile under fourteen years of age is not responsible under the law. Between the ages of fourteen and eighteen, a juvenile's responsibility must always be investigated. If the investigation indicates that the individual is mentally and morally mature enough to understand what he was doing and the wrongfulness of his act at the time he committed it, he may be punished as prescribed in the Juvenile Courts Act. The act sets down permissible disciplinary and educational measures and the limits on those of a disciplinary nature. Offenders over eighteen years of age are treated as adults.

Prosecutors, counsel, and judges concerned with criminal proceedings against juveniles are chosen from those who have the necessary educational qualifications and who have experience with youths. Juvenile trials are not open to the public. Whenever possible, educational, rather than disciplinary, sentences are handed down by juvenile courts.

Punishments are resorted to when it is determined that educational measures could not succeed or after they have failed. These may consist of confinement in a juvenile prison. Sentences may designate a specific or an indefinite term of confinement. Indefinite term sentences permit prison authorities to hold the individual until they consider that he has responded favorably to their rehabilitation efforts or to release him early when they consider it would best serve the individual and the community. The minimum sentence in juvenile prison is three months; the maximum is ten years.

Lesser disciplinary sentences can restrict juvenile offenders to their homes, schools, and places of work. Extra duties or warnings suffice in other situations. Educational measures include supervised probationary study or reformatory schooling.

SUBVERSIVE POTENTIALS

Authorities are aware, but not overly fearful, of the subversive potential of radical political groups, and they do not appear to be afraid that incidents of group lawlessness and rioting involve enough of the people to constitute an immediate danger to the country. They are also concerned that the longer term effects of the rapidly expanding population, vastly changing economic conditions, and evolving moral and social standards may be so little understood that they could constitute a threat to stability, albeit difficult to define and of unknown magnitude.

The federal Ministry of Interior's Office for the Protection of the Constitution is charged with monitoring actual and potential subversive activities against the country. The office records memberships and activities of all organizations advocating basic changes in the economic system or governmental institutions, although only a few such organizations employ, or advocate the use of, violence or terrorist tactics. The 1973 report listed over 100 organizations the office considered right-wing extremist, over 300 it considered left-wing extremist, and about 225 foreign extremist groups. It reiterated the opinion that neither right-wing nor left-wing extremist efforts from within the country were serious threats. It stated that a somewhat more serious threat did exist from foreign extremist organizations having operating branches in the Federal Republic. The 225 such organizations in 1973 had about 1,000 regional branches scattered throughout the country, with memberships totaling slightly over 50,000.

The local right-wing National Democratic Party of Germany, which has succeeded the outlawed Socialist Reich Party, had about 12,000 members in 1973. Another 106 right-wing organizations had memberships totaling about 10,000. Of the members about 2,000 were in youth groups.

The German Communist Party had approximately 39,000 members in

1973. Another 316 left-wing extremist organizations had approximately 48,000 members. The German Communist Party adheres to the Soviet model. The most rapidly growing extremist groups are those of the so-called new left that are inspired by Mao Tse-tung and Leon Trotsky. These groups were reported to have memberships totaling about 18,500 in 1973.

Left-wing youth organizations also had memberships of about 18,500. Of these, approximately 12,000 were Socialist German Youth Workers, supported by the German Communist Party. The remainder were divided almost equally between the sports-oriented Spartakus Marxist Student Union and the Socialist University League. With the exceptions of the youth organizations and the new left groups, the extremist organizations—both left-wing and right-wing—had decreasing membership rolls during the early 1970s.

The Office for the Protection of the Constitution also maintains records of individual extremists employed in certain selected occupations. Its report lists about 1,350 right-wing and 1,425 left-wing extremists who were employed in public service and about 135 right-wing and 325 left-wing extremists who were employed in teaching positions. It also indicated that left-wing activists were prominent in university student governments. They occupied nearly one-half of the seats in student parliaments and about two-thirds of the seats on other student committees.

The office's report indicated that terrorist acts and violent incidents were fomented or participated in by several of the foreign underground organizations, including Palestinian and Croatian guerrilla groups. Of thirty-one people convicted of espionage, spying, or treason in 1973, twenty-seven were in the employ of agencies of the Democratic Republic.

YOUTH PROGRAMS

Alert to the restlessness and impatience of youth and the tendencies to resist the less satisfactory facets of society and its institutions and to look responsively toward any promised reform measures, authorities expend much effort on channeling youthful energy into constructive endeavors and studying the directions in which young people move when left to their own initiatives. There are approximately sixty youth organizations. Most of the groups are associated with the German Federal Youth Ring (Deutscher Bundesjugendring) and the Ring of Political Youth (Ring Politischer Jugend). Individual groups in the two major ring organizations vary in size from a few hundred to more than 600,000 and have a total membership of more than 4 million. Religious youth organizations have about 2.2 million members in two organizations, the League of the German Catholic Youth and the Working Party of the Protestant Youth of Germany.

With the exception of those groups fostered by extremist political parties, authorities encourage youth organizations, maintaining that they "assist in the development of personality" and "develop a consciousness of youth responsibilities in maintaining a free and democratic social order." Some of the groups are active in welfare, social work, vocational training, special juvenile assistance projects, student hostels, and other student affairs. Several are affiliated with their own or associated international organizations.

National incentives have been developed to encourage young people to participate in worthwhile activities or to become involved in creative efforts. Federal Youth Games—in which all children of school age are encouraged to participate—attract 4 to 5 million competitors each year. The German Youth Film Prize encourages the making of films suitable for church and youth groups. The German Youth Photograph Prize, the German Youth Book Prize, and the Young People Make Music program attract groups of more specialized participants and competitors.

Sporting events and participation in group and individual sports are popular. German sociologists see recreational time increasing and gaining in significance as the workweek shortens. Football (soccer) is the most popular sport, followed by gymnastics. The German Gymnastics Festival which, from years of tradition, is held each five years is—as are the Olympic games—an occasion when business and politics retreat from the front pages of the newspapers. Winter sports (skiing in particular), tennis, swimming, bicycling, handball, hiking, and auto racing are also popular.

The various organizations within the German Sports Federation claim 10 million members, about 17 percent of the population. They are distributed among nearly 40,000 gymnastics and sports clubs. The football federation is the largest, having some 2.8 million members. The gymnastics federation, having 2.2 million members, is the only other club having a membership greater than 1 million.

All schools have compulsory sports programs. Primary schools devote about two hours a week to physical education, and secondary schools about three hours a week. A widely coveted sports badge is awarded students who have a good average performance in five or more different sports.

BIBLIOGRAPHY

Section I. Social

Adams, Marion (ed.). *The German Tradition: Aspects of Art and Culture in German-Speaking Countries.* Sydney: John Wiley and Sons, 1971.

Adenauer, Konrad. "Germany and Europe," *Foreign Affairs,* XXXI, April 1953, 361-366.

————. "Germany, the New Partner," *Foreign Affairs,* XXXIII, January 1955, 177-183.

Altenstetter, Christa. "Intergovernmental Profiles in the Federal Systems of Austria and West Germany." (Unpublished paper prepared for the Center for the Study of Federalism and the Urban Studies Center.) Philadelphia: Temple University, 1973.

American Jewish Yearbook. (Ed., Morris Rine.) New York: American Jewish Committee, 1973.

Arendt, Hannah. *The Origins of Totalitarianism.* New York: Harcourt, Brace, 1951.

"Are the Germans Coming?", *Newsweek,* January 14, 1974, 58.

Arntz, Helmut. *Germany in a Nutshell.* Wiesbaden: Press and Information Office, Federal Republic of Germany, 1963.

Asimov, Isaac. *Asimov's Biographical Encyclopedia of Science and Technology.* Garden City, New York: Doubleday, 1964.

Baier, C. *Deutschland und die Deutschen* (Germany and the Germans). London: Methuen, 1952.

Bainton, Roland. *Here I Stand: A Life of Martin Luther.* Nashville: Abingdon Press, 1950.

Balfour, Michael. *West Germany.* New York: Praeger, 1968.

Barraclough, G. *The Origins of Modern Germany.* Oxford: Basil Blackwell, 1947.

Becker-Carsten, Wolfgang. "Current Chronicle: Berlin," *Musical Quarterly,* LVII, No. 2, April 1971, 314-317.

Beck, Lewis W. *Early German Philosophy: Kant and His Predecessors.* Cambridge: Belknap Press of Harvard University Press, 1969.

Bently, J. E. *Visual Outline of Philosophy.* (Student Outline Series.) Philadelphia: David McKay, 1939.

Binder, David. "Births Are Down in West Germany," *New York Times,* January 28, 1973, 4.

Binkley, Robert C. *Realism and Nationalism, 1852–1871.* New York: Harper, 1935.

Bithell, Jethro. *Germany: A Companion to German Studies.* Alva, Scotland: Robert Cunningham and Sons, 1959.

——. *Modern German Literature, 1880–1950.* London: Methuen, 1963.

Bochenski, Innocent M. *Contemporary European Philosophy.* (Trans., D. Nicholl and K. Aschenbrenner.) Berkeley: University of California Press, 1957.

Boesch, Bruno. *German Literature: A Critical Survey.* (Trans., Ronald Taylon.) London: Methuen, 1971.

Brack, Hans. *German Radio and Television: Organization and Economic Basis.* Geneva: European Broadcasting Union, 1968.

Brandes, O. Jean. "Effect of War on the German Family," *Social Forces,* XXIX, December 1950, 164-173.

Brazill, William. *The Young Hegelians.* New Haven: Yale University Press, 1970.

Bruck, Werner Friedrich. *Social and Economic History of Germany from William II to Hitler, 1888–1938.* Cardiff: Oxford University Press, 1938.

Brunn, Geoffrey. *Europe and the French Imperium, 1799–1814.* New York: Harper, 1938.

Bucher, Felix. "Twenty Years of German Post War Films," *Camera* [Lucerne, Switzerland], XLV, November 1966, 56.

Bullock, Alan. *Hitler: A Study in Tyranny.* New York: Harper, 1953.

Caponigri, A. Robert. *A History of Western Philosophy: Philosophy from the Age of Positivism to the Age of Analysis,* V. Notre Dame: Notre Dame Press, 1971.

——. *A History of Western Philosophy: Philosophy from the Renaissance to the Romantic Age,* III. Notre Dame: Notre Dame Press, 1963.

——. *A History of Western Philosophy: Philosophy from the Romantic Age to the Age of Positivism,* IV. Notre Dame: Notre Dame Press, 1971.

Carr, Jonathan. "Survival of a Strong Point," *Financial Times* [London], February 18, 1974, 27.

Carsten, Francis L. *The Origins of Prussia.* London: Oxford University Press, 1954.

Cohn, Arthur. *Twentieth-Century Music in Western Europe.* Philadelphia: J. B. Lippincott, 1965.

Collinson, William E. *The German Language Today.* London: Hutchinson's University Library, 1953.

Coon, Carlton S. *The Races of Europe.* New York: Macmillan, 1939.

Craig, Gordon A. *From Adenauer to Bismarck: Aspects of German Statecraft.* Baltimore: Johns Hopkins University Press, 1958.

Crossland, Norman. "Reform of Education," *Financial Times* [London], October 8, 1973, 22.

Dahrendorf, Ralf. *Society and Democracy in Germany.* New York: Doubleday, 1967.

Dampier, William. *A History of Science.* New York: Macmillan, 1949.

Davidson, Eugene. *The Death and Life of Germany: An Account of the American Occupation.* New York: Knopf, 1959.

Dehio, Ludwig. *Germany and World Politics in the Twentieth Century.* (Trans., Dieter Pevsner.) New York: Knopf, 1959.

Demographic Yearbook, 1971. New York: United Nations, Department of Economics and Social Affairs, Statistical Office, 1972.

Deutsch, Karl W., and Edinger, Lewis J. *Germany Rejoins the Powers: Mass Opinion, Interest Groups, and Elites in Contemporary German Foreign Policy.* Stanford: Stanford University Press, 1959.

Dickinson, Robert E. *Germany: A General and Regional Geography.* London: Methuen, 1953.

Diesel, Eugen. *Germany and the Germans.* (Trans., W.D. Robson-Scott.) New York: Macmillan, 1931.

Documentation Center of the West German Rectors' Conference. *Westdeutsche Rektorenkonferenz: Documentation Concerning University Reform.* Bad Godesberg: July 1969.

―――. *Westdeutsche Rektorenkonferenz: Documentation Concerning University Reform II, 1969–1970.* Bad Godesberg: June 1970.

Dopsch, Alfons. *The Economic and Social Foundations of European Civilization.* New York: Harcourt, Brace, 1937.

Dorn, Walter L. *Competition for Empire, 1740–1763.* New York: Harper, 1940.

Ebenstein, William. *The Nazi State.* New York: Farrar and Rinehart, 1943.

Edinger, Lewis J. *Politics in Germany: Attitudes and Processes.* (Little, Brown Series in Comparative Politics.) Boston: Little, Brown, 1968.

Editor and Publisher International Year Book. New York: Editor and Publisher, 1974.

Elkins, T. H. *Germany: An Introductory Geography.* New York: Praeger, 1968.

Elon, Amos. *Journey Through a Haunted Land.* New York: Holt, Rinehart, and Winston, 1967.

Emery, Marc (ed.). "Munich '72: Jeux Olympiques," *Architecture d'Aujourd' hui* [Boulogne], No. 162, June–July 1972, 87–112.

Engel-Janosi, Friedrich. *The Growth of German Historicism.* Baltimore: Johns Hopkins University Press, 1944.

"Enter the Heavy Mob," *Economist* [London], CCL, No. 6810, March 2, 1974, 34.

Erler, Fritz. *Democracy in Germany.* (Jodidi Lectures at Harvard University.) Cambridge: Harvard University Press, 1965.

Ernst, Richard. *History of German Civilization: A General Survey.* (2d ed.) New York: Macmillan, 1911.

Esslin, Martin (ed.). *The Genius of the German Theater.* New York: Mentor, 1968.

The Europa Year Book, 1972, I. London: Europa Publications, 1972.

Federal Republic of Germany. *Facts About Germany*. Bonn: Press and Information Office, 1972.

————. *Mass Media in the Federal Republic of Germany*. Bonn:Inter Nationes, 1971.

————. *Recommendations by the Science Council for the Structure and Expansion of Higher Education after 1970*. (Trans., K.D. Gottsdalk.) Bonn: Bundesdruckerei, June 1970.

Federal Republic of Germany. Report by the Federal Chancellor. *The State of the Nation, 1971*. Kassel: Druck-und Verlagshaus Schneider und Weber, November 1971.

Feurstein, Gunther. *New Directions in German Architecture*. (Trans., Thomas E. Burton.) New York: George Braziller, 1968.

Fijalkowski, Jürgen. "Carl Schmitt." Pages 58–60 in David Sills (ed.), *International Encyclopedia of the Social Sciences*, XIV. Riverside, New Jersey: Macmillan and Free Press, 1968.

————. "The Structure of German Society after the Second World War." Pages 84–110 in J.P. Payne (ed.), *Germany Today*. London: Methuen, 1971.

Fodor, Eugene (ed.). *Fodor's Germany, 1972*. New York: David McKay, 1972.

Friedrich, Carl J. *The Age of the Baroque, 1610–1660*. New York: Harper, 1952.

Friedrich, Otto. *Before the Deluge: A Portrait of Berlin in the 1920s*. New York: Harper and Row, 1972.

Fuller, B.A.G. *A History of Modern Philosophy*. (3d ed., rev., Sterling M. McMurrin.) New York: Holt, Rinehart, and Winston, 1962.

"German Science Looks for International Role," *Business Week*, November 16, 1968, 108–112.

"German Sponsors Fight for TV Time," *Business Week*, January 21, 1967, 92–96.

"Germany." Pages 277–360 in *Encyclopaedia Britannica*, X. Chicago: William Benton, 1969.

Gilbert, Creighton. *History of Renaissance Art: Painting, Sculpture, Architecture Throughout Europe*. New York: Harry Abrams, 1972.

Goshko, John M. "Europe's New Immigrants," *Washington Post*, July 28, 1974, C-1.

Great Britain. Admiralty. Naval Intelligence Division. *Germany: Physical Geography*. (Geographical Handbook Series, No. 1.) London: 1944.

Grosser, Alfred. *Germany in Our Time: A Political History of the Postwar Years*. (Trans., Paul Stephenson.) New York: Praeger, 1970.

Guilland, Antoine. *Modern Germany and Her Historians*. New York: McBride Nast, 1915.

Hamilton, Clarence. *Outlines of Music History*. Boston: Oliver Ditson, 1924.

Hammer, John C. "Review of Drama 'Nach Brecht: Eine Einführung in dramatische Probleme der Gegenwart' by Rainer Taeni," *Modern Drama*, XIII, No. 1, May 1970, 105.

Hartmann, Johannes. *Das Geschichtsbuch: von den Anfangen bis zur Gegenwart* (Book of History: From the Beginning to the Present). Frankfurt: Fischer Bücherei, 1955.

Hayes, Carlton J. H. *A Generation of Materialism, 1871–1900*. New York: Harper, 1941

Heiden, Konrad. *A History of National Socialism*. New York: Knopf, 1935.

Heine-Geldern, Robert. "One-Hundred Years of Ethnological Theory in German-Speaking Countries: Some Milestones," *Current Anthropology*, V, No. 5, December 1964, 407–418.

Henderson, Ernest F. *A History of Germany in the Middle Ages*. New York: Haskell House, 1968.

———. *A Short History of Germany*, I: 9 A.D.–1048 A.D., New York: Macmillan, 1944.

Hertz, Frederick. *The Development of the German Public Mind: The Middle Ages, the Reformation*. London: Allen and Unwin, 1957.

Hiscocks, Richard. *The Adenauer Era*. Philadelphia: J.B. Lippincott, 1966.

Hofer, Walther. *Der Nationalsozialismus: Dokumente, 1933–1945* (National Socialism: Documents, 1933–1945). Frankfurt: Fischer Bücherei, 1957.

Hoffman, G.N. *A Geography of Europe*. New York: Roland, 1953.

Hoffmann, Joseph. "Situation et Problèmes du Catholicisme Allemand Aujourd'hui," *Revue d'Allemagne* [Paris], II, No. 2, April-June 1970, 194–230.

Hurd, M. *An Outline History of European Music*. London: Unwin, 1968.

Huyghe, Rene (ed.). "Art and Mankind." *In Larousse Encyclopedia of Modern Art from 1800 to the Present Day*. New York: Prometheus Press, 1965.

Iggers, Georg G. *German Conception of History: The National Tradition of Historical Thought from Herder to the Present*. Middletown, Connecticut: Wesleyan University Press, 1968.

"In Democratic Europe the Honors and Titles Still Mean A Lot," *Washington Post*, October 14, 1973, K-7.

Jaspers, Karl. *The Future of Germany*. (Ed. and trans., E.B. Ashton.) Chicago: University of Chicago Press, 1967.

Jennings, Gary. "Bavaria: Mod, Medieval, and Bewitching," *National Geographic*, CXLV, No. 3, March 1974, 409–430.

Kaufman, Friedrich. *German Dramatists of the Nineteenth Century*. Freeport, New York: Books for Libraries Press, 1970.

Keyser, Erich. *Bevölkerungsgeschichte Deutschlands* (Demographic History of Germany). Leipzig: n.pub., 1949.

Kleining, Gerhard von. "Struktur-und Prestigemobilität in der Bundes-republik Deutschland," *Kölner zeitschrift für Soziologie und Sozial-psychologie* [Cologne], XXIII, No. 1, 1971, 1–31.

Knight, Maxwell E. *The German Executive, 1890–1933.* Stanford: Stanford University Press, 1952.

Kochan, Lionel. *Russia and the Weimar Republic.* Cambridge: Bowes and Bowes, 1954.

Kohn, Hans. *The Mind of Germany: The Education of a Nation.* New York: Scribners, 1960.

Kohn, Hans (ed.). *German History: Some New German Views.* Boston: Beacon Press, 1954.

Krieger, Leonard. *The German Idea of Freedom: History of a Political Tradition.* Boston: Beacon Press, 1957.

Kuhn, Charles. *German and Netherlandish Sculpture, 1280–1800.* Cambridge: Harvard University Press, 1965.

Kunbull, S.F., and Edgell, George H. *A History of Architecture.* New York: Harper and Brothers, 1918.

Kunstler, Gustav. *Romanesque Art in Europe.* Greenwich, Connecticut: New York Graphic Society, 1968.

Lamousé, Annette. "Family Roles of Women: A German Example," *Journal of Marriage and Family,* XXXI, No. 1, February 1969, 145–152.

Landgrebe, Ludwig. *Major Problems in Contemporary European Philosophy.* (Trans., Kurt F. Reinhardt.) New York: Fredrich Unger, 1966.

Lane, Barbara. *Architecture and Politics in Germany, 1918–1948.* Cambridge: Harvard University Press, 1968.

Lang, Paul H., and Broder, Nathan (eds.). *Contemporary Music in Europe: A Comprehensive Survey.* New York: G. Shirmer, 1965.

Lehmann-Haupt, Hellmut. *Art Under a Dictatorship.* New York: Oxford University Press, 1954.

Lessing, O.E. *Masters in Modern German Literature.* (Essay Index Reprint Series.) Freeport, New York: Books for Libraries Press, 1967.

Linderman, Gottfried. *History of German Art: Painting, Sculpture, and Architecture.* (Trans., Tessa Sayle.) New York: Praeger, 1971.

Linz, Juan. "Robert Michaels." Pages 265–272 in David Sills (ed.), *The International Encyclopedia of the Social Sciences,* X. Riverside, New Jersey: Macmillan and Free Press, 1968.

Lippit, Ronald. "Kurt Lewin." Pages 266–271 in David Sills (ed.), *The International Encyclopedia of the Social Sciences,* IX. Riverside, New Jersey: Macmillan and Free Press, 1968.

Littell, Franklin H. "The Protestant Churches and Totalitarianism (Germany 1933–1945)." Pages 108–119 in Carl J. Friedrich (ed.), *Totalitarianism.* Cambridge: Harvard University Press, 1954.

Longyear, Rey M. *Nineteenth-Century Romanticism in Music.* Englewood Cliffs, New Jersey: Prentice-Hall, 1969.

Lowenstein, Hubertus zu von. *The Germans in History.* New York: Columbia University Press, 1945.

Lowenthal, Marvin. *The Jews of Germany: A Story of Sixteen Centuries.* Philadelphia: Jewish Publication Society of America, 1936.

Lowie, Robert H. *Toward Understanding Germany.* Chicago: University of Chicago Press, 1954.

Ludwig, Emil. *The Germans.* (Trans., Heinz Norden and Ruth Norden.) Boston: Little, Brown, 1941.

Lueschen, Guenther, et al. "Family Organization, Interaction and Ritual: A Cross-Cultural Study in Bulgaria, Finland, Germany, and Ireland," *Journal of Marriage and Family,* XXXIII, No. 1, February 1971, 228–234.

McElheny, Victor K. "Genetics at Cologne," *Science,* CXLVI, No. 3646, November 13, 1974, 904–907.

Mann, Golo. *The History of Germany Since 1789.* (Trans., Marian Jackson.) Washington: Praeger, 1968.

Marcel, Franciscono. *Walter Gropius and the Creation of the Bauhaus in Weimar: The Ideals and Artistic Theories of its Founding Years.* Urbana: University of Illinois Press, 1971.

Mehl, Roger. "Le Protestantisme Allemand d'Aujourd'hui," *Revue d'Allemagne* [Paris], II, No. 2, April–June 1970, 170–193.

Meinecke, Friedrich. *1848, eine Säkularbetrachtung* (1848, A Secular Reflection). Berlin: Blanvalet, 1948.

––––––. *The German Catastrophe: Reflections and Recollection.* Cambridge: Harvard University Press, 1950.

Merkl, Peter H. *Germany: Yesterday and Tomorrow.* New York: Oxford University Press, 1965.

Meyer, Henry Cord. *Mitteleuropa in German Thought and Action, 1815–1945.* (International Scholars Forum.) The Hague: Martinus Nijhoff, 1955.

Midgely, John. *Germany.* (Modern World Series.) Oxford: Oxford University Press, 1968.

Miller, Hugh M. *History of Music.* (2d ed.) (College Outline Series, No. 55.) New York: Barnes and Noble, 1953.

Mommsen, Hans. "Historical Scholarship in Transition: The Situation in the Federal Republic of Germany," *Daedalus,* C, No. 2, Spring 1971, 485–508.

Morgan, Roger (ed.). *Germany, 1870–1970: A Hundred Years of Turmoil.* London: MacDonald, 1970.

Muhlen, Norbert. *The Return of Germany: A Tale of Two Countries.* Chicago: Regnery, 1953.

Muller, Theodor. *Sculpture in the Netherlands, Germany, France, and Spain: 1400–1500.* Baltimore: Penguin Books, 1966.

Munke, Stephanie. *Die Mobile Gesellschaft.* Stuttgart: W. Kohlhammer Verlag, 1967.

"Nobel Prizes." Pages 548–552 in *The Encyclopaedia Britannica,* XVI.

Chicago: William Benton, 1969.

Ogrizek, Doré. *Germany.* (World in Color Series.) New York: McGraw-Hill, 1956.

Organization for Economic Cooperation and Development. *Classification of Educational Systems: Germany, Finland, Japan.* Paris: OECD, 1972.

———. *Directorate for Scientific Affairs, Reviews of National Policies for Education: Germany.* Paris: OECD, November 1971.

———. *Educational Policy and Planning: Germany.* Paris: Directorate for Scientific Affairs, OECD, 1972.

———. *Education Committee Reviews of National Policies for Education: Germany.* Paris: OECD, November 4, 1971.

———. *Education Committee Reviews of National Policies for Education: Germany.* Paris: OECD, November 15, 1971.

———. *Innovation in Education: Germany, Technical Report,* by Helga Thomas. Paris: OECD, June 1971.

———. *Reviews of National Policies for Education: Germany.* Paris: OECD, 1972.

Passant, E.J., et al. *A Short History of Germany, 1815–1945.* New York: Cambridge University Press, 1962.

Payne, J. P. (ed.) *Germany Today.* London: Methuen, 1971.

Peck, Reginald. *The West Germans: How They Live and Work.* New York: Praeger, 1970.

Peterson, Iver. "500 Germans, Own Colleges Full, Will Study in U.S.," *New York Times,* February 2, 1974, 1, 27.

Pinson, Koppel S. *Modern Germany: Its History and Civilization.* New York: Macmillan, 1954.

Pollock, James K., et al. *Germany in Power and Eclipse.* New York: Van Nostrand, 1952.

Pounds, Norman J. G. *Divided Germany and Berlin.* (Searchlight Books.) New York: Van Nostrand, 1962.

Priebsch, R., and Collinson, W. E. *The German Language.* (3d ed.) (The Great Languages, ed. by L. R. Palmer.) London: Faber and Faber, 1938.

Prittie, Terence. *Germany.* (Life World Library.) New York: Time, 1965.

Rand McNally Historical Atlas of the World. Chicago: Rand McNally, 1965.

Ranisden, E. H. *Twentieth-Century Sculpture.* London: Pleides, 1949.

Reitlinger, Gerald. *The Final Solution: The Attempt to Exterminate the Jews of Europe, 1939–45.* New York: Beechhurst Press, 1953.

Ritter, Gerhard. *The Schlieffen Plan: Critique of a Myth.* New York: Praeger, 1958.

Robertson, J. G. *A History of German Literature.* (6th ed., rev. by Dorothy Reich.) Elmsford, New York: London House and Maxwell, 1970.

Roh, Franz. *German Art in the Twentieth Century.* (Rev. ed.) Greenwich, Connecticut: New York Graphic Society, 1968.

Rothfels, Hans. *Die deutsche Opposition gegen Hitler* (The German Opposition to Hitler). Frankfurt: Fischer Bücherei, 1958.

Rovan, Joseph. *Germany.* (Trans., Jonathan Griffin.) (Vista Book, W3.) New York: Viking, 1959.

Ruberg, Rudolf. "Autorität in der Familie," *Ehe: Zeitschrift für Familien und Ehekunde* [Zurich], VI, No. 6, 1969, 145–163.

Ruhm von Oppen, Beate (ed.). *Documents on Germany Under Occupation, 1945–1954.* London: Oxford University Press, 1955.

Ryan, Paul Ryder. "Notes on Theater in Germany," *Drama Review,* XVII, No. 4, December 1972, 92–99.

Ryder, A.J. *Twentieth-Century Germany: From Bismarck to Brandt.* New York: Columbia University Press, 1973.

Schaffner, Bertram. *Father Land: A Study of Authoritarianism in the German Family.* New York: Columbia University Press, 1948.

Schalk, Adolph. *The Germans.* Englewood Cliffs, New Jersey: Prentice-Hall, 1971.

————. "Putting the Starch in the German Press," *Saturday Review,* March 25, 1972.

Schalluck, Paul. *Germany: Cultural Developments Since 1945.* Munich: Max Hueber Verlag, 1971.

Schewe, Dieter. *Survey of Social Security in the Federal Republic of Germany.* Bonn: Ministry of Labor and Social Affairs, 1972.

Schorske, Carl E. *German Social Democracy, 1905–1917.* (Harvard Historical Studies, LXV.) Cambridge: Harvard University Press, 1955.

————. "Postwar Religious and Intellectual Trends." Chapter 10 in Hoyt Price and Carl E. Schorske (eds.), *The Problem of Germany* (Studies in American Foreign Relations. No. 5.), New York: Council on Foreign Relations, 1947.

Schuster, George Nauman. *The Germans: An Enquiry and an Estimate.* New York: Dial, 1932.

Sewall, John Ives. *A History of Western Art.* New York: Holt, Rinehart and Winston, 1961.

Shayon, Robert Lewis. "West German Broadcasting: House of Cards," *Saturday Review,* LI, August 17, 1968.

Sheehan, James J. "Liberalism and Society in Germany, 1815–48," *Journal of Modern History,* XLV, No. 4, December 1973, 583–604.

Sitwell, Sacheverell. *Gothic Europe.* London: Weidenfeld and Nicholson, 1969.

Snyder, Louis L. (ed.) *Documents of German History.* New Brunswick: Rutgers University Press, 1958.

Sozialstatistik: Bildungsstatistik. Luxembourg: Statistisches Amt der Europäischen Gemeinschaften, 1972.

Speier, Hans, and Davison, W. Phillips (eds.). *West German Leadership* and *Foreign Policy*. Evanston: Row, Peterson, 1957.

Spiro, Herbert J. *The Politics of German Codetermination*. (Harvard Political Studies.) Cambridge: Harvard University Press, 1958.

The Statesman's Year-Book, 1972–1973. (Ed., John Paxton.) New York: St. Martin's Press, 1972.

Statistisches Jahrbuch für die Bundesrepublik Deutschland, 1962. Wiesbaden: Statistisches Bundesamt, 1962.

Statistisches Jahrbuch für die Bundesrepublik Deutschland, 1973. Wiesbaden: Statistisches Bundesamt, 1973.

Steefel, L. D. *The Schleswig-Holstein Problem*. Cambridge: Harvard University Press, 1932.

Stein, M. L. "West Germany's Adversary Press," *Saturday Review*, May 8, 1971.

Steiner, Peter. "The World of Gunter Eich's Radio Plays," *Germanic Review*, XLVI, No. 3, May 1971, 210–227.

Straus, Richard. "Postwar Development of the German Press," *Department of State Bulletin*, February 23, 1953, 294–301.

Stuckenschmidt, H. H. *Twentieth-Century Composers: Germany and Central Europe*, II. New York: Holt, Rinehart and Winston, 1971.

A Survey of Europe Today: The Peoples and Markets of Sixteen European Countries. New York: Reader's Digest, 1970.

Taylor, Donald L. "The Changing German Family," *International Journal of Comparative Sociology* [Leiden], X, Nos. 3 and 4, 1969, 299–302.

Thoene, Peter. *Modern German Art*. (Trans., Charles Fullman.) Harmondsworth, England: Penguin, 1938.

Tonnelat, Ernest. *A History of the German Language*. (Trans., D.P. Inskip.) London: George G. Harrap, 1937.

UNESCO Statistical Yearbook, 1970. Paris: United Nations Educa-Educational, Scientific and Cultural Organization, 1971.

United Nations. Department of Economic and Social Affairs. Statistical Office. *Population and Vital Statistics Report*. (Statistical Papers, Series A, No. 1.) New York: UN, 1974.

United Nations Educational, Scientific and Cultural Organization. *World Survey of Education*, V. Paris: UNESCO, 1971.

Vagts, Alfred. *A History of Militarism*. New York: Meridian Books, 1959.

Victor, Lange. *Modern German Literature, 1870–1940*. Port Washington, New York: Kennikat Press, 1967.

Von Klemperer, Klemns. *Germany's New Conservatism*. Princeton: Princeton University Press, 1957.

Von Rintelen, F. J. *Contemporary German Philosophy and its Background*. Bonn: H. Bouvier, 1970.

Wachenheim, Hedwig. *Public Health Administration in Germany, 1919–1945*. New York: Institute of World Affairs, 1945.

Waidson, H. M. *The Modern German Novel.* London: Oxford University Press for the University of Hull, 1959.

Walsh, John. "German Science Policy: Bund Shifts the Balance," *Science,* CLIX, No. 3021, March 22, 1968, 1340–1341.

Warner, Karl. *History of Music.* (Trans. and supplemented by Willis Wagner.) New York: Free Press, 1973.

Warren, Richard L. "The Classroom as a Sanctuary for Teachers: Discontinuities in Social Control," *American Anthropologist,* LXXV, No. 1, 280–291.

Waterhouse, Gilbert. *A Short History of German Literature.* London: Methuen, 1952.

Westerbrook, Colin. "The Screen: Deutschland Unter Alles," *Commonwealth,* November 9, 1973.

Whitney, Craig R. "Papa, Who Was Hitler?", *New York Times,* October 28, 1973, Section 6, 24–25, 96–100.

Winter, Helmut. "A Note of History and Politics in Recent German Drama," *Modern Drama,* XIII, No. 3, December 1970, 247–253.

"Workers of the Nine Unite," *Economist* [London], CCXLVI, No. 6750, January 6, 1973, 46.

Worldmark Encyclopedia of the Nations, V: Europe. (Ed., Moshe Y. Sachs.) New York: Worldmark Press, Harper and Row, 1967.

The World of Learning, 1972–73, I. London: Europa Publications, 1973.

World Radio-TV Handbook, 1974. (28th ed.) (Ed., J.M. Frost.) Hvidovre, Denmark: World Radio-TV Handbook, 1974.

Section II. Political

Altenstetter, Christa. "Intergovernmental Profiles in the Federal Systems of Austria and West Germany." (Unpublished paper prepared for the Center for the Study of Federalism and the Urban Studies Center.) Philadelphia: Temple University, 1973.

Anthon, Carl G. "Germany's Westpolitik," *Current History,* LXII, No. 396, May 1972, 234–238.

Ashkenasi, Abraham. "The Federal German Executive and the Foreign Policy Process: The Political Party as the Only Significant Internal Opposition." (Unpublished paper prepared for delivery at the 1973 Annual Meeting of the American Political Science Association.) New Orleans: September 1973.

Balfour, Michael. *West Germany.* New York: Praeger, 1968.

Brecht, Arnold. *Prelude to Silence: The End of the German Republic.* New York: Oxford University Press, 1944.

Carr, Jonathan. "Brandt Fends Off Party Criticism of Leadership," *Financial Times* [London], March 13, 1974.

Carter, Gwendolyn M.; Herz, John H.; and Ranney, John C. *Major Foreign Powers.* New York: Harcourt, Brace, 1957.

Conradt, David P. "Electoral Law Politics in West Germany," *Political Studies* [London], XVIII, No. 3, September 1970, 341–356.

Dahl, Robert A. (ed.) *Political Opposition in Western Democracies.* New Haven: Yale University Press, 1966.

Dahrendorf, Ralf. *Society and Democracy in Germany:* New York: Doubleday, 1967.

Davidson, Eugene. *The Death and Life of Germany: An Account of the American Occupation.* New York: Knopf, 1959.

Dill, Marshall, Jr. *Germany.* Ann Arbor: University of Michigan Press, 1970.

Dittmer, Lowell. "The German NPD: A Psycho-Sociological Analysis of Neo-Naziism," *Comparative Politics,* II, No. 1, October 1969, 79–110.

Drummond, Stuart. "West German Youth in the 1970s," *World Today* [London], XXVIII, No. 8, August 1972, 360–369.

Edinger, Lewis J. "Political Change in Germany: The Federal Republic After the 1969 Election," *Comparative Politics,* II, No. 4, July 1970, 549–578.

———. *Politics in Germany: Attitudes and Processes.* (Little, Brown Series in Comparative Politics.) Boston: Little, Brown, 1968.

Edinger, Lewis J., and Luebke, Paul, Jr. "Grass-Roots Electoral Politics in the German Federal Republic: Five Constituencies in the 1969 Election," *Comparative Politics,* III, No. 4, July 1971, 463–498.

Erler, Fritz. *Democracy in Germany.* (Jodidi Lectures at Harvard University.) Cambridge: Harvard University Press, 1965.

The Europa Year Book, 1972. I. London: Europa Publications, 1972.

Federal Republic of Germany. *Facts About Germany.* Bonn: Press and Information Office, 1972.

———. *Jahresbericht der Bundesregierung, 1972.* Bonn: Herausgegeben vom Presse- und Informationsamt der Bundesregierung, 1973.

Federal Republic of Germany. Federal Ministry for Intra-German Relations. *The State of the Nation, 1971.* Kassel: Druck-und Verlagshaus Schneider and Weber, 1971.

Fisher, Joel M., and Groennings, Sven. "German Electoral Politics in 1969," *Government and Opposition* [London], V, No. 2, Spring 1970, 218–234.

Flenley, Ralph. *Modern German History.* London: J. M. Dent, 1959.

Gillessen, Günther. "The Social Democrats and the Young Left," *Encounter* [London], XXXIX, No. 4, October 1972, 85–90.

Golay, John Ford. *The Founding of the Federal Republic of Germany.* Chicago: University of Chicago Press, 1958.

Graebner, Norman A. "Germany Between East and West," *Current History,* LXII, No. 396, May 1972, 225–228.

Great Britain. Foreign Office. *Manual of German Law,* I. London: His Majesty's Stationery Office, 1950.

Grosser, Alfred. *La Démocratie de Bonn* (The Bonn Democracy). Paris: Libraire Armand Colin, 1958.

————. *French Foreign Policy Under De Gaulle.* New York: Praeger, 1967.

————. *Germany in Our Time: A Political History of the Postwar Years.* (Trans., Paul Stephenson.) New York: Praeger, 1970.

Gunlicks, Arthur B. "Intraparty Democracy in Western Germany: A Look at the Local Level," *Comparative Politics*, II, No. 2, January 1970, 229–250.

Hanf, Kenneth. "Administrative Developments in East and West Germany: Stirrings of Reform," *Political Studies* [London], XXI, No. 1, March 1973, 35–44.

Hanreider, Wolfram F. *West German Foreign Policy, 1949–1963.* Stanford: Stanford University Press, 1967.

Heidenheimer, Arnold J. *The Governments of Germany.* (3d ed.) (Crowell Comparative Government Series.) New York: Thomas Y. Crowell, 1971.

Hirsch, Felix E. "Ostpolitik in Historical Perspective," *Current History*, LXII, No. 369, May 1972, 229–233.

Hiscocks, Richard. *Democracy in Western Germany.* London: Oxford University Press, 1957.

Horne, Alistair. *Return to Power.* New York: Praeger, 1956.

Huddleston, John. "Trade Unions in the German Federal Republic," *Political Quarterly* [London], XXXVIII, No. 2, April-June 1967, 165–177.

Jaspers, Karl. *The Future of Germany.* (Ed. and trans., E.B. Ashton.) Chicago: University of Chicago Press, 1967.

Joll, James. *Europe Since 1870.* London: C. Tinling, 1973.

"Jusos Attack," *Economist* [London], CCXLVI, No. 6760, March 17, 1973.

Kaiser, Karl. *German Foreign Policy in Transition.* New York: Oxford University Press, 1968.

Keesing's Research Reports Staff. *Germany and Eastern Europe Since 1945.* New York: Charles Scribner's Sons, 1973.

Lippmann, Walter. *The Communist World and Ours.* Boston: Little, Brown, 1959.

Meinecke, Friedrich. *1848, eine Säkularbetrachtung* (1848, A Secular Reflection). Berlin: Blanvalet, 1948.

————. *The German Catastrophe: Reflections and Recollections.* Cambridge: Harvard University Press, 1950.

Morgenthau, Hans J. (ed.) *Germany and the Future of Europe.* (Harris Foundation Lectures, 26th Institute.) Chicago: University of Chicago Press, 1951.

Neumann, Robert G. *The Government of the Federal Republic of Germany.* New York: Harper and Row, 1966.

Northrop, F.S.C. *European Union and United States Foreign Policy.* New York: Macmillan, 1954.

Pinson, Koppel S. *Modern Germany: Its History and Civilization.* New

York: Macmillan, 1954.

Pollock, James K., et al. *Germany in Power and Eclipse.* New York: Van Nostrand, 1952.

Pollock, James K. (ed.) *German Democracy at Work.* Ann Arbor: University of Michigan Press, 1955.

Prittie, Terence. *Germany.* (Life World Library.) New York: Time, 1965.

Pulzer, Peter G. J. "The German Party System in the Sixties," *Political Studies* [London], XIX, No. 1, March 1971, 1–17.

Reitlinger, Gerald. *The Final Solution: The Attempt to Exterminate the Jews of Europe, 1939–1945.* New York: Beechhurst Press, 1953.

Ritter, Gerhard. *The Schlieffen Plan: Critique of a Myth.* New York: Praeger, 1958.

Ryder, A. J. *Twentieth-Century Germany: From Bismarck to Brandt.* New York: Columbia University Press, 1973.

Schmidt, Helmut. *The Balance of Power.* (Trans., Edward Thomas Obe.) London: William Kimber, 1971.

Seagle, William. *The History of Law.* New York: Tudor, 1946.

Segal, David R. "Classes, Strata, and Parties in West Germany and the United States," *Comparative Studies in Society and History* [The Hague], X, No. 1, October 1967, 66–84.

Serfaty, Simon. *France, de Gaulle, and Europe.* Baltimore: Johns Hopkins University Press, 1968.

Shell, Kurt L. "Extraparliamentary Opposition in Postwar Germany," *Comparative Politics*, II. No. 4, July 1970, 653–680.

Snyder, Louis L. (ed.) *Documents of German History.* New Brunswick: Rutgers University Press, 1958.

Speier, Hans, and Davison, W. Phillips (eds.). *West German Leadership and Foreign Policy.* Evanston: Row, Peterson, 1957.

Statistisches Jahrbuch für die Bundesrepublik Deutschland, 1973. Wiesbaden: Statistisches Bundesamt, 1973.

Tatu, Michel. *Le Triangle Washington-Moscou-Pekin et les Deux Europe (s).* Paris: Casterman, 1972.

Tilford, R. B., and Preece, R.J.C. *Federal Germany: Political and Social Order.* London: Oswald Wolff, 1969.

Ullman, Richard K. *German Parliaments.* New York: Praeger, 1954.

Vetter, Heinz Oskar, "Trade Unions Role in Contacts with the East," *Bulletin* [Bonn], XVIII, No. 6, February 24, 1970, 39.

Wallach, H. G. Peter. "Leadership Styles in West German Political Parties." (Unpublished paper prepared for delivery at the 1973 Annual Meeting of the American Political Science Association.) New Orleans: 1973.

Wechsberg, Joseph. "Profiles: The Outsider," *New Yorker*, XLIX, No. 47, January 14, 1974, 35–37.

Williams, Philip. *Politics in Post-War France.* New York: Longmans, Green, 1954.

Zink, Harold. *The United States in Germany, 1944–1955*. Princeton: Van Nostrand, 1957.
(Various issues of the following periodicals were also used in the preparation of this section: *Financial Times* [London], February-May 1974 and *New York Times*, October-December 1972, January-June 1974.)

Section III. Economic

Arntz, Helmut (ed.). *Industry in the Federal Republic of Germany.* (3rd ed.) Bonn: Press and Information Office, Federal Republic of Germany, 1967.

Bruck, Werner Friedrich. *Social and Economic History of Germany from William II to Hitler, 1888–1938.* Cardiff: Oxford University Press, 1938.

Commission of the European Communities. *Agricultural Income in the Enlarged Community.* (Working Document No. SEC [73] 900.) Brussels: March 7, 1973.

Deutscher Raiffeisenverband E.V. 1971 Jahrbuch, XXIV. Bonn: Deutscher Raiffeisenverband, 1972.

Ebenstein, William. *The Nazi State.* New York: Farrar and Rinehart, 1943.

Federal Republic of Germany. *Agrarbericht der Bundesregierung.* (Deutscher Bundestag, 6. Wahlperiode, Drucksache 6/3090.) Bonn: Bonner Universitäts-Buchdruckerei, 1972.

————. *Agrarbericht der Bundesregierung, 1973.* (Deutscher Bundestag, 7. Wahlperiode, Drucksache 7/146 and 7/147.) Bonn: Bonner Universitäts-Buchdruckerei, 1973.

————. *Agrarbericht, 1974.* (Deutscher Bundestag, 7. Wahlperiode, Drucksache 7/1650 and 7/1651.) Bonn: Bonner Universitäts-Buchdruckerei, October 3, 1973.

————. *Die Energiepolitik der Bundesregierung.* (Deutscher Bundestag, 7. Wahlperiode, Drucksache 7/1057.) Bonn: Bonner Universitäts-Buchdruckerei, October 3, 1973.

————. *Facts About Germany.* Bonn: Press and Information Office, 1972.

Federal Republic of Germany. Der Bundesminister für Ernahrung, Landwirtschaft, und Forsten. *Bericht über die Verbesserung der Agrarstruktur in der Bundesrepublik Deutschland, 1971.* Bonn: Landschriften-Verlag, n.d.

Grosser, Alfred. *Germany in Our Time: A Political History of the Postwar Years.* (Trans., Paul Stephenson.) New York: Praeger, 1970.

Heaton, Herbert. *Economic History of Europe.* New York: Harper, 1948.

Heiden, Konrad. *A History of National Socialism.* New York: Knopf, 1935.

IFO-Institut für Wirtschaftsforschung. Abteilung Landwirtschaft. *Agricultural Marketing Systems in the EEC-Member Countries.* (Studien zur Agrarwirtschaft, I, Heft 10.) Munich: IFO, 1971.

Klein, Burton H. *Germany's Economic Preparation for War.* (Harvard Economic Studies, No. 109.) Cambridge: Harvard University Press, 1959.

Langsam, Walter Consuelo. *The World Since 1914.* New York: Macmillan, 1950.

Mayhew, Alan. "Structural Reform and the Future of West German Agriculture," *Geographical Review,* LX, January 1970, 54-68.

Midgley, John. *Germany.* (Modern World Series.) Oxford: Oxford University Press, 1968.

Organization for European Cooperation and Development. *Agricultural Policies in 1966.* (Agricultural Policy Reports.) Paris: OECD, 1967.

————. *The Industrial Policies of 14 Member Countries.* Paris: OECD, 1971.

Passant, E.J., et al. *A Short History of Germany, 1815–1945.* New York: Cambridge University Press, 1962.

Pinson, Koppel S. *Modern Germany: Its History and Civilization.* New York: Macmillan, 1954.

Rosenthal, Glenda. "Interest Groups and Decision-Making in the EEC: An Agricultural Case Study." (Paper prepared for delivery at the 1973 Annual Meeting of the American Political Science Association.) New Brunswick: Rutgers University, 1973.

"Russian Uranium Agreement Okayed," *Report from Europe,* I, No. 3, November-December 1973.

Schnitzer, Martin. *East and West Germany: a Comparative Analysis.* New York: Praeger, 1972.

Statistical Yearbook, 1969. New York: United Nations, Department of Economic and Social Affairs, Statistical Office, 1970.

Statistical Yearbook, 1970. New York: United Nations, Department of Economic and Social Affairs, Statistical Office, 1971.

Statistical Yearbook, 1972. New York: United Nations, Department of Economic and Social Affairs, Statistical Office, 1973.

Statistisches Jahrbuch für die Bundesrepublik Deutschland, 1962. Wiesbaden: Statistisches Bundesamt, 1962.

Statistisches Jahrbuch für die Bundesrepublik Deutschland, 1973. Wiesbaden: Statistisches Bundesamt, 1973.

Stolper, Gustav. *German Economy, 1870–1940.* New York: Reynal and Hitchcock, 1940.

U.S. Department of Agriculture. Economic Research Service. *The Agricultural Economy and Trade of the Federal Republic of Germany. (ERS-Foreign 325.) Washington:* GPO, November 1971.

————. *Structural Changes in West German Agriculture.* (ERS-Foreign 339.) Washington: GPO, June 1972.

U.S. Department of Agriculture. Foreign Agricultural Service. *The Common Agricultural Policy of the European Community.* FAS M-255.) Washington: GPO, November 1973.

Wallich, Henry C. *Mainsprings of the German Revival.* (Yale Studies in Economics, No. 5.) New Haven: Yale University Press, 1955.

Year Book of Labour Statistics, 1973. Geneva: International Labour Office, 1973.

Section IV. National Security

Adenauer, Konrad. *World Indivisible with Liberty and Justice for All.* (*World Perspectives*, ed. Ruth Nonda Anshen, V.) New York: Harper, 1955.

Alexander, Edgar. *Adenauer and the New Germany.* New York: Farrar, Strauss and Cudahy, 1957.

Benton, William. "Germany." Pages 277–359 in *Encyclopaedia Britannica*, X. Chicago: William Benton, 1969.

Brewer, Carey. "The General Staff of the German Army," *United States Naval Institute Proceedings*, LXXXII, February 1956, 157–166.

"Career Officers' Colleges," *Military Review*, LIV, No. 6, June 1974, 94–95.

Craig, Gordon A. *The Politics of the Prussian Army, 1640–1945.* Oxford: Clarendon Press, 1955.

Cramer, James. *The World's Police.* London: Cassell, 1964.

Dahrendorf, Ralf. *Society and Democracy in Germany.* New York: Doubleday, 1967.

Erler, Fritz. *Democracy in Germany.* (Jodidi Lectures at Harvard University.) Cambridge: Harvard University Press, 1965.

The Europa Year Book, 1972. I. London: Europa Publications, 1972.

Federal Republic of Germany. *Facts About Germany.* Bonn: Press and Information Office, 1972.

———. *The Force Structure in the Federal Republic of Germany.* Bonn: Force Structure Commission, 1973.

Federal Republic of Germany. Ministry of Defense. *White Paper 1973/1974: The Security of the Federal Republic of Germany and the Development of the Federal Armed Forces.* Bonn: 1974.

Federal Republic of Germany. Report by the Federal Chancellor. *The State of the Nation, 1971.* Kassel: Druck- und Verlagshaus Schneider und Weber, November 1971.

"The German Aerospace Industry on a Tightrope," *Interavia* [Geneva], XXIX, No. 5, May 1974, 415–431.

Görlitz, Walter. *The German General Staff: Its History and Structure, 1657–1945.* London: Hollis and Carter, 1953.

Great Britain. Foreign Office. *Manual of German Law*, II. London: His Majesty's Stationery Office, 1952.

Grosser, Alfred. *The Colossus Again.* New York: Praeger, 1955.

Habe, Hans. *Our Love Affair with Germany.* New York: Putnam, 1953.

Hart, B. H. Liddell. *The German Generals Talk.* New York: Berkley, 1956.

Hudson, James (ed.). *Law and Judicial Systems of Nations.* Washington: World Peace Through Law Center, 1968.

Jane's All the World's Aircraft, 1969-70. (Ed., John W.R. Taylor.) New York: McGraw-Hill, 1969.

Jane's Fighting Ships, 1969-70. (Ed., Raymond V.B. Blackman.) New York: McGraw-Hill, 1969.

Jane's Weapon Systems, 1969-70. (Eds., R.T. Pretty and D.H.R. Archer.) New York: McGraw-Hill, 1969.

The Military Balance, 1973-74. London: Institute for Strategic Studies, 1974.

Rosinski, Herbert. *The German Army.* (2d ed.) Washington: Infantry Journal Press, 1944.

Schröder, Jürgen. *Das Deutsche Heer* (The German Army). Bonn: Athenäum-Verlag, 1957.

Shanahan, William O. *Prussian Military Reforms, 1786-1813.* (Studies in History, Economics, and Public Law, No. 520.) New York: Columbia University Press, 1945.

Snyder, Louis L. *German Nationalism: The Tragedy of a People.* Harrisburg: Stackpole, 1952.

Speier, Hans. *German Rearmament and Atomic War.* Santa Monica: Rand, 1957.

The Statesman's Year-Book, 1972-1973. (Ed., John Paxton.) New York: St. Martin's Press, 1972.

The Statesman's Year-Book, 1973-1974. (Ed., John Paxton.) New York: St. Martin's Press, 1973.

Statistisches Jahrbuch für die Bundesrepublik Deutschland, 1973. Wiesbaden: Statistisches Bundesamt, 1973.

Stern, Frederick Martin. *The Citizen Army.* New York: St. Martin's Press, 1957.

Vagts, Alfred. *A History of Militarism: Romance and Realities of a Profession.* New York: W.W. Norton, 1937.

Warburg, James P. *Germany: Key to Peace.* Cambridge: Harvard University Press, 1953.

Worldmark Encyclopedia of the Nations, V: Europe. (Ed., Moshe Y. Sachs.) New York: Worldmark Press, Harper and Row, 1967.

Young, Desmond. *Rommel.* London: Collins, 1950.

GLOSSARY

BRD—Bundesrepublik Deutschland (Federal Republic of Germany). Commonly referred to as West Germany.

CDU—Christlich-Demokratische Union (Christian Democratic Union). One of the two major political parties in the Federal Republic. *See also* SPD.

CSU—Christlich-Soziale Union (Christian Social Union). Bavarian sister party of the CDU *(q.v.)*. Maintains separate organization and elects its own officers.

DDR—Deutsche Demokratische Republik (German Democratic Republic). Commonly referred to as East Germany.

DM—Deutsche Mark. The basic unit of currency (DM1 equals 100 pfennigs). In the fall of 1974 DM1 equaled US$0.3759.

ECSC—European Coal and Steel Community. *See* European Community.

EEC—European Economic Community (also known as the Common Market). One of the associations of countries collectively known as the European Community *(q.v.)*.

EURATOM—European Atomic Energy Community. *See* European Community.

European Community—EC (often, European Communities). Includes ECSC, EEC, and EURATOM. Member countries are Belgium, Denmark, France, the Federal Republic of Germany, Ireland, Italy, Luxembourg, the Netherlands, and the United Kingdom. Institutions common to the EC are the Commission, the Council of Ministers, the European Parliament, and the Court of Justice.

FDP—Freie Demokratische Partei (Free Democratic Party). The only minor party that has won seats in the Bundestag (Federal Diet) in every national election. Has usually been a coalition partner to one or the other of the two major parties.

hectare—10,000 square meters. Equal to 2.471 acres.

Land—state; pl., *Länder*. Federal Republic is made up of ten *Länder* plus West Berlin. West Berlin is administered separately and has no voting representation in the federal legislature.

metric ton—1,000 kilograms. Equal to 1.1 short tons, 0.98 long ton, or 2,204.6 pounds.

Nazi—derived from the German pronunciation of the word *national* in the formal title of the Nazi Party (National Socialist German Workers' Party.)

Raiffeisen, Friedrich Wilhelm (1818–88)—German economist who founded agricultural cooperative credit unions and a system of agricultural banks during the nineteenth century. Some banks and agricultural unions still bear his name.

SPD—Sozialdemokratische Partei Deutschlands (Social Democratic Party of Germany). The second major political party in the Federal Republic. *See also* CDU.

WEU—Western European Union. An alliance designed to coordinate defense matters among member states and to foster cooperation in cultural, legal, political, and social affairs. Members are Belgium, France, the Federal Republic of Germany, Italy, Luxembourg, the Netherlands, and the United Kingdom.

INDEX

303, 305, 313; sales, 7
aviation. *See* air force; air transportation
Axis partnership: 41; pact, 39
Azores high-pressure air mass: 63

Bach, Johann Sebastian: 19, 153, 167, 169
Bach, Karl Phillip Emanuel: 167, 168
Bad Godesberg Party Conference: 241
Bachmann, Kurt: 230
Baden: 24
Baden-Württemberg: 47, 50, 57, 61, 64, 68, 70, 71, 92, 93, 229, 285, 286, 309; and industry, 305; population of, 84, 85, 88
Bahr, Egon: 243, 244, 245, 246
balance of payments: viii, 265, 280
Balkans: 22, 106
Baltic Sea: vii, 57, 61, 91, 284
banks and banking (*see also* German Federal Bank): 207, 266, 275–279, 318; central bank, 264, 265–266, 275; commercial banks, 264, 278, 279; and government policy, 264; mortgage banks, 278; savings banks, 277, 279; union cooperatives, 278–279
Baptists: 2
Barbarossa, Friedrich. *See* Friedrich I
Barth, Karl: 157
Barth, Paul: 166
Basic Law (Grundgesetz) (*see also* constitutions): viii, 3, 4, 7, 47–48, 137, 205–207, 208, 213, 218, 219, 220; and armed forces, 323, 325, 329, 331; and civil defense, 349; and economy, 261; and judicial branch, 214, 216; and media, 192; 193, 198; and politics, 221, 230; and rearmament, 248
Basic Political Treaty: 222, 223, 245–246
Basic Program: 226
Bastian, Adolf: 166
Bauer, Bruno: 156
Bauhaus group: 171, 172, 173, 175, 187
Baumeister, Willi: 187
Bavaria and Bavarians: 2, 11, 12, 18, 24, 29, 47, 54, 57, 58, 61, 64, 70, 71, 83, 92, 93, 106, 107, 108, 113, 114, 123, 218, 229, 273, 305, 307; and Basic Law, 206; Bavarian People's Party, 225; farming in, 284, 285, 286, 288, 291; population of, 83, 84, 88
Bavarian Alps: 53, 54, 55, 58, 61, 62, 64, 68, 70
Bayern-Kurier: 197
Bayreuth: 169
Bebel, August: 32, 33
Becker, Walter: 188
beer: 104
Beethoven, Ludwig van: 3, 153, 168, 169; *Eroica,* 24

Bender, Hans: 181
Belgium (*see also* Benelux): vii, 7, 71, 252, 338; and foreign relations, 238, 323; migrant workers from, 2, 111
Benelux: 238, 250, 251
Berges, Werner: 188
Berlin: 10, 24, 26, 45, 47, 51, 76, 88, 94, 107, 113, 164, 169, 243, 244; agreement of 1971, 245; and arts and sciences, 164, 169, 170, 171, 175, 177, 179; crisis of 1961, 339
Berlin, East: 51, 223, 243
Berlin Industrial Bank: 279
Berlin Quadripartite Agreement: 51
Berlin Wall: 49, 89, 242, 243, 269
Berlin, West: vii, viii, 3, 50, 53, 79, 84, 92, 142, 185, 186, 222, 223, 243, 244, 339; access agreement of 1971, 245; banking, 278; government, 211, 216, 219; and media, 195, 203; Philharmonic Hall, 186; population of 84, 85, 88
Berliner Morgenpost: 195
Bernstein, Eduard: 33
Beuys, Joseph: 187
Bialas, Günter: 185
Bible, The: 158, 159
Bild Zeitung: 195, 196
Bingen: 55, 60
Birgfeld, Detlef: 187
birth control: 91
birthrates: 79, 83, 86–87, 91, 119; infant mortality, 86, 87, 99; and military draft, 328
Bismarck, Otto von: 9, 27–35, 101, 123, 240
Blacher, Boris: 185
Black Forest (Schwarzwald): 55, 56, 59, 61, 68, 69, 93, 172
Black Sea: 76
Bloch, Ernst: 180
The Blue Angel: 176
Böckh, August: 166
Böcklin, Arnold: 174
Bodensee: 55, 58, 61, 70
Bohemia: 15, 42; Bohemians, 13
Bohm, Gottfried: 186
Böhmerwald: 55, 62, 70
Böll, Heinrich: 181, 189
Bolshevism: 39, 40
Bonn: 3, 47, 55, 60, 70, 73, 177, 193, 194, 219, 347
books: 112, 178, 203–204; and youth, 354
Borchert, Wolfgang: 181
Bothe, Walther: 184
bourgeoisie (*see also* middle class: social stratification): 16, 19, 25; medieval burghers, 120

306, 307
Comerzbank: 278
Committee of Professional Agricultural Organizations (COPA): 288
Common Market. *See* European Economic Community
communications (*see also* books; films; freedom of expression; libraries; newspapers and periodicals; press; radio; television): viii, 6, 191–204; state control of media, 218
communism and communists: 10, 36, 40, 50, 51, 123, 221–222, 226, 230–231, 241, 243, 247, 250, 251, 352–353
The Communist Manifesto: 156
concentration camps: 40, 109, 343
Confederation of the Rhine: 24, 25
Conference on Security and Cooperation in Europe (CSCE): 244
Congress of Vienna: 24, 25, 26
Conrad II: 13
conscription: 7, 324, 326, 329, 340; and conscientious objectors, 207, 329, 331; and unemployment insurance, 102
conservatism: 26
conservatories and academies: 146
Constitution of 1867: 28
constitutions (*see also* Basic Laws; Parliamentary Council; Weimar Constitution of 1919): 26, 27, 31, 36, 46–47, 117, 206, 323
construction industry: 260, 261, 303, 304, 314–315, 317
consumerism: 100, 129; and social status, 125
Conze, Werner: 184
cooperatives: credit 278–279
Corinth, Lovis: 175
Council for European Agriculture (CEA): 287
Council of Experts for the Evaluation of Overall Economic Development: 262
Council of States: 45
Council on Science and the Humanities: 138
Counter-Reformation: 18, 19, 172
counties (Kreisen): 218, 219
courts (*see also* judicial branch); viii, 205, 214–216, 350, 351, 352; Federal Administrative Court, 216; Federal Constitutional Court, viii, 4, 192, 193, 205, 208, 214, 216, 221–222, 261; Federal Court of Justice, 205, 214, 350; Federal Finance Court, 216; Federal Labor Court, 216; Federal Social Security Court, 216; Federal Supreme Court, 197, 215; Juvenile Courts Act, 351–352
crafts and craftsmanship: 117, 120, 122, 127, 132; medieval guilds, 120–121; training in, 146

Cranach, Lucas, the Elder: 173–174
Credit Institute for Reconstruction: 277–278
crime: and judicial process, 215, 350–352
The Critique of Judgment: 155
The Critique of Pure Reason: 155
crops (*see also* fruits and vegetables, grains): 54, 57, 284, 285, 297–299; root, 285
Cuba: 242
cultural life (*see also* arts; intellectual life; philosophy; science): 14, 15, 18–19, 22–23; after World War II, 154
currency (*see also* Deutsche Mark): 37, 46, 51, 263–264, 265, 274–275, 303, 318, 339–340; exchange rates, 265; gold, 275
curriculum: 133, 134, 136, 142, 143, 144, 145, 147; Nazi, 135 customs (*see also* tariffs): custom union, 26
Czechoslovakia: vii, 41, 42, 62, 70, 88, 108, 244, 246, 347; and Soviet coup, 247, 248

Dahmen, K. F.: 188
Dahrendorf, Ralf: 124, 125, 126–127, 128, 129, 130
dairy products: 297, 299, 300
Daladier, Edouard: 41
Danube River: vii, 10, 53, 54, 55, 59, 61, 62, 91
Danzig: 16
Das Kapital: 156
Dawes Plan: 37
death rates: 79, 86, 87, 98, 99
Declaration of Fundamental Rights: 27
The Decline of the West: 157
defense. *See* security, national
deGaulle, Charles: 251, 253–255
Dehio, Ludwig: 34
democracy: 10, 28, 33, 35, 36, 38, 45, 46, 49; and armed forces, 330; and education, 135; and police, 343; and social status, 124, 130
Denmark: vii, 16, 27, 110, 255–256; Danes, 1, 85, 105, 106, 109
dentists: 100; training, 150
depression: 40
Der Spiegel: 50, 191, 193, 195, 196, 197
Der Stern: 197
détente, international: 50
Deutsche Bank: 278
Deutsche Mark (*see also* currency): viii-ix, 249, 259, 274, 279
Deutsche National-Zeitung: 197
Deutsche Welle (The Voice of Germany): 191–192, 199
Deutsche Zeitung: 197
Deutscher Werkbund: 171
Deutschlandfunk (Radio Germany): 191, 199, 200

Marshall Plan: 4, 48, 241, 247, 251; repayment of, 272
Martel, Charles: 11
Marx, Karl: 26, 33, 123, 149, 153, 156, 161; Marxism, 32, 33, 180, 184, 226, 241
Mataré, Ewald: 186–187
Maurer, Hans: 186
Max Planck Society for the Promotion of Science: 183
Max, Prince of Baden: 35
Maximilian, Emperor: 172
Mayer, Julius: 165
mayors: 219
meat supply: 297, 299
media. See communications
medical care: 97, 101, 103; and military, 335–336; training, 148, 150
Mein Kampf: 39, 42, 52
Meissen: 112
Meistermann, Georg: 187
Meistersinger: 158
men (see also conscription): 116–117; in labor force, 269; marital relationships, 118–119; patriarchal tradition, 116, 117, 119; in population, 79, 80–83, 84, 90, 328–329; wages, 316
Mendelssohn, Felix: 168–169
Mendelssohn, Moses: 155, 160
Mendes-France, Pierre: 252
Mennonites: 2
Menzel, Adolf von: 174
Mercedes-Benz: 313
merchant marine: 77
Merovingians: 11
Messiah: 167
Methodists: 2
metric system: 24
Metternich, Clemens von: 26
Meuse River: 60
Michels, Robert: 167
Michelson, Hans: 182
Middle Ages: 93, 113, 122, 153
middle class (see also social stratification, working class): 19, 20, 21, 22, 25, 26, 27, 32, 52, 113, 122, 123, 124, 125, 126, 127, 128, 129, 130; bureaucrats, 126, 128, 130; false, 125, 127, 128; freemen, 12; lower, 122, 127; and politics, 227; service class, 125, 126, 127, 128; white-collar, 122, 130; workers, 126, 129
Middle East: 89, 256–257, 310
Middle Kingdom: 12
middle school: 134
Miës van der Rohe, Ludwig: 172, 185–186
migrant workers (see also Gastarbeiter): 85,

86, 110–111, 269–270, 316
migration: 88–90; to United States, 249
military. See armed forces
mineral resources (see also mining; resources, natural): 37, 54, 69, 93, 106, 306
mining (see also coal; gas, natural; iron and steel; petroleum; potash; salt): 260, 304, 307, 308, 314, 316, 317; barites, 306; lead, 306; zinc, 306
ministries: vii, 48, 206–207, 208, 209, 210, 211, 214, 325; agriculture, 138; culture, 220; defense, 322, 325; education and science, 137, 138, 139, 142; finance, 266, 267, 273, 348; foreign affairs, 240; housing, 100; information, 192; interior, 177; 341, 342, 346, 347, 349, 352; justice, 216–217; labor and social affairs, 102, 103; science, education, and public instruction, 135; transport, posts, and telecommunications; 348–349
Minnesänge: 158, 159
Mittelgebirge: 284
Mittelland Canal: 75, 76
Molotov, Vyacheslav: 42
Mommsen, Theodor: 166
monarchy: 11, 12, 13, 14, 15, 26, 27, 28; and Bismarck, 31
Mönchen-Gladbach: 306
Monnet, Jean: 251
Moravia: 42
Morocco: migrant workers from, 2
Moscow: 4, 25
Moselle River: 55, 60, 62, 75, 76; valley, 61
Mossbauer, Rudolf: 184
motion pictures. See films
mountains (see also Alps, Bavarian Alps): 53, 54, 56, 60, 61
mud flats (Watten): 56, 57
Müller, Johannes: 164
Multilateral Nuclear Force: 248
Munich: 3, 36, 39, 41, 47, 73, 74, 77, 84, 94, 104, 108, 183, 216, 347; and arts and sciences, 171, 175, 179, 186, 188; and media, 195, 197, 203, 204; and military training, 334
Murner, Thomas: 159
museums: 153, 179
music: 153, 158, 167–170, 184–185; education, 146; folk, 159, 168; opera, 185; support of, 177
Muslims: 11
Mussnug, Martin: 229
Mussolini, Benito: 41

Nahe River: 62; valley, 60
Napoleon Bonaparte: 14, 15, 22, 23, 24, 25,

Parzifal: 158
Peasant War: 18
peasants (*see also* social stratification): 13, 16, 17–18, 21, 22, 24, 120, 121, 122–123, 125, 130; and taxation, 19
Pechstein, Max: 175
pensions: 101, 102
Pepin the Short: 11
periodicals: 112
petroleum (*see also* Arab states): 70, 306, 307, 309, 310, 311, 313, 316, 319; crude oil, 307–308
Petschnigg, Hubert: 186
Pfalzerwald: 55, 60
Pfenning, Richard: 188
Pforzheim: 109, 186
pharmacists: 100; training, 148
Philip the Bold: 15
philosophy (*see also* absurdists; existentialism; expressionism; humanism; political systems; romanticism): 3, 23, 105, 154–158, 179–180; Frankfurt School, 180; mysticism, 154, 158, 160, 161; naturalism, 163; phenomenology, 157; rationalism, 159, 160; realism, 161, 163, 175
physicians. *See* doctors
Piene, Otto: 187
Pieper, Joseph: 179
Pius XII, Pope: 182
Planck, Max (*see also* Max Planck Society for the Promotion of Science): 165
Plessner, Helmuth: 179–180
Pleven Plan: 251
Plievier, Theodor: 180
poetry: 112, 158–159, 160, 161, 178, 180, 181
Poitiers: 11
Poland: 5, 16, 18, 21, 36, 42, 76, 88, 108, 222, 244, 245, 246; Poles, 12
polders: 67–68
police: (*see also* Elite Guard; land, Secret State Police; Storm Troops): ix, 38, 341–349; Criminal Office, 348; customs officials, 348; Emergency Police, 343, 344; Federal Border Police, ix, 343, 346–348; manorial police power, 25; miscellaneous duties, 348–349; training, 344–345; uniforms, 344, 347
political extremist groups: 341–342
political interest groups: 232–234, 235; peak associations (Spitzenverbände), 232, 233
political parties: 31, 37, 38, 46, 195, 208, 209, 211, 216, 220, 221–231; Catholic Center Party, 31–32; Center Party, 31, 32, 35, 36, 46, 224; Christian Democratic Union (Chrislich—Demokratische Union—

CDU), 4, 5, 46, 47, 49, 50, 197, 221, 222, 224–226, 227, 229, 230, 233, 235, 240, 243, 245, 248, 250; Christian Social Movement, 31; Christian Social Union (Christlich—Soziale Union—CSU), 5, 197, 224–226; Communist Party of Germany (Kommunistische Partei Deutschlands—KPD), 10, 35, 38, 230; Conservative Party, 31; Democrats: 35, 36; Free Conservative Party, 31; Free Democratic Party (Frei Demokratische Partei—FDP), 5, 49, 50, 192–193, 221, 222, 224, 228–229, 235; German Communist Party (Deutsche Kommunistische Partei—DKP), 230–231, 352–353; German Young Democrats (Deutsche Jungdemokraten—DJD—Judos), 229; National Democratic Party of Germany (Nationaldemokratische Partei Deutschlands—NPD), 229–230, 352; National Liberal Party, 31, 37; National Socialist German Workers' Party (Nazi Party), 10, 36, 38, 40, 342; Nationalists, 35, 38; People's Party, 35; Social Democratic Labor Party, 32; Social Democratic Party of Germany (Sozialdemokratische Partei Deutschlands—SPD), 5, 31, 33, 35, 36, 38, 40, 46, 50, 51, 192–193, 196, 197, 221, 222, 223, 224, 226–228, 229, 230, 233, 235, 238, 240, 241, 243; Socialist German Youth Workers, 231, 353; Socialist Labor Party, 33, 123; Socialist Reich Party, 352; Socialist Unity Party of (East) Germany (Sozialistische Einheitspartei Deutschlands–SED), 226, 241; Young Socialists (Jungsozialisten—Jusos), 227–228; Young Union (Junge Union—JU), 225–226
political systems. *See* authoritarian rule; Bolshevism; capitalism; communism and communists; conservatism; democracy; imperialism; Marxism; monarchy; nationalism; philosophy; socialism; totalitarianism
political values and attitudes: 234–235
Pomerania: 20, 26
Pommer, Erich: 176
Pompidou, Georges: 255
population (*see also* ethnic groups): vii, 1, 56, 79–95; growth, 86–88; and religious wars, 18; trends, 90
pornography: viii, 192
ports: ix, 56, 77
Portugal: 248, 332; migrant workers from, 2
Postal Union Membership: 270
potash: 70, 306, 309

potatoes: 57, 286, 288, 297, 298
Potsdam: 88, 323
poultry: 299, 300
Prague: 15
precipitation: 54, 63, 64, 284
Preller, Friedrich (the Elder): 174
Pren, Heinred: 188
president (*see also* executive branch): vii, 48, 50, 51, 205, 207–209; impeachment of, 208, 216; and veto, 208
press (*see also* freedom of expression; newspapers and periodicals): viii, 27, 191, 192, 193, 194–198; conferences, 194
Press and Information Office (BPA): 193–194, 211
princes and principalities: 18, 19, 22, 24, 27, 119, 120, 121, 134
printing: 17, 159
prisons: 351–352
private schools: 133, 137, 138, 139
propaganda: 39, 40, 41, 170, 176
Protestant Press Service (Evangelische Pressedienst—EPD): 198
Protestant Union: 18
Protestants (*see also* Evangelical Church in Germany; Lutherans): vii, 2, 9, 18, 20, 104, 107; and arts, 159, 174; and media, 197, 198; and politics, 224, 229; Working Party of the Protestant Youth of Germany, 353
Prussia (*see also* Junkers): 9, 16, 19–22, 24, 25, 26, 27, 28, 29, 38, 114, 121, 123, 172; East Prussia, 16, 21, 29; Prussians, 108; West Prussia, 21, 29
Prussian Army Corps: 121; Prussian General Staff, 322
Putsch of 1923: 36

Quakers: 2

racism (*see also* anti-Semitism; Hitler, Adolf; Jews): 1, 39, 135, 153–154, 157, 163, 207
radio: viii, 2, 114, 191, 193, 194, 195, 198–200; and education, 152
Radio Free Europe (RFE): 192, 204
Radio in the American Sector (RIAS): 200, 204
Radio Liberty: 192
Radio Moscow: 200
railways: 32, 72–74, 309; *Bonzenschleuder*, 74; and budget, 273
rainfall. *See* precipitation
Ranke, Leopold von: 166
Rapallo policy: 37; treaty, 38
Rathenau, Walther: 38
Rauch, Christian: 172–173
recession: v, 266

Reding, Josef: 181
Reformation: 17–19, 121; and arts, 158, 159, 174
refugees: 89, 91, 97, 108–109, 129; and budget, 272
Regierungsbezirke (districts): 71
regionalism: 107–109
Reichstag: 18, 28, 33, 38
Reinhardt, Max: 163
Reitz, Edgar: 189
religion (*see also* Christianity, clergy, Counter-Reformation, Jews, Lutherans, Protestants, Reformation, Roman Catholic Church): vii, 9, 12, 13, 15, 17–19, 32, 118, 154, 155; and birthrate, 83; church architecture, 170–171, 186; church schools, 137, 139, 152; control of German princes, 18, 19; freedom of, 24, 207; and painting, 173; state vs. church, 9, 12, 13, 15, 17, 18, 19; youth groups, 231
Remarque, Erich Maria: 162
Renaissance: 17
reparations: 37
resources, natural (*see also* crops, mineral resources): 69–70; and Basic Law, 207; restoration, conservation, and development, 292; water, 309
retirement: farmers, 292, 294–295
reunification: 220, 239, 244, 245
Reval: 16
Revolution of 1848; 27
Revolution of November 1918: 35, 36
Rheinfelden: 75
Rheinische Merkur: 197
Rheinische Post: 195
Rhine River: vii, 10, 11, 55, 61, 62, 70, 75, 76, 91, 106, 250
Rhine Valley: 53, 54, 55, 58–59, 61, 93, 94, 284; rift valley, 59
Rhineland-Palatinate: 47, 71, 93, 123, 251, 273; and farming, 285, 286; population of, 84, 85, 88; Rhinelanders, 107, 108
Rhine-Main: 76, 94
Rhine-Main to Danube Canal: 76
Rhine-Neckar: 94
Ribbentrop, Joachim von: 42
Richelieu, Cardinal: 15
Richter, Hans: 181
Riemann, Georg: 165
Riga: 16
Rilke, Rainer Maria: 161
Ring of Political Youth: 353
Ring of the Nibelungen, The: 168
riots (*see also* police): 341, 345–346, 347, 352, 353

police): ix, 239, 321–354; budget, 271, 273; civil defense, 349–350
Seeckt, General Hans von: 36
Senft, Haro: 189
Sengbusch, Rheingold von: 183
serfs (see also social stratification): 21, 22, 25, 120, 121, 123
servants, 120; domestic, 119
Seven Years' War: 22
ships and shipping (see also navy): 72, 76; merchant marine, 77; and oil, 311
Sicily: 14
Siebs, Theodor: 113
Sieg River: 62
Siegfried: 158
Siemens electrical manufacturing: 37
Silesia: 21
Simmel, Georg: 166
Siodmak, Robert: 189
Slavs: 12, 15–16, 40, 106
Slevogt, Max: 175
Slovakia: 42
Smithsonian Agreement of 1971: 274
social secuirty (see also welfare): viii, 97, 101; budget, 271; and central bank, 264; and farmers, 283, 293
social stratification (see also aristocrats; bourgeoisie; elite; middle class; peasants; serfs; working class): 5–6, 20, 119–131; castes, 25; estates, 18, 22; and industriali- zation, 121–122; and language, 113; lessening of class marks, 103; mobility, 129–131
social system: 115–132
social welfare. See welfare
socialism and socialists: 32, 33, 34, 35, 40, 46, 101, 156, 157, 221, 226, 353
Socialist International: 33
Socialist University League: 353
Society for the German Language: 178
soils: 54, 56, 58, 64–66, 67, 283–284; loess, 284; peat bogs, 65; podzols, 284
Soldiers Act: 330
Solingen: 306
South Africa: 90, 280
South Asia: 257
Soviet Union (see also Russia): 4, 5, 37–38, 39–40, 42, 49, 51, 54, 59, 71, 88, 239, 308, 310, 311, 313, 314, 337; and foreign rela- tions, 222, 240, 241, 242, 243, 244, 245, 246, 247, 248, 250, 251, 323; occupation, 1, 10, 45, 53, 346; and World War II, 322–323
Spain: 17, 18, 28, 106; migrant workers from, 2, 85, 111
Spanish Civil War: 41

Spartacists: 33, 35
Spartakus Marxist Student Union: 231, 353
Spaziergang (family walk): 104
special education: 147, 150
Spengler, Oswald: 36, 39, 157
Spieker, Franz: 189
Spinoza, Benedictus de: 160
sports: 104, 354; soccer: 104, 354
Springer, Axel: 194, 195, 196, 197
Stalin, Josef: 42, 241
Stalingrad: 42
Stamitz, J. W. A.: 167
standard of living (see also consumerism): income, 129
states. See Länd (pl. Länder)
Staudinger, Herman: 184
Staudt, Klaus: 188
steel: 32, 48; industry, 305
Stein, Heinrich vom und zum: 25
Steinthal, Heymann: 167
Stemmle, R. A.: 189
stereotypes: 108, 116, 119, 131
Sternberg, Josef von: 176
Sternheim, Carl: 163
Stirner, Max: 156
Stockhausen, Karl: 185
Stöher, Walter: 188
Stoph, Willi: 50
Storm Troops (Sturmabteilung—SA): 40, 343
Strassburg, Gottfried von: 158
Strauss, David Friedrich: 156
Strauss, Frans-Josef: 193, 196, 197, 225
Strauss, Richard: 169, 185
Strecher, Paul: 188
Stresemann, Gustav: 37, 184
strikes: 270–271; and police, 345
students (see also youth): 6, 135, 137, 146, 148, 232; activism, 148–149, 231; and Jusos, 228; and Marcuse, 180; organiza- tions, 353, 354; Spartakus, 231
Sturm, Helmut: 188
Sturm und Drang: 160, 162
Stuttgart: 3, 47, 76, 94, 104, 203, 270; Academy, 187
subversion: 352–353
Sudan: 256
Sudetenland: 41–42
Sueddeutsche Zeitung: 195, 196
sugar beets: 57, 286, 297, 298
Supreme Allied Commander Europe (SAC- EUR): 252
Suso (or Seuse), Heinrich: 154
Swabia and Swabians: 2, 12, 93, 107; Alemanni, 107, 113

Wolf, Friedrich August: 166
Wolff, Christian: 154–155, 159
women: 116, 118, 119; and education, 144, 147, 148, 151, 152; on farms, 289, 294; in government, 211; and labor force, 269; marital relationships, 118–119; maternity care, 97; in medical studies, 100; and Nazism, 118, 124; and politics, 225; in population, 79, 80–83, 84–85, 90; and wages, 316
wood products (*see also* forests): 304, 305, 315; lumber, 68
working class (*see also Gastarbeiter*, labor force, migrant workers, peasants, serfs, social stratification): 115, 123, 125, 126, 127–129, 130, 161, 269–271; blue-collar, 115, 130; and codetermination, 222–223, 268–269; and cultural life, 153; elite, 127, 128; industrial, 125; and politics, 227, 241; skilled, 130; and universities, 148
Working Party of Broadcasting Stations under Public Law in the Federal Republic of Germany (Arbeitsgemeinschaft der Offentlichrechtlichen Rundfunkanstalten der Bundesrepublik Deutschland—ARD): 199, 200, 201, 202

World Bank: 48
World Disarmament Council: 41
World Health Organization: 48
World War I: 9, 28, 32, 34, 36, 49
World War II: 1, 43, 77, 100, 105, 115, 124, 322–323, 330; Allies, 3, 10; and the family, 118
Wundt, Wilhelm: 167
Wuppertal: 306
Württemberg: 24, 29

Yalta Conference: 45
Yemen, Arab Republic of: 256
Young People Make Music program: 354
Young Plan of 1929: 37
youth (*see also* juvenile delinquency; political parties; students): 103, 104; and Hitler, 118, 124; and politics, 225–226, 227–228, 229, 231; and values, 131; youth programs, 353–354
Yugoslavia: 50, 244; migrant workers from, 2, 85, 110; and trade, 280

Ziegler, Karl: 184
zinc: 69, 70
Zuckmayer, Carl: 189
Zugspitze (peak): 55, 58

PUBLISHED AREA HANDBOOKS

550–93	South Africa, Republic of	550–80	Turkey
550–171	Southern Rhodesia	550–74	Uganda
550–95	Soviet Union	550–43	United Arab Republic (Egypt)
550–27	Sudan, Democratic Republic of	550–97	Uruguay
550–47	Syria	550–71	Venezuela
550–62	Tanzania	550–57	Vietnam, North
550–53	Thailand	550–55	Vietnam, South
550–89	Tunisia	550–99	Yugoslavia
		550–75	Zambia

396

☆ U.S. GOVERNMENT PRINTING OFFICE : 1977 O—237-193